PRAISE FOR

HYDE

"This spellbinding first novel is an ingenious revision of a classic Gothic tale ... Narrated by Hyde, the book delivers a new look at this enigmatic character and intriguing possible explanations for Jekyll's behavior ... [*Hyde*] offers many surprises and rich, often intoxicating prose."
— *Washington Post,* **Five Best Thrillers of 2014**

"An elegantly woven retelling ... The story is deeply psychological and unapologetically dark."   — *Ellery Queen Mystery Magazine*

"This rich, allusive, erudite novel is a welcome reminder of what a tour de force really is."— **David Leavitt, author of** *The Indian Clerk*

"Daniel Levine locates the strange beneath the familiar in this intricately imagined, meticulously executed debut. You may think you know Dr. Jekyll, but this *Hyde* is a different beast altogether."
—**Jon Clinch, author of** *Finn*

"Daniel Levine's intelligent and brutal first novel, *Hyde,* puts a fresh spin on the well-worn material ... It goes beyond a companion piece to an independent novel worth reading in its own right."
— *Columbus Dispatch*

"Levine's evocation of Victorian England is marvelously authentic, and his skill at grounding his narrative in arresting descriptive images is masterful."   — *Publishers Weekly,* **starred review**

"Prepare to be seduced by literary devilry! Go back to Victorian times to find a very postmodern whodunit. Visceral prose, atmosphere you could choke on, characters who seem to be at your very shoulder."
— **Ronald Frame, author of** *Havisham*

"Levine's masterful in his surrealistic observations of Hyde subsuming Jekyll . . . Cleverly imagined and sophisticated in execution."
— *Kirkus Reviews*

"A gloriously disturbing portrait of man's animal nature ascendant, *Hyde* brings into the light the various horrors still hidden in the dark heart of Stevenson's classic tale of monstrosity and addiction. It's Daniel Levine's extraordinary achievement to give voice to a creature capable of indulging every impulse of transgression, while driving its higher self to damnation. Devious and ingenious, *Hyde* is a blazing triumph of the gothic imagination."
— **Patrick McGrath, author of** *Asylum*

"*Hyde* is masterfully told, with plenty of damp and spooky London gothic atmosphere . . . A haunting yarn with a sumptuous Victorian atmosphere exquisitely re-imagines Stevenson's 'monster,' the maligned Hyde."
— *Shelf Awareness*

"Ambitious and imaginative . . . Taking the parameters of Stevenson's story, but deepening and extending the details, Levine allows us to view Hyde not merely as the venal incarnation of Jekyll's soul, but as a fully fledged character in his own right."
— *BookPage*

"A fascinating companion piece to a classic story."
— *Booklist*

HYDE

A Novel

DANIEL LEVINE

MARINER BOOKS
HOUGHTON MIFFLIN HARCOURT
BOSTON   NEW YORK

First Mariner Books edition 2015
Copyright © 2014 by Daniel Levine

For information about permission to reproduce selections from this book,
write to Permissions, Houghton Mifflin Harcourt Publishing Company,
215 Park Avenue South, New York, New York 10003.

www.hmhco.com

Library of Congress Cataloging-in-Publication Data
Levine, Daniel G.
Hyde / Daniel Levine.
pages cm
ISBN 978-0-544-19118-1 (hardback)   ISBN 978-0-544-48402-3 (pbk.)
1. Missing persons — Investigation — Fiction. 2. Self-experimentation
in medicine — Fiction. 3. Psychological fiction. I. Title.
PS3612.E92383H93 2014
813'.6 — dc23
2013044255

Book design by Alex Camlin

Printed in the United States of America
DOC 10 9 8 7 6 5 4 3 2 1

for Hilary

Man is not truly one, but truly two. I say two, because the state of my own knowledge does not pass beyond that point. Others will follow, others will outstrip me on the same lines; and I hazard the guess that man will be ultimately known for a mere polity of multifarious, incongruous and independent denizens.

— Dr. Henry Jekyll in Robert Louis Stevenson,
The Strange Case of Dr. Jekyll and Mr. Hyde

Sir, if that was my master, why had he
a mask upon his face?

—Poole in Robert Louis Stevenson,
*The Strange Case of Dr. Jekyll
and Mr. Hyde*

CONTENTS

LONDON
March 1886

DAY ONE

Morning

Henry Jekyll is dead.

I whisper the words and then listen, as if I've dropped a stone into a well and await the plunk and splash . . . But inside my head there is only silence. All around me a chorus of celebratory noises fills the void: the simmering pop of the coals in the stove, the nautical creak of the whole wooden cabinet, and a faint, high-pitched cheeping from beyond the windows that sounds almost like baby birds. Here I sit in Jekyll's chair by these three encrusted casement windows, with his mildewed overcoat draped about my shoulders like a travelling cloak. My journey's end. The transformation has never felt so smooth before. No spinning sickness, no pain. Just a gentle dissolution: Jekyll evaporating like atomic particles into the air and leaving me behind in the body. This time for good.

Extinction. That was the word Darwin used in his book, which Jekyll befouled weeks ago and then dumped from the chamber pot out the window (no doubt it still lies down there in the yard like a spine-broken bird tumbled from flight). *Extinction. Do the races of men,* Darwin said, *encroach on and replace one another, so that some finally become extinct?* Jekyll refused to explain this concept to me. But now I begin to glimpse what *extinction* really means. I have been singled out. Selected for survival.

The fine hairs along my forearm rise into filaments. I look down at my left hand, resting in my lap like a pale crab, belly-up, the fingers loosely curled. The fraying cuff of Jekyll's shirt is folded back once, revealing the lavender tail of the vein that runs to my wrist. Gingerly I draw the cuff farther up the arm and see the purple lines of infection fork and branch into darkened tributaries that reconverge at the crook of my elbow, which I bare with a hissing wince. The abscess in the notch has gone black, juicy and fat, like a blood-gorged spider at the heart of its web, its abdomen a-throb. I brush my thumb down the cubital vein, hard as a violin string under the skin and scattered with systematic punctures, some scabbed over and some red and fresh, my various points of entry. Look at what he's left me. What he's made me do. All those experimental powders, those double injections — and for what? The end is the same.

My pulse thumps in vindication as I turn in the chair and stare across the cabinet laboratory at Jekyll's writing desk. The white envelope sits propped up against the brass-and-bell-glass lamp. Just as he left it an hour ago. Even in this wan light I can read the elaborate contour of ink across the envelope face: *Gabriel John Utterson*. For the past week I have watched Jekyll scratch out those buckled pages of frantic confession that are folded inside this envelope. Henry Jekyll's Full Statement of the Case. Possessed by his own demented monologue, Jekyll would scribble, lips twisting, for hours — and then he would stop cold and glance up, as if he'd detected a furtive footstep from behind. Amazed, I peered out, surrounded by the pump of his blood, the fizzling whisper of his thoughts, and watched him ease open the lowest drawer of the desk, lift the false wooden bottom, and stash the accumulating pages in the secret under-space compartment. As if he somehow hoped to hide them from me. As if he believed I could not read through his own eyes every word he was writing — believed I would rip his precious manifesto to scraps if he were to leave it lying in the open. Lunacy! And yet after all that, this very morning when he is finally finished, what does he do? He stuffs the pages into that envelope, addresses the crazy thing to his best friend and solicitor, and props it up right bloody there on his desk for me to destroy at my leisure!

I won't destroy it, of course. I have no reason to touch it. Let Utterson find it and read it. The solicitor is no fool. From the moment he first heard my name fall from Jekyll's lips, Utterson knew he was not being given the story entire but rather a carefully manicured account. Why should Jekyll's written confession be any different? From the first line, Utterson will see that the statement is anything but *full*, that it is little more than his friend's dying, desperate protestation of innocence. Why should I waste the effort? No, I won't deny Jekyll his pathetic self-exoneration. But neither will I let him have the final say.

I don't know how much longer I have before Poole realises it's me festering up here — the wanted murderer Edward Hyde — and not his master. Jekyll's man to the last, trusty old Poole. Twice a day for the past two months, he's been ferrying his master's meals on a tray with a domed silver cover across the gravel courtyard from Big House: charred bangers and glutinous eggs and a leaky slice of grilled tomato for breakfast, then a chop or chicken or minced pie sometimes for supper. But this arrangement won't continue indefinitely. Surely this evening, the moment Poole throws open the rusty steel door, he will feel the change, like a temperature drop, in the gloomy depths of the surgery block below me. With chilled breath he will stand at the foot of the stairs, holding the tray, staring up the dark rickety ascent at the cabinet door behind which I crouch. Will he climb up to the door himself and knock? Or will he fetch Utterson to do it? Yes, it will be Utterson who knocks, Utterson who shouts out, Harry, open this door at once! Jekyll knew his friend would be coming, of course. Jekyll knew how it all would end: Utterson pounding at the door and Poole a step below, armed with some implement to smash the door down, that black-headed axe with a silver gleam along its lip. Take it down, Poole! Utterson will cry, and the door will jump and crack as the blade bites in. Our saviours, who will arrive far too late to save anyone.

I shake off a ripple of goose flesh and peer out one of the three iron-framed casement windows that overlook the white gravel yard. A low stratum of morning fog moves like dense liquid over the stones. Above the boxy, silhouetted back end of the surgery block, to the east, the sky is soft cerulean blue, ribbed with pink fire. My breath mists up the glass, and I draw back, wipe the pane with the squeaky meat of my palm. Seven o'clock. Jekyll stopped winding his pocket watch over a month ago, but I can tell the hour by the light and by Poole's comings and goings. Breakfast at half past eight, and supper at six. I have some time yet. And anyhow, the end will not come today. I am oddly certain of this. I have been selected. Granted this final spell of solitude, alone in the body, to set our story straight. I don't want to die with Jekyll's hectic lies echoing in my mind like the jeers of a mob at an execution. I don't want to die at all, but if there's no escaping it, then at the very least I want to remember everything properly first, the way it truly happened. The truth is inside this head. I simply must extract it. In the end no one will know it but me, but that will be enough. I shut my eyes, blow out a trembling breath. A nerve in my hand is twitching an erratic pulse, like a telegraphic code. *Tap-tap, tap*, down the wire.

I am alone, I whisper.

I am all alone.

Winter, then. Not this winter past but the one before it, the first, euphoric winter. December of 1884. The early days of my awakening. I had been roused from my long hibernation just that summer, in June, July. And on the full October moon, Jekyll finally cooked up the first injection and ejected me into the world. By December, then, I was still newborn, naïve. Everything was simple, at this primary stage. Up here in the cabinet after dark, Jekyll would prepare the twin syringes, strip off his clothes, and slide the needle into his arm; the floor would flip in a sickening spin and I'd stagger out into the body. I'd climb into his huge hand-me-down suit and descend the rear stairs and slip from the back door onto Castle Street. Before dawn I would return, take the second syringe, and give the body back. Receding inside Jekyll was a necessary respite from the overwhelming enterprise of existence, and the end of each evening found me stumping happily down spindly Castle Street to the blistered door in the old limestone block of the surgical theatre and the cabinet laboratory on the upper floor. Home, such as it was.

That particular night in December of 1884, though, something was off. As I plodded back to Castle Street, a kind of restlessness still teemed beneath my skin. I wasn't unfamiliar with Jekyll's occasional dissatisfaction, an itch my seedy adventures had failed to scratch. I could feel Jekyll's urgings, but I couldn't always decipher what precisely he desired me to do. It was late, however, and my legs were dead from tromping around Soho, and my toes in Jekyll's draughty boots were nubbins of ice. I was approaching Castle Street from a poky, poorly lit side lane, hands buried in Jekyll's overcoat pockets, breathing steam through the chink in his upturned collar. The dark rooftops almost converged overhead, like the edges of a chasm, and the slot of sky in between was raw pink, like blood mixed into milk. I was gazing upward as I turned the corner onto Castle Street, and when I heard the quick slap of bare feet on stones I spun in surprise. A small hurtling body hit me in the belly with a yelp.

It was a girl. I caught her arms and hoisted her into the air, as if I were her father returned from distant travels. A black tangled mane covered her face as she squirmed in my grip, kicking her naked feet at nothing. She wore only a nightshirt. I could feel her sliding skin prickled into points. Where was she going, dressed like this, with no shoes, in such hurry? *Easy, lassie*, I said, giving her a shake. She stopped struggling. Through her tresses she breathed fiercely at me, a frightened, defiant animal. I caught a hint of odour from her nightclothes, medicinal, urinous, obscurely arousing. Then she shrieked and kicked me square between my legs. I dropped her, doubling over with belly nausea, and she fell and tripped backward onto the stones. As she tried to scramble up, I put my foot down on her chest.

I did not *stamp* on her, as everyone would later accuse me of doing. I placed my foot lightly on her chest, with just enough pressure to pin her down. It was reflex, like stepping on a news sheet before the wind snatches it away. The girl beat at my leg with tiny fists. I could feel her frail rib cage under my boot sole. I returned her glower a moment, then stepped off and hobbled away, my lower belly and bollocks sick with that specific pain. The surgery block, a squat cube of pitted limestone, was just across Castle Street. Three cement steps led up to the stoop and the peeling door, and as I approached, fishing from under my collar the chain with my keys dangling from it, I heard a loud manly holler from behind. My pulse spiked and I broke into a panicky scurry, but heavy feet were clapping up quickly, and as they came closer I froze, shoulders hunched. A hand grabbed my collar and wrenched me around.

A man with black muttonchops spilling down his ruddy cheeks gripped my coat lapels. Where are you going, eh? Where d'you think you're going?

My mouth was dry. I could not respond. I lacked the strength to even knock his hands away. This wasn't anonymous Soho, where I could bolt off from whatever escapade, madly laughing. I was standing right outside our back door. The man narrowed his eyes at me. You come along, he said, and by the collar he towed me across the lane. I compliantly followed, knowing I should simply twist free and pelt off yet impelled by a queer curiosity. For to my amazement, a scene had materialised back where I'd left the girl. She was on her feet now, with a man and woman — her parents, presumably — kneeling and fussing at her, and I could see a

third party limping up the dark poky lane. I stood as if shackled
to the spot by my muttonchopped captor while they surrounded
me. Where had these people come from? They all seemed to be
jabbering at once. My eye fell on the bent old crone who had just
arrived and was crowing toothlessly what sounded like Touch
'im! Touch 'im! Soon yet another figure shuffled up and inserted
himself into the circle: an oldish, ashen gentleman with a black
bowler and a black doctor's bag in his grip. His basset-hound eyes
fastened upon me as my captor began explaining to him that he
had seen me snatch up this girl and try to carry her off and then
throw her down and trample her body before passing calmly on.

I could not protest. The scene had all the nonsensical sponta-
neity of a nightmare. And behind my breastbone, I was beginning
to feel Jekyll's excited reverberation, that pleasurable buzzing I
had been seeking all evening. An insuppressible smile was curling
my lips. Still clutching my collar, my captor gave me a shake and
said, Well? How do you answer for yourself?

Ah, I thought. Money.

From under the brim of my topper, I gleamed at him. *How
much?* I said.

What — the man snorted — money? You want to buy these
good people off?

How much?

My captor looked at the girl's father, who was holding her
wrist. Then he looked at the old doctor. All right, he announced.
One hundred pounds.

One hundred pounds! I had little concept of currency in
these early days, but I knew a hundred pounds was exorbitant ex-
tortion, the price of a whole house. *Ten,* I replied. Ten? he cried.
Ten is an insult — look what you've done to this poor girl! I did
not glance down at her; I knew I'd done her no damage. *Twenty,*
I countered. The muttonchopped man took my lapels in his grip
and yanked me close. This is not a negotiation, he snarled, do you
hear? One hundred pounds. A fleck of spit hit my cheek on the

word *pounds*, and I blinked. My gaze slid down now to the girl, manacled to her father by the wrist and staring up at me with a small, vengeful smile, a dark wicked fairy. *One hundred pounds*, I heard myself say. *All right, then.*

I knew that we didn't have one hundred pounds up in the cabinet. I knew it was impossibly reckless to let them see me enter the surgery-block door, my portal. But Jekyll was guiding me now, his confidence suffusing my breast like a slug of good brandy. *Over there*, I said, and led the way to the warped, paint-chipped door. On the first step I paused, spoke over my shoulder: *Wait here.*

I shut the door behind me and turned back the bolt. Heart slamming, I leant against the wood as my pupils dilated in the blackness of the dissecting room. It was just an empty corridor now. But bodies had been preserved and prepared in this room when the great surgeon John Hunter had owned Big House and built the surgery block out back, and a sweetish, chemical fragrance still lingered one hundred years later. I groped up the steep rear stairwell to my left. I had only two keys on my chain at this time, the Castle Street key and the cabinet key, and I could tell them apart by feel. The Castle Street key was old and wrought intricately in iron, and the cabinet key was new and thick steel. Jekyll had installed the twin lever-tumbler detector locks on both the cabinet doors, front and rear, just a few months before. In the dark I fitted the key into the slot, snicked it open, and let myself into the cabinet.

The room always made me think of the hold of a ship: narrow, low ceilinged, and timbered in varnished oak. I hurried down the length of the walnut laboratory table to the wardrobe in the corner and opened its doors. Jekyll's suit hung from the bar; I slid it to one side and pulled out the main drawer, jerked it loose from the slot. I carried it to the table, surveyed the assorted coins scattered across the felt bottom. Ten pounds I counted, plus a bob or two. Then I noticed the pale green folded paper neatly tucked in the drawer's corner.

I peeled it open. It was one of Jekyll's bank cheques. He must have removed it from his pocket at some point and placed it here, though I couldn't remember him doing so. It looked complicated. Several blank lines to be filled in. How could I give them one of Jekyll's cheques, anyhow? Wasn't it a very bad idea, connecting his name to this business, to me?

Yet that warm assurance glowed now in my limbs as I retrieved Father's fountain pen, heavy and sleek, from Jekyll's trousers hanging in the wardrobe. I had not so much as held a pen since the childhood, and the polished mahogany thing felt clumsy and sinister in my fingers. When I unscrewed the cap, baring the needle-sharp nib, for a flash I saw Father in his hospital wheelchair, the pen held loose in his withered hand. I transferred it to the fingers of my right hand as I bent over the cheque on the table and tentatively touched the nib's point to the signature line. Instantly my hand scribbled out an elegant tangle of ink. Astounded, I drew back. A plausible autograph. Had I done that? I touched the nib to the cheque again and my hand dashed in the remaining lines, making it out to *Bearer* for *ninety pounds*.

I was back outside a minute later. By now the women had withdrawn, and just the three men waited on Castle Street, below the stoop: my captor, the girl's da, and the old doctor with his black bag. I had the ten pounds in coins in my fist, and I held it out to my former captor. Don't give it to me, he sneered, and he jerked his head at Da. A stocky, unshaven fellow with a brush moustache wearing braces and no collar, a common working bloke, trying his best to meet my eye. I tipped the coins into his hands. What's this? my man said, peering at the pile. *Ten pounds*, I replied. Da was looking down at his fortune, and I placed the cheque atop the pile of coins. My erstwhile captor snapped it up and held it before him, inspecting the slim paper, for an agonisingly long time. Then he lowered it and looked at me. The arrogant bluster in his eyes slipped into uncertainty as he now studied my face. I did not like to be looked at directly. But I suffered the man's scrutiny, trying to hide under the shade of my hat brim. Did he know Jekyll? I suddenly wondered. In my excursions I hadn't yet met anyone who knew Jekyll.

Sir, the man said, what is your name?

My name. My name? I did not have a name. No one had ever asked me for one. I was just — me. My mind spun in search of some reply. *Why do you ask?* I said. Why? he repeated. Because I met Dr. Henry Jekyll some years ago. And you are not he.

Relief flashed in the heart of my panic: he didn't know, he couldn't see. He could see only me, a stunted, stark-eyed creature with a cringing grin in a bigger man's suit. But a name! The hackles along my neck pricked up as if Father's shadow were falling over us again, and the old protective impulse surged in my throat —

Hide, I whispered. *Hide!*

The man frowned. Mr. Hide?

I gaped at him. *Yes,* I said. *Mr. Hide. And yours?* He was inspecting the cheque again. I am Enfield, he answered. Enfield. The name sounded familiar. I could feel the immense complex of Jekyll's memory absorb it.

Mr. Hide, Enfield said, how can you expect me to accept this cheque if it is not your own?

Mr. Hide. It had a certain ring to it.

The cheque is good. The bank will tell you so.

Enfield folded the paper in half and slipped it into his inner pocket. In that case, he said, you would not object to waiting with us until the bank opens? I had known he would say this. *Wait where?* Enfield glanced up at the limestone wall of the surgery block, windowless, splotched with lichen. A flicker of unease crossed his face, and he murmured, My rooms aren't far. We'll wait there. He glanced at the doctor and Da, as if he had forgotten they were still there. I'd most appreciate your company, gentlemen, he said. The doctor was watching me again, his mouth wrinkled sour with distaste. He gave a curt nod. No one waited for Da to answer. We set off, all together.

Enfield did live nearby, in a posh flat off St. Martin's. His stooped manservant opened the curtains and built up the fire in the sitting room, and we settled down to wait for daylight. I chose a tall leather wingback and crossed my legs, letting one boot dangle in midair the way Jekyll would sit in the lounge at the Grampian Club. Enfield produced a cigar case and offered it to the doctor, who raised a hand and turned his face aside. Next to him on the voluptuous sofa sat Da, perched uncomfortably upright, hands on his knees. He hesitated at the cigar before darting forward and plucking one out. Enfield moved the case halfheartedly to me. I didn't particularly like cigars, but I slid from the leather slot a slim tapering perfecto and rolled it between my finger and thumb like a connoisseur. Enfield snapped a silver lighter for Da and then offered the steady flame to me. I sucked the earthy end until the butt began to blossom, then sank back into the wing chair, recrossing my legs. A euphoric wave was cresting in my chest. I let a milky curl of smoke unfurl from my mouth, casting a languid eye at Da again. He was frowning at his cigar as if it weren't drawing right, picking discreetly at the tip.

Someone must be dying, I heard myself say, and he looked up with an alarmed little start. I nodded at the doctor. *You sent the lassie for our good doctor here, dead of night. Someone must be dying. Your old man, maybe? Your lady's old man? Yet here you are. Waiting for the bank to open.*

Enough, Enfield broke in. Don't tell him anything, he instructed Da. In fact, I propose we all cease speaking, for the present.

He was in a wingback like mine, one leg thrown over the other. For the first time I took in his odd attire. He wore a blue plaid suit and a preposterous, almost prismatic purple waistcoat buttoned snug over his belly. *These two are accounted for,* I said. *We know why they were out and about in the middle of the night. But what about you, Enfield? What've you been up to?* His expression was hard to read behind the sizzling ember of his cigar. *Naughty boy, Enfield. What's your fancy, then?* He lifted a hand and waved the smoke aside. I'll have you know, Mr. Hide, that I happen to be an informal member of the London Society for the Protection of Young Females. *An informal member,* I repeated. *That sounds very impressive. You go about dressed like that protecting young females, do you?*

His eyes were glittering points. A response seemed to play on his lips like a trace of smile. Then he sniffed and looked off at the ash of his cigar, and victorious, I let my gaze lift to the windows. Beyond the rise of black rooftops, the sky was suffused with fuchsia. Dawn. I had never held on to the body long enough to see the sun rise. I had never been exposed to the daylight. The skin on the back of my hands was shrinking with excitement. This was new. A change was coming, inevitable as the sun itself. I could feel Jekyll close inside, abuzz in my blood, as if *this* were exactly what he'd been craving all evening. This very adventure, upon which everything would pivot, as on a hinge.

We kept the rest of the vigil in silence broken only by the old doctor's occasional snore. I was hoping I might see the sun ascend from the rooflines and hang in the window frame like the molten eye of God. But the flush gradually cooled to blue, and the room lightened until I could make out the gritty detail of Enfield's cheek. He rubbed his jaw with a sandpapery rasp, then dipped into his waistcoat pocket for a gold watch. It sprang open at his touch. He snapped it shut, gave me a sidelong glance, and with a grunt pushed up from his wingback and left the room. When he returned, breakfast followed him on a trolley. Coffee, rolls, cold meat, and cheese. Da hungered at the fare, but he was obviously following Enfield's lead, and Enfield just took coffee and then pretended to read some papers at his desk. I ripped open the rolls and packed beef and cheese inside and stood breathing through my nose as I chewed. I slurped down two cups of hot black coffee and was vibrating with vim. I was going outside into that cold clean morning for the first time. As we gathered together to leave, I clapped Da enthusiastically on the back, making him almost stumble. *Now, sir, let's go get you your hush money.*

Stepping out into the sunshine, I braced myself, half expecting the light to sear my skin with a hiss of steam. But it greeted me like I was anyone else, its alien heat on my upturned face. I felt bleached by it, purified, as we strolled toward the Strand. It was a different city by daylight, crisply divided by shadows and sun, the stony lanes thick with rumbling carriages and bodies plodding to work. Shards of light winked off the shop windows and clopping cabs and nickel-headed walking sticks and made me squint. Soon we reached the great pillared façade of Coutts Bank, corniced like a Greek temple. We trooped inside and stood blinking in the vaulted grandeur of its lobby, all of us red-eyed, unshaven. Enfield took off one floppy leather glove and gestured with it to a wooden bench. As if they were dogs, the old doctor and Da obediently sat down. Easing off his other glove a finger at a time, Enfield said quietly to me, I would prefer to handle this alone, if you don't mind.

My mouth tasted of soot and earth, from the cigar. All at once I was nervous. I shrugged, lightheaded, but trying to seem dismissive, and Enfield was led away by a young flunky to one of the many huge mahogany desks beyond the barricade of the lobby. I tried not to watch the transaction. My shirt, Jekyll's billowy shirt, was pasted nastily to my shoulder blades.

A hoarse voice spoke: And if it clears?

I turned and looked down at the doctor on the bench, baggy-eyed, his bristly dewlap dangling under the wrinkled chin. And if it clears? he repeated. Then what? This never happened, I suppose?

I glanced away, as if from something I had accidentally trodden upon and crushed. With relief I found that Enfield was walking back toward us already, and he was holding some papers in his hand. Sir, he said to Da, and handed the man the banknotes. Ninety pounds, as promised, Enfield pronounced, watching me curiously. Da puzzled dully down at the money, as if he didn't know what it was for. The old doctor stood up, black bag in his rope-veined hand. Bah, he said to the floor, then turned and left. And that was that.

I trudged through the stabbingly bright morning back to Castle Street, all at once exhausted, one eye squinched against an impending headache. Upstairs, I bolted the rear cabinet door behind me and went around the table to the cherrywood glazed press, the antique bureau in which Jekyll kept his magic. One of its twin glass-paned doors stood ajar, as he had left it. The slim jewellery-box drawers inside were lettered from A down to H on the left side, from I down to P on the right. From E drawer, I removed the coil of black rubber tubing and the black Milward box.

Within, the two syringes lay nestled in their beds of red baize, pointing in opposite directions. The upper, empty syringe pointing right was Jekyll's. The lower one pointing left was mine, the barrel loaded with the pale transparent green serum. I stripped off my sticky clothes, tied the tourniquet round my left biceps, and pulled it tight with my teeth as I flexed up the vein in the crook of my arm. I took the syringe by its steel loops. Down the room, on the wall, hung Father's portrait. A young man, he sat on a stool with his beloved violin perched on one knee, his long deft fingers cradling the scrolled pegboard. The eyes watched me askance, wide set and grey, so exact, so alive.

Mr. Hide.

I eased the needle into the vein and pressed the plunger.

Here I sit in my chair by the cabinet windows, staring into the past, squeezing the vein below the abscess, which contains the pulsing pain. But the pain is merely a background nuisance as I nod in quiet triumph. That night of the little girl *was* the true beginning. A pivotal point, upon which everything would turn. There was the bank cheque, of course. That would be part of the trouble later on. But much more than the cheque, it was the name. It was the name that shifted our double life in a new, irreversible direction.

Later that morning, after I had given the body back to Jekyll, he slipped from the surgery block and crossed the gravel courtyard to the handsome brick back of Big House, entering by the glass conservatory door. Upstairs in his bedroom, he bathed and shaved, humming tunelessly between his pressed lips. He splashed some bay rum into his palm and patted it lightly over his cheeks and throat, and I could feel its exotic sting as it set his face in place. Mornings were ritualistic for Jekyll. After his bath and meticulous blade work, he would hang his dressing gown on its hook and cross, naked, to the bureau, keeping his eyes off the long oval swinging mirror, always tilted up in its frame. Only when he had his drawers on did he tilt it down and regard himself. He could not look at his nakedness, the hair and the dangling thing. Even when he urinated, I'd noticed, he did not quite touch or look at it, as if it were a scarred-over wound he didn't want to remember. But he was proud of the rest of his body. A large, heavy-boned, athletic body, so opposite my own stunted essence, his torso robust, shoulders broad, quadriceps braided with muscle. I had been amazed when I'd awoken that summer of 1884, after thirty-six years of hibernation in the mind wherein I had nested during the whole of his adult life. The years between thirteen and forty-nine were a black smear across the span of my memory. I had left Jekyll a hollow-eyed, skinny, cropped-headed boy and returned to find a giant blond god. His clothes enhanced the effect. His ivory linen was tailored precisely to his chest and wrists. Each of his numerous waistcoats bore some subtle, unique stamp of fashion — lavender stitching along the pockets, or a paisley design to the inner silk lining. And when he drew his jacket snug by the satin lapels and shot his silver-linked cuffs and posed with his handcrafted shoes parted like a dancer's, his transformation into the character he had forged was complete.

I thought he was merely going for a walk when he set out from Leicester Square. But ten minutes later he stopped before a drab stone building on a busy street and went inside. The Blackhaven Banking Company consisted of a large dingy room with musty drapes and threadbare carpeting, and the clerk who led Jekyll back to his desk was a spectacled imp with a wisp of fair hair swept over his shiny pate. Jekyll sat, crossed his legs, brushed something from his knee, and said he wanted to open an account for a second party. The clerk was unscrewing his fountain pen. The name of the second party? Jekyll's heartbeat was quickening. *Hyde*, he said, *Edward Hyde. H-y-d-e.*

Edward? What was this? Yet the clerk was writing the name on his papers as if it belonged to a real person. Jekyll's foot wagged up and down as he watched the clerk's pen transmute my anonymity into official existence. Mr. Hyde's residence? the clerk asked. Jekyll said that Mr. Hyde had recently moved to the city and was staying at the Donne Hotel until he found more permanent accommodations. He dipped a hand into his inner breast pocket and drew out a slip of paper. The clerk unfolded it as I recognised the pale green colour. It was another of Jekyll's cheques from Coutts. The clerk stared for a moment. Five thousand pounds, he said. He looked up. Of course, Doctor, he said, and bent eagerly over his papers again.

Five thousand pounds? When had Jekyll written that cheque? I had no memory of him doing so. Jekyll just watched the clerk's scritching pen. He could shut me utterly out of his thinking, back in these early days. The mind was a complex asylum in which I had my nestled residence, with a front window onto his world. But the majority of the mind, vast regions of cells in the wings and rear, remained sealed off from me, and back then I didn't try to pry into the inaccessible corridors. Though some things, I suppose, I knew innately. That summer when I first awoke, almost immediately I knew that we were living in London and that Jekyll had returned to Big House after two years at the Paris hospital where he had been treating a French patient, Emile Verlaine. Jekyll was in the surgical theatre below the cabinet when I first blinked to the surface. He was prying open some wooden crates with a jimmy bar, taking out the bottles inside, and placing them on the dissecting table. When the crates were empty, he set them upright and shattered them to slats with an axe. I knew that it was June or July of 1884. I knew I had awoken because Jekyll needed me. But I didn't know why. I did not know his plans. I found I didn't know what Jekyll was going to do until he did it.

After the Blackhaven Banking Company, Jekyll went to his fencing club and then to the Grampian, as was his routine. Sometimes he ate dinner at the Grampian, but usually he just sat in the baroquely chambered bar and lounge drinking his soda water with a handful of the old boys whom I didn't really try to tell apart. That evening, John Utterson was sitting across the room with a few of the boys when Jekyll came in. Utterson lifted his hand and Jekyll threaded through the labyrinth of ponderous furniture to join his circle. He met the solicitor's eyes, milky grey and steady under overgrown iron eyebrows, and gave his friend a private nod. Twenty minutes later Jekyll met Utterson's gaze again and inclined his head toward the door. They stood up simultaneously and made their apologies. *Come on, old man*, Jekyll said as they crossed the lounge together, *I'll escort you home.*

A block from the Grampian they encountered a dapper, elderly man in a tall stovepipe sauntering down the sidewalk. Utterson stopped to greet him. I did not notice much about Sir Danvers Carew on this first incidental meeting. Except perhaps for his silky white hair, spilling from under his topper, and his

colourless, crystal eyes. Sir Danvers Carew, Utterson said, this is
Dr. Henry Jekyll. They shook hands. Carew knew Jekyll's name.
He said he had attended one of Jekyll's lectures many years ago
in Vienna. The rest of the conversation is blurred, for I was focused on figuring out what Jekyll was up to. He had sought Utterson out, it seemed, for some special purpose. The three men
stood talking on the sidewalk for several minutes, then parted
ways. But there it was. That was the moment Carew entered our
lives, that narrow window of time on the sidewalk. Had Jekyll
ushered Utterson out of the club even a minute later, we might
have missed the man, and then who knows where we'd be now?
And yet, that is faulty thinking. Because it wasn't incidental, of
course, it wasn't merely coincidence. There are no coincidences,
not in this story.

Sir Danvers, eh? Jekyll remarked afterward. Rather high company you keep, old man. Utterson replied that he had handled some
business for Carew, and Jekyll said, A client? Good gracious, John, I
wonder if your roster is becoming too eminent for the likes of me.

But there was something forced in his jovial tone. I could
sense his inscrutable design as they entered Utterson's dreary
house and climbed to his study. A dark room with carved rafters reaching to a domed wooden ceiling shuddering with gar-
goylesque shadows from the fire. It might have been transplanted
from some baronial hunting lodge in the Black Forest, this lair.
Utterson sat low in his wingback, long legs outstretched and
crossed at the ankles, fingers interlaced on his chest, a brooding pout to his glistening lips. Yes, I was watchful of the solicitor,
even this early in the game. He had known Jekyll longer than anyone alive, aside from Hastie Lanyon. The three of them had gone
to school together back in Edinburgh, and I could sense the depth
of the friendship when Jekyll sat alone with Utterson, their history yawning below me like bottomless water. Jekyll watched his
friend too, even as he feigned absent-minded reflection while gazing into the fire. At last he lifted his eyes to the portrait gloom-

ing over the mantel. An older, thicker, fiercer Utterson glowered down: John Utterson Senior, no doubt. Jekyll said with a small laugh, *Just imagine, John, the psychological damage we've endured, sitting under those eyes all these years.*

Utterson looked up from the fire. You'll have to imagine it for me, Harry. You're the expert.

What is it he disapproves of? I wonder. Jekyll paused, musing. *Do you think that your bachelorhood would have troubled him, if he had lived to see it?* I think, Utterson replied hesitantly, he would have been glad if I'd had a family. *That isn't what I asked.* Jekyll let a moment pass. *He knew I wasn't married, you know. My father. When I went to see him. He looked at me from that wheelchair, and he said, Kept yourself a bachelor, have you, boy?*

I caught an unexpected flicker just then: a young blond woman playing the piano. It was like a bubble wobbling to the surface and bursting, leaving a name hanging on the air. Georgiana. Jekyll shook his head, cleared his throat. *Of course my father would have briefed himself beforehand. Wormed some information out of his Dr. Pinter. The good doctor was fairly infatuated with him. Nevertheless, I've been thinking about it. Not of marriage. But the idea of having an heir. Leaving something of myself behind. A legacy.* He let another pause swell the silence, and with a thrill of fright, I could suddenly see what was coming. *There is someone in particular, you see. A protégé.*

A protégé, Utterson repeated.

Yes. A younger man. I've taken him under my wing, I suppose. He is from hard beginnings; he hasn't had any advantages. But his mind is quite unique. He could do great things, given the proper support and encouragement. That's what I want to provide, the support for him to flourish. Well, Utterson said, Harry, you are free to support whomever you like. *Thank you. But I had something specific in mind. I'd like to include him in my will.*

Include him to what extent, if I may ask?

I want to leave him the house on Leicester, Jekyll said, *and what-*

ever's in Coutts, and the securities. And Pent Manor, I'd like to leave him that too —

Utterson made an astounded noise. Harry, what on earth are you talking about? *I'm talking about revising my will, John.* Leaving everything you own to some — some protégé? Your house? Your family estate? Who even is this man? *First of all, as it stands, Je-*kyll said calmly, *at my demise, the family estate will fall to my fa-ther's sister's step-grandchildren. They're not blood. And if you are concerned that I'll be cutting you out in the process, my friend, I hope you know* — Stop it, Utterson interrupted. That's not remotely my concern, and you know it. Harry, who is this man? *You mean,* Jekyll said, *his name?* Yes, all right, his name. What is his name? *His name is Hyde. Edward Hyde.*

Edward Hyde.

Utterson murmured it to himself. This Mr. Hyde is a student of some kind? *Yes,* Jekyll said. *But he teaches me things too.* Utter-son sighed. Harry, look. You wish to support this disadvantaged young man, and that is commendable. There are a variety of ways this can be done. You could establish a trust, which I could hold in escrow. Or an annuity, from which he would receive regu-lar payments. You could do any number of things, each of them more immediately beneficial to Mr. Hyde than making over the whole of your estate to him in your will, which doesn't do him any good until you are dead. Why would you wish to place yourself in such a position with respect to anyone, let alone a man you have known, what, since you've been home? Six months, at most? *John,* Jekyll said gently, *I've known him far longer than that. I knew him many years ago. Then he left for a while, and now we've become reac-quainted. And it isn't about the money. Those options you mentioned, they are practical, yes, but I want to give him something more than money. I want him to inherit what is mine; I want him as my heir. It may not seem — legally pragmatic, but that's because it is a symbol. A gesture.* And here Jekyll lifted his hands and opened them out-ward to the fire.

A gesture, Utterson repeated. And you wish me to help you put this gesture into a legally binding document. Is that correct? Jekyll didn't reply. Well, I'm sorry, but I won't do it. It would be greatly irresponsible on my part. *Irresponsible*, Jekyll said. Yes, irresponsible. Harry, forgive me, but you haven't considered this properly. Your will at present identifies a number of beneficiaries, all of whom you propose to oust in favour of a total stranger. There will be complications. And then — well, let us be frank. I'm not certain that you are in the proper frame of mind to execute such consequential decisions. The events of this year, you cannot tell me they have been without effect. I don't know what happened in Paris, and I respect your desire not to speak of it. But losing a patient under any circumstances — and then, shortly after your return, losing your father as well. I did not tell you this, but I corresponded with Dr. Pinter after your father's death. There were some details the hospital wanted to clear up. He told me, Harry, the manner in which your father . . . It must have been tremendously disturbing for you to witness such a thing. I am sorry. Obviously it's on your mind. This idea of yours seems to stem rather directly from this last contact with your father. And now you come to me wishing to leave the whole of your fortune and property to a man whose name I have never heard until tonight, a man who has suddenly reemerged out of the past — Utterson paused, lips parted, at a momentary loss. *So what are you telling me? That you question my sanity? That you consider me legally incapable of making decisions for myself?* Utterson shook his head and said, reproachfully, Harry. Can't you understand? I'm concerned. You can be truthful with me. Are you in some kind of trouble? This Hyde. Did he put you up to this?

Jekyll looked away, across the room. A smile was fighting its way onto his face, an odd, reflexive smile. *You insult me, my friend. You think I'd let myself be bullied into this? I make my own choices. And I have chosen to do this of my own will. If you don't wish to help, I'm capable of writing it myself. Or finding another solicitor to do so.*

Utterson stood from his chair and posed before the fire, head down, hands clasped behind him. You make your own choices, indeed. You still haven't seen Lanyon, have you. Jekyll said nothing. So I thought, Utterson said. You sit there and speak of gestures, and still you haven't been to see Hastie, not once in the six months you've been home. Have you even written him your condolences?

A flush bled into Jekyll's face. The coals hissed and popped.

Utterson shook his head. Such a shame. Such a waste of friendship. Like it's some common thing to be thrown away.

I didn't come tonight for a lecture, John.

No, Utterson said. No, you didn't.

Back at Big House on Leicester Square, Jekyll went up to his study on the second floor. He shed his jacket and crossed the plush rug to his massive desk, then eased into the swivelling chair. He removed a few sheets of paper from a drawer and reached into his trouser pocket for Father's fountain pen. Jekyll bent over the blotter and began to write, his intricate script scrolling from the scratching nib. I read in growing bewilderment and horror. The houses, the accounts, the stock funds, all were to pass to me, Edward Hyde; *my friend and benefactor,* he called me. Benefactor? Wasn't I his protégé a moment ago? But that was not all. *In the event of Dr. Henry Jekyll's disappearance or unexplained absence for any period exceeding three calendar months, Mr. Edward Hyde should step in without further delay and assume Dr. Jekyll's residence and possessions.*

At last Jekyll flashed off his ornamental signature and dropped the pen to the blotter. He sat back, flexing his hand. That odd, guilty smile was again inching its way onto his face.

The surgery block across the courtyard glowed against the misted dark like a white pebble on a forest path. Jekyll stepped from the conservatory and crossed the gravel yard to the steel block door, and as he climbed the steep creaking stairs to the cabinet, I was leaping in his breast with apprehension. I didn't know what to expect or to think. In the cabinet, Jekyll moved to the glazed press and fitted in the antique little key. He slid E drawer from its slot and set it down on the long walnut table. I had watched him prepare the syringes fifty, sixty times by now. Yet this night I felt an echo of the first night: the first time I'd watched him pour the transparent green solution into a phial, punch the hypodermic through the rubber stop, tip the phial upside down, and suck out the fluid to the half line on the glass barrel. Now Jekyll filled one syringe and then the other, and then he began to undress. He hung his clothes in the wardrobe and retrieved from his jacket pocket a folded wad of papers — banknotes — which he slipped into the trousers of *my* black misshapen suit, which was hanging alongside his. Naked, Jekyll passed before the mirror without looking and took up the coil of rubber tourniquet. I felt myself teetering on the brink of something new as he slid the needle into the vein, and then he pressed the plunger, and the floor flipped upside down, flinging me into the sickening fall. I groaned as blood filled my head and a billion needles rained through the skin as if to shred us to particles, and then the room whipped upright once more and I staggered into the body, seasick, momentarily blinded, and back again.

I went to the Toad. The sleazy, subterranean Toad, off Greek Street, hot and loud, voices ricocheting in an indistinguishable din. A youngish, gaudy crowd sharked about the room, releasing the yeasty stink of beer and bodies in heat. By the sticky bar I watched a pair of handsome twits in yellow checked jackets, Oxford boys, gleaming with oily assurance and chatting up a trio of ostentatious tarts. Jekyll always drew my attention to these types, the slummers, the gentlemen from high town, Mayfair, Belgravia, St. James's, out for a taste of the low life. Tourists, impostors. Jekyll could instantly see through their disguises, and these two schoolboys playing at being scoundrels were particularly transparent. Even I could imagine them huddled with their chums in an oaken dining hall telling their tales of scummy London town. Crammed in the crush at the bar, I was observing them, more out of habit than genuine interest, when a shrill of laughter cut through the clamour. I glanced down the busy plank and saw her. She was just a girl to me, on this night. Just some young piece of dolly shaking her head and touching her collarbone as another bout of laughter fluted from her throat. A man was talking to her, cupping his mouth with one hand as he spoke into her ear, and she was laughing and tossing her burnished red head and patting his arm as if telling him to stop. Fifteen, sixteen maybe, young even by the Toad's standards. I had only this glimpse, through this opening, before the sound and bodies moved back in to swallow her from my senses.

Georgiana.

The name welled up out of Jekyll again to the surface. And for an instant I saw another flash of that small, honey-haired woman, this time in a powder-blue evening dress laughing in a marble ballroom, a musically rising laugh, as she touched Jekyll's sleeve and helplessly shook her head.

I blinked rapidly, then looked down into my gin. My heart was clenched, a stricken, winded sensation. I glanced back for another glimpse of the girl, but instead I found a man standing a few paces down, blocking my view.

He had one fist propped against his hip; his overcoat flared open to reveal an iridescent emerald waistcoat shimmering like lizard skin. Black chops framed his smug, rosy face. He brought a shot of whisky to his lips and tipped it back with a stylish toss of his chin. A tourist, obviously, the kind who hardly took any trouble to hide it, who flaunted his lavish foreignness. I watched him knock back two more drams of whisky as my heart gradually released, and blood began to pound in my cheeks, and I forgot about the girl and Georgiana and even the mystifying business with Jekyll's will. For my attention followed Jekyll's, and his

was riveted upon this ridiculous impostor. The man slipped a finger into his waistcoat pocket and produced a coin, which he set
on the bar, and then he turned and pushed through the crowd toward the rattletrap stairs. I felt a jerk behind my breastbone and
followed after him.

Fogbound night, not many people about. I tried to match his
footsteps from thirty paces behind, impelled by a curiosity and
an instinctive disliking I did not need to understand. He led
me across Soho Square and down a deserted road to a blind alley lined by dead-eyed brick tenements. At the corner I waited,
watching him approach a door, which he knocked on, in a kind of
code, four times, with a pause after the third. There was a metal
grating sound, then the door opened and the man slipped inside.

I tarried, shifting on my feet, needing to urinate. This was
no simple dolly shop. I had followed gentlemen to the Frenchie
houses with their red-shaded windows and frilly dolls, and this
was something altogether different. In my trouser pocket, my
hand gripped the wad of banknotes Jekyll had transferred there.
Was *this* what he'd intended me to use it for? I looked over my
shoulder, then crossed the decrepit alleyway to the battered door
and lifted my fist. *Knock-knock-knock,* pause, *knock.* A slot scraped
open above my head. A pair of examining eyes peered out. I didn't
look away, bold in Jekyll's high-buttoned greatcoat, hat brim
screwed low over my brow. Ten pounds for entrance, sir, said the
voice behind the door. I poked a tenner through the slot, and then
I was inside.

A narrow corridor. The hulking doorkeeper motioned me
down it. At the end I found, with some surprise, a small, warm
sitting room, two flowered armchairs by the fire, and a red tea-
pot hanging by its handle from the hob. Charily I stepped into
the empty room, eying a wooden cuckoo clock on the wall that I
expected to explode open at any moment. Framed photographs
hung around the room. In one, a girl in a white nightshirt stood

holding one arm behind her back, regarding me with washed-out eyes. Another girl in the next frame was moving, in two places at once with a ghostly blur in between. I heard a sound behind me and turned.

An elderly lady had materialised from the far doorway. Iron-stranded hair moulded to her scalp, navy dress with lace at the throat, hands clasped before her. Watching me, head cocked. She too struck me as familiar. I could feel another memory welling upward. I shook my head to dispel it, and the lady lifted her eye-brows. Good evening, sir, and welcome. This would be your first visit? I nodded. Delightful. Her eyes seemed wholly black in their nested wrinkles. I was trying not to look at her hands, liver-spotted, shot through with tendons, talons hooked at the ends. How had I come to learn of their establishment? I cleared my throat. *A friend.* She nodded. Would you care to sit down, sir? I did not move, and she gave me a trace of smile. To business, then. Have you any preferences with respect to colouring? I stared at the ivory brooch at her throat. The cuckoo clock was minutely ticking, springs winding tight. Room three will do, the lady said, moving her eyes behind me, and I turned to find the massive doorkeeper wedged inside the tiny room. Ivan here will lead you. Do enjoy your stay with us. She bowed and withdrew. Ivan bestowed upon me his stony glare. Just this way, sir.

Room three was off another narrow corridor. Hooded gas brackets stuck out from papered walls lumpy with shadows. Ivan unlocked the door, pocketed the keys, and stepped back. I entered.

The girl was sitting on the edge of the bed, her back to me. The room was a cube: four walls, low ceiling, carpeted floor, and the four-poster bed in the middle. A wooden crucifix hung above the headboard, Jesus carved in His agony upon it. I stood with my back against the door. The girl did not look over. Her dark shiny hair was braided down her spine and tied with pink ribbon. Her dress was pink with white sleeves, scooped away in back to reveal her delicate scapulas. The silence was thick, and as my eye fell on the wall I realised the room must be soundproofed under the paper. I took a step onto the padded carpet. The girl was looking down at something in her lap. From the bedpost I could see it was a doll of some kind, wearing a bonnet; she held the rigid thing in both hands. I had an obscene inclination to laugh. The girl sniffed and moved her eyes to me.

Her face was rouged. Soot rimmed her lashes, then ran and stained her cheeks like dirty rain down a window. Her brimming eyes were large and remote, gazing through me into the glassy distance. She set her doll on a bedside vanity table and came to me, her feet in white patent shoes. The top of her glossy head just reached my chest. She said, in a soft mechanical voice, Let me help you with your coat, sir. Her hands rose as if on puppet strings and a quick, unaccountable terror surged within me. I caught her by the wrists.

That old lady's hands — tendons hard under the spotted skin — all at once I knew what I was remembering. Auntie Gorgon's hands, shapely and strong as Father's yet with those iron talons that curled like a falcon's and dug into the underside of an arm. Oh God. How could I have forgotten Auntie Gorgon? Her grim house on the edge of that wind-scoured hillside where we had gone to live after they'd taken Father away. That house was the last thing I *could* remember, in fact, before the long, black intermission.

I was still gripping the girl by the wrists. She was beginning to breathe rapidly through her nostrils. I pushed her away and she tumbled back onto the bed, her skirts in a ruffle. With arms outstretched she lay there, head to one side, breathing, waiting. What did Jekyll want me to do? Until now it had merely been women he wanted, the novelty of women, after a life of virgin control. I pressed my fingers to my left eye, where a lance of pain was starting to spike. I couldn't understand what he was trying to tell me. *Stop*, I said. My voice sounded distant. I cleared my throat.

Sit up. The girl shifted her head to look cautiously at me. She slid herself up with a rustle. *What's your name?* I felt queer and faint and barely heard the girl's reply — Violet. *Violet,* I repeated. The spike was pressing into the back of my eyeball, making me flinch. My other eye rolled to the crucifix: Jesus's head tipped to the cross, mouth open, as if crying at the sky. I fumbled in my trouser pocket, pulled out a crumbled banknote. *Here, take this. Hide it.* The girl just stared at the paper rattling in my fingers. *Take it,* I snarled. *Hide it good.*

Then it happened. This was the first time, the first lapse of blankness. One moment I was holding out that banknote to little Violet and the next moment I was outside on an icy broken lane in northeast Soho scurrying after the man with the emerald waistcoat. The time in between was a blink.

I was not overly alarmed. I felt much better, actually, as if I had fallen asleep for a totally revitalising second: the pain in my eye was gone; my brain felt recharged and alert. The body was moving confidently ahead as I rejoined it, and I slipped into the present moment with a kind of reinvigourated purpose. There was a reason I was following this man, a reason I would remember as soon as we arrived at our destination. His stout, top-hatted silhouette turned onto Crown Street, and at once the dingy alleys of Soho disappeared, as if we had passed from some backstage into the respectable world. For several blocks the man led me north, eventually arriving in Bedford Square, where he turned into the gate of a large, pleasant white-brick house with a green door and a welcoming lamp. Rather than climbing the stone front steps, the man let himself into a side entrance on the ivied ground floor. And just like that the chase was over. I stood rooted to the pavement, pulse quickening, staring at the unsuspicious house, the comfortable castle into which my man had vanished. An epiphany was unfurling in my mind. That money. That five thousand pounds Jekyll had put in my bank account. Suddenly I knew what I was meant to do with it. He wanted me to buy my independence from Big House, the cabinet, the back door off Castle Street. A house. I should get myself a house. That was what the will was about, that was the gesture, his hands opening outward to the fire. Liberation. *The support for him to flourish.*

He wanted me to grow.

DAY ONE

Afternoon

Time moves. It must be four o'clock: the weak sunlight's begun to creep up the brick back of Big House, the line of shadow rising like dark water. That is the amazing thing about time. You do nothing, yet you're propelled into the future. In spite of my optimism this morning, I hadn't been entirely certain that I would make it this far alone, unmolested. I hadn't been certain I would make it past Poole's delivery of Jekyll's breakfast. I can say it, now that the dirty tray is sitting on the steps down there again, where I put it for Poole's removal. Part of me really believed he would detect the change the instant he stepped foot in the surgery block. How quiet I was as he clumped across the boards and began his climb up the rickety stairs. I could hardly believe it when I heard him set down the tray, descend, and then crunch back across the courtyard. Will I actually be permitted to do this, to simply remember, the mind like an empty cathedral? I do not trust the emptiness. That stifled quality of silence — of something biding its time.

The abscess pulses. A second, sickly heart.

The day after my visit to Auntie Gorgon's girlie shop, I dropped by the Blackhaven Banking Company and withdrew five hundred pounds from my account. I scratched a maze of ink on the signature card and accepted a green leather booklet of cheques, and several days later an obese, flame-headed agent from a Soho leasing office led me up to the old manse on Ghyll Road. The house looked dark and rundown in its sunken recess between its neighbours, like a book pushed in deeper than others on a shelf. I followed the wheezing agent into the cobbled courtyard. From atop the empty fountain a disintegrating stone angel watched me, eyes eroded, mouth open. We climbed the sagging portico steps, pushed into the entrance hall. It was cold, the floorboards carpeted in dust. A pair of ornamented doorways opened left and right into other rooms, and a staircase climbed to the upper floors. The oddest feeling was creeping over me, as if I had been here before. Lived here in another life, one I had forgotten. The agent was explaining how the house had been built more than two hundred years ago, when rich people had fashioned Soho before moving on farther west. The rooms were dirty and smelt like mice droppings, but indeed I could make out the abandoned grandeur, the moulded ceilings and plaster medallions where chandeliers had hung. On the top floor I opened a door and the sense of recognition returned: a long garret room with scarred parquet and double verandah doors giving onto a rotting balcony. The iron parapet clung to the house forty feet above a spinal back lane and overlooked the mad tumble of rooftops and weathervanes inked in black against the platinum sky. Exhilarated, I stood clutching the rusted rail. I was home. I signed the lease on the spot, at thirty quid for the year.

Workmen from a warehouse nearby carried in a score of random heirlooms to furnish the place, and I filled a Chinese wardrobe with new tailored clothes. I didn't expect to enjoy that as much as I did, ridding myself of Jekyll's dragging hand-me-downs. I posed before the huge Gothic mirror in my bedroom as the wizened tailor scuttled around marking me with chalk, making me into a real person before my very eyes. That first experimental jacket that he slipped up my arms and snugged around my shoulders — the yellow stitching was still exposed and the pockets flapped, but it did not matter. In fact, it suited me, half-formed creature that I am, fish pale, compressed, as if grown in a jar in the dark. Jekyll's fine, big body somehow contorted itself to my runtish nature, my fetal curl, but his clothes of course could not change. Now I had a costume of my own. I stared into my bright, haunted blue eyes and grinned, baring two rows of tarnished, ground-down teeth. I ordered suits and waistcoats and two heavy wool greatcoats, and except for the linen, I kept the fabric black. None of Jekyll's touches of plumage for me. I wanted to slip into the world, into its slimy seams.

Next Mrs. Deaker. I still don't understand why I went to that agency to ask for a charwoman in the first place. Yet one day she appeared on my porch, in her black frock ringed with feathers at the neck, like a vulture. She looked about seventy, with silver hair and ice-grey eyes and a tiny stained smile. Her upper spine was stooped, so she had to crane her neck to peer up at me, but she tipped a dignified nod and said, Master, in her precise, whispery voice. Years ago, in her prime, she must've been a fashionable lady. She fit the house perfectly, I had to admit. I gave her the spare room off the kitchen and she moved in the next day.

Just like that, I was a legitimate human being. I was Mr. Edward Hyde of Ghyll Road, an untethered entity. In fact, I hadn't been back to the cabinet for well over a week, I realised with a jolt. It was time for Jekyll to show his face at Big House again. After midnight I returned to the Castle Street door with one of my new suits bundled under my arm and proudly hung it in the cabinet wardrobe alongside Jekyll's. In the Milward box the second syringe lay loaded with the transparent, ever-reliable serum. As I took it up by its steel loops, I deliberately did not look at Father, on the far end, those eyes looking at me askance, always watching.

• • •

The next morning, Jekyll was in his blue silk dressing gown shaving away the heavy crust of beard accumulated in his absence when Poole knocked on his bedroom door. Every so often Poole would do this, always when Jekyll was shaving, never when he was still abed or in the bath. Poole had been managing the business of Big House since Jekyll had bought the place, twenty years ago, and from the beginning of my reemergence into Jekyll's world, I had been wary of him, warier even than I was of Utterson. For in his subdued, sphinxlike manner, the man seemed to know everything.

Poole stationed himself in the dressing-room doorway, as usual. He had some questions concerning Christmas and Jekyll's fiftieth birthday party, both approaching. Jekyll listened and made his replies without breaking from his scrupulous work. When a pause fell, he said, *You seem to have everything thoroughly handled without me, Poole. I'm sure you've noticed I've been away these past few days.* Jekyll pared a few hairs from his upper lip. *I've been working again. A comprehensive psychological study of London. For the present I'm drawing up profiles of various characters, case studies that catch my attention. To study them properly I'm required to remain in their company for several days at a time. Anyhow, if I happen to be absent when any decisions need to be made, you know I have utter confidence in your discretion.*

Jekyll rinsed the razor blade in the basin and flicked his eyes sideward in the glass to Poole, standing in the reflected doorway. It was a casual glance, but Jekyll held it until Poole dipped his head. Thank you, sir, I shall do my best. Congratulations on your work, sir.

Ah, Jekyll said, *indeed. I daresay it will be quite something, when I'm finished.* He lifted his chin and dusted the shaving brush over his throat. *I am a fortunate man, am I not, Poole?* I should say so, sir. *And would you consider yourself a fortunate man as well?* Poole hesitated. I would indeed, sir. Jekyll drew the skin of his throat

taut with his thumb. *Fortunate men like us must remember the un-*
fortunates. In the course of my work, you see, I've made a new ac-
quaintance. He's come from unfortunate beginnings. I suppose I've
taken him under my wing. He has a promising mind, but he wants —
refinement.

Jekyll's pulse was thumping under his thumb as he lifted the
blade and carefully trimmed his Adam's apple, and just beneath
the surface, I cringed as the hairs crunched and popped. *His name*
is Hyde, Jekyll said, swishing the blade clean. *Edward Hyde. I've*
invited him to call on me here at the house. It would do him some good
to see how a gentleman lives. The problem is my schedule has lately
been so erratic, I can't be certain I'll be here to receive him. So if he
should call while I'm away, I'd like you to let him in regardless. Let
him have the run of the place, in fact. Could you do that for me?

Of course, sir.

I should warn you, his manners are a trifle rough. He's come from
hard beginnings, as I said, and he has what you might call an artis-
tic disposition. Don't pay it any mind. Just let him have the run of the
place. Feel at home.

Poole remained motionless at the mirror's edge. As you wish,
sir. Will there be anything else?

Anything else? Why would I show my face here at Big House?
Wasn't this why he'd given me all that money to lease a house of
my own — to keep our lives separate and distinct?

Jekyll remained at Big House through Christmas, the yearly
dinner for his whole staff, all eating as equals in the dining room.
The next morning I was allowed to return to my house on Ghyll
Road — to Ghyll, as I'd taken to thinking of it. Yet I couldn't stop
gnawing over the invitation he'd issued me. Did it relate to that
will Jekyll had drawn up — to that peculiar clause about my re-
placing him if he should disappear? What could he foresee? It was
a frustrating, blinded feeling, my ignorance. I wanted to know

what my purpose was, what Jekyll *needed* me for. If it was to live a new, ulterior life, why introduce me into his own?

I tried to divert us both over the next few days. I dropped into the Great Cornelius Luce's hypnotism demonstration on Poland Street and stood in the beery hall while onstage the tailcoated maestro cast mental spells over his volunteers. I visited a dolly shop and let a blonde reeking of ambergris slap her rump up and down on my thighs on a pink circular bed. Afterward I lurked outside until a tall gentleman emerged and took a satisfied pinch of snuff, and I followed him into a side street with some vague notion of mischief, of teaching the geezer a lesson of some kind. But my heart wasn't in it. I knew I could put it off for only so long.

The morning of 1 January 1885, Mrs. Deaker knocked on my bedroom door at around noon, as usual, and bustled in with the breakfast tray. Her breakfasts ran the gamut. Some days there was fresh bread, jam and butter, coffee. Other days she'd serve me a broken, runny egg and oversteeped tea. I ate whatever she brought me. I found it rather refreshing, after Poole's predictability. This morning, breakfast was warm earthy tea and a stale currant scone that crumbled into the sheets when I bit in. My mouth was dry with hangover, and the pastry turned to paste, impossible to swallow. Mrs. Deaker went to the verandah doors and wrenched the curtains aside, and I flinched in the winter glare. She turned to behold me in my tangle of satin bedclothes. I couldn't see her expression, but I knew her cosy smile by now, servile and yet craftily insubordinate. Happy New Year, Master, she said. Big plans for the day, I take it? I forced down the lump of scone and tried to grin, the stuff sticking to my teeth. *Always, Mrs. Deaker. Tick-tock, tick-tock.*

I dressed in my black suit and examined my face, with its disguising growth of rusty scruff. Then I swiveled my top hat down on my head and set off south for Leicester Square. I had never actually been on the square before in the body. I had seen it only

through Jekyll. The sky was low with pewter light over the irregular line of houses. A rime of dirty snow crusted the ground in
the central park. A dog was yapping. Hotels spelled their names
in large vertical letters; houses looked shut up for the season. The
air had a damp chill, and I clenched my teeth to keep them from
chattering as I approached Big House, standing grandly distinct
from its shabbier neighbours. The brick façade soared from the
front steps; black shutters and ivory trim adorned the many windows, and symmetrical chimney stacks stood erect against the
shifting sky. The huge black door had a brass knocker and a bell
button. I grasped the brass ring, shockingly cold, and rapped on
the plaque.

As the clicking footsteps approached and then the door
swung inward, I was seized by a fierce impulse to avert my face.
I crouched on the stoop, leering up from under my brim at Poole
in the doorway. His black uniform was immaculate, with a perfect V of crisp white shirt front. His head was sleek and small but
the eyes large and zinc-white against the black rims, as if he had
outlined them, like an Arab. His velvety irises rested on me. The
muscles of his face did not move. You must be Mr. Hyde. I nodded. Poole stepped back from the doorway. I'm afraid Dr. Jekyll is
not at home at the moment. But won't you come in?

The entrance hall was long and low, paved in slate flagstone.
Walnut panelling trapped the heat from the giant hearth. Firelight flickered off the glass in the cabinetry opposite, the polished
gloss of the blackwood bench. Sir, Poole said from behind me,
and I guardedly let my overcoat slide from my shoulders. *I'll keep
the topper*, I said quickly, holding the brim, when he extended his
hand to accept it.

I followed Poole into the main hall, with the burgundy staircase spilling down and the marble pillars ascending to the fres-
coed ceiling and dazzling chandelier. He led me to the right, into
the cool green parlour. Please make yourself comfortable, Poole
said. Might I offer you some refreshment? Protected by the shade

of my topper, I surveyed the handsome room, scalloped in creamy trim, bright pictures on the walls. *Wine*, I said, and Poole left me alone.

My breastbone was humming like a tuning fork. Poole had bought it. He really thought I was a distinct person. I *was* a distinct person. I was Mr. Edward Hyde of Ghyll. Was this what Jekyll was trying to show me? I sank into a velvet chair as Poole reentered with decanter and glass on a tray. This he set on the low Japanese tea table nearby, and he filled the glass with ruby claret. I sat watching the deft precision of his hands. *It's Poole, isn't it?* Yes, sir, he replied, letting his eyes travel up to my face, shaded by my hat brim. *Well, thank you for the refreshment, Poole.*

It came out laced with sarcasm. The briefest flicker of pique crossed Poole's placid expression. He slipped the silver tray behind his back and bent minutely at the waist. You are welcome, sir. Do alert me should you require anything further.

When he was gone I leapt to my feet, swooped up the glass, and drained the wine. Everything seemed so vivid, as if a transparent layer had been peeled away, like skin, from the parlour. I wandered down the archway that led into the dining room, trailing my hand along the silken wall, which sizzled under my fingertips. In the dining room I stood behind Jekyll's chair at the head of the long table and then leant over until my reflection hung beneath me in the shadowy polish. From my lips I let a thread of spittle glisten down toward the surface, then sucked it up swiftly before it snapped. I strolled down the narrow connecting corridor back into the main hall and jogged up the winding staircase. The house was disconcertingly silent; I paused on the landing, listening. A slim naked statue stood in an alcove, missing arms and a head, and I caressed its cold curving hip as I passed. On the second floor I paused again outside the white double doors to Jekyll's study, then I pushed one open and peeked in. I was almost expecting to find Poole pretending to clean to guard the room against my trespass. But it was empty. Books lined the white shelves in the crimson walls. Two leather wingbacks were angled invitingly toward the fire. Above the mantel hung a large picture in a knotted frame; I hadn't noticed it before. It wasn't like the pictures downstairs in the parlour, pastoral landscapes and portraits. This one was just a black and brown mass of paint dizzyingly aswirl around the canvas. I eyed it uneasily as I crossed the Persian carpet to Jekyll's desk. Letters were aligned on the green leather blotter, arranged by Poole in order of arrival. I studied them upside down and then reached out and turned the closest one around.

Across the envelope was scrawled in a tight, sinuous hand *Dr. Henry Jekyll.* The corner was printed in letterpress: *Danvers X. Carew, MP.* The name was familiar. I tore the envelope open and let Jekyll read the first few lines of the letter, and it came back to us: Jekyll had met him outside the Grampian Club with Utterson. He was asking for permission to call upon Jekyll. I dropped the letter back on the blotter and sidled around the desk to Jekyll's swivelling chair. I lowered myself into its embrace, stacked my feet on the desk, and watched the half-open door.

Let him have the run of the place.

I left the study and continued down the second-floor corridor toward Jekyll's bedroom, at the far end. I had been in his bedroom before, on the first night. My throat was dry and my palms moist as I reached for the doorknob. I turned it and tipped the door inward.

One of the maids knelt before the fireplace, picking through dead coals. She was relatively new at Big House, ghostly and unnoticeable, with dark hair pulled under her white bonnet. The name came to me — Lizzie. She wiped her forehead with the back of her wrist and looked up. She froze, wrist still lifted, staring at me, and I stared back in sudden recognition.

All at once I was seeing her from the corner of Father's study where he made us stand: the girl kneeling before him, Father with his long fine fingers pulling the bonnet from her dark mass of hair and bringing it up to his face, crushing it there, eyes closed.

Sir, Lizzie murmured now, and flicked her eyes down. She crouched there by the fireplace, her hands black with coal dust, a smoky wisp of hair escaping the bonnet at the nape of her neck. Yet the image of Father lingered on my retinas like a photographic flash, leaving shards of pain buried in my eyeballs. I winced, gripped the door frame. I felt myself listing forward into the room. This was Jekyll's house. I gave my head a violent shake and jerked myself back a step from the doorway. Then I hurried down the corridor toward the stairs. The hairs on my neck were prickling; I wanted to get out of here — something bad was going to happen if I didn't. The entrance hall was dim and as I passed into it, my balance went askew. I staggered, making a rattling clatter.

It was the wooden stand for walking sticks. Nearly a dozen of them slotted into separate compartments. I had grabbed one by accident, reflex, and I drew it from the slot. The warm brass knob fitted snug in my palm, and the stout oak shaft tapered to a brass cleat at the tip. I tapped a few times it on the flagstone, then shrugged and carried it down the hall to where my coat was hanging by the bench. I put down the stick, flung the overcoat on, snatched up the stick again, and turned to find Poole standing just behind me. Beg your pardon, I didn't mean to alarm you, sir. His gaze dipped to the stick clutched in my hand, then rose to my shaded eyes, peering wildly out from under my topper. His brow tensed, ever so slightly. Then he moved past me to open the front door. I squinted at the silver daylight, not quite believing I'd be allowed to leave. With hope, Dr. Jekyll will be here to receive you, Poole said, when you call on us again. I tittered out a nervous laugh. *With hope.* I edged past him and out the door.

DAY ONE

Nightfall

For the second time today, I turn back the bolt and ease the cabinet door open. Gaslight cuts down the stairwell and throws my shadow across the pitted brick wall. Halfway down, a glimmer of silver catches the light — the domed cover of the dinner tray. You see? All is well. Poole suspects nothing. As if the steps descend underwater, I take a deep breath and steal down in my stockings.

Poole always sets his tray down here, on this precise step, twelve from the top. It seems to be the exact centre step, though I haven't been the rest of the way down since we started living up here, two months ago. I take hold of the wooden rail and peer into the vaulted dark of the surgical theatre. Through the murky glass cupola high overhead, a funnel of twilight filters down onto the stone dissecting table, cluttered with bottles. Beyond the spotlight is gloom, thronging shadows. My eyes adjust as they scan the space, picking up the packing straw that scatters the floor around the table, an empty crate standing upright.

The axe. The axe Jekyll was using to smash the crates into slats and tinder when I awoke that summer. Is it still down there? Poole isn't permitted to tidy up in the theatre. If Jekyll didn't remove the axe, which I don't think he did, then it's down there, somewhere.

I hunker down next to the tray on the twelfth step. I should just go down there, sniff around. The axe is probably propped someplace in plain sight; I could take it with me up to the cabinet, lock it inside. How will they break the door down then? Yet I do not move. For this twelfth step, here, I'm beginning to realise — it is a boundary line. Why does Poole place the tray here *every* time? Every day for the last two months he has set the tray down here and never ascended a step above it, as if he too knows it is a boundary line. As if Jekyll and I have been living within a protected bubble in the cabinet that extends down to this precise step, separating our world and Poole's. Cross the boundary, and the spell of protection pops. I let my eye travel down the remaining steps that vanish into the blackness at the bottom, like a reflection of the steps rising behind me. As if I am kneeling at the rim of a dark mirror world, above my own blurred double luring me down.

No, I do not trust it. I rise, lifting the dinner tray by its scrolled-silver handles.

In the cabinet I set the tray on the laboratory table, peek under the cover. Steam billows out. A lamb shank leaking its juice into the boiled, bloodless vegetables. I shut the cover and turn away from the smell, repulsed by the very idea of eating. From the shelf above the glazed press, I haul down the two-gallon jug of ethanol. I pour some water into a graduated glass, and from the cumbersome jug I tip in a splash of the clear, pure alcohol. Bracing myself, I take a sip — boom! A blue flame bursts in the gastros and roars up my esophagus into the sinus and I cough, blinking tears. There's dinner for you! Burn off all the scum inside.

Carew came to Big House for his first visit soon after Jekyll's fiftieth birthday party, on 8 January. I suppose I can't blame Jekyll for inviting him. I had opened Carew's letter myself and tossed it back on the blotter. I could have burned it or something, but I didn't, I left it there for Jekyll to find. I don't really recall having any particular feeling at the time about Carew's visit, aside from my customary wariness of new characters.

He wore a royal-blue velvet jacket, very beautiful against his silvery hair. His face was laced with a network of delicate wrinkles. His eyes moved around Jekyll's study, crystal eyes, like disks of quartz. Poole brought in a decanter of pale sherry and two tiny glasses, bowed, and withdrew. Jekyll poured the sherry and said, *So that lecture you said you attended, my lecture in Vienna ten-odd years ago. I happen to remember it. It was on demonological fixations in early-dementia patients. I don't imagine there were many politicians in the audience.*

Carew made a wry little smile. No, I imagine not. But politicians would do well to attend the occasional psychiatric lecture; many I know could use the insight. He raised his sherry glass, then took a sip. I was in Vienna, Carew continued, for a conference, but my interest in your lecture was purely extracurricular. I was very interested in hearing you speak of your work on the Haemler case. *Yes,* Jekyll said, sitting back, *Erwina Haemler. I haven't thought of her case in years.* Ah, but it was groundbreaking. The most lucid presentation of circular insanity I had heard since Falret first described it.

Jekyll regarded him, suppressing the flush of flattery.

I assure you, Doctor, I'm not trying to charm you. I've merely maintained an amateur's interest in your field for many years. I find that your field of study and mine, you see, at times intersect. *And what is your field of study, if I might ask?* You are welcome. Tell me, have you heard of the Society for Psychical Research? Jekyll nodded. *I have. Gurney, Sidgwick, Myers, yes?* Very good, Carew said. He took another careful sip of his sherry, watching Jekyll over the crystal rim. *So, you investigate psychic phenomena.*

Carew nodded. Exactly.

Investigate: I didn't like the sound of that. I didn't like this man, with his clever eyes and private smiles. You do not care for the comparison, he said, our field to yours. Jekyll shrugged. *You're not the first to draw it. The mind cannot be seen, spirits cannot be seen, there is a seeming desire to conflate them.* Yet you consider them to be wholly distinct? *I find considerations of the spiritual realm unnecessary to psychiatry. The mind is quite enough on its own.*

Except, Carew said, surely you can't dismiss the issue out of hand, can you? Mrs. Haemler, for instance, believed herself to be infested by a demonic spirit — the Egyptian spirit Apep, if I recall correctly. Can you begin your analysis with the assumption she is deluded? *I begin with the assumption that the idea — in this case, possession by an Egyptian god of chaos — has a point of origin. The patient had the idea put into her head. I assume that it is the idea that is troubling her, not an actual spirit. Mrs. Haemler's husband was an archaeologist; she had visited Egypt with him several years earlier, which is where, I soon discovered, she heard stories of spiritual possession, deities entering mortal bodies. It obviously made a strong impression on her. And a year later, when she began to manifest certain symptoms — severe mood fluctuations, nightmares, disturbing daydreams — her mind sought an explanation and ultimately fixated upon the notion that she too had been ... infested, as you put it, by a spiritual entity. It is simpler for the mind to externalise causes of distress. The attachment to this idea stimulates her symptoms, and they worsen, confirming her suspicions. A self-perpetuating delusion.*

I had never heard Jekyll speak of his work like this. His work was sealed off in regions of the mind well beyond me, whole wings of memories I was curious about but also leery of. Jekyll's voice was calmly pedantic, but his pulse was picking up. Carew listened patiently. Except, he said, that does not absolutely rule out the possibility of an external cause, does it? Just because Mrs. Haemler had the idea put in her head that possession was possible does not mean, speaking logically, that possession is factually impossible. Especially when you are dealing with a patient who is not merely fixating upon the idea but actually transforming in appearance and behaviour. A patient who actually becomes, at certain times, a different person entirely. Surely — Carew paused, and then turned his eyes to the fire. It had gone horribly quiet. Jekyll had stopped breathing. Surely, Carew continued, when you are dealing with a patient such as Mr. Verlaine, you cannot rule out the possibility of possession until you've confirmed that it is definitively false.

It was as if Jekyll had been waiting to hear the name. Emile Verlaine, his French patient. His heart clenched tight and then opened with a hot rush of blood to his face. *Ah*, he said, like a sigh.

Carew glanced over. I can understand that you are hesitant to speak of the case, Doctor. And I hope you don't think I've come tonight to weasel the details out of you. *Why have you come tonight?* Carew took a breath. I've come because I would like to tell you something. I understand how these matters work. When there is publicity, public expectation, and then things go badly, a scapegoat is required. It is ancient behaviour, driving the goat from the village burdened down with the collective guilt. You were the obvious choice in this case, you were the head doctor, and an Englishman. But you are back in England now. You are amongst peers. There is sympathetic, admiring interest in your work. And if you should have any wish to unburden yourself, to share your accomplishments, I would consider it a great honour to hear of them.

I did not like this. I knew this racing in Jekyll's veins. I had felt it each time he'd spoken my name aloud, to the bank clerk, to Utterson, to Poole. It was the terrible thrill of trespass. And yet in spite of my increasing unease, I was gripped by it too. I wanted to hear, to learn. Jekyll just sat in his wing chair, legs crossed, one finger at his chin, the shell of his face cool and intact.

What precisely would you like to know, Sir Danvers?

Carew lifted his gaze to that picture hanging above the mantel. He seemed to contemplate it a moment, that blackish, swirling mess of paint. I would like to understand how you determined, if indeed you did determine, the origin of Mr. Verlaine's other personalities. How you eliminated the possibility that they derived from some external source. Jekyll did not say anything. Carew kept his eyes on the picture, waiting. Perhaps, he said, you might tell me something of your initial experience with the personalities. It would have been Pierre you met first?

Pierre, Jekyll repeated softly. *Yes. Although Emile didn't have a name for him when he was first admitted to the hospital, about six months before I arrived. Emile was having episodes, lapses into unaccountable, childlike behaviour. He had no memory or awareness of these episodes; they were blacked out. He was frightened. But he put on a brave show, welcomed me very warmly, wanted to speak English. Told me he was eager to address the problem. Handsome young man. Talented painter.* Jekyll stopped. Something lightly gripped him at the throat.

It was Mr. Verlaine's father, Carew prompted, who admitted him?

The father. Monsieur Verlaine. He had just gotten remarried, to a younger woman. Emile's mother had died nearly ten years before. Emile was reluctant to speak of her, his mother. But he wanted to cooperate, he wanted to get better. For the first month he didn't have any episodes. Then one of the orderlies came to fetch me. Emile's room appeared to be empty when I entered. I looked under the drawing table, and there was this boy, cowering under there. Staring at me as if I were a stranger. He looked at least ten years younger than my patient. Only because I knew it was Emile could I recognise him.

Did he speak to you? Carew asked, after a silence. *No. Not that first episode. The second time, he spoke to me. I was ready. I had prepared an experiment. One of the orderlies came to fetch me again and I brought a box of chocolate truffles. Emile, you should know, did not care for sweets of any kind. The boy was in bed facing the wall, crying. I opened the box and ate a chocolate. The boy stopped crying at once, turned around. He slid from the bed and came over. Not all the way, he kept his distance, but when I extended the box, he plucked one out and stuffed it in his mouth. Pure joy in his expression as he chewed. He swallowed and then eyed the box in my hand as if he were a cowering dog. Emile always held himself straight and graceful; he met your eyes squarely. Yet here was this cringing child begging for another sweet. I said that I would give him the entire box if he told me his name. And that is when he said, Pierre.*

For a moment I could almost see the boy's face in the shimmer of the fire, eyes closed, dreamy with rapture. A room with wrought-iron bars over the windows and pictures hung on the walls. Then Jekyll shook his head. He lifted a hand to touch his face, below his eye. *Please excuse me. I didn't expect to speak of this tonight.* Carew was silent. Of course, he said at last, of course, I understand. He patted the arms of his wing chair and pushed himself to his feet. Jekyll stood as well. Carew's eyes lifted again to the picture above the mantel as he buttoned his velvet coat. Jekyll contemplated it too: a hideous thing, whirlpools of paint in the knotted frame. Carew turned to Jekyll and extended his spidery hand. Dr. Jekyll, thank you. This has been a most intriguing conversation. To be continued, I hope?

Jekyll stood in the entrance hall after closing the door on Carew. A piece of coal lay on the flagstone hearth, its shadow flickering long and struggling to escape. It was giving me a vertiginous sense of disproportion, as if the chunk of coal were in fact a huge boulder we were looking down upon from a sickening height. There was so much I did not know. All at once I was realising it, the magnitude of my ignorance. How little I knew about the years, the life that yawned like an abyss behind me.

About Emile Verlaine I knew what Jekyll needed me to know, what memories he had selectively shown me to explain what the powder and syringe could do. But listening to Jekyll tonight was like hearing the young man's case for the first time, filling me with a revelatory fear, a dizzying sense of expanding dimension. What had happened to Emile Verlaine? How had Jekyll lost him?

I stared at the coal, feeling on the brink of a dark premonition — before Jekyll stiffened and strode from the entrance hall. Ten minutes later I was locking the Castle Street door behind me.

Jekyll felt distant as I stumped north to Soho. I knew he was thinking about his conversation with Carew. I knew he had let me loose to distract me whilst he pursued his own thoughts. I didn't like this secrecy, this feeling of a dark, open doorway widening behind my back.

I arrived at the Pig and Gibbet without even realising I'd been headed there. Fondly I peered up at the gold-flaked letters, then pushed inside. Ah, the Pig and Gibbet. Even though they betrayed me, all the regulars and Vic in particular, I can't seem to hold it against them. They were such a weary, brokenhearted lot. Not the weekend crowd, but the regulars who'd chosen the place decades back for whatever reason and stuck grimly with it. I can see them ranged down the chipped bar, nursing their milds, old men and a few rawboned whores, and fat surly Vic reading his daily up against the dusty bottles. Dead and quiet, that's the way I liked it best. I wasn't a regular — the regulars had been coming for years — but my presence was acknowledged by them with a kind of begrudging obligation in their mucosal old eyes. When I took my seat and placed a sovereign on the bar, Vic would bring me the gin bottle and a glass. His face was a fleshy splintered sack with two sad mistrustful eyes gleaming out. He would tip me the faintest of nods and trudge back to his post, leaving me with the bottle. I had to earn that, him leaving me the bottle, and as I sat there pouring out my own shots at my own corner of the bar, I felt like a man of substance.

This night, however, there was a man sitting at the far end of the bar, *my* end of the bar. And not a regular either. He had a pink elderly face with a white moustache and wore a dark plain suit and cheap collar. They did not match, the face and the suit. I took a stool at the middle of the bar and tossed down a coin.

The gent was drinking neat whisky. His hand had a slight, elegant palsy as he brought the glass to his lips. I could picture him perfectly in the Grampian lounge, in tailored tweeds, chuckling along with the old boys. So what was he doing here, of all places? The Pig didn't generally attract many tourists, and it irritated me that this tame old party had even found the pub, obscure as it was, and then presumed to take *my* seat. I felt unguarded, sitting at the middle bar, with my back to the foul corridor leading to the jakes and the alley. Hunched over my elbows, I watched the old gentleman, his eyes wandering unobtrusively around the room, brows politely lifted. When he encountered my seething stare he paused and then raised his whisky with a weak smile and that genteel tremour in his hand. That spike of pain was beginning to pierce my left eyeball again. I pressed the ocular hollow with my fingers. My skin felt clammy, and my other hand was gripping the gin glass so hard it was trembling. It did not seem like my hand, with that bifurcate vein branching over the knuckles, I didn't feel quite in control of it. Suddenly the glass slipped out of my hand, wobbled to the edge of the bar, and dropped onto Vic's side like a drunk off a high wall. Vic lowered his paper and looked morosely up at me. I tried to grin and caught sight of myself in the warped mirror behind the bottles, a bulging face crowded with teeth. Startled, I looked away, at the gent at the end, and found him on his feet counting out coins from his cupped palm. He tipped a gracious nod to Vic, picked up his hat from the stool, and made his way to the door, sending a wave of goose flesh over my back as he passed.

Then I was outside on the misty lane following after him. I didn't remember leaving the bar — I was just there, cracking my stick down the cobblestones. I could see the old man's rounded hat in perfect silhouette against the gas lamp's halo ahead, his careful jerky gait. I could feel the brass knob of my stick moulded to my grasp, and the pricks of fine rain on my face. Yet the body's impetus seemed beyond me, as if I had drifted off for a moment and was trying now to catch up. Against the greenish curtain of gaslight, the old man stopped and peered into the lane behind him, and I kept coming, smacking the brass cleat to the stones. My sternum was starting to vibrate. It felt like the centre of my momentum, surging forward as if to something magnetised — and I realised that Jekyll was no longer at the far reaches but now ringed intently around me. The old gent was making for Dean Street, which intersected our empty lane ahead, and as I closed in I could hear his wheezing and see his plumes of breath. He looked back at me again and tried to run. Then he clutched his leg, braced himself with a hand on the wall. He coughed, then straightened as I strolled up.

The edges of his moustache quivered as he gave me a firm, patrician stare. Evening, he said with a rough nod. I lifted my stick and pressed the brass cleat into his padded shoulder. Excuse me, he said, and I backed him up against the brick wall, with just enough pressure to pin him there. I could smell his sweet, powdered flesh, the old impostor. My molars were grinding together and blood was beating in my temples, spotting the edges of my sight. Where had this rage come from? It had taken hold of me like a fever. The old man swallowed and stammered, Wh-what do you want? Is it money you want? *What do you want?* I said, leaning into the stick. *Cunny? Pretty young cunny? Is that what you're after, old man?* He shook his head, swinging the dewlap under his chin. His mouth flapped in protest. *Oh yes, that's what you want, old man like you, nice young cunny, fresh as cream.* A fiery-haired, laughing phantom flickered across my mind just then, indistinct as a passing scent, and I looked off down the lane as if to catch it: burnished curls, a bare white throat, head thrown back in merriment . . . That name again, *Georgiana.* The old man was gripping the end of my stick, trying to dislodge it from his shoulder socket as he grunted and said, No, no, a drink is all I wanted, please. I swung my gaze back to him, blinking off the vision. *Then drink where you belong. Not here. Don't ever come here again. I see you here again and I'll ram this stick into your arse and snap it off. You think you're fooling anyone? Stay where you belong. You got that, dying old man?*

I could hear myself snarling out these words; it was as if someone were speaking through me in a choked voice. The man was nodding vehemently. The stick twisted in my hand, then I pulled back and released him. He grabbed his shoulder, gasping. His eyes rolled up, and for a second I saw another phantom: Father in his wheelchair, ash-white hair hanging to his shoulders, holding that pen and watching us, a final moment. Then my stick leapt up and smacked the old man in the mouth. His head snapped back as something jumped from his face and clattered at my feet. Teeth. A row of teeth. The man was making muffled noises, covering his mouth as he cringed to the wall. I bent down and picked up the teeth, set into a mould of pale gums. I held them up and the old man goggled at me, bareheaded, his bowler now on the stones. He reached his bloody shaking hand from his mouth, now collapsed and dark, his moustache stained. I drew the teeth back. *These are mine now.* I jerked my head at Dean Street. *Go. Go before something bad happens to you.*

I watched him stagger off, then turned and went the other way. My knees felt shaky; I had to resist the woozy urge to hunker down on the stones. I was still pinching the man's teeth, I realised, and I stuffed them disgustedly into my coat pocket. Why had I taken them? But I hadn't. I hadn't struck him; the stick — it'd just leapt up on its own. As if I were a puppet with someone's hand inside. I hadn't even decided to go after the old man to begin with, I had simply . . . How *had* I gotten from the barstool to the street outside? A sliver of time was missing. When had this happened before?

It had happened at Auntie Gorgon's girlie shop. I see that now, of course. But as I wandered away into the drizzle that night, I could just dimly remember the other episode — that room with the Christ, the broken street outside, the white-brick house on

Bedford Square. I did not want to remember. I didn't want to start piecing things together, not when my new life had only just begun. I didn't want to think anything might be amiss. Perhaps Jekyll *had* taken control of the body, scared the old man off our turf. The notion was perturbing, that he could reach through me, into me . . .

But it wasn't my function to question the existence I'd been granted. It seemed the easiest solution was to forget about the old impostor and his teeth. Which I did, especially after Jekyll's encounter with Utterson at the Grampian several days later. Jekyll was crossing the cavernous granite lobby as Utterson descended the steps from above, tucking his muffler into his coat. Jekyll hadn't seen the solicitor since his birthday party, and even then they hadn't spoken more than a dozen words. Utterson stopped at the foot of the stairs. *You're leaving?* Jekyll said. *Bosh, come up and sit with me.* But Utterson shook his head, still fussing with his muffler. Dining with a client. He glanced into Jekyll's eyes, a rueful, guarded look. How are you, Harry? *I'm well, how are you, John?* Utterson held the glance from under his shaggy eyebrows. And Mr. Hyde? How is he?

The skin over Jekyll's cheekbones tightened. *Mr. Hyde is also well, last I saw of him.* And when might I see him? Utterson asked. *You'd like to meet him?* Of course I'd like to meet him. Given the terms of your will, I should think it necessary that I meet him, don't you agree? *Perhaps,* said Jekyll slowly. *I'll propose it to him, next I see him. I warn you, I doubt he'll consent. He's suspicious of new people. Our kind of people, especially. They intimidate him.* Well, it's only me. Just a brief chat, that's all. Any place of his choosing. *Yes, as I said, I'll propose the idea. No promises, I'm afraid.*

Utterson nodded, the shrewd old dog. No, he said. No promises.

It was out of the question, of course. There was no way I was showing my face to suspicious Utterson. That will — that stupid, insane will — I had almost managed to forget that Jekyll had actually sent the thing to the solicitor, that by now it was most likely locked in Utterson's safe, festering at the back of his mind. What was Jekyll trying to do — did he *want* Utterson to find our secret out?

He seemed to have no intention of letting Utterson meet me; I could read that clearly enough, with some relief. Yet the encounter left him pensive in the days following. It was his friend Hastie Lanyon he was thinking of. I knew a little about Dr. Hastie Lanyon by now, absorbed from the general atmosphere of Jekyll's mind. Something had happened in recent years between Jekyll and Lanyon; something had soured. Wisps of memory were adrift: I could see the two friends as young men, on a ferryboat chopping through northern seas, bellowing gloriously at the rail into the tearing wind as Lanyon's pale hair whipped his happy, pretty face. But I also caught a glimpse of him years later, red in the face like an impotent despot, standing in some drawing room and shouting, I won't have it, Harry, I won't have you putting your hocus-pocus on her!

I wasn't surprised when, about a week after his run-in with Utterson, Jekyll wrote Lanyon a letter asking his friend to dinner. It seemed an oblique but clever piece of strategy. Utterson could not be allowed to meet me, but at least Jekyll could see Hastie, as Utterson had been urging him to do. Perhaps the man would be mollified by that.

They met in a restaurant, low lit like a wine cellar, bottles slotted into the walls. Lanyon was already seated in a side room next to a fireplace, a slight man in a canary-yellow waistcoat gazing vaguely off into the air. He gave a start as Jekyll approached, then stood up and offered a shy smile and his strong little hand. He had a brick-red, elfin face, curly flaxen hair. Hesitantly, his faded blue eyes met Jekyll's. Hullo, Harry, he said. Awkward silence after they sat down. Lanyon had been drinking. A soft, bifurcate vein stood under his eye. He considered for an unfocused moment the crystal rim of his glass, then glanced up and waved his finger for the waiter. Some wine? You'll have a glass with me, won't you, Harry?

The waiter poured Lanyon a quarter of a glass, which he gave a swirl then sniffed above the rim before holding it up to the fire-light. He tipped the burgundy back at a swallow, eyes briefly shut. Jekyll watched the performance with a tightness in his throat. When both glasses were full, Lanyon lifted his and said, Well, Harry, what to? Jekyll had not yet reached for his glass. *Hastie. I'm sorry. I'm so very sorry.*

Lanyon tried to smile but it broke, and his eyes went glassy — and all at once I knew, with a kind of *ah, yes.* Lanyon had lost his wife. Utterson had written to Jekyll in Paris. Suddenly I could see her, a plump woman with rich marmalade hair pinned up in a bun, sitting in Jekyll's study before the fire, red-nosed and sniff-ing, twisting a handkerchief. Then Jekyll blinked and I saw Lan-yon across the table still holding his wine with a wavering smile. Yes, Lanyon said, I'm sorry too. His gaze fell to Jekyll's wine. He wagged his finger at it. Now, come on, then, don't leave me in the lurch. What to, Harry? Jekyll looked at his glass, lifted it. *To us, I suppose.*

He brought the glass to his lips but did not let the warm sweet wine enter his mouth. He never swallowed alcohol. Just took these careful, feigned sips in company when required.

After they had ordered, another silence fell. Everything seemed sensitive ground. *How's the practise?* Jekyll asked eventu-ally, and Lanyon shrugged. It's been better. Been a difficult year, of course. I've been paying some house calls, though. They keep me out and about. *That's good. What are people ailing of, these days?* Oh, the usual. Rheumatism, gout, tuberculosis. Breast can-cer, quite a few cases of breast cancer, actually. Nothing I can do for them, of course, except prescribe laudanum and a good sur-geon. Lanyon frowned, shrugged his shoulders again. *My mother,* Jekyll said after a long pause. *Breast cancer for her as well.*

Goodness. I didn't know that, Harry.

I was very young. Five or six. Nothing the surgeons could do either. My father made me drink a big glass of whisky, and when I came to, the butchers had gone. They had a sheet over her, upstairs, but my father drew it down for me. Held the back of my neck, so I could see. Both breasts, it was.

Goodness, Lanyon said again, Harry! He looked down into his wine, translucent in the firelight. John told me, he began tentatively. John told me about your father. His passing. Jekyll nodded. Lanyon cleared his throat. John told me that you were in the room, his hospital room, when it happened.

I was. Except it didn't merely happen. *Did John tell you that too?* Lanyon was silent. *His fountain pen was lying on the table near the windows. He asked me to bring it to him. Said he had something for me, something to sign over to me.*

I could see it again: the gleaming wooden pen on the table. I could see Father's hand, yellow-nailed and palsied, as he reached to take it from us. Father unscrewed the cap, beheld the steel nib. Then he looked up at us, from his wheelchair, with his overgrown hair and naked, moustacheless mouth, a stranger except for the eyes. *Henry,* he whispered.

He took the pen from me, Jekyll said. *And he* — Jekyll lifted his chin and jerked his fist at his throat. He held Lanyon's horrified gaze, head tipped back, as a geyser of blood hissed through our mind, Father blinking, gurgling. Good Lord! Lanyon said, eyes wide, as if seeing it too. Good Lord, Harry, he — he must've been utterly senile. Jekyll shook his head. *I don't think so. His doctor had written to me, said my father had been asking repeatedly to see me. He had planned it out. He had set the pen on that table so that I could carry it to him.*

But, Lanyon said, but why?

Jekyll gazed at him. *Atonement.*

At that moment, the waiter arrived with the first course, cold prawns in aspic. Both of them considered the scalloped mounds, still aquiver. *Well, I'm just famished,* Jekyll announced, and Lanyon let out a snort of laughter. *Look,* Jekyll said, leaning forward, *why don't we knock off the morbid talk. What do you say, Old Gooseberry?* Lanyon looked puzzled for a moment, then his face lit up and he roared out a laugh. Old Gooseberry! I'd forgotten all about Old Gooseberry! And who was his wife, Old Gooseberry and — ah, don't tell me — who was it again? *Lady Halibut,* Jekyll said, and Lanyon threw his head back in laughter and banged the table with his hand. Holding his tiny fork, Jekyll watched him, that ache swelling again in his throat. Poor old Lanyon. He sniffed and wiped his sparkling eyes with his linen. This one we can handle, I remember thinking. This one is no Utterson.

Lanyon had port instead of coffee. The talk had turned to their schooldays, more silly nicknames, a story about their anatomy professor, Utterson in his nightshirt and slippers demanding quiet. At one point Lanyon was gasping with laughter and waving his hands. No more, he pleaded, ah, no more! The tablecloth had somehow gotten tucked into his waistcoat, and when they stood up at last, he nearly dragged all the plates and glasses off. Jekyll steered him through the restaurant and helped him into his coat at the door. The maître d' was wishing them good evening and Lanyon was pumping his hand and then came her voice from behind — Henry.

Instant recognition. Jekyll turned and there she was at last, just outside the archway to the main dining room. Georgiana. A dainty bird in pink silk with a white-blond bun and blue eyes, her quick lively face tilted up with an amused little smile. Henry, she said, I knew it was you. Jekyll stood there, coat over his arm, pulse slamming against his cool outer shell. He crossed the foyer and took the hand she offered, fragile-boned and cold. *Georgiana.* She gazed up at him with that amused, half-sad little smile. Up close, we could see that fine age lines touched the edges of her eyes, the wings of her mouth. Listen, she said, patting his hand, I'm with people, back in there, but I saw you and — and that's Hastie Lanyon, isn't it? She leant to look behind Jekyll, and then she straightened, said quietly, Henry, I've been, it's funny, I've been — could I come to see you, do you think?

It came out in a rush, and she made a hesitant, wincing face. *See me? Of course. When?* When I can get away, in a week, perhaps. I'll write to let you know. Is that — is this horribly inappropriate? *No, not at all. I'd be delighted.* Georgiana raised a hand as if to press it to his chest. Thank you. Her brow creased in slight pain, and she said softly, Henry. Then she turned and swished back into the dining room.

Was that not Miss Floris? Lanyon said slyly when they were outside. Jekyll stood rigid looking across the road at nothing. *It's Waller now.* Lanyon said, Right, right. There was silence. Well, he said brightly, what does the evening hold in store for a pair of old bachelors? Jekyll looked down at Lanyon. *Hastie, forgive me, but home.*

Back at Big House Jekyll wandered into the parlour and pretended to browse through a book he picked off the shelf. He listened for Poole, then snapped the book shut and crossed the room to the far doorway that led into the powder-blue side parlour, which never seemed to be used. He went to the wall and found the faint vertical line running from ceiling to floor, where the secret panel was, and gave the wall a push. There was a click and the panel fell open, and he slipped through the gap into the servants' pantry. Dim shelving, smell of silver polish and sawdust. I knew the smell. I'd been in here before, on the first night. I had crept across the courtyard and entered Big House by the servants' door, the tall black door down the corridor to our left. I could see it through the slim doorway now, as Jekyll stood in the pantry. He went down the servants' corridor, with its many doors on either side, to the black door at the end and the foggy courtyard beyond.

Why didn't he leave through the conservatory as usual? It

seems significant to me now, that he should go in there, into the servants' corridor, on this particular night, the night he sent me out to find Jeannie.

It was the clearest impulse I had ever received. The moment I lurched into the body I knew what he wanted me to do. That girl we had seen in the Toad, weeks and weeks ago, the girl who had flashed through my mind just the other night — laughing, shaking her burnished head. I wanted to find her, to see her again. It was as if I had walked past a tiny silver key in the road miles back and suddenly realised what lock it might fit.

At the Toad I stood crushed to the bustling, sticky bar, peering about. When the barman passed, I snagged his sleeve and shouted, *There's a girl, little redheaded thing with a big laugh. Know her?* The barman had pig eyes embedded in his baby face. What, he said, Jeannie? *I don't know,* I shouted, *little redheaded thing with the laugh?* The barman just gave me his squalid gaze, eyebrows lifted. I put a quid on the bar. He told me to try the Gullet. And there she was.

The Gullet was the proper name. The place was dark and narrow and at the back fell down a steep staircase to a basement room. She was down in that candlelit grotto, leaning on the bar talking to the barman, gesturing expressively. One of her feet was curled round her other ankle. The barman was cleaning a glass with a filthy rag as he half listened to the girl. He glanced at me as I approached. *Gin,* I said. *And one more for the lady.* He sniffed a laugh, poured a gin for me in the glass he'd been cleaning. The girl held out her glass and he splashed some in there. One more for the lady — where had that come from? The girl looked at me and slit her eyes, and I saw the resemblance at once: Georgiana's quick sharp face, the disconcertingly direct blue eyes. The girl's hair was dyed deep vermilion and her front teeth were gapped, but the way she was looking at me was strikingly familiar, a kind of mock-sceptical appraisal. *How does you know I's a lady?* she said with an exaggerated accent. She was having me on. I couldn't think what to say. I knocked off my gin at a swallow. She took a sip from her glass then tipped her chin back and gargled it, almost spitting it back out and then covering her mouth and coughing. *You're a funny girl.* No, I'm not, she said, I'm very, very sad, if you must know. Tragic story, mine is. Her voice skipped drunkenly along, picking up accents and putting them down. She leant on the bar, head propped on her hand. Slit her eyes at me again. You don't talk much, do you? I grinned down at the floor. *I lack practise.* Oh dear, she said. She yawned hugely, and sighed. Do you have a tragic story too?

I took her back to Ghyll. I'd never taken anyone there. We didn't speak on the walk over. She followed me with her hands in her pockets, humming to herself. She wore a shabby coat and slipperlike shoes, in spite of the ice on the stones. When we came to Ghyll's front gate, she stopped in the road behind me, looking doubtfully up at the unlit house slotted into its shadowy recess. I was fishing my chain of keys from under my collar. *It's all right. This is home.*

The entrance hall was cold and laced with its distinctive odour that struck me every time I returned after a few days away. Like ammonia, or whatever Mrs. Deaker used to clean, if she cleaned at all. I was ushering the girl toward the stairs when the old woman's voice crooned, Master returns, and we froze. Mrs. Deaker bobbed in the dim drawing-room doorway. Good evening to you, Master. Welcome back. She chuckled, a wet treacly sound. She was drunk. *Good evening to you, Mrs. Deaker.* The old lady scuffled a step forward. I saw a flash of her eyes, reflective, like a cat's. And young missy, welcome to you as well. What a treat. We don't receive many visitors, do we, Master? *Thank you, Mrs. Deaker, that'll be all.* Yes, time for bed, isn't it. Well, good night to you, Master, and young missy. She swayed there, at the far end of the entrance hall, eyes shining and then winking out. I gave the girl a nudge and led her upstairs to my room.

A slant of blue light fell through the verandah doors, slicing across my canopied bed. I let my greatcoat drop to the floor as I went to the sideboard. I held up the bottle to see how much Mrs. Deaker had nipped in my absence, then sloshed gin into two tumblers. My hand was unsteady. I could hear the girl behind me stepping tentatively over the creaky floor. This was new. Bringing this girl here, up to my room, my sanctum. This girl who seemed so familiar, as if I'd known her in a dream. I was almost afraid, a voluptuous fear thickening in my throat with Jekyll's urgency pounding behind it. I turned.

She stood with hands in coat pockets, watching me, her face very still and white. I held out her gin. *Nightcap.* She came slowly over, took the tumbler in both hands. The top of her head barely reached my chest as she stood before me. I watched my hand rise as if on a string; the crook of my finger found her chin and lifted her tense white face. She breathed through her nostrils, eyes fixed upon me, trying to look cool and detached. But I could see her behind that, alive with wary fright, reckless excitement. I had an urge to lean down and kiss her on the mouth. The impulse welled in me like music; I lowered my head and she took a step back, slipping off my finger. She eyed me over the rim of her glass as she brought it to her lips. I walked past her, toward the bed, loosening my tie.

Naked under the satin sheets I waited, shivering, as she undressed. When the baggy drawers had dropped she stood, turned away, marble blue. I followed the knobs of her spine and dimpled coccyx to the lavender bruise on the back of her thigh. She sat on the edge of the bed and lay down as I swung the sheet over her. It settled like silky oil over her contours. She was shivering too. I held myself up on one arm, looking down at her. I felt on the brink of something, an exhilarating fall. *Jeannie. It is Jeannie, isn't it.* She nodded, eyes wide upon me. *How old are you?* She swallowed. Sixteen, she whispered. *Sixteen,* I repeated. Then I let myself go.

•   •   •

I truly did. In the midst of it I sucked down her trim length and spread her legs, kneeling in between as before a sacrificial altar. Oh, I did it, the thing that Father taught us, forcing our head into Alice's lap. As if his hand were gripping my head now, I knelt before her and lapped and slurped at her neat, musky quim. She squirmed and twitched and tried to get away, and then she squealed and ground the slippery flesh against my teeth as something quaked inside her and Father whispered, *Good, good boy.* From behind I buried my face in her hair and twisted handfuls of satin sheet, and when the end came I crushed shut my eyes into sparkling blackness.

I woke before dawn. Jeannie was sleeping with her face pressed into the pillow, mouth open, snoring faintly with each breath. I sat up and watched her. I had found this girl for a reason, as if she were indeed a key to a lock opening into the unknown, into Jekyll's past. There had been no women in that past, I knew. There could be no women, no lovers. For Jekyll there could be no nakedness, no vulnerable soul. His costume had to be impenetrable, a monk's mantle. This Georgiana, this flirtation, friendship, whatever it was, had turned out to be, in the end, yet another failed experiment. A failure, it seemed, I was now being offered the chance to rectify. Jeannie's eye opened, and she focused upon me. She lifted herself onto an elbow. The side of her face was seamed with a scar from the pillow. I got to get home, she said. She slipped from the bed and, covering her breasts, began collecting her clothes from the floor. I watched her, unable to speak. At last she had her shabby coat back on, and she stood at the edge of the bed, picking the thready hem of her sleeve. You said a fiver after too.

I have to see you again, I whispered.

DAY TWO

Before Dawn

Have to see you again. I said it as though I hadn't any choice. This is what strikes me, increasingly, as I dredge out these details and reassemble them into their proper, murderous order: that they could not have happened any differently. It wasn't just coincidence that Georgiana was dining in that particular restaurant that evening, that Jeannie was drinking exactly where I had been told to look. I'll say it again: There are no coincidences.

Why does it obsess me so, that idea — that everything happens the way it was always going to happen? Because it means that there is no escape? Yet I already know there is no escape, from this cabinet, from the ending that awaits me. Utterson banging at the cabinet door, then the axe, the door splintering apart, me cringing by the windows clutching the phial of cyanide. That's how I'll do it. With the cyanide. Jekyll cooked up the dram of clear, colourless extract a month ago. As if he could see the ending too. As if the cyanide were to be his parting gift to me. That is what I'm saying. Inevitability. You cannot evade what is going to happen because, in a sense, it already *has* happened. It's just a question of perspective. Even as I lie here on my bed of hard floorboards, atrophied, exhausted, but perfectly alive — even now I am already dead.

◆ ◆ ◆

I met Jeannie at the Toad the following night and again took
her back to Ghyll. After the climax, Jekyll receded, sinking like
a body into watery depths after thrashing for life at the surface.
Yet his mind still rang like ripples in the air. Propped against the
headboard, Jeannie and I devoured the remains of a ragged lamb
joint and a loaf of crusty bread I had scrounged from the kitchen,
and as I surreptitiously watched her chew, I slipped inside a memory. A parlour, cup of tea on Jekyll's knee. Young Georgiana was
playing the piano, and her mother beside the bench was singing
Italian opera in a terrible soprano. The sounds were muted as he
focused on the girl, just a few years older than Jeannie, sharply
pretty with honey-white hair piled up in a bun. Her clavicle
jumped as she played. Her eyes slid askance and met Jekyll's, a
cryptic, intricate look, eyebrows lifted as if in question.

The scene dissolved. With a lump of meat in her cheek, Jeannie eyed me as I stared at her, a tang of tenderness in my throat.
It was quiet in the bedroom. The fire low with big shadows minutely atremble. *The thing is,* I found myself saying, *you remind
me of someone.* Your daughter? Jeannie said, brushing crumbs
from her belly. She glanced quick at me, as if the quip had just
slipped out. *I don't have a daughter.* I looked down at the bloody
plate between us. Who do I remind you of? Jeannie asked quietly. *Someone from another life.* Jeannie nodded. I get that all the
time. *Really. How many lives have you lived?* She thought hard for
a moment, squinting. Four, she said. Somehow I had known she
was going to say that: four. She giggled, tickled by herself, and I
reached for her hair. Already I was mad for her hair, magenta-
dyed, like a disguise, and heavy with unwashed odour. I reached
to take a strand and she allowed me, watching my fingers as I let
the hair run through. Then I reached for the back of her neck and
she pulled away. No, sir, no more, I got to get home. She made
to throw off the sheet and I took her wrist. *Stay.* I can't, she said.
Her eyes flicked up to me, flat and hard, wary again. I can't. My
da. I held her a moment longer, then let her go.

Stay? I'd never felt this way about a dolly, never wanted anything to do with any of them afterwards. Yet when I had closed the front door on the girl, down in the entrance hall, a fresh pain whistled through me like air sucked through a rotten tooth. I stood in the gloom savouring it, the sharp, sweet ache.

I saw her the next night as well, and when she left in the early hours I almost snuck after her to see if indeed she had a home — and a da. I went as far as Ghyll's front gate and then stopped, gripping the iron spears of the fence, listening to her high aimless humming dwindle down the road. Back in my room, I tried to sleep and could not. At last I threw off the sheets and dressed, found my stick, and stalked back to Castle Street.

Jekyll was anxious to see if Georgiana had written. A day or two later, she did. Poole brought the letter up to Jekyll in his study. It had been delivered, Poole said, by the boy from the wine merchant. Yet it was addressed to the London Ornithological Society, and the letter inside was written in code, confirming the date two days hence as acceptable for an outing, provided the weather held. Jekyll folded the letter back into its envelope and stood at his study window, hands behind his back, and for a second I glimpsed into a yellow sitting room with a pair of ugly wing chairs and Georgiana standing very close, with a sad smile of pity. Henry, she said gently, it's all right.

Jekyll flinched, turned from the window, and glared at the envelope on his desk. The familiar script looped across its face. He hesitated, then reached out and lifted it by the corner. He opened his desk drawer and dropped the letter inside. And did nothing. He was standing at his study windows again when she came two days later, as promised.

It was the first or second of February, a dark morning on the verge of sleet. Jekyll had taken an hour to decide on a beige twill suit with a knitted burgundy waistcoat. He turned from the windows as Poole entered the study to say that Miss Georgiana had arrived. *Very good, Poole. I'll come down with you.* Poole followed him down the corridor. *Mr. Hyde tells me that he's felt very welcome here,* Jekyll said. *I'm sorry I haven't been home to receive him, but I saw him the other night and thought I'd pass his compliments along. Thank you, Poole, it means a great deal to me for him to feel at home here.* From behind, Poole murmured, Sir. *You do not care for him, do you.* I do not offer an opinion, sir. *Well, you aren't alone. I don't imagine there are many who do care for him. He has much to learn in the way of manners. But he is a kind of genius. And genius must be nurtured, must be protected.* Jekyll turned and gazed into Poole's languid, Arabian eyes. *Can you understand that?* Poole met his gaze. Perfectly, sir. Jekyll considered him a moment longer, then nodded. *Good man.*

Downstairs he found Georgiana in the parlour reading the spines of the books in the case. She held out her hand. She looked older than she had at the restaurant; the lines at the edge of her eyes and mouth seemed deeper, and for a moment I couldn't quite recognise the woman with her shining head cocked and her knowing smile. Henry, she said. Jekyll bowed over her hand, and she pressed his thumb with hers underneath. He let her go, cleared his throat. *Perhaps . . .* Georgiana nodded. Yes, that's what I was thinking.

I knew he was going to bring her up to the cabinet. Jekyll had been upstairs an hour before, warming the stove, scanning for anything that might seem suspicious. It struck me as madness to take her up there. This was *our* room. The cabinet was the nexus of our lives. And yet I also knew that the cabinet had not always been our room. It had been Jekyll's private consulting room, many years ago. He met with patients up there. He had met with Georgiana up there, several times, when he was young and fresh from his training and success on the Continent, full of promise. Now he led Georgiana across the courtyard to the surgery block squatting in the midmorning damp. The steel door gave a rusty shriek, and something flapped about the glass cupola, trapped. Jekyll lit the lantern and offered his hand.

He unlocked the cabinet door, lined on the outside with a layer of thick red baize, and Georgiana stepped in behind him. In her navy dress and shawl, flushed in the cheeks, she gazed about the room, running her eyes past the windows and around the furniture until she came to the blank space of wall near the corner where Father's portrait hung. She went over, stopped a few paces from Father. Perpetually young, with his rich brown hair, his full drooping moustache and nether-lip tuft, his collar raked open beneath the black velvet jacket, he sat on a stool with his precious violin propped on his knee. His expression remote, yet at the same time wet and sentient in the lachrymal ducts. This is your father, Georgiana said.

It is. Jekyll was standing by the table. It's quite remarkable, she said. How did you come by it? *He left it to me. He's dead.*

Oh, Henry, I'm so sorry. When did he die? *In August.* Not this August past? *This last summer, yes. He left me the portrait, and the violin he's holding in it.* He gestured at the mirror, where the black violin case was leaning up against the wall behind it. *It's a Stradivarius. Quite valuable. It has its own name, some Italian name.* You told me he was a conductor, I believe? Georgiana said. *Yes. Of the Edinburgh Orchestra. The youngest they'd ever had. Unconventional too; he would sometimes play the violin solo himself, or so I heard. Fame, travel. Then my mother died.*

I am sorry, Georgiana said.

I'm not. I'm not the least bit sorry. He lived far too long. I had begun to think he was really going to outlast me, like some perverse joke.

Georgiana turned to Father's picture again, his sedate and constant stare. Mother made me sit for a portrait, she said. I'm playing the piano. I had to sit there for hours and hours. Now it's in the parlour. Opposite her own picture. So they just look at each other, from across the room. Mother goes on and on about the likeness. That's her word, the *likeness*. I don't think it looks like me at all. Something in the face is wrong. Georgiana let out a nervous laugh. Now we'll both outlast ourselves, Mother and I. Isn't that why people have these portraits done? So they can hang there on the walls, staring out at whoever's left? Sometimes I imagine taking the picture down in the middle of the night and cutting out the face. My face. Then hanging it back up and pretending to be horrified in the morning. She'd probably think it was one of her spirits. We have spirits living in the house, according to Mother. Three of them. *Somehow that doesn't surprise me. She lives with you too, then.* Oh yes, Georgiana said. The house is quite large, too large for the three of us. There was a sensitive pause. *So, you have no children?* Georgiana met his eyes for a moment, then looked down at her hands. *Georgiana, would you like to sit?*

They sat in the chairs by the windows. Jekyll crossed his legs and rested two fingers at his temple. Georgiana frowned at her hands in her lap, twisting her ring round and round the finger. I know what I'm doing isn't right. Coming here again. Asking you to listen to me, involving you in a deceit. I would never have contacted you — I mean, I thought of contacting you, but I wouldn't have. I even saw someone else so I wouldn't have to impose on you. But then I saw you in that restaurant, and I thought, It's fate. So here I am. And not just for myself. You asked if I have children. I don't. Georgiana glanced up, out the window, still twisting her ring. But I'm pregnant.

Jekyll's eyes involuntarily slipped down to her belly. It was trim behind the tiny-buttoned front of her dress. *How far advanced are you?* Six weeks or so, I'd guess. *Have you been examined?* She shook her head. Not yet. But I just know. I can tell by now. Jekyll watched her profile, the little twitching frown at the edge of her mouth. *Have you miscarried before?* She nodded, her eyes going glassy. *How many times?* Eight, she replied.

Jekyll stared at her. *You've miscarried eight times?* She nodded. *At what stage?* Jekyll asked, holding on to his voice. It varied, she said. In the second or third month, usually. One of them — one of them made it almost to the very end. Jekyll looked out the window, at the grim courtyard growing darker still. Georgiana sniffed. It feels good just to say that, you know. I've never said it to anyone. That one — they just took him away; I didn't get to see. They didn't even want to tell me it was a he. Georgiana wiped her eyes, let out a sobbing laugh. Oh, poor Henry. A nice hysterical woman to start off the day.

Outside the window, flakes of snow were beginning to straggle down like bits of ash. Georgiana took a breath. There's something I'd like to ask you. It's something I've been thinking, and I'd like to know if you think there's any validity to it. She waited, as if for Jekyll's permission. He motioned with his hand: go on.

I've been trying to be scientific. To analyse my, my condition. One conclusion is that the problem is physical. That something is wrong, misshapen, inside me. Sometimes I think this must be the answer, that I'm deformed inside, in which case there's really nothing I can do differently this time that will matter. But then, there's a second possible conclusion. What if the problem isn't physical, but mental? Psychological, I mean. What if there is something in my mind that is causing the — the miscarriages? Like a poison? It doesn't sound very scientific when I say it like that. But you told me, all that time ago, that emotions and thoughts are not merely mental, that they have a chemical aspect as well. You spoke of the body having its own chemistry. Which is why I thought you, of all people, might understand what I'm saying.

You are asking me if it's possible for a woman to psychologically sabotage her own pregnancy? Well, *sabotage* makes it sound deliberate, Georgiana replied. I suppose I'm asking if a woman could be doing it involuntarily? *Why would it be involuntary?* I don't know, she said. The poets make it seem that feelings are these insuppressible forces storming through the body. That is how it feels to me sometimes. And so much of what I'm feeling recently seems so — poisonous. I can taste it, this acridness. Georgiana dropped her eyes. How can that be good for a baby? To be feeding on that? Maybe that's been the problem all along.

Do these poisonous thoughts ever concern Mr. Waller?

Horace is a good man, she said. A good husband. He just — She shook her head.

He just doesn't understand.

Georgiana glanced up, warily, to see if he was mocking her. No, I suppose he doesn't.

Have you told him you are pregnant?

I have. She gave a strange little laugh. It was a slight fiasco. *Would you tell me about it?* If you like. It was about a week ago, just before I saw you. Mother was holding a benefit for some psychical society. She hadn't picked a good time. Horace had been away in Belgium for almost two weeks and had just returned that morning, and now all these guests were arriving and he had to dress up and play host. I'd planned to wait to tell him. But there he was, buttoning up his waistcoat before the mirror. And I just blurted it out. Immediately I regretted it. He looked so hopeful, so innocently happy. It's exactly how a woman would want her husband to look, isn't it? But it seemed so foolish, so naïve. Every time, he looks at me as if it's the first time, as if everything that's happened hasn't actually happened. Sometimes I think he's managed to forget, in a way, all the disappointments. I'm not supposed to talk about it. He doesn't even like me to think about it. Like if we pretend together, it will all just disappear.

Anyhow, after dinner, Mother comes up behind me and takes my arm and leads me off. I can tell at once that Horace has told her. She's gripping my arm. Why hadn't I told her? Why did she have to hear the news from my husband? With this frantic smile on her face, clutching my arm. She leads me into the sitting room, where this man is waiting. I've met him before, one of Mother's psychics. She tells me she's asked the man to examine my aura, to make sure it is healthy. He says, Please, showing me where he wants me to stand. I walked out of the room. I was shaking, I was so angry. I made it back to my bedroom and Mother blows in right behind me, and — it's hard to describe. She changes, her face changes. She grabs my arm and sinks in her nails, and she's all white and splotchy in the face, saying things — you wouldn't believe me if I told you. I'm a whore, I can't have a baby because I'm a whore and I've been damaged inside. At some point I realise we've been shrieking at each other because Horace is there trying to pry Mother's hand off my arm. She backs off and stands there. In this daze, as if she didn't know where she was. But I could see through it. I could see her in there, behind the confusion, looking out at me, this cunning thing. And I thought, I have her blood. She made me. So what am I?

She held Jekyll's gaze, waiting for an answer. *You are not she. That's what you tell yourself.*

And do you tell yourself the same, Henry?

Yes. I do.

Georgiana smiled, faint and soft. Who are you, then? Who is this secretive Dr. Jekyll? Her tone was playful, but her eyes were not. *What makes you think I have a secret?* Everyone has a secret. At least one. *How many do you have?* She thought for a moment. Four, she said, and laughed. Then she looked down. Sometimes, I feel like I am the secret. Like I am inside myself. Inside the self everyone thinks is actually me. But the true me is . . .

She didn't continue. It was very quiet. Icy flecks of snow tapped the pane.

I want to show you something, Jekyll said. He rose from his chair and went around the long table to the shelves above the glazed press. The second level held the glass vat with the human intestine coiled fat and pale inside, and Jekyll reached up for the smaller jar alongside it. It made a clinking noise as he took it down and carried it back to Georgiana. He set it on the little table under the windows. She bent to peer into the jar. Are those — are those teeth? She furrowed her brow and picked up the jar in both hands.

The old man's teeth hung vertical in the clear liquid, just touching the bottom. When she turned the jar around, they shifted to one side with a click.

Are these yours? she asked. *They've become mine. I took them. As a souvenir.* She wrinkled her nose. A souvenir of what? Jekyll reached out his hand and accepted the jar. A tiny bubble slipped loose from a tooth and rose to the top. *An unexpected incident. I surprised myself. It's good to surprise yourself now and then. You should try it. Do something unexpected. Something the true you wants to do. And take a souvenir. We are all secrets, Georgiana. All hiding inside, self within self within self. When we pretend this isn't so, that is what poisons us. Do you understand?*

She was gazing at the jar in Jekyll's hand. I think so, she said.

Jekyll opened the steel surgery-block door, and a blast of icy air made them stop. It was dark as late afternoon. *May I ask you something?* Of course, she said. *Earlier, you said that you had seen someone else. You had considered contacting me, but then you'd seen someone else so as not to impose. Was it someone I might know?* Oh, she said, well, perhaps. A pause. *May I ask his name?* She gave her nervous laugh. I'm slightly embarrassed to tell you, Henry. He's not a doctor. He's a hypnotist. A very good one, I had heard. Cornelius Luce?

Cornelius Luce. We knew the name. We had been to his hypnotism show on Poland Street. *I've heard of him,* Jekyll said neutrally. *Where, if I may ask, did you go see him?* Well, at his house, off St. James's. That's where he sees his clients. *Where did you hear of him?* He came to the house this summer. For one of Mother's affairs. We spoke; he left me his card. I kept it. Do I feel the need to apologise right now? *No. I'm merely curious. So he lives off St. James's. Where, exactly?*

Georgiana looked up as Jekyll stared ahead. Why? she said carefully. *It's professional curiosity, Georgiana. I'm not going to do anything, I merely like to know where everyone operates. Is it such a secret, where he lives?* She sighed. Dury Street, Dury and King, I believe, off the square. He has a plaque out front. *Thank you,* Jekyll said.

I had never been to St. James's before. Yet an hour later I strode from Castle Street as if I knew the way, as if it were my own impulse I was following. Soon I came upon the open expanse of the square, stately houses boxing it in. Dury Street I found by chance, a smaller side lane off the far end of the square. I stood at the brick gatepost to a giant house and read the brass plaque:

Cornelius C. Luce, Hypnotist and Spiritual Consultant
By Appointment Only

The house was brick with black shutters and a huge black door, rather like Big House, except bigger. It soared against a silver rent in the sky. A purposeful rage gripped me as I stood in its shadow. I remembered this Luce. His show on Poland Street, the rowdy crowd, laughing and shouting. Luce onstage with four volunteers whom he'd put in a trance. He made one of the men believe himself afflicted with horrible flatulence and the other three believe they could smell it; they wrinkled their noses and looked suspiciously around as the crowd roared with laughter. Luce stood to the side, watching the antics with an indulgent smile. Jekyll and I had been dubiously amused. But now I stood below his house grinding my teeth, twisting the bit of my stick into the pavement. The man was a showman, an entertainer, probably a fraud. The idea of this man feeling around inside Georgiana's mind — rifling through her thoughts with his filthy fingers — filled me with exultant fury as Jekyll expanded inside my skin.

A girl opened the door. A lovely thing, in a black maid's dress with a white apron and bonnet, white stockings and shiny black shoes. Good day, she said. *Good day. I'd like to see Mr. Luce.* Do you have an appointment? She knew I didn't. *I don't. But the name is Hyde. Inspector Hyde. Scotland Yard, ma'am.*

I said it as easily as if I'd planned it. But it surprised me; I almost winced. The girl studied me a moment. Green eyes in a heart-shaped face, fringe of dark red under the brim of the bonnet. I could imagine her in one of Jekyll's parlour pictures, a riverside café in full bloom. She would remember me, months later. She would witness everything. She studied me with her canny eyes, then made up her mind and let me in.

Front hall like a ballroom, black-and-white-checkered floor. Giant ferns flanked the grand stairs. A tapestry at the landing. The girl led me across the hall and into a burgundy waiting room. She said she would let Mr. Luce know I was here and, with a last cagy glance, left me alone.

I strolled to one of the photographs on the wall. A grim old woman sat in a chair gazing out with blind-seeming eyes. Behind her, in the murky blackness, a white transparency, tall like a man, reached out for her. A fake, of course. Yet it unnerved me. I turned away and caught sight of myself in a gold-veined mirror on the opposite wall, a hunched, nocturnal thing, pale as a vampire. I approached my reflection, lifting my hand. Our fingers drew close enough to touch. I glanced at the door and found the girl was back, watching me. Inspector, she said, Mr. Luce has ten minutes before his next appointment. If you'll come with me. I followed her upstairs to the first floor, to a pair of white double doors. She knocked and opened them inward.

The spacious moss-green room ran down to huge latticed windows; the white ceiling arched and segmented. Cornelius Luce stood waiting with hands clasped behind him, a small dapper man in a pale grey suit, hair slicked back, immaculate black moustache. Thank you, my dear, he said in his leisurely voice. Behind me, the girl murmured, Sir, and closed the doors. Luce was looking at me with his eyebrows lifted pleasantly. Inspector Hyde, is it? My throat was dry. Beyond Luce, a fireplace, two chairs, a low brown leather piece of furniture, like a bed. *Just Mr. Hyde, for tonight. An unofficial chat, is all.* He gestured at the chairs and the fire. We sat. My eye fell again on the low leather bed, with its arm like a sofa's at one end and a red velvet pillow. I jerked my chin at it. *Do your clients lie there?* If they choose, he replied. His eyes were calm and almond brown. *Mr. Luce,* I said. *A woman came to see you, several weeks ago. Mrs. Georgiana Waller.*

He seemed to be watching my lips as I spoke. I waited. Forgive me, was that a question? I'm sorry, Mr. Hyde, but I'm afraid I cannot divulge the identity of my patients. *The identity of your patients?* Indeed, Luce said. This is a discreet process, and my patients generally rely upon that discretion. *You're a doctor, then?* Of a kind. *Well, Mrs. Waller did visit you.* He lifted his shapely eyebrows again. So you say. We regarded each other. Then I looked away at the fire, the glassy smelting coals. I could hear the trickling, pinging sound they made as they burned. *Mr. Luce, what if I told you Georgiana Waller was dead.*

I felt a giddiness saying the words, a pleasurable loosening. I looked back at Luce, who sat lightly struck, eyes widened, lips pursed. Oh dear, he said quietly. *Ah. Now we're getting somewhere. She did come to see you, then.* Evidently you know that she did, Luce said. *Evidently.* I settled back in my chair with a smug little smile. I put my elbows on the arms and touched my fingertips together, as Jekyll might have. *So, what did she say to you when she was here?* Luce shook his head. That is confidential, I'm sorry. *Was it incriminating? Are you concerned for the lady's reputation?* Frankly, I'm concerned for my own. How do you imagine my other patients might feel about my revealing their private business to the police? *They might feel worried. Quite worried, I imagine. They must tell you all sorts of things, your patients.* Luce looked at me steadily for a moment. You did say, Mr. Hyde, this was an unofficial chat, did you not? *I did. It's a courtesy. We can make it official if you like.*

I had a crazy urge to cackle. Instead, I pushed up from the

chair and strolled to the fireplace mantel. I had never known such articulate control. On the mantel something had caught my eye, a tomb-shaped wooden box with an upright silver pendulum. A metronome. Father had kept one like it in his study. I reached out a finger and tapped the pendulum into motion. I expected the quick tocking to start, but this one made no sound; the silver disk slipped silent back and forth. *Mrs. Waller,* I mused, without turning round. *She didn't just die. She did herself. Very nasty. Want to know how? She cut out her own stomach with a carving knife. Like the Japanese do. Before she did that, she carved a word into her arm.* Whore. *Carved it right into the skin.* I turned and looked at Luce, staring aghast back at me. Dear God, he said. *Yes, dear old God. Now, here's what I'm wondering. How's a lady take it into her head to do a thing like that? You'd have to be a stark raving lunatic.* Luce just stared at me. *Tell me, Mr. Luce, what's it you do exactly? What is a spiritual consultant, anyhow?*

I'm a guide, he said, after a moment. I guide lost spirits to people. And lost people to realisation. I cocked my head. *Realisation of what?* Whatever it is they are looking for, Luce said. *So what was Mrs. Waller looking for?* Luce sighed, moved his eyes across the long room. He sat with his legs crossed and one grey leather shoe dangling, his smooth-shaven chin angled as if defiance. An answer, he said at last. *An answer to what?* To a question, he said, she did not know she was asking. *Is that a riddle?* You might call it a riddle. We are all asking questions, Mr. Hyde, are we not? *You're the expert, you tell me. What do you think she was asking?* Luce sighed again. I think she was asking how to be happy.

The answer startled me; the cords of my throat tightened. *Was she unhappy?*

She seemed cheerful, Luce said, but sad. Like many people I see. Mrs. Waller had a difficult family situation, from what I could understand. Her mother lived in her house, and she seemed to be a difficult mother, overprotective, self-absorbed, unpredictable, possibly unstable. Mrs. Waller felt responsible for her. *And the husband? What about him?* Luce lightly shrugged. She didn't really discuss her husband. *We met only once, for an hour.* But overall, it seemed to me the woman felt — constrained by her circumstances. *Marriage? Living with her mother?* That, Luce said, and her circumstances more generally. *What circumstances?* He moved his eyes back to me. The lids were hooded, the gaze cool with disdain. Perhaps you fail to appreciate what a complicated time it can be for women in our modern age. They are beginning to grasp that they are entitled to more. Yet they do not know what precisely more is, or how to attain it. *I see. You're telling me Mrs. Waller was suffering from the modern age. Is that it?* Isn't that enough? Luce replied. I shrugged. *Did she tell you she was pregnant?*

He held my eyes, a calculating inspection. Then shook his head. I looked back at the metronome. Still the disk slipped back and forth without a sound and with no sign of slowing down. I reached out a finger and stopped it. *Well, she was. Does that spoil your theory?* Not at all, Luce said, it supports it, in fact. I laughed, a short bark. *Oh, it would, wouldn't it. That's your scientific method: find a theory, then find evidence to support it. But I've a theory of my own. Would you like to hear it? We have a perfectly healthy woman, carrying a child, pays you a visit, looking for an answer. A realisation. You hypnotise her. Put her under your spell. And a few weeks later the lady carves* whore *into her arm and slices open her uterus. That's some realisation, I'd say.* Luce made a sound. He was regarding me incredulously, his mouth partly open. That is an outrageous imputation. And a gross misunderstanding of how hypnosis works. *Oh, I've a fair notion how it works. Wealthy ladies lie here on your leather bed, asleep, and you rifle through them. Learning their secrets. Leading them to realisation. I've been to Poland Street, Mr. Luce, I've seen what sort of realisations you lead your patients to.*

Luce uncrossed his legs and slowly rose from his chair. I watched him, vibrating with triumph. Inspector Hyde, may I see your identification? *No,* I said. My voice quavered. *You may not, Mis-ter Luce.* He nodded briskly. In that case, I am going to ask you to leave. Immediately, please. The fire snapped and festered at my feet. There was a knock on the door, and then it opened. The girl stood there with her hand on the knob. Penelope, Luce announced, Mr. Hyde was just leaving us. I grinned. *She's a proper darling, isn't she. But she's no maid. Why've you got her dressed like one, then?* Penelope, Luce said again, go get Oswald, please. *No need,* I said hurriedly, *no need. I was just leaving, as you say.*

They followed me halfway down the grand stairs, then stood on the landing watching me. My stick was propped against a bench by the front door, my hat sitting beside it. I turned around to face the tremendous entrance hall with my stick in one hand, hat in the other. They beheld me from above, my audience, and an operatic thrill swelled in my gorge. *You haven't seen the last of me!* I cried, and dipped a giddy bow.

I wanted to see Jeannie, wanted to celebrate. I tried the Toad, then the Gullet. But she was not there. Outside I stood in the trampled mud, a twist of panic in my heart. What if I couldn't find her again? The thought wrung the wind out of me. I retreated to the Pig and Gibbet to sedate myself and wait. And there she was. I stopped in the door, not believing it, the sight of her perched on a high wobbly stool at the bar, chattering at Vic. I had told her I drank here, I'd said if not the Toad or Gullet then try the Pig and Gibbet — and yet still I didn't believe it, didn't trust it. Her chattering was the only sound in the place, not loud but constant, and some of the regulars down the bar were eying her almost appreciatively. Even surly Vic wore a puzzled half smile as he watched her from under his lumpish brow. She didn't notice me until I'd leant up right next to her, at which point she turned and gave a little yip. The blue fractured eyes studied me, as if she were trying to remember who I was. Her shawl had slipped down from one shoulder, revealing the freckle on her neckline, her skin milk white against the crimson hair. I wanted to plunge my face into her throat; the delicate cup of her clavicle pulled me like gravity. I peeled my eyes away to Vic, who was giving me a dull, sullen stare, realising she was mine. I nodded at him. He gruffly poured me a gin. I knocked it back and told him I wanted a bottle of champagne. He shook his head. No champagne. Have to send the lad off. I waited, brows lifted, and he glared at me out of his pocky, sacklike face before trudging off. I reached down and took Jeannie's hand off her knee, and pressed her palm to my face, inhaling its grubby spice. She wore a confused, crumpled smile, and she drew her hand away when I slid the fingertips down to my lips. Touching her neck, she looked off, and I gleamed down the length of the bar at the regulars. All the haunted eyes were fastened upon me like the eyes of animals, each in its cage, yearning at something wild and free. *Look at all these friends you've made*, I said quietly.

Well, that's what I do, she replied, isn't it. She shrugged her shawl up to cover her shoulder. Make friends.

It was only a matter of time before I followed her home.

It was the next evening, in fact. I had met her in the Pig and Gibbet again, to rub their faces in it. But she was distant, evasive, and in my bedroom later she stood looking stiffly off as I undressed her. I saw the bruise when the underthings dropped. Left flank, side of the thigh. Fresh with broken vessels, swollen. She always seemed to have a bruise or two, her skin so pale and sensitive, faded yellow or indigo dings. But never one like this. I tried to ignore it, but she just lay unresponsively on the bed until it began to feel like I was feasting on a corpse and I stopped. I sat up against the headboard next to her. She had begun to cry, fiercely, in silence, sheets tucked into her armpits. *Was it your da*, I said at last. She didn't answer. *Jeannie. Did your da do that?* She nodded, wiped her nose with her arm. I watched myself reach out and put my hand on her head. She braced, resisting, as I tried to pull her toward me. *Ssh*, I said, and drew her head down to my bare chest. After a few seconds, she started to weep in earnest. I stroked her hair and stared across the room, a ring of darkness tightening round my heart. Eventually she fell asleep on my chest. Her head rose and fell as I breathed.

I must have fallen asleep because I woke when the weight on my chest lifted. I could hear her sliding on her clothes. I whispered her name. She came to the bed's edge and found my fingers, gave them a clumsy squeeze. Then she tiptoed out. When the front door all the way downstairs creaked shut I threw off the sheets and scrambled into my clothes. I snatched my stick and picked up her trail halfway down Ghyll Road. We were alone on the lane and I crept a good distance behind, keeping to the shadow side. She left Soho to the northeast, took Theobald's Road a long way until it turned into Clerkenwell, then hooked into the side streets. Tight lanes, few gas lamps. She led me up a climbing alley with gaping stalls and black workshops. Washing lines crisscrossed overhead, and clothes bellied in the breeze. Uphill, to a wider street lined with narrow houses jammed together. She turned up some steps and went inside. I waited, then entered a lobby with a cracked tile floor, a smell of mildew and soup. She was clumping up the old wooden column of stairs, and I followed, my back to the wall. She stopped on a landing, and I stole up to the switchback below it. Saw her feet, through the railing, her shabby slippers. The key clicked in the lock and she closed the door behind her.

I slipped up and listened at the door. Low voices, indistinct vibrations from inside. I could make out Jeannie's frequency, and another, deeper. I hovered. Hell with it. I banged on the door. Silence. I banged again, and a slim man in shirtsleeves wrenched it open. He had a full, drooping moustache just like Father's, chin and cheeks grizzled with stubble. The stink of whisky wafted from him as he ogled me, unsteady on his feet. Who're you supposed to be? he said, and then Jeannie stepped into my narrow view of the peeling room behind him. I met her eyes. Father swayed, turned half around to look back at her, and I shouldered the door open, slammed him against it, jamming the shaft of my stick under his chin. I gripped the stick at either end, pinning him to the door as he grimaced and gasped and kicked the hollow wood. My head was pounding; I could hardly hear my voice as I leant in and snarled, *You know me, old man.* He flashed his teeth, emitting a croak as the thick oaken shaft ground the crushable cartilage of his windpipe. How easy it would be. My knuckles were blanched. With a grunt of effort I tore myself away.

He clasped his throat and coughed, pressing himself to the door. I reached into my pocket and pulled out a fistful of coins. *You know me now, old man?* His eyes moved over my shoulder and I said, *Don't look at her, look at me.* I let the coins fall to the floor; they bounced and rattled at my feet. *Pick them up.* He took a hand from his throat and turned the placating palm out to me. *Pick them up.* He nodded, slid down to his knees, and began to blindly feel for coins on the floor. *All of it,* I said, and when he got down on all fours like a dog, I kicked him in the thigh. Another punt to the ribs flipped him back against the door. Ah, he gasped, clutching his side, ah God, please, sir. I lowered myself to my hams to look him level in the eyes. Please, he said. I reached and took a handful of his oily hair. *I've always wanted to scalp a man. Rip his rug off by the scalp, like the Indians do. How'd you like that, old man?* He tried to shake his head but I gripped tighter. *Touch her again, touch any part of her, and I'll come back here with something sharp and take a souvenir. Understand?* I knocked his head back against the door, twisted his hair. *Understand?* Yes! he cried. Yes, I understand, please, I understand.

I released his hair and wiped my hand on his shirt. When I stood up a dizzy wave rolled under my feet and my vision went grey. I blinked rapidly, startled by the dingy room behind me. Jeannie was backed against the kitchen table, her expression wide with alarm and wonder. Beyond her shoulder stood a flimsy door, cracked inward ever so slightly. I had the feeling that a person was crouched behind it, one glistening eyeball to the gap. *It's all right,* I said, glancing uneasily back to Jeannie. *I'm all right.*

By the time I got back to Ghyll it was morning, unseasonably warm and smelling of mud and dung. I dropped my coat in a heap on the floor and wandered into the drawing room. I was going for the sideboard, I think, but I stopped, struck by the light filtering like dust through the great front window. There was something in a pot on the table beneath it. Suspiciously I approached. A flower, with a large brown face and golden crowns, turned up to the light like a sunbather. I was almost afraid. It was as if the thing had materialised from thin air, from the morning itself, all the way from some other dimension. Very pretty, Mrs. Deaker crooned behind me. Very pretty, doesn't Master think so? I whirled to the sound of her voice and found the old lady watching me from the depths of an armchair by the doorway. She drew the blanket off her legs and with a soft groan pushed herself from the chair, shuffled over to stand beside me. Master must permit the indulgence. Does he find it pleasing? *It's going to die,* I said. *It's still winter.* She clucked her tongue and reached a long-nailed hand to the flower. I could smell her, unbathed and gamy, beneath her clothes. Of course it will die, she said softly, running a fingernail down its furry stalk. Young missy will like it. You'll see.

DAY TWO

Morning

You'll see.

I bang awake, the words ringing. A dream — people trampling me into the muck, Mrs. Deaker kneeling beside me, pushing my face into the ooze, whispering. I sit up and look around: I'm on the floor by the stove, where I must have curled up to sleep, leaving the old woman and her flower frozen in the past. Daylight fills the dusty windows. I lie back on the floorboards, gasping. A cobweb is strung between the bench and the underbelly of the walnut table. With both hands I cover my face and scratch my bristly beard, then give myself a hard smack. Get up.

On my feet, I grit my teeth and arch my spine till there's a nice fat *pop* from the lumbar vertebrae. Then I grab the edges of the table and hunker down to crack my knees. The body stiffens up more every day, the muscles bowing my spine, pulling my pelvis askew. Hyde the Hunchback. I limp toward the glazed press, the jug of ethanol on the shelf above it. But as I pass the little writing desk, my eye falls on the envelope propped against the lamp. The line of ink engraved on its face: *Gabriel John Utterson.*

I do not like this thing. The way it just sits there, mocking me with its immunity, so certain I won't burn it or shred it. How did Jekyll know I wouldn't? I don't know that I *could* even touch it. My fingers tingle at the thought, as if the paper carries the trace of some contagion, of Jekyll's insanity. Yet insane as he was, he still knew I would obey him in this last command, to leave his confession as it lies. How I long to prove him wrong! To pick the thing up and slowly, painstakingly rip it into scraps . . .

My lower eyelid starts to twitch, an erratic tapping under the skin — I touch it with my fingertips, alarmed.

Just as quickly, it stops.

I edge away from the desk. Nothing to be frightened of. There is nothing in that envelope but desperate lies that Utterson will not believe. He knows far too much to be taken in by Jekyll's incomplete account. He must have nearly all the pieces by now, enough to get a rough idea at least. Has he seen it yet? The whole picture — the truth?

He surprised me, Utterson did. In spite of my chariness of the man, I'd still underestimated him, the power of his curiosity. He'd said he wanted to meet me — it was *necessary* that he meet me. Yet I never thought he would do what he did. How long had he been watching the Castle Street door? How many nights? He knows how to wait, Utterson does. Even now, with the puzzle all assembled before him, and that envelope sending out its siren song, he waits for Poole to come and beg his help. Today? Maybe not. But tomorrow? Day after? How much longer will they let me live like this?

Utterson's perseverance paid off not long after my visit to Jeannie's flat. I was almost convinced she wouldn't show at the Pig and Gibbet the following night, convinced I had scared her off. But to the Pig she came, and when I woke early the next morning, for the first time, I found her still in my bed, her brow intently furrowed in sleep. In the chill light her skin was like ivory, inset with tiny gemlike pimples on her chin and forehead. I had never seen her in such sober, meticulous detail, inches away, breathing softly on my face. A strand of hair was caught at the edge of her mouth, and delicately I plucked it free and placed it behind her ear. One agate eye flickered open and fixed upon me. I half expected her to recoil, to sit up in a hurry and grab her clothes. Instead, her eyelid dipped shut again, and she smacked her mouth and sleepily mumbled, G'morning.

A day or two later on my rambles I passed a chic shop window with a pink dress displayed on a smallish wooden mannequin. It had white puffy sleeves and lacy embroidering around the collar and waist. I went inside and bought the thing for a whopping five pounds — for my daughter, I explained. It fit Jeannie as if tailored for her. I took her to the Hotel Grand for dinner. A three-piece orchestra performed brightly in the centre of the room like an elaborate wind-up mechanism. Jeannie had washed her wonderful hair and pinned it up; her neckline was flushed as she gazed about, trying to look unimpressed. I told the waiter it was my daughter's birthday and he brought her a sherry-size glass for her wine, which she took down in quick, covert gulps. When the waiter dropped by to inquire how mademoiselle was enjoying the consommé, Jeannie placed her hand over mine and said, in a posh little voice, Daddy says it's too fishy. I snorted a spoonful and started coughing, and she patted my hand and whispered to the waiter, It's the worm, Daddy's never been the same since Inja. Later, she spooned up a glob of my lemon custard and when it plopped into her lap, she cried, looking down in dismay, Oh shit!

Christ, these details, these futile details.

It was the next night, or the night after that, when I returned to Castle Street. I had not intended to, I'd just been wandering aimlessly, for Jeannie had taken the evening off to spend with her sister at home. When I looked up and took stock, I realised my roaming had landed me very near Trafalgar, a few blocks south of Leicester Square. I felt a tug at my navel, a jerk of the reins, and with a shrug I turned toward Castle Street.

I came up the cobbled lane and approached the surgery block from the south rather than the north, the way I usually did. I was fishing my chain of keys from under my collar as I passed the

narrow alley that led from Castle Street into Big House's courtyard. Utterson must have been hiding in there, just inside the alleyway. I'd like to say that I stopped, nose lifted, eyes sharp, de-
tecting some watchful presence. But in truth I divined nothing as
I climbed the three encrusted steps. I sensed approaching movement below only at the last quarter-second, just before he touched
my elbow and said, Mr. Hyde?

Hissing, I raised my stick to strike blind at the voice. Yet Jekyll held my arm. The nearest lamp was behind me, and from under my topper I peered out at Utterson's grave, horsy face, its startling detail: the close-set grey eyes, the wiry chops bristling from
his cheeks, the flesh-coloured mole on his long upper lip.

I stood rooted to the spot. You are Edward Hyde, Utterson
said, and I found myself nodding. *I am Hyde.* His eyes narrowed,
slightly. He could not see me, I realised. I was just a dark figure
above him. I am Utterson, he said. *I know who you are. What do
you want?* I was hoping to see Dr. Jekyll. Perhaps you might let
me in? *Jekyll's not home.* I see, he said, and glanced up at the windowless wall of the surgery block. Are you living here? *I've a house
of my own. Now excuse me.* I turned for the door. He touched my
arm again. Wait. I stopped with the key extended. *What do you
want?*

I want to see your face.

My beard growth stiffened. My face. No, I could not show
him my face, not Utterson. Yet with a riveted helplessness I was
lowering the key and turning, my own hand involuntarily rising
to the brim of my topper. Then I lifted it off. I stood above him,
head steaming, a cold halo round my scalp where the band had indented my hair. Utterson stared up. He swallowed. Could you, he
said faintly, could you step down, please? I laughed, a little hysterical. *This is all you get, Utterson. Now go home.* And as if released
from his spell, I spun for the lock and crunched in the key.

Up in the cabinet I collapsed in a chair, shaking. What had
just happened? How did he know to wait for me by that door? I

felt queasy, exposed, as if a curtain had just been yanked away to reveal a busy backstage spying operation. I watched the courtyard out the window, the slim opening of the alleyway, almost expecting to see Utterson emerge leading a mob. Why had I taken off my hat? Had Jekyll made me do that? Why would he want the solicitor to see my face?

Jekyll sank naked onto the bench, unwrapping the rubber tourniquet from his left arm. The vein was getting hard and discoloured in the elbow crook, pocked with dried tiny punctures down the forearm. Jekyll flexed the hand open and shut as he held the left arm out against his right — that one smooth and clean, veins flowing fresh beneath the skin.

From the wardrobe he retrieved the razor and porcelain bowl, which he filled with cool water, and shaved before the mirror. The hairs pulled and crunched under the blade. Jekyll dipped a cotton ball in ethanol and smeared his raw face with the scorching stuff. Then he dressed in his own clothes, descended from the cabinet, and crossed the courtyard to the conservatory.

Poole was in the dining room, arranging silver along a cloth. Jekyll came up the two steps from the conservatory and stopped when he saw him across the table. The gas was turned down to a sepia stain. It was nearly midnight. Yet here was Poole, doing the silver. He looked up, as if surprised. Oh, sir, good evening, welcome home. Guardedly, Jekyll nodded. *Evening, Poole. Up late, I see.* Poole dipped his head. Yes, sir. Can I get you anything? *No, no, I'm up to bed. You can catch me up in the morning.* Very good, sir, Poole said, and waited until Jekyll nearly reached the far doorway before he added, Mr. Utterson called for you, sir.

Jekyll paused. Poole's tone sounded unnatural. *Oh? When was this?* Just now, sir. He left perhaps ten minutes ago. Jekyll turned. *Did he say what he wanted?* Not really, sir, it seemed he just wanted to see you. I thought you would like to know, as he left so recently. *Indeed. Past Mr. Utterson's bedtime, I should have thought.* Poole dipped his head with a trace of a smile, and then met Jekyll's eyes. *True, sir.*

Jekyll was halfway down the corridor leading to the main hall when he paused again. Softly he snapped his fingers, then turned around and went back to the dining room. Poole was standing by the table, holding a fork, gazing into space. *Sorry, Poole, it's just occurred to me. Mr. Hyde plans to spend the night in the cabinet. Could you bring him back some water and wine? Don't disturb him, just leave it on the stairs. Would you?*

Poole looked down at the fork in his hand. *Certainly, sir. Shall I bring Mr. Hyde some breakfast in the morning as well? No,* Jekyll said, *I imagine he'll take off fairly early. Just the water and the wine.*

Had Poole positioned himself there, in the dining room, with the silver? Had Utterson told Poole that he'd seen Mr. Hyde go in the back door of the surgery block? *He's back there right now,* Utterson might've said. *Are you aware he has a key, Poole?*

Jekyll lay in the bath with a towel over his face. The question beat in the blood-warm water: How had Utterson known to wait for me by the Castle Street door? How did he know I came and went by that door? Utterson had helped Jekyll buy the house twenty years ago when he first moved to London, so he would have known about the door itself, the connection of Big House to Castle Street. Yet how could he know that *I* used it? He had been waiting there. Poole might possibly suspect I had access to the cabinet. But would he share this with Utterson? Who knew how much those two said to each other? They could have been exchanging notes on Mr. Hyde for weeks now.

Everything felt precarious, as if the structure of our lives had been built up too high and was starting to sway. Yet Jekyll's veins fizzed with zest the next morning as he drew on his velvet smoking jacket and jogged downstairs and crossed the courtyard. He wrenched open the surgery-block door, and again something exploded into frantic flapping in the glass cupola high overhead. The silver tray with decanters of water and wine sat upon its step, halfway up the stairwell. Jekyll lifted the tray and carried it up to the cabinet, set it down on the table, and locked it inside.

The newspaper was still warm from Poole's ironing when Jekyll sat down for breakfast. As Poole poured his tea, Jekyll frowned, bending close to read some small print, then flipped the page. *I say, Poole, I've been thinking about getting some of the old gang together for supper, the way we used to. This Friday, perhaps. Would you feel up to it?* Jekyll lifted his teacup and glanced into Poole's eyes with a hint of challenge. I'm confident we could manage it, sir. Good. *Then it's settled.*

Jekyll wrote out the invitations himself that afternoon. Utterson, Lanyon, three other names I dimly knew. I was awestruck by his attitude. Poole and Utterson were conspiring, and he was going to throw a party? Yet the five invitations appeared, one by one, conjured out of Father's fountain pen. Afterward Jekyll reclined in his chair, holding a card Carew had sent several days before. *Requesting the pleasure of another reception*, read its sinuous line, *any night of your convenience*. Jekyll wagged the card by its corner.

I didn't think Jekyll should be seeing anyone just now. We had been careless. We needed to be scaling back, securing everything before moving on — certainly not inviting the inquisitive likes of Carew into the house yet again. Jekyll could feel me twisting as he gazed out the window, tapping his knee with one finger. That tic of a smile was tugging at the edge of his lips.

Responses to his invitations all flew back the next afternoon. Five yeas to dinner Friday night. Carew simply wrote, *Wednesday evening it is.*

This time he requested a tour. You know, Carew said in the main hall, my grandfather visited this house once, a hundred years ago. He was an amateur naturalist, this young unknown Irishman. He just knocked on the door and John Hunter answered it, the

great surgeon himself. My grandfather loved to talk about the gi-
raffe in the main hall — do you know where it stood?

Jekyll led him through the ground floor, indicating all the details he had preserved from the olden days. At the dining room,
Carew paused and said, And through here? *The conservatory.*
After a moment Jekyll lifted his hand and said, *Please, after you.*
Carew went down the two steps, and Jekyll stood in the doorway
above him. In the unlit room we could see through the glass into
the misty courtyard, the limestone block hulking in the northeast corner. Oh, how splendid, Carew said, the old surgical theatre. Except if I'm not mistaken there was a glass arcade connecting it to the main house, an exhibition wing? *The former owner
tore it down. The whole block is on the verge of collapse, in fact; I've
been trying to rescue it. I would show you, but it's havoc in there, with
the construction.* Jekyll touched the switch and the gaslight rose,
and the glass wall turned into amber mirror. Ah, Carew said, how
disappointing. Have any of Hunter's preparations survived? *A
few. Though the majority were carted off after he died. Debts and so
forth.* A pity, Carew said, gazing down the length of the greenhouse room. He nodded at the wicker chairs and hanging plants
at the far end. Do you mind if we sit a moment? I rather like it
here.

They arranged themselves in the creaky wicker chairs. Jekyll
brushed something from his knee and said, *I dropped by the library and was pleased to find several issues of your psychical society's
journal. I was particularly intrigued by the case of the Gorley sisters.*
Yes, of course, Carew said, Agatha and Maggie. *Did you have the
opportunity to examine them yourself?* I did, in fact, though unoffi-
cially, for it was after our report had been published. Which was
unfortunate, I suppose, as my visit yielded a rather curious result. Jekyll lifted his eyebrows. You see, Carew began, the report
in the journal focused primarily on the sisters' transmission of
visual images from one room to another. Maggie was the artist;
she would sit in the drawing room while Agatha in the parlour

would be instructed to communicate an image with her mind, which Maggie would sketch. There were some striking instances of accuracy, as you read. The omnibus prompt, for instance, resulted in a fairly indisputable rendering of an omnibus in Maggie's sketchbook. But I wanted to increase the distance between the sisters. I wondered if their telepathic ability, if that's indeed what it was, had a range. And I also wanted to see if the immediate atmosphere, the house itself, was somehow a facilitating factor. The sisters had grown up in the house; it was intimately familiar to them. So I prepared a number of experiments that involved removing Agatha from the house. I took her into the garden, then for a stroll around the block, and finally for a cab ride, and this is where I had my curious result. As we rode along I read a poem to her, the same poem, several times. Browning, "My Last Duchess." Meanwhile, back at the house, Maggie was with my assistant. I'd told her not to draw but to speak aloud whatever came to her mind while I was out with her sister. My assistant would write it down. When I returned, I read the transcript. There was nothing seemingly related to the poem in what she'd said. Much of it was random imagery, things you might plausibly see on the street. I looked up and saw Maggie watching me. And then this confused look came over her, and she said, Curtain? Like a question, softly. Curtain?

Carew paused, relishing the moment. Have you read the poem "My Last Duchess"? he asked. It's a monologue, an Italian duke is showing us a portrait of his late wife, up on the wall. And he keeps the portrait behind a curtain. No one is allowed to draw it back except he. Curtain.

Jekyll watched him, waiting. Carew smiled. Very curious, is it not? I puzzle over it still. I spent two additional days with the sisters, and no other result approached it. But for that singular instant, I tell you, it seemed as though the idea itself had leapt across the air, from one mind to another. He paused. You find the incident suspicious. *Every such incident is suspicious*, Jekyll said. So

Maggie Gorley duped me? She somehow discovered what poem I'd read to her sister? Is that what you believe? *I suppose I just believe it's in our nature to deceive and to be taken in by deception when we desire to believe. I've seen too often the amazing lengths people will go to to deceive their believers.* I've seen it too, Carew said. I've exposed more frauds than anyone, I assure you. But I won't say that what the frauds pretend to conjure is false. I won't dismiss the principle, you see, in the face of false evidence. *Evidence of what? What are you trying to believe?*

Carew sat back in his chair and looked off across the room. You speak of human nature. I think of it often too. I think of the human animal. This hairless primate, walking around on two feet and wearing its elaborate costume as it goes about the business of survival. We deceive each other, oh yes. Cheat, torture, kill each other, deliberately, occasionally with pleasure. Other animals live in fear and awe of us. What makes us so special? The mind. The grotesque power of the human mind. Carew turned to look at Jekyll, his eyes bright as glass. It is a ruinous mutation, this excessive intelligence. It has fooled us into imagining that we are above nature, that nature is subservient to our demands. And this arrogance will destroy us, unquestionably, unless we can learn its purpose. You see, perhaps the human mind is something more than simply the workings of a brain, of overadapted muscle matter. Perhaps it is part of something else, some larger, universal consciousness to which we are all connected. We are all one fluid mind, and have only to realise it . . . I suppose I am trying to believe in that.

The individual mind as part of an interconnected network. It's an appealing idea. Do you imagine we shall come to this realisation collectively, as a species? It would take time, Carew said. A great deal of time. I'm not speaking of my lifetime, or any lifetime. But I can still make my contribution. If there is one person out there who can indisputably tap into this network, as you say, this flow of thoughts and experiences, then I would like to find that person. It would be a start, would it not? Jekyll shrugged. *Toward what end? Another way of living, surviving? We live the way we live. We don't change? We don't progress? We progress, certainly. But do we change? The way we talk, the way we dress, the way we move about, yes. But does the nature of us change? Can it?*

Carew shook his head. I confess, I'm surprised. From you of all people, Doctor, such cynical certainty. We are what we are. Evolution stops with us, is that it? Jekyll didn't reply for a long, careful moment. *I can say only what I said to you last time we spoke. The notion of the mind being something more, having mobility, permanence, beyond the brain matter. It's unnecessary to my work. The mind's function is complex enough on its own, and these additional theories — they are simply redundant.* Redundant, Carew repeated. It's redundant to even consider the possibility that people afflicted with, say, a dissociative disorder may be acting and speaking under the influence of minds beyond their own? How do you dismiss such a consideration? How did you dismiss it in the case of Mr. Verlaine, one man with three distinct personalities, all apparently inhabiting his head? I want to understand this. Truly, I do.

Jekyll exhaled a steadying breath. He had known it was coming back around to this, of course; even I had been waiting for it. He regarded the sideboard against the wall, the cut-glass decanter of sherry. Then he stood and went over to it. He poured the pale red sherry into two tiny glasses, carried them back, and gave one to Carew. One hand in his pocket and the other holding his glass, Jekyll stood next to the wicker chair pretending to admire the dangling vines and spade-shaped leaves of the hanging plant. *I don't believe that evolution stops with us. Out in the world, humans are evolving as we speak. What does it require for a thing to evolve? Unique, often harsh conditions, and the urgency to survive. Physiological mutation can take generations to develop. But a psychological mutation, an evolution of the mind. That can happen over the course of a childhood. While the mind is still shaping itself, still adapting.*

Jekyll looked down into his glass, its ruby facets. He lifted it and let the vinegary sherry run to his lips. Then he drew the dram into his mouth, and swallowed. I had never seen him do this. The burn of alcohol rose to his eyes. Carew below murmured, Your health. Jekyll took Carew's empty glass and returned to the sideboard. *Emile's mother*, he said, lifting the glass stopper, *died when he was ten years old. For the ten years following her death, Emile lived with his father without disturbance. The lapses into the child personality I would come to know as Pierre did not begin until he was twenty. That is, not until Monsieur Verlaine remarried and his new wife moved into the house.* Jekyll handed one of the sherries to Carew, then lowered himself into the creaky chair. *The mind works sometimes in life as it does in a dream. It makes substitutions, places emotion and meaning upon a substitute object. Monsieur Verlaine's second wife was young and attractive, but otherwise different from his first wife, Emile's mother. Yet in Emile's mind, as it happens in a dream, here was his mother again, resurrected, or reincarnated, if you like. And there was a violent reaction. Parts of his mind, regions of memory Emile had locked away, burst open. For almost ten years Emile had trained himself to live in the front of his mind, the part that amassed new experience, absorbed itself with art, society. He had managed to lock away everything he didn't want to remember, about his mother, his childhood. But suddenly, it was as though his mother had returned to live in the house again. And the memories returned as well.*

Jekyll's face was already warm with the wine. He turned his fresh glass by the stem. Emile's mother, Carew said. She traumatised him, you are saying. Jekyll nodded. *That's a good word. Traumatised.* Carew waited. What did she do, exactly?

Much of it seemed to be sexual in nature. She had sewn a sort of chastity belt—like contraption that she made him wear under his clothes, very tight and painful. She would wash him in the bath and hold his head under the water, insert soapy fingers into his rectum to clean him there. The boy's father, Monsieur Verlaine, remained oblivi-

ous to what was happening, from what I could determine. *The mother held the boy in fear of some horrifying threat, and the boy never spoke of it to his father. Instead, he developed alternative means of defending himself. Pierre, as the personality would come to call itself, was one of those adaptations.*

What was his function? Carew asked. Jekyll turned the crystal stem between his fingers, the liquid winking. A thirst at the root of his tongue, a heady recklessness. *His function was to bear the pain. The discomfort, the humiliation, to bear it when it became unbearable. He was a whipping boy. He took the punishment for the prince. Emile forced him to the front of the experience, as a buffer. And then he locked him away, for almost a decade. Until their mother returned, so it seemed. When Pierre returned too.*

And the other, Carew said. He returned as well, did he not? L'inconnu. That is what you called him?

I didn't call him that. That was the hospital board's silly invention, and the papers picked it up. L'inconnu. No, I — I didn't really have a name for him. He never gave himself one, nor did Emile. But he was created. The same way as Pierre. As an adaptation. *Yes and no. I think he developed over the years. Accumulated. Like a dark pearl. Or a tumour. Pierre was different; he had been trapped in stasis as a child. But the other had matured in the back of Emile's mind. Waiting, it seemed to me in retrospect, for the perfect moment to emerge.*

He wanted an audience. To announce himself. The board gave him an opportunity. They wanted to interview Emile. From the beginning I'd made it clear that I alone would treat Emile, but now the board was insisting upon an interview. So I took two of the doctors, Queneau and Petit, to meet with Emile in his room. They questioned him about his comfort, his perceived progress. Then they began to ask about Pierre, and I could see something shift in Emile's manner. He became fidgety, bouncing his knees, scratching his arms. His facial muscles were behaving oddly. I could see Queneau and Petit exchanging glances. At last they nodded and stood up, and Petit put out his hand for Emile to shake. That's what he was waiting for. I watched Emile take his hand, and a convulsion ran through him, like he was going to sick up. Then Emile was biting into the back of Petit's hand. Tearing at it, shaking his head, growling. Petit was shrieking, Queneau hollering bloody murder. I stepped up and smacked Emile on the back of the head. He looked up at once. It wasn't Emile anymore, and it wasn't Pierre. There was blood all over his mouth, his teeth. He was grinning. His eyes had changed, the colour, the pupils had constricted to black points. He said, Doctor. In English, in this rasping whisper, Doctor. Then the door banged open and the orderlies rushed in, and I watched this creature go scampering around the room like an ape, making them chase him, hooting and laughing as he crashed about. Somehow he got out the door; they cornered him down the hall. Got him in a straitjacket and hauled him up to the fourth floor. High security. The violent and deranged. They had him in a padded room, still in the jacket, hours later when they finally let me up to see him.

The board blamed you for the attack, of course? *They held me responsible. And I was responsible; he was my patient. But Queneau and Petit were acting as if I'd led them into an ambush. I had to put the matter in perspective for them. A third distinct personality. The case had just expanded by another dimension. No other hospital in France was treating such a case. Prestige, publicity — I had to frame it in such terms. And Petit's hand was not deeply injured. It was a provocation, not a true attack. The personality wanted our attention; we couldn't simply lock him up on high security. At last they let me up to see him. By then, of course, there was just Emile, confused and frightened. He had no awareness of what had happened?* He claimed to have none. It was a blank. Suddenly he was in a padded cell, just like that. I had to leave him there overnight. Early in the morning, however, an orderly came down to fetch me. He was asking for me. Not Emile. The other.

He was hunkered down in the corner of the cell when I came in. He seemed smaller, skinnier than Emile. Like an animal kept in a *cage. Hungry, calculating, watching me. I had brought a needle, a sedative, in case. But he stayed there in the corner. He wanted to talk. He knew who I was, who Emile was. He knew about Pierre, he knew why they were in the hospital. He knew I wanted to study him. And he was willing to cooperate. But he wanted things in exchange. Off the fourth floor, for starters, back in Emile's room. Later it was other things. When I was able to oblige him, he would tell me about Emile's mother, about what she had done to them. He had the clearest recollection, I soon learned, this unknown other. He had stored the memories, all those years, away from Emile's conscious mind. All that horror, all that rage and disgust for the father, so willfully oblivious. It had to go somewhere. So rage turns inward. If it can't be inflicted on others, it afflicts the self. A malignancy. Pierre was created as a whipping boy, but this other held the lash, and Emile was caught helpless in between.*

Mortification of the flesh, Carew mused. A kind of self-flagellation. So you are saying that L'inconnu's function was — for Emile to punish himself?

Jekyll was staring into the jewel of wine in his glass, wide-eyed, mesmerised. *Punish himself,* he repeated softly.

For what? Carew asked.

Jekyll ran his tongue along his lower lip. His mouth felt very dry. He carefully set his full glass on the wicker table. *For pretending, perhaps. All that time. Pretending to be a normal person. I don't know.* A trace of impatience had entered his voice. He touched his temple, where a thumping had begun. *You'll forgive me. It's been a long day.*

Carew was silent, gazing at the dark reflective bank of glass, the invisible courtyard beyond. Of course, he said. It's late. You've been most accommodating. Thank you.

In the entrance hall Carew put out his spindly hand. Jekyll, he said.

Sir Danvers. Jekyll slid into his grip, and then added out of nowhere, *You know, I'm throwing a little dinner party this Friday.*

* * *

It was too much to process. This whole story of Emile Verlaine was also about us. I had accumulated over the years, like a dark pearl. I had been his whipping boy. Yet I had no desire to punish Jekyll. Quite the opposite, in fact: I wanted to protect him. *He* was the one taking all these risks, drawing these investigators into our sphere, flirting with exposure.

He plunged ahead with the plans for his dinner party. He designed a menu with Fanny, the meaty, florid-faced cook. He ducked around the cobwebby wine cellar with Poole in search of special vintages. He selected glassware and silver. This dinner party had once been a regular tradition at Big House. The same six guests year after year: Utterson, Lanyon, Percy and Osgood from the Grampian, McClure from the fencing club, and Talbot. Talbot was now dead, but the other five were returning, with Carew making six. By Friday afternoon I was starting to writhe in my confinement. I missed my house, my bed, my Jeannie, even old Mrs. Deaker. My life felt far away, illusory, as if it were simply something I had dreamt one magnificent night.

Resentfully I watched Jekyll button up his quilted waistcoat and draw on his lustrous cutaway tailcoat. He tugged the lapels and touched his cuffs, smoothed a palm across his impeccably parted hair. Minutes later he leant in the doorway of the card room downstairs.

Poole was at the sideboard pouring wine from the bottles into carafes. The card room was scarlet with scalloped white trim. I had never seen it used before now. *How's the nose on that Lafite?* Jekyll asked, strolling in. Poole twisted off the last drizzle of wine and handed the vase to Jekyll, who gave it a swirl and sniffed the spouted opening. He met Poole's eyes over the crystal rim. *Oaky,* he said, handing it back. He gazed at the table, set for seven, the crimson napkins folded into flowers on each plate. *Just like old times, eh, Poole?* Yes, sir, Poole said. Just like them.

◆ ◆ ◆

Jekyll sat at the head, Utterson at his left hand and Lanyon at his right. I was very aware of Utterson. I could hear him eating, speaking with Carew to his left. A sustained chatter and clatter filled the card room. Jekyll propped his elbow on the padded arm of his chair and moved his fixed, pleasant smile around the table. But he was attending Utterson too. Utterson had been the last to arrive. When Jekyll had shaken his hand in the parlour, the solicitor had not met his eyes. He had continued to avoid Jekyll's eyes all evening. Now Jekyll and I both watched him, his white tie ever so slightly askew, sombrely cutting his beef fillet and nodding at whatever Carew was saying. He felt our scrutiny. His eyes slid over. The pink glistened in his lower rims as he held the stare, chewing. He swallowed and tried a hesitant smile. Then Lanyon grabbed Jekyll's right hand and squeezed.

His face was red to the roots of his flaxen curls. Ho there, Old Gooseberry! D'you know I was remembering that the other day? I was with a patient, very bad case, and *Old Gooseberry* just popped into my head. I almost burst out laughing! Lanyon's words were slurred, his voice too loud. *Yes*, Jekyll said distractedly, *that must have been awkward.* Harry! Lanyon cried, then hiccoughed and swayed in his chair. Harry, a toast! Give us a toast, would you? He turned to the table and announced, Eh, boys, how about a toast, what d'you say? A toast from the host! There was a short silence. Then Osgood and Percy and McClure filled it in: Oh yes, a toast, come on, Doctor, let's see if you've lost your touch! Lanyon was chanting, Toast! Toast!, gavelling the table each time. Jekyll lifted his hand. *All right, all right.* He stood with his wineglass. Suddenly it was quiet. Every eye in the room was trained upon him.

His voice was clear and calm. *Friends. Old friends. And new.* He nodded at Carew, who was watching, a finger to his lips. *It has been too long. I was trying to determine it today. It was 1876. That was the last year we had dinner together like this, in this room. Nine*

*years. I won't pretend nothing has changed. These are the years when
everything begins to change. We have amassed. And now we begin to
lose. I don't think it's too much to say that each of us has lost something
already. Loss is the nature of life. The inevitable rule. But that doesn't
mean we must be complacent. We can take things back. This, here,
what we once had, we can reclaim, old friends. What is valuable, we
must reclaim.* Jekyll held the pause, staring into the candlelight.
He lifted his wine. *To friendship. To the end.*

A pure second of silence. Then Lanyon sobbed out a laugh
and cried, Cheers! Everyone lifted his glass and together they
all said, almost gravely, To friendship — and they drank. Jekyll
looked down at Utterson and found a wary kind of wonder in
his eyes. *To your health, old friend.* Utterson nodded once. Your
health, Harry.

During dessert Lanyon excused himself and didn't return. Jekyll
found him in the darkened drawing room at the other end of Big
House. He was sitting on a sofa with his face in his hands, shaking. It's no good, he moaned, waving off the handkerchief. It's no
good, please just leave me, Harry, I'm begging you. Jekyll helped
him lie down, and Lanyon turned to face the back of the sofa. I'm
so stupid, he said, groaning, so stupid, stupid. I just want her back.
I want her to come back. Jekyll sighed, and then Lanyon reached
and grabbed his wrist. Harry. He gasped. I — I should have —
I — should have let you — His wine-stained mouth opened and
closed like a fish's, his eyes strained. *It's all right,* Jekyll said. *Everything is going to be all right.*

Everyone had moved to the parlour for cigars and brandy.
After an hour the guests began to say their goodbyes, and Jekyll
slipped away to check on Lanyon. He was sleeping on his side,
curled toward the back of the sofa, lightly snoring. When Jekyll
stepped out of the drawing room, he found Utterson and Carew
alone in the main hall.

They were at the far side, by the doorway to the entrance hall.

Jekyll stood unseen by a large urn, straining to hear their murmuring. Carew was leaning into Utterson as he spoke, and Utterson looked away, listening, reluctantly it seemed, even leaning back a little, as if his shoes were nailed to the floor. They broke apart when Jekyll's footsteps clicked across the marble floor. Your Dr. Lanyon, Carew said, he is feeling better, I hope? *He'll be fine.* There was a pause. Well, Carew said, then this is good night. Thank you, Dr. Jekyll. I am flattered to have been included this evening. Mr. Utterson, always a pleasure. Jekyll showed him to the door, and when he closed it and turned, Utterson was behind him in the entrance hall. His eyes glimmered in the low firelight. He was breathing heavily through his nose. *Come, John.*

In the parlour, the dirty glasses had been cleared and the ashtrays dumped out. A fuggy haze of cigars still hung on the air. Jekyll poured some port into a large snifter and handed it to Utterson, then dropped into one of the wingbacks before the fire. His pulse was knocking rapidly. Utterson's shadow passed and then he sat in the other chair. The coals trickled like broken glass as they burned and popped. At last Utterson said, That was some toast you gave, Harry. Did you mean it? *Yes. I did.* You did. So that means you truly want your friends? Jekyll looked at him. *Yes. I do.* Then, Harry, let me be your friend. Let me be your friend and help you.

Help me. What makes you think I need help, John? Because you do, Utterson said. I know you, Harry. As much as any man can. And I know something is not right. And we both know it's to do with Edward Hyde.

Jekyll gazed at his friend, tapping a finger on the leather. *I heard about your introduction. He told me. I didn't believe him at first. The idea of you lying in wait for him outside that door—I couldn't quite imagine it.* No? Utterson said. You couldn't imagine it? How else was I supposed to meet the man, Harry? *But why must you meet him? What does it matter?* What does it matter? Utterson repeated incredulously. Harry, you've handed your entire life over to this man. If you disappear — that is your word, *disappear* — that man is meant to simply step into your life! Are you really asking what it matters if I meet him? Utterson's face was thick with vehemence. He looked down into his port. It is not idle curiosity; I'm not snooping into your affairs, I never have. But there is talk. Concerning Mr. Hyde. His behaviour, his character. I've heard things. *Go on*, Jekyll said. *What things? Surely you know his character for yourself. I do. And I know how character is misconstrued by gossips. So please, enlighten me.* No, this isn't what I came to say. *John, I want to know what you've heard. What behaviour?* Oh, damn it, right outside your back door, Harry, the man tried to carry off a young girl, a child. Or so I heard. All right? Satisfied?

Jekyll stared at him as a valve opened in the mind. Of course. Enfield. Richard Enfield, that little girl's saviour. Utterson knew him. They were obscurely related, distant cousins. They took Sunday strolls together. Jekyll had met him years ago. This was how Utterson had known to wait outside the Castle Street door. He hadn't heard it from Poole. Enfield had told him I'd gone in a back door and Utterson knew exactly what that door was.

He was watching Jekyll's reaction. Jekyll cleared his throat. *Listen. I've heard this story too. He wasn't trying to carry that girl off. That is a lie, I'm sure of it. You see, this is exactly what I mean about gossip, how character is* — I don't care, Utterson broke in, I'm not interested in the gossip either, as I told you. Harry, listen to me. This is what I came tonight to tell you. Whatever it is that you've done, I don't care. Whatever led to this situation, whatever you did that brought him to you. I have never judged you; I have no right. Whatever it is that binds you to this man, I can help you break it. You don't have to do this on your own. Harry, for God's sake, let me help you!

His face trembled, and Jekyll had to look away at the shining cap of his dangling shoe. For a long moment he could not speak. *John*, he said at last. *I'm moved. Forgive me for my tone earlier. You are concerned, and that is a great comfort. To know that you would do everything in your power to help me. If I needed help. But as it happens, I do not. Edward Hyde has no hold over me. I am interested in him, and I want to see him succeed, reach his potential. The details of that will are peculiar, I admit, but there is reason, very good reason, behind it. I'm sorry I can't explain it to you. But I can't. Why?* Utterson cried. *Why can't you? Because you will not understand. Don't say that you will, because you won't. It's not your fault. Mr. Hyde is not a likable man. He disturbs people. I'm aware of that. Most people, almost all people, are repulsed when they flip over a large rock and see all the slimy things. People don't want to be reminded that things can grow and thrive in such conditions. But that is how they were made. That is how they look. And to a certain eye, they look very interesting. So* he is a scientific specimen, is that it? *If you like. But a very rare specimen, in danger of extinction, without the —* The support for him to flourish, yes, yes, Utterson interrupted wearily. He shook his head, glaring into the fire. Jekyll let him simmer a moment, then he leant forward and grasped Utterson's forearm. Utterson looked at Jekyll's hand, large-veined and firm, then up into his eyes. *John, if you truly want to help me, if you want to give me peace of mind, then do this. Promise me you'll see to my instructions if anything should happen. Promise you'll see that he gets what I've left him. Trust that I know what I'm doing, and promise. That's how you can help me.*

Slowly Utterson nodded, once, as if hypnotised.

All right, he said. I promise.

DAY TWO

Dusk

The sky is bruised behind Big House's silhouetted chimney stacks. Poole won't be long with dinner now. Not that I could eat anything; my stomach still roils at the idea of food. But I'm starting to find comfort in his regularity. He is like the heart of a vast cuckoo clockwork, popping twice daily from the conservatory door with his domed silver tray. This morning, in fact, as I crept down the stairs to the breakfast tray on the middle step, I realised this ticking clockwork is the measure of my life. As long as Poole continues to ferry Jekyll's meals across the courtyard, I am still alive.

There is something distinctly ritualistic in it. Up to that exact middle step he climbs — the membrane between his world and mine — and then kneels to set down his offering, like the worshipper of some terrible god in his temple. He descends and retreats to the house, and the terrible god slinks from his lair to retrieve his bounty. For breakfast: a gelatinous egg, a ribbon of fatty rasher, a slice of char-grilled tomato, and a few small boiled potatoes wobbling about. I haven't been able to eat, but I don't want Poole to think Jekyll is starving himself, so I have been cutting everything up and tipping the plate out the window onto the gravel below, where Jekyll used to empty his chamber pot. (I suspect Poole has trained himself to ignore the mess along this side of the building, which he does not directly pass on his trips to and from the house.) Then I cover the plate and carry the tray back down the stairs, to the altar, for Poole to replace with dinner. A ritual. A cycle of life.

See that he gets what I've left him.

How prophetic the words sound now. As if he knew precisely what my inheritance would be. This. He left me this.

After the party Jekyll guided Utterson from the parlour to the front door. The solicitor stood on the stoop, defeated and slumped, a gleam of petulance on his lower lip as he looked back at Jekyll in the doorway. Jekyll lifted his hand and closed the door, then went in search of Poole.

Could not find him upstairs or downstairs. At last Jekyll went into the side parlour and up to the slit in the wall. He pushed and the panel clicked and fell open, and he drew the door wide enough to slip into the servants' pantry. The long servants' corridor ran down to the left, to the black courtyard door at the end, but instead Jekyll ducked through the narrow doorway to the right. A shorter corridor, with a single door at the end. Jekyll knocked, and after a moment Poole opened it. He was adjusting his cuffs, looking as if he'd just thrown on his jacket. His eyes changed immediately when he saw Jekyll standing there. Sir, forgive me, has Mr. Utterson gone?

Beyond Poole lay his tranquil quarters: a desk, bookshelf, leather chair and hassock, little table with a glass of amber liquor. Jekyll put his hand on the man's shoulder, gave a slight squeeze. Poole had not betrayed him. *You're done for the night,* Jekyll said. *I just wanted to thank you. Everything was perfect.* Poole lowered his eyes. Most welcome, sir. Jekyll held his shoulder another moment, then let him go. *Also, I'm going to be leaving tomorrow morning for a week or two. I have to go back to Scotland, I'm afraid, something has come up with the estate. I thought I might turn it into a little holiday. So you might not see me in the morning.* Poole lifted his eyes, and something rippled over his face, like movement behind a curtain.

It's always a pity to see you go, sir. Until your return, then.

Yes. Until then.

I need to remember this carefully. Up in the cabinet Jekyll slid E drawer from its slot in the press and set it down on the table. He picked up the stoppered powder bottle, hefted it in his hand. It was almost empty. One dose of white residue at the bottom. Jekyll turned back to the press and pulled out H drawer, at the lowermost left. Now how many bricks remained?

Jekyll had ordered the original store of the powder from Maw's, in London, while he was treating Emile Verlaine in France; there had been six of the silver-foil bricks left, packed shoulder to shoulder in the wooden crate, when Jekyll had shipped his supplies back to Big House from Paris. We had been depleting this quantity since October, and it was now February or early March. There must have been four of the bricks remaining. Four silver bricks, a rectangular pound each, stocked in H drawer that night. Enough to last us another year, perhaps. But what was Jekyll planning to do when the stock ran low? Order more? Or did he know even then that there wasn't any more, that this was the last in existence?

I wasn't concerned with how long the powder would last or what would happen when it was gone. That was Jekyll's realm, and I still trusted him. I wanted only to get out — back to my life! Impatiently I watched him unpeel one of the foil bricks and cut up the crumbling block of chalk-white powder and scrape it into the stoppered bottle. He crushed the silver wrapping into a tight ball, which he tossed into the rubbish bin beside his desk, then threw off his tailcoat and lifted the bottle of crimson, whisky-smelling spirit lying flat in E drawer. He drew the cork and poured a precise portion into an Erlenmeyer flask. With the bronze spoon he scooped out the white powder, scraped the excess off the rim, and tapped it into the flask. Instantly the crimson started to froth and deepen to purplish black before fizzling out into a pale, perfectly transparent green. Into a slim glass phial he transferred the serum and popped in the black rubber plug, then he picked up the first syringe by its cold steel loops. The needle punched through the plug, and like a hummingbird's beak, it sucked out the fluid to the white middle line of the barrel. He fitted this syringe back in the red innards of the Milward box and picked up the second. His nimble hands performed the operation on muscular automatic — he could have done it blindfolded. At last he shed the rest of his clothes, hung them in the wardrobe, and bound the chill rubber tourniquet around the left biceps. I could feel the pressure hissing into the vein in the cleft as he flexed his fist, then the steel punching through skin. I teetered on the brink — before the plunger was depressed — and then pitched forward into the centrifugal spin as the room whipped around on its axis, flipping me up and into the body with a sick, dizzy lurch.

Clumsy, I stumbled around, air tingling on my skin like dissolving snowflakes. I pulled my clothes from the wardrobe and fumbled them on, not caring which button went through which hole. Down to the groove on my brow I screwed my old topper; I retrieved my trusty walking stick and then paused as always before the long mirror. My hand quivered as I reached out toward myself in reflection, then I pressed it flat to the cold palm on the nether side of the glass. When I peeled my hand away, a humid stain shrank into its centre and vanished.

Fresh gorgeous air rushed through my misbuttoned clothes; the smells of coal smoke and mist and beery yeast sang in my nostrils. There was a sliver of moon; rags of cloud raced overhead; and Soho glistened as if a slime of black seaweed coated the stones. A homing instinct pulled me back to Ghyll. I had to assure myself it was real. I plunged around the crooked corner and there it was,

slotted into its recess, a ripple of pale light down its roof scales —
and my heart expanded so fast I had to lean against the wall, weak
with gratitude.

As I crossed the cobbled courtyard, the decaying stone angel
atop the fountain seemed to turn its head to watch me. I mounted
the sagging steps and let myself in. The sepulchral entrance hall,
its familiar, ammoniac odour. I drifted into the drawing room,
where an underwatery light was sifting through the front windows. The flower was still there, on its moonlit table. The thing
seemed to be sleeping, its nodding head crowned with golden petals. I extended a finger, stroked the curving stalk and furry down.

Master returns, Mrs. Deaker croaked behind me.

I spun around. The witch was sitting in that wingback by the
doorway — yet again I had walked right past her. I almost giggled, I was so relieved to see her. Everything was just as I'd left
it. Master returns, Mrs. Deaker whispered again, from his long
travels.

I threw my hat on the sofa and let my stick fall to the rug
with a dull *whunk. Returned indeed. Do you live in that chair, Mrs.
Deaker?* She chuckled, whispered something to herself. Then she
held out her hand to me. Help a lady up. Her skin was shockingly
soft, but the bones and tendons gripped me with falcon strength.
I hoisted her up, and as she swayed I caught a whiff of her fecund
body. She staggered and put a hand on my chest, then looked up
at me, her eyes like disks of ice, her tiny teeth bared in a new, suggestive smile. She chuckled again and murmured, Master, like a
reproach. Her fingers were spider-walking down the front of my
waistcoat.

I stepped back. For half a second, the prospect flashed
through my mind — then I suppressed a shudder and made for
the sideboard, poured a glass of acidic sherry and downed it. I
brought Mrs. Deaker one and she accepted it, head inclined, teeth
glistening. There is a surprise, she said. *Oh?* She nodded. Come.

She led me upstairs, holding forth the shaky oil lantern she carried around at night. I followed her up to the top floor, where my bedroom was, and when we got to the landing she glanced back at me, and I saw that she was afraid. Suddenly I was afraid. She turned and led me across the landing to the far end, to where the empty room was. It was just an empty room. At the door she lifted a finger to her lips and went, *Shh.*

The big velvet chaise longue had been pushed in from my bedroom. It lay under the window in the slanted ceiling, and the same underwatery light swam over the curling arm, where someone was asleep. I looked at Mrs. Deaker, then stepped into the room. It was Jeannie, her slim ivory arm thrown over her face. I tiptoed toward her and then stopped cold as the shadowy half of the chaise longue took shape. Something was wrong; there were too many limbs. I squinted. There was another body sleeping there too, sprawled the opposite way. A little girl, arm tossed off the edge and a leg thrown over Jeannie's knees. I crept up. The girl's face was turned away, and I could see only a tiny, opalescent ear, involuted like a seashell, a birthmark below it. I glanced at Jeannie and found her eyes open and fixed on me. I felt oddly guilty, as if caught in some furtive act. She lifted the little girl's leg from her knees and slipped off the longue. On her bare feet, she reached and took hold of my finger, hanging at my side, and led me back to the doorway. Mrs. Deaker was waiting there with her lamp. Young missy, she whispered, and placed her old hand on top of Jeannie's head. They both looked up at me.

In my bedroom I poured a gin and stood at the verandah doors. All at once I was suspicious of this homecoming. It was all wrong — I was being offered too much, too quickly; first Mrs. Deaker's suggestive smile, and now this. There was a conspiratorial element in play. I turned to the bed and found Jeannie seated on the edge, bare shinned and feet dangling, watching me with cautious, sleep-ringed eyes. God, those shapely feet — I was struck by the long-ing to sink before them, press them to my senses. But I stood firm across the room, strangling my drink. *Well, let's hear it, then.*

After we had parted, a week or so ago, Jeannie said she had gone home to find her sister Dorie alone in the flat. For two days their da did not return. Then a well-dressed elderly lady arrived claiming to be their da's auntie, explaining that he had written to her, that he'd gotten into some trouble, and would she look af-ter the girls, in her own house, until he was able to fetch them? Somehow she convinced Jeannie and her sister to climb into the waiting carriage downstairs, and off they went to the west, arriv-ing at a large house in some obscure square. That's when Jeannie had a terrible presentiment. It was not a real house. It looked like a *dummy house*, she said. As the driver helped them down to the kerb, she managed to kick him in the shins and grab Dorie and run off and hide behind some rubbish bins.

What'd you think it was? This dummy house?

A girlie shop, Jeannie said, obviously. They set 'em up in posh places like that, get girls in the same as they nearly got us. Girls locked in cages, I've heard, men can do 'em through the bars if they fancy. You don't believe me? You never heard of a girlie shop?

I've heard of them.

Jeannie braved my scrutiny for another moment, daring me to disbelieve her. Then she looked down at her hands in her lap. I drained my gin, dropped the glass on the rug, and approached her slowly. Her flesh tensed as she felt me coming, but she did not look up until I was standing over her, breathing heavy now, vine-ripe desire coagulating from my crux to the root of my tongue. She lifted her face — determined, even faintly defiant. Yet when she met my eyes, an uneasy doubt fell across her defiance, as if she had seen something looming behind me. I caught a dark glimpse of movement to my left and turned, to the giant mirror banked against the wall. For a moment it seemed like a doorway into another room, another dimension, where my pallid stunted double stood, reaching a stealthy hand toward the bed. I looked at my own hand. It was rising, fingers poised to take a strand of Jeannie's hair. As if *I* were the reflection. I jerked my hand back. My brain was thudding.

You'd better get back to bed.

Next morning I staggered onto the rotting verandah and retched a torrent of gin and undigested scraps over the railing, spattering the stones far below. I swayed there in the warm breeze, head awhirl. What had I eaten last night? I couldn't remember a thing from the moment Jeannie had left my room. A total blank. Exploring my sour mouth with my tongue, I fetched a bit of something from my molar which I spat into my hand. A slimy thread of grey gristle. Disgustedly I wiped it on the rail and yanked my gown shut and lurched across the top-floor landing to the empty room. The door was ajar.

It was empty. Just the chaise longue, a blanket draped neatly over the back. A shaft of sunlight angled through the window onto the floor. I could smell the girls on the air like cooling bread.

The three of them were downstairs in the kitchen. The table was set for four. Jeannie and Dorie sat across from each other while Mrs. Deaker worked the stove. Coffee, crackling grease; my stomach rolled with nausea. They all looked at me, in the doorway, as I peered blearily at little Dorie perched on the big wooden chair. I was sure I had seen her before, in a painting somewhere, this breathtaking child with white-golden hair and feline green eyes. Jeannie gave her a stern, meaningful nod and the little girl sighed and hopped dutifully off her chair and came around the table to me. She made a little curtsey, murmured, overpolitely, Sir. Then she reached for my hand, huge and wormed with veins, and took it with her perfect miniature fingers. I watched dizzily as she bent and just barely kissed the back of it. Then she ran to her chair and climbed on again. Mrs. Deaker was eying me, holding a black twisted spatula. Good morning, Master. Breakfast is served.

The egg yolks were intact. The rashers weren't burnt, and the bread fried just brown. I watched Mrs. Deaker daintily cutting her egg up with knife and fork. I felt sick, and mistrustful, and yet strangely moved by all the production, on my behalf it seemed. There was even fresh cream for the coffee in a little blue jar. The ladies ate in comfortable silence, as if having breakfast together was something we did every morning. Dorie ripped off bits of rasher with her fingers and dabbed them in the yolk, examining the ceiling with bright interest as she chewed. I could see a birthmark under her exquisite ear, a larger brown dollop on her throat. What was she doing in my house? Hadn't I just been thinking that everything was becoming too big, too complex, that we needed to scale our lives down? I glanced at Jeannie and found her watching me intently, as if reading my thoughts. Was I really expected to believe their da had tried to sell them off to a girlie shop? Did it matter? She had come here — to me — for my help.

Jeannie carried the plates to the sink and started the washing up, while Mrs. Deaker sat across the table with her spotted hands regally crossed. When I met her gaze, she lifted her silvery eyebrows and, like an echo, I heard her whisper, You'll see. I scraped back my chair and stood, unsteadily. *Well*, I announced, *that was delicious. I believe I need a nap.*

Jeannie had turned with a dripping dish in her hand. *When you're done.*

Her dress laced up the back; I tore the knot and yanked the strings open, peeled the garment down to the bedroom floor. Later, with her nimble leg hooked over my shoulder, I smeared my lips up her throat, her chin, mashing them into her lips. She pressed back with her tongue, and electricity jolted through this wet, new contact; our first true kiss. Angrily, thirstily we sucked at each other, clicking teeth. Afterward she lay turned away on her side, a curve of light tracing her contour. I touched my lower lip and brought away a dab of blood.

Your da. Where do you think he is?

Her skin tightened. She shrugged a shoulder. *Jeannie,* I said, and she rolled over toward me. Her fingers played with the satin edge of the pillowcase. Do you want us to go? No. *I don't want you to go. I want you to stay. But I want to know if that da of yours is going to change his mind and come looking for you.* He doesn't know where you live, Jeannie said. *Are you sure of that?* She shrugged again. As sure as I can be. Anyhow, he's not in London, like I said, he's gone off. He hates it here, he's always saying so, how he wants the country and all that. Now's his chance.

And that's it? You never see him again?

She slid her eyes up to me. I fingered a strand of hair away from her forehead. *He won't forget about you. You should know that. He'll try to find you eventually. He'll want to say he's sorry.* I let my finger rest on Jeannie's cheek. *Father had this door, at the far end of his study. It opened into a winding stairwell. At the foot of the stairs was another door. Very small. Like a tiny cupboard inside. Knees to your chest. The chokey, Father called it. He'd put us in there. Like a kind of training. For endurance, he'd say. Sometimes he'd make us take whisky first. Or cocaine. Have you ever had cocaine?* Jeannie solemnly shook her head. *That's good.* I looked away, out the verandah door, at the dull white sky. *The last time, he left us in there two whole days. Carlton got us out in the end. Carlton was the butler. He got all the men in the house together, and they broke down the study door. Like a mutiny. I'd've liked to see that.*

My eyelids were heavy. I let them close. A rushing in my ears—I could hear Father shouting, throwing and smashing things, but muffled, faraway. *Don't worry,* I murmured. *We're all safe now.*

◆ ◆ ◆

But I didn't believe that. When I woke later, Jeannie was gone, and the verandah door was groaning on its hinges in the wind, rapping the curlicued desk chair. I'd had a dream about Ghyll the way it used to be, hundreds of years ago in its glory days, when a happy, innocent family had lived here, oblivious to its doom. I had carried from the dream a realisation, a kind of dire prophecy. But as I swung my eyes around the bedroom, I couldn't remember what it was. Things were changing. Evolving in complexity. While Jekyll had been planning his dinner party all this last week — while I'd been stuck inside fretting over Utterson and Poole — my life here had been metamorphosing into something almost unrecognisable. This farce of family life, in which I had my role to play. I did not trust it. I was no father, no great provider. And yet — it seemed as if I was changing as well, evolving from within. I did not feel like myself, not like my own self at all.

I wandered down from the eerily quiet top floors and into the drawing room, where I could hear voices. Mrs. Deaker and Jeannie were seated on the sofa and Dorie on the floor, with the flowerpot on the low table between them. They were playing a game, taking turns speaking to the flower. Dorie was whispering into its face with both hands cupping her mouth. Mrs. Deaker glanced up and saw me in the doorway, and then the girls were looking at me too. I went to the sideboard and trembled sherry into a glass. Doris, Mrs. Deaker said, perhaps Master would like to say something to Mr. Sun?

I turned and found the little girl clutching the flowerpot in both hands. Doris, said Mrs. Deaker, why don't you let him try? It's Master's flower, after all. The girl continued to give me her cold, sulky glare until Jeannie said, Dorie, a note of warning in her voice, and the girl shoved the pot across the table to the edge, where Jeannie stopped it before it toppled off. A small silence. *Very well*, I said, examining the flower. It seemed to be flourishing, actually. The golden petals crowned its earthy upturned face like a mane. Its head was slightly cocked, as if asking a question.

You have to *talk* to him, Dorie said, in that same obnoxious way Jeannie did when a thing struck her as especially obvious. I smiled at the little girl. *But I am talking to him. I'm talking with my mind. That's the only way he can hear you.* Her eyes screwed to slits. *This way,* I whispered, *I can hear him too. I can hear him right now, in fact. How interesting. Want to know what he's saying about you?*

Dorie appraised me for another moment. Then she stood and picked up a feather duster from the sofa and drifted over to the windows, humming under her breath.

That afternoon I spent inspecting the outside of Ghyll. If I was actually meant to protect these precious gems in my draughty fortress, I wanted to see how secure the house really was. I locked the front door and tried to jimmy and force it open. I peered through the brass letterbox into the slot of entrance hall, then jammed my hand in until it stuck at the meat of my thumb. I edged down the slender alleyway alongside of the house, to the skewed cobbled lane beneath my verandah where the bits of my vomit were drying on the uneven stones. A rusted drain-pipe scaled the house to my balcony high above, and I tugged at it, wondering if it could be climbed. As I backed away blinking flakes of rust from my eyes, I felt something against my legs and found a mangy tabby cat grinding itself against my shins with a contented rumble. I shooed the beggar off and turned to Ghyll's unused back door, which was down a few disintegrating steps from the street. The lock felt flimsy, as if a good shoulder shove would break it. I returned to the front of the house and went through the kitchen to the steps that descended into the stor-age cellar, which this back door opened into, and I pushed an an-cient chest through the dust to brace against it. Wiping cobwebs from my face, I slumped down on the chest. I had accomplished nothing, of course. Whatever was coming, it wouldn't sneak into my life by this back door or shimmy up the drainpipe to my balcony. But what else could I do? The threat was too diffuse and indefinable. And the house was rather larger than I'd re-alised.

Over those next few days I was to become aware of all the empty space within Ghyll. After breakfast Mrs. Deaker would take the girls exploring, into the middle floors between the ground level and my upper bedroom landing, to play their pe-culiar games. The silence seeped like a lethal gas from the walls, making me skittish, hypersensitive to every squeak and groan. I would search them out in my stockings, so that I might observe them undetected. In the desolate parlour on the second floor, I spied them sitting in a triangle on the threadbare carpet, hold-ing their hands up to an imaginary fire in the centre, eyes closed, swaying, a coven of witches. In a barren bedroom on the third floor I found Dorie lying on the boards, hands crossed over her chest, playing dead, while Jeannie and Mrs. Deaker stood at the head of the grave delivering her eulogy, trying to make her laugh. These games unnerved me. I didn't like to see these empty cells of my house, places where a person might hide, might live, slink-ing about unsuspected. As if to prove it, the ladies would some-times simply disappear, vanishing for hours into some nightmare version of hide-and-seek in which everyone was hiding and no one seeking. Except me. I would creep from floor to floor, open-ing stray wardrobes and cabinets, yanking curtains aside, peer-ing into crooked closets, and once even pressing my pounding ear to the floorboards when I heard a rustle from under there. In the second-floor parlour I stared at a picture on the wall, a silvery beachscape by moonlight with a distinct black figure far away. I squinted at this figure, struck by the mad fancy that one of them was hiding *inside* the picture. I turned away and did not let my-self examine the beachscape again for fear the figure might have moved. Yet where *were* their impossible hiding places? Where was I not seeking?

Then I remembered the storage cellar and spent a fruitless hour poking amongst the abandoned cobwebs and clutter of lumber and broken furniture, headboards and chairs and a lady's gilded vanity table left behind by that grand family when they'd fled this place. I checked inside the ancient chest bracing the back door, then clumped back upstairs to the kitchen. I longed to escape this stifling house. It had been days since I'd been out for a proper ramble. Yet I didn't like the idea of leaving the ladies alone. In the cellar I had torn through a sticky spider web, and I was swiping it from my face as I crossed the kitchen when I heard a bump, a knock, and I froze. The noise had come from the sink. The pipes? My eyes moved down from the spigot and ceramic basin and took in the drain-cupboard door underneath. A white wooden door with a black knob. My throat went dry. I lowered myself to a squat before it, reached for the knob. It stuck at first, then screeched open — and I gaped at Dorie curled up inside hugging her knees behind the looping U-bend of iron drainpipe. Shut it! she hissed at me. I'm hiding! But I could only stare, agog. Father's chokey. It was here in my house, lurking behind the drain-cupboard door. Had Dorie been hiding in here all along? Shut it, shut it! she hissed again. I'm hiding! She reached out to grab at the door, and I saw Father hunkered outside the dark frame, outlined against the light of his study behind him. The light thinned as he closed us in, thinned to a strip, a few golden grains. The cupboard door squeaked into place and I scrabbled back over the kitchen floor.

I hauled myself into a chair. My hands were shaking, and my left eyelid was twitching crazily, making it seem like the thick orange sunlight in the filthy windows was oscillating. Pressing my eyeball I stared at the door again — the chokey door with steel braces at either end and a heavy wood plank propped across. It had come back. I had spoken its name and conjured it, like a curse. I shut my other eye and ground the heels of my hands into the sockets, willing it to go away, feeling the chair suddenly tipping back, as if the whole room was off balance and on the brink of flipping —

And then I was stumping down the road. My stick rhythmically smacked the stones of the lane, and cool air was slipping into my collar. I touched my clammy face, my hat brim, blinking at the pitted brick house fronts bathed in peach haze, the row of black pigeons on a wire strung in between, the people ambling by. The deceptive casualness of everything. I was moving with purpose, hooking into a narrow lane, then turning again, until at last I found myself on a tumbledown byway, peering at a sign above a steep descent of steps. The painted lettering was illegible. It looked like people had been stabbing the wooden sign as they went down. I glanced behind me, then eased down the slippery steps to the open drain at the bottom and ducked into the pub.

Low and compressed, smelling of chamber pot. A few men sat on stools along the bar, and I shuffled behind them, brushing the brick cellar wall, until I came to an empty stool, which rocked to one side when I sat down. The bearded geezer behind the bar limped up, and I asked him cautiously for gin. He set before me a glass of clear stuff that smelt like whatever Mrs. Deaker used to clean.

I had been guided here, it seemed, to this vile nameless place. As if by some dark hand plunged into my brain, manipulating the impulses. Yes, something was undeniably infiltrating my life, like curlings of ink in water. I stared into my glass, chipped and clouded, and took a wincing sip. Then I glanced to my left, at the man who'd just brushed behind me. He stood at the bar pulling off his gloves, finger by finger.

The gloves he slung inside his topper, which he set upside down on a stool. He unbuttoned his overcoat and propped a fist against his hip as he leant at the bar, and the murky light caught the scaly emerald texture of his waistcoat.

I knew this man . . . but from where? He was compact, ruddy, with black muttonchops framing the mild, pleasant face. The barman had shambled over and the man was speaking to him, slipping two fingers into the iridescent emerald pocket of his waistcoat. A coin was extracted and snapped onto the bar. The old geezer moved away and then the man looked over at me. He dipped me a dubious nod.

Of course.

Auntie Gorgon's girlie shop. Room three, the carved Christ crying out to His God. It was the very same man — in the very same emerald waistcoat. My scalp was shrinking over my skull. This could be no accident. No. The man was lifting a shot of whisky and tossing it back — and I recalled it exactly, that jaunty tip of his chin. He did not sit down; he just stood at the bar five paces away, his chest flashing like the puffed-up front of some exotic bird. He was speaking with the barman again, gesturing at the whisky bottle. The bearded geezer murmured some response, and the man pulled out another, larger coin that he set in the wrinkled palm. The whisky bottle was left on the bar, and the man poured himself another shot, lifted it leisurely to his lips.

Big night? I heard myself say.

I hardly recognised my own voice: it was choked, strained. The man drank and lowered his glass. Pardon? *Big night*, I said again, nodding at the bottle. He eyed me uncertainly, then shrugged and gazed away. The usual.

Yes, the usual. My ears were starting to ring, as if the bottles and glasses behind the bar were vibrating. I gripped my glass, in which gin was rippling with the same, minute tremour. A sharp pain was pressing into the back of my eyeball. I screwed the eye shut, resisting the urge to cover my ears with both hands as the ringing increased. What was I meant to do? Wasn't this the very kind of man I was trying to protect my girls back at Ghyll against? The beast in his finery, whetting his appetite before the feast. He poured himself a third shot, knocked it back, and bunged the cork in the bottle. Right, then, he said to himself, taking up his topper. He grabbed the whisky bottle by the throat, smacked his gloves on the bar, and strolled off toward the back of the room, the exit in the rear.

At the back door, a set of steps ascended to an alleyway rigged with high washing lines. Sheets like sails, dyed by the apricot sunset. The man was gazing up, swigging from his bottle. As he lowered the whisky, he turned. A fawning smile of fear lit up his face. I had the sense it was not me he saw but something behind me, something that moved through me and punched him in the solar plexus. He went down to his knees and retched. My palm swung across his cheek with a meaty *crack*. I could hardly feel the sting of contact. Only the spike of pain in my eyeball. The man sprawled on his side on the stones, coughing. I took the gurgling bottle from his fingers. *Open up*, I heard myself say as my boot rolled the man onto his back. A splash of whisky spattered his face. He spluttered, gasping. *Get undressed.*

I stood in Ghyll's hall, dazed, entranced by a last lozenge of orange melting on the floor. I could hear voices and a clattering of plates from the kitchen, down the corridor. I shook my head, touched my left cheek. The pain was gone. The ringing in my ears had stopped. Bile burned at the back of my throat. I climbed to my bedroom and shut the door.

I shed my coat and took a breath, then stepped into the giant frame of the mirror. The emerald waistcoat fit me snug as a corset. It flashed and shimmered as I turned my torso, transfixed. The face staring back at me was not quite my own. The eyes had an alien, darkened luster. My hands stank of whisky. The waistcoat was soaked in it. Yet through the booze, I could smell the sharp whiff of shit from my thumb, which I held splayed from the other four fingers. *Drink up!* I heard the choking voice roar. *Drink up, boy!*

I shuddered, fumbled with the waistcoat buttons and ripped it off. Wiping and twisting my thumb in the fabric, I stuffed the thing in the bottom drawer of my wardrobe. From the bottle on the sideboard I splashed gin onto my hands and scrubbed them together. Panting, I listened into the depths of the house and gradually discerned the muted sounds of dinner all the way downstairs.

I did not want to be alone.

They had started without me. Edging into my seat, I took elaborate care scraping into the right position, looking pointedly away from the sink and the chokey door below it. I held my breath and looked up at Mrs. Deaker, chewing quietly, who gave me a polite, inscrutable smile. I slid my glance to Dorie, glaring at me with chill marble eyes, like a cat harbouring thoughts of revenge. What had I done? Found out her hiding place? Jeannie meanwhile had taken my empty plate and now set it down before me, loaded with food: lamb chops, potatoes, peas, some kind of gloopy pudding. I blinked at the inedible mess, heart in my stomach. Then I looked at her. Her crimson hair was frazzled, as if from steam, and her complexion flushed. She took me in, her brow furrowed, inquiring. Then she reached out and touched my hand, limp on the table edge.

By reflex I almost jerked back at the sweet, unexpected contact. But I held my hand there as she slid her fingers under my palm and then squeezed, and a rush of heat flowed up my arm. All at once I felt like weeping — like slumping to the floor and burying myself in her lap to muffle my gulping cries. Instead I looked away, at the sink and the white door underneath. Just a drain-cupboard door, I told myself. Just a white wooden door with a harmless black knob. The chokey was not here. It was hundreds of miles north in a dead, abandoned house, boarded up for good.

The next morning at breakfast I had my appetite back. I speared one banger after another, devouring them off the end of my fork, juice bursting into my mouth. Curiously, the meat itself had no flavour, and the coffee was just scalding black water, but I chewed and slurped away, actively avoiding little Dorie's eyes to my right. She was acting peculiar still, fussing with her food, fixing me with frosty, vengeful glares. But I was determined to behave as if un-fazed. At last the little girl shoved her plate aside and crossed her arms. We never do anything fun, she said. We want to do some-thing *fun*.

Mrs. Deaker watched me with a forked slice of sausage poised in the air. I speared another — the last — from the oily platter, though the grease was congealing in my throat. I took a bite, and with the tasteless wad in my cheek I met the girl's accusatory glower. *What's your idea of fun, then?*

That evening found me in a sprung velvet seat in a grandly shabby theatre watching sweaty pirates dance across the garish stage. Mrs. Deaker sat next to me jerking in her seat and patting the armrests to the music. As we walked home afterward the girls ran ahead down the busy lane, chasing each other and swash-buckling, and Mrs. Deaker slipped her arm inside mine. Mas-ter, with your permission, I was thinking we might move the ar-moire from the parlour up to the girls' room. Or a chest, at the very least. They have nowhere for their clothes.

I was only half listening. I was scanning the street and the faces of passers-by, expectant, but of what precisely, I did not know. *How many clothes do they have?* I asked absently. Yes, said Mrs. Deaker, well, they will need more clothes. Her arm tight-ened around mine, and I reluctantly turned to her grimly rigid profile. Not for the first time I wondered where *Mr.* Deaker was. What had happened to him?

So we just keep them? Is that the idea?

You have other plans for them?

There was a bitter, cryptic implication to her tone I did not like or understand. She stared sternly ahead as we strolled along. I clucked irritably and looked off down the lane, after the girls, who had disappeared from view. Shops were still open, and the evening sky overhead was deep blue, and the Soho locals were ambling about, lovers arm in arm, flashy swells in rowdy packs. I felt a surge of vexation for the bony arm hooked through mine like a shackle, binding me. What was I even doing, talking about wardrobes, playing the family man? And what did she mean, *other plans?* I craned my neck, searching through the gaps of bobbing hats and shoulders. Then Cornelius Luce passed across the lane, just ten paces ahead.

An alleyway intersected our lane and he was crossing that intersection. Recognition instantaneous: the gleam of immaculate moustache, the placid mien beneath the black bowler. My heart hitched and Luce strolled on and vanished into the other side of his alleyway.

I hurried to the corner, hauling along Mrs. Deaker, who would not let go of me. The alley was tall and narrow, and Luce picked his way down, tails of his charcoal coat flapping. I could almost feel the wake of possibility he'd left behind him. This was what I'd been waiting for. This was no coincidence, no more than finding that man in the emerald waistcoat was. No, they were being placed in my path. I could not simply ignore it. I was straining toward the alleyway as if sucked in by the undertow, yet something was holding me back. I looked down at Mrs. Deaker's clasping hands curled around my forearm, digging into the tender vein at the cleft, and with a snarl I ripped my arm free. She gawked at me, elbow lifted, as if I'd made to swat her. I stepped back; then the alleyway sucked me in and I stumbled down its lopsided stones after Luce.

At the next intersection Luce turned onto a wider lane, and I slipped through the rambling crowds with his rounded bowler bouncing in sight. I had left my stick behind tonight and felt empty-handed, defenceless, as I swiveled and dove between the oncoming walkers — once getting stuck in that absurd pedestrian dance with some idiot who mirrored my attempts to get past him until I shoved him from my path. Several blocks later Luce came to the Black Shop Pub, and I followed him inside. Irish bar, crowded and loud, fogged in smoke. I lost sight of Luce at once in the crush of big milling bodies. I threw myself into the current and was carried to the bar, where the barman slopped a black foaming beer before me. I fought with it against the tide until I spied an opening, a wooden railing, and hauled myself free.

The bar area was lifted a few feet above the main room and corralled by the wooden banister to which I was now pinned from behind. But I had an excellent view of the floor below. Booths on both ends, high chairs and tables in the centre, and darts in the back. Sipping my sludge, I searched the room for Luce. Quickly I picked him out. He had removed his bowler, and his slick hair shone in the overhead light as he stood at a high table speaking to a man who was seated with his back to me. The man wore a blue checkered jacket and a tall black topper.

My position at the railing was far too exposed; any moment Luce might look up and see me. But I could not seem to move — the herd of bodies weighed me in place. And that blue checkered jacket, that tall stovepipe hat. Had I seen this outfit somewhere before? Luce took off his own charcoal coat, which he slung on the back of a chair, and then dabbed his forehead with a handkerchief, eyes swinging around the room. *Turn!* I told myself. *Hide!* But there was nowhere to turn or hide. I gripped the banister as Luce's gaze passed over me, sucking in my breath as if to make myself unnoticeable. I saw his shaded eyes falter, then flick back to mine. His white silk handkerchief was still lifted toward his brow, a sham truce, as we stared fast at each other from across the floor. Then a pair of men blundered between us, and when they'd passed, I saw that Luce was leaning over the seated man, speaking hurriedly. As the man began to turn his shoulders, a white tail of tied hair slipped out from his collar. I knew whose face it would be beneath the black brim. Though I strained to wrench away from the rail, my body was riveted to it. The sharp cheekbone came around and the crystal eyes found me. All sound evaporated.

Even after Carew turned back to the table, still I could not move, clutching the rail and my pint glass. I felt as if I'd glimpsed into some blinding heart of truth in which everything momentarily melded and made sense. Of course Luce had led me to him. Luce had taken his coat and bowler and was pushing through the crowd toward the door — but Carew remained in the high chair with his checkered back to me, that white tail curling over his collar. The roaring of the bar was dimmed in my ears beneath the dark gongs of blood. Carew now reached to lift off his topper, and as if he could feel my eyes, he ran a hand through his hair and pulled the tail loose. He stepped down from the chair and, holding his topper by the brim, began to make his way across the floor in my direction. His eyes were down on the obstacles in his path. I strained at the body, gritting my teeth, but it would not budge. A lock of silver-white hair swung before his face as he manoeuvred between the chairs and he tucked it behind his ear and at the same moment looked up and sank his gaze into me like a sabre. I could not even blink.

A second or two later he turned away, and my heart kicked back into gear with a double whump. The pint glass slipped from my grip to the floor, and the *clunk* released me from paralysis. I unpeeled my blanched fingers from the banister. Carew was heading for the door. His checkered shoulder disappeared between incoming bodies. I turned and elbowed my way after him, pawing through Irishmen, dragged along by the body's reins as it lunged ahead. I staggered outside into drizzling rain.

The Black Shop occupied a corner, and I looked wildly around before sighting Carew, striding up the lane twisting north. It rose between grey tenements, dripping sporadic from the eaves. The left side was darker and I hugged the rough wall, while Carew marched sure-footed up the slippery centre, hands in his overcoat pockets. Up ahead the lane climbed to a set of crooked steps and pipe railing outlined against a streetlamp's greenish nimbus in the mist. Carew ascended and I saw him emerge in silhouette, the outlandish topper first, then the rest. Near the top he paused, and I pressed myself to the wall. He stood listening before turning around to survey the sloping lane below. A lean black figurine, a chess piece. He took in a great breath and then shouted in triumph, Mr. Hyde!

I almost cried out.

Carew remained motionless, framed against the green evil mist. I could see his fuming breath. He drew in and shouted again, Mr. Hyde! Shivering on the wall, I clamped a hand to my mouth, fighting the awful, swelling impulse to yell back. The eaves above spattered. He waited. I shut my eyes. When I opened them, I was alone.

Alone? No, I wasn't alone. As I tromped home through the rain, I could feel Jekyll's imprint on my brainstem, where he had gripped me. *I* had not stood rigid at that banister for Carew's perusal, *I* had not followed him up that lane and then tried to cry out some reply! It could only have been Jekyll. There was no denying it anymore. His control was evolving. He could influence me — reach into the body, or into my mind — and *move* me. I did not like this. Why would he want Carew to see me — why pursue him? What did it mean that Carew knew my name?

Up in my room at Ghyll I stripped off my sopping clothes and shivered into my dressing gown. I climbed into a tattered armchair in the corner, feeling strangely suspicious of my bed, as if I might be hacked to pieces in my sleep if I slumbered there. Paranoid, yes. But I could not shake Carew's triumphant echo from my head, as if he had been seeking me for a long while and then found me, hiding, at last. Yet how could that be? Even if Luce had told him my name — what could he possibly want with me? And what did Jekyll want with him in return? My mind felt pregnant with obscure motivations moving behind the membrane. From a rip in the armchair, the stuffing was bulging out, and my fingers tugged at the white hairy tufts, rolling it into tiny wads. My nose was running; absently I wiped it with the back of my hand and was startled by the warm, silky slime smeared across my wrist. My wrist? My room? Was any of this actually mine?

When I woke with a snort it was morning, and a figure was standing a few feet away with a silver tray. For a confused, terrified moment I thought it was Poole. I fisted the gum from my eyes and saw it was Jeannie there with the breakfast tray, watching me. I was splayed in the chair, one leg hooked over its arm, dressing gown spread open. I yanked it shut and sat up, pulse racing, brushing little balls of white upholstery from my lap. Jeannie had averted her gaze, was looking for somewhere to set the tray. She bent and put it on the floor. Would Master care for his coffee now? she crooned in eerie mimicry of the old lady as she rose with the cup and saucer. I wagged my fingers and guzzled the stuff back, gasping as it scorched through me.

Where'd you go last night? Jeannie asked. She had moved to the sideboard by the wall and was tracing the involutions of its edge with her finger. Against the silver glare streaming through the verandah doors, she was just a slim outline, a downcast cheek. I cleared my throat. *A pub. Black Shop Pub.* She waited. What for? I frowned, looking down into the silty dregs of my cup, as if to read the mystifying answer in its runes. *I had to meet someone,* I said slowly. *Someone was waiting for me.* Who? Jeannie asked. I shook my head.

You've been — Jeannie began. You've been different.

Different how?

Jeannie traced the scalloped edge of the sideboard. Just different. Dorie said —

Dorie said what?

Dorie said the other day — she said you trapped her under the sink. When she was hiding, you pushed a chair or something against the door?

Th-that, I stammered, *that — but that's nonsense. I found her —*

she was — *she told me to shut it.* I touched my temple, seeing again that closing strip of light. *I didn't* —

Jeannie scratched the wood with her fingernail, making a tiny, gnawing sound, then dropped her hand and sighed. Never mind. Dorie lies an awful lot. Call it imagination. Do you want your egg?

I shook my head. I hadn't pushed any chair to the cupboard door. Why would she lie about that? I stared at Jeannie, stamped in silver, looking down. Gently she brought her hand to her tummy. I have to tell you something, she said in a small precise voice. But she did not continue. Instead she sighed again, and then she glanced up at me with a certain determination, a coy inclination of her head. Hey, she said. What say we go out tonight? Just you and *moi*. Someplace rum, like we did that once. All right?

Someplace rum?

Yeah. Someplace posh. I wanna do me hair.

She did do her hair. Washed it in the kitchen sink and curled it into a pile of burnished ringlets. Then Mrs. Deaker made up her face, rouged the cheeks and lined the lashes and painted the eyelids blue. Biting a tentative lip, Jeannie led the way into the entrance hall wearing the frilly pink dress I had bought her, followed by the old lady, who gave me a chilly, cordial nod. Very pretty, she said, fixing me with a raptor's eye. Doesn't Master agree?

Dorie threw a tantrum before we escaped. She wrapped herself around Jeannie's ankles, swiping a claw at Mrs. Deaker, who made a rueful *tsk* of disapproval. I wanna go I wanna go I wanna go! the girl wailed. I pottered by the door, watching the antics. I had no sympathy for the histrionic little liar. Dorie caught my sneer, and she suddenly scrambled up and took two alarming steps toward me and then stopped, clenching her tiny fists, complexion hectic and blurred. Sparkling hatred blazed from her matted gaze. Die, it commanded. Die. I stood mesmerised. The girl drew a trembling breath and removed a strand of hair from her feverish lips, then turned and, with a kind of stately dignity, climbed the stairs. That was the last I saw of her.

I took Jeannie to the George. Like a nobleman's hunting lodge, wooden rafters and a roaring fire in the stone hearth and stags' heads mounted round the walls. I told the waiter it was my daughter's birthday and ordered a bottle of champagne. But my smile felt false and stiff, and my face wore a greasy sheen. She was right. I was different. I was changing. But into what? Jeannie sipped from her flute and eyed the room. Look at these people, she whispered. She jerked her chin at a prim man dining alone. I'll bet he pays ladies to yoke him and whip him, she said, I'll bet he's got lashings all over. And that one there! That one's a surgeon, see. He goes round at night cutting up stray cats and leaving 'em on geezers' doorsteps!

The waiter glided up with the snails, gave us each a pair of silver tongs and a tiny fork. I watched Jeannie struggling to grasp one of the slippery bastards, which leapt from the tongs onto the table and rolled over to reveal its slimy underside. At last she managed to plunge in her fork, twist, and pluck out the meat like an eyeball. With my tongs I turned a snail over, probed the frilled, grey flesh. So, Jeannie said, chewing the rubbery thing. What's it you do, then? *Do?* Yeah, do. When you go off. Your other life. *My other life*, I repeated. I set down the tongs. *I'm a doctor. I live in a great big house. Lots of servants. All new clothes. You wouldn't even recognise me.*

Jeannie watched me, a lump of snail on her fork. What kind of doctor?

A head doctor. An alienist, it's called. I treat the insane.

She gave me a sad smile. That's not true.

It is true, it's all true. Ask me anything.

She put her fork on her plate, and looked down at her lap, gathering courage. All right. In this big house of yours, d'you have a wife?

No. No wife.

Why not?

Because. I'd make her very unhappy.

An effervescent pain was expanding in my breast, as if I'd swallowed a gulp of champagne down the wrong pipe. Jeannie nodded vaguely at the tablecloth between us, and I ached to reach over and smear the speck of pepper from the wick of her mouth with my thumb. Instead I tugged the napkin from my collar and stood up, muttered something about the loo, and lurched off toward the back of the room as if across a pitching ship. In the gentlemen's I unfastened my collar and splashed my bristly face, regarded my dripping reflection. My eyes were pink and glassy; a squiggly vein stood on my temple. A wife! Why would she ask me that? What did she think I could do? I couldn't protect her. I didn't even know what I was protecting her from. Myself, it was beginning to seem. I gripped the porcelain basin, struck by the urge to punch my reflected face in the glass and splinter it. We did not deserve her. We were only dirtying her with our soiled hands. And something far worse was going to happen if we held on to her much longer. I could feel it coming like a cloud about to cross the sun and throw the world in shadow. She was not safe. *No one is safe!* I whispered, like a fervent prayer. From a stall behind me came a thunderous flush.

I looked up in the mirror to see the stall door open and a man stroll across the tiled floor toward me: heavyset, brown beard going grey at the chin. At the sink next to mine he began washing his hands, squelching the soap into a lather. I watched his reflection, the root of my tongue beginning to stiffen like a ramrod down my throat.

Oh God. Not another one.

I knew this man too. For a numbed moment I could not think how, and then the secondhand knowledge trickled in. Horace Waller. Georgiana's husband.

The man meant nothing to me. Yet I could not stop staring. He wrung his hands and shut off the tap and glanced up in the mirror and found me watching. A broad, common face behind the thick beard. He tipped me a doubtful nod, accepting a towel from the old attendant in uniform. Have we met? he asked, wiping his paws. My larynx was locked. For an instant I saw Georgiana in the chair by the cabinet windows, touching her belly, hair shining. I looked down at the gushing sink, twisted off the tap. The gents' door swung shut. I was alone with the ancient attendant, shuffling toward me with a towel and a sweet, encouraging smile.

Back at the table, Jeannie had moved on to my snails. I had made a mess of refastening my collar. A vessel thumped at my temple. I did not want to be drawn into yet another addling misadventure. What did I care about Georgiana's husband? Yet even as I struggled to concentrate on Jeannie I could feel my eye veering off, scanning the dining room for Waller. Soon I had spotted him over Jeannie's left shoulder, his thickset back and low scruffy head, at a table with three other men. Of all the loos in London. What did this sequence of appearances mean? One after another, these men were being placed in my path, as if by some hidden arranger, like those three ghosts in Dickens leading the old miser to enlightenment. Enlightenment! This was its opposite — murky, baffling implications. I was being toyed with. It was all interconnected, like a web. And here was Jeannie snagged at the centre of it, oblivious to the danger. I had to let her go. Get her far away from me.

Bring me the bill, I told the waiter when he sidled up with our wine. I shakily refilled my glass, downed it, and caught the desperate glass eye of the stag's head affixed to the timber above our table. The bill arrived in its elaborate leather portfolio. How much, then? Jeannie asked. *A lady shouldn't inquire*, I quipped, attempting a smile. Then I offered her the bill and when she snapped it up I snuck a glance at Waller's table, where the men were pushing back their chairs and getting to their feet. I groped in my pocket for the wad of banknotes, peeled some off and dropped them on the spotted tablecloth. I stared at the remaining stack and then with a wobble of grief presented it across the table to Jeannie, still examining the bill in amazement. She saw the money in my hand. What's that for? I shrugged, grinning miserably. *You might need it. Never know.* Her fingers accepted the lump of crumpled paper. My eyes were starting to smart, the candlelight blearing. *Ready, then?*

The four men came out of the George and dallied on the kerb, shaking hands and clapping shoulders. I held Jeannie by her coat lapels, teetering in her tall shoes. She had the hiccoughs. I can't stop, she complained, as another one seized her. You have to help me, she said, gasping, you have to say my name and tell me to hiccough. Dorie — *hic!* — Dorie does it and it works. Tell me to hiccough — say, Jeannie, hiccough!

Two of the men climbed into the first hansom by the kerb and went clopping off. Another man got into the second. Waller waved as the cab pulled away, big-bellied in his overcoat, breathing rags of steam. A third hansom was rolling forward to take him, but he turned to plod off down the street.

Do it! Jeannie was pleading with me. Just try it — *hic!* — say my name and tell me to hiccough, it works, I promise. Pleeease? *Jeannie,* I snapped, giving her a rough shake. She looked at me, startled, tottered a step. I think that did it, actually. *Good. Let's go.* I hooked my arm through hers and tugged her down the pavement after Waller. A quiet, well-tended lane behind Regent with regular trees and lampposts and shops all shut for the night. Waller scuffed along, a model of shambling innocence, the family man ambling tipsily home to his wifey. Jeannie clip-clopped at my side. What're we doing? She panted. *Listen,* I said, my throat hard with heartache. *There's something I want you to do.*

She slid her arm from mine, and looked at me with slow, disgusted bewilderment. As if I had pulled off my face like a bandage and bared the real, raw flesh to the air. She stepped back, her mouth sour, her eyes starting to shine. Why would you want me to do that?

Because, I answered recklessly. *Why's it matter? It's a simple thing, isn't it?*

And what're you gonna do? You gonna watch me with him?

No. My voice felt clotted. *Maybe. What's the difference? This is what you do, no? Make friends? With me, with him, with anyone. How many have there been, eh? How long you been at it? I feed you and your bitch of a sister, I keep you safe. I'm not your da. Not your sweetheart. I'm just some bloke you let lick your cunny for room and board. Am I wrong?*

Jeannie looked at me. Her bewildered brow had loosened into a kind of disappointment, mature and tired. As if she had known all along that this was who I was and yet had wanted to pretend otherwise. I'd been trying to make her angry. This was so much worse. My eyes were smarting again. A nearby lamp lent Jeannie's hair a russet corona. She moved back another step and again touched a hand to her belly. Yes, she said. You're wrong. Then she turned and walked away.

Sprawled on damp grass, I awoke. Early morning. Someone was standing over me, prodding my shoulder. I shielded my eyes, smacking my rancid mouth. The man held a blunt stick in his hand, poised to prod me again. Thick leather belt, gold buttons down his tunic, a rounded hat like a riding helmet. I sat up in cold panic. A park. A wine bottle on the grass beside me. Wakey, wakey, sir, the copper was saying, you can't sleep here. I nodded, wincing. *What park is this?* I tried to say, but I could murmur only *Park.* That's right, sir, this is Hyde Park, you can't sleep here. What's your name, sir? I touched my fragile head. *Hyde.* That's right, sir, the copper said, Hyde Park. He sighed. Let's get you on your feet.

The earth rocked like a boat. I clung to him, swallowing back the rising bile. *Apologies. Last night, an argument, the old lady. Took things a little far, it seems.* I tried to smile and imagined my dark-ringed mouth and wine-stained teeth. He was inspecting me, my clothes, my boots, my bloodshot eyes. Where's your residence, sir? *Ghyll. Ghyll Road.* He frowned, his brigadier's moustache pulling down. Then he nodded brusquely, slid his stick into his belt. In that case, sir, might I suggest you go home.

Home. A drizzle was falling as I stood in the stone courtyard, looking up at the grey house, fighting a mean, heartbroken urge to find a stone and smash it through the drawing-room window. A cat was yowling out of the mist, repetitive and mournful. The stone angel atop the fountain mutely echoed the sound from its corroded open mouth. When I stepped into the entrance hall I sent a pair of cockroaches scuttling across the floor. I trudged upstairs to the top landing and pushed open the girls' bedroom door. The chaise longue lay askew under the window and its dingy shaft of morning. Downstairs I wandered into the kitchen, stared blankly at the table and chairs. The door to Mrs. Deaker's room, beyond the stove, was partly ajar; there was flickering within. I went over and eased it wider with one finger. The room was high and windowless. The leaves and pearls of scalloped moulding leapt with shadows. *Mrs. Deaker?* I said, stepping into the bedroom, peering uneasily about. I could smell her sharp, musty tang. My eye found the oblong flash of a mirror, in the far corner—a vanity table. Mrs. Deaker was sitting before it with her back to me. Her long silvery hair was down, as if she had been brushing it. But she was not moving now. Her stillness was frightening. I had the ghoulish notion that it was not actually her but a stuffed mannequin, with glass eyes and horse hair. *Mrs. Deaker?* I whispered. With a soundless swivel she turned on her stool, then rose and began to shuffle toward me like a sleepwalker, her dressing gown flowing, her eyes eerily vacant. Gin hazed the air around her; I stepped back in alarm. *Eudora,* I said, and she stopped, swaying, a few paces away. Her zombie eyes focused upon me, and her lips drew back.

We just keep them, she whispered. That was the idea. We keep them.

Listen, I said. *Listen.* Uselessly I shook my head. *They had to go. It has to be this way.*

It seemed the old woman might laugh. You men, she said, in almost a kind of wonderment. You made it this way. *I didn't*, I cried. *I don't have any control over this. It's just — how it is.*

She stared at me, her eyes filled but not spilling over, her little teeth bared. Then she spat on the floor at my feet. A speck struck my cheek, wet and intimate. I blinked.

Get out, she said.

DAY THREE

Before Dawn

I'm convinced of it now: there is a bird's nest in some cranny of the surgery block. I'd wondered if I was imagining things when I first heard it, but there it is again, that tiny hopeful cheeping. I would like to stick my head out the window and have a peek, but that wouldn't be wise; it's almost light and Poole might be watching the windows. Listen to them, though — the minuscule things, all feathers and beaks and quivering hearts, chirruping in the half dark for their breakfast. Remarkable, to think of life growing in the cracks of this cursed workshop. You could almost take it as a sign of something good. But I know better. I am being taunted again with these birds. All those birds dead in Ghyll's courtyard fountain. That's what I am meant to remember, all those inexplicable little bodies. Birds are like tiny minions flung here and there by the handful. To die in my fountain, to build a nest under my window and lay eggs — like it's all the same, birth and death, interchangeable.

As I move from the windows my eye falls on last night's chicken dinner. The carcass gives me an unpleasant start — the flayed skin glistening in the early light and a shredded hole hacked into the breast; the legs awry. This looks like the left-overs of a lunatic. When did I do this? Gingerly I bend one of the legs back into place, feel the gristle click in the socket. When

I release it, the leg begins to rise again on its own. No, this is no good, I can't have Poole see this. Bracing myself, I take hold of the knobby bone end and lift the weighty carcass from the plate with one hand, ease the window open a bit wider with my other. I dangle the thing through the aperture and let it drop to the courtyard below. It hits with a damp, meaty thump. At least it won't go to waste out there. The birds have been pecking up everything I drop.

Chicken, though. Is it cannibalism for a bird to consume another bird?

Oh, who cares. Birds eat each other every day. Everything devours its own kind.

Get out, Mrs. Deaker said, and I did. I went back upstairs to the girls' room. Feverish sleep on the chaise lounge: I woke bathed in sweat, parched, head pounding. I couldn't tell if I had slept for a day or a minute—the grey drizzle pattering the slanted skylight was unchanged. I flopped back to the cushions and dreamt of digging through moist, falling earth, and when I woke again, the morning sun was roasting me alive.

I was famished. I staggered heavy-legged from the house into the sparkling day. Silver clouds shifted over the sun; a warm breeze gusted up the road. I bought a sausage roll from a stand, piping hot and bursting with gorgeous bits of fat. I devoured it on the spot and dragged a sleeve across my mouth, invigourated, and continued on. I was heading eastward; soon I'd crossed Crown Street and left Soho behind. I knew where I was going. I did not question it. Yet I couldn't remember the exact route Jeannie had taken that night. Everything looked different in the daylight. The lane was crowded: a swaying omnibus groaned with people clinging to its sides, the air thick with noise and plaster dust. I ducked into an alleyway lined with open stalls and workshops, furnaces glowing molten. Women kept pulling my arm and trying to show me their wares—jewellery, urns, enamel saints, candlesticks, leather harnesses, seat cushions — I stumbled away through the milling throngs. At last I found myself climbing an uphill lane strung with washing lines overhead, sheets and linens flapping in the high breeze. Spurred by recognition I clambered to the top and came onto a wide street of dreary brownstones sealed together in a barricade on either side. Yes, this was her street. I went up some steps and pushed into a stinking lobby, but I could tell it wasn't the right one. I tried another, and another, before stepping into that specific smell of mildew and soup, with a pattern of broken tile on the floor. This was the place. I climbed the stairs to the third landing. A yellow stain spread over the bloated wallpaper like a country on a map. I tiptoed to the first door on the left, pressed my ear to the wood, and listened. Silence. I tried the knob — it was locked, but the lock was flimsy; the door gave a little when I weighed my shoulder against it. Hell with it. I backed up and kicked it open: splintering *crack* and a ping of something metal clattering off. The front room was empty. Four mismatching chairs at the tilted table; flies stitching the air above it. It stank of rotting vegetables, bad plumbing. I stood panting, waiting. Two peeling doors stood opposite each other, one partly ajar. I crunched across the gritty floor and nudged it open.

A large bed took up all the space in the box of a room. Yellowed, rumpled sheets; an oniony stink on the air. A greasy undergarment was slung over the bedrail, and from the missing drawer of the bureau, a shirtsleeve lolled like a pale tongue. I crossed the front room to the other door, twisted the knob, and let it swing inward. A low double bed, a bookshelf, a school desk with a crippled leg. I approached the neatly made bed. An impression upon the pillow and coverpane; I bent and sniffed and caught a faded trace of them, that warm bready odour, overlaid by Da's gamy scent. A doll was slumped against the wall, forlorn, and I tentatively picked it up. A strange fabric thing, floppy, with rough, loose stuffing. It must have had hair and a face once, but now the head was bare except for a few nubs of yarn along the scalp, the face blank but for a single brown-button eye. It gazed up at me, lopsided and somehow hopeful, and it occurred to me rather oddly that the orphaned thing was naked and that between its legs ran a small seam. I brought it to my face, pressed my nose to its navel, and saw Jeannie standing in my bedroom again with a hand on her belly, looking down. I made a stifled, moaning sound into the fabric. I lowered the doll and thrust it back onto the bed. Then I turned and hurried over grainy boards of the front room to the door, hanging open on its hinges. I pulled it shut behind me and found Jeannie's da on the landing.

He looked ill, stubbled and sallow. He had shaved off his moustache; for a second I hardly recognised him. His head quivered as he gaped at me, clutching a paper sack to his chest. L-listen, he stammered, they're not — they haven't ... I thought ... His grizzled chin trembled, and his eyes filled. They're not with you, then? I had to look away. *No.* I pitched past him down the stairs as he cried brokenly after me, Then where? Then *where?* I blundered out into the blinding day.

In the drawing room at Ghyll, sunlight fell through the front window, dancing with dust motes. The flower basked on its table. I turned the pot to make it look up at me; its rich brown face was lifted and slightly cocked, questioning. My thumb and forefinger plucked a petal from its golden crown. The petal fluttered down when I let it go, and I took the flower's whole head in my hand. I felt its neck pop and split and its face crumble like earth. I pulverised it between my fingers, then yanked it loose from the pot by its stalk with a shower of sod, dropped it to the carpet, and ground the veiny roots under the toe of my boot. I lifted my foot and stomped down on the mash, again, again, finally smearing it under my heel. A sob hitched from my throat; crouching, I scooped up the remains. Cupping the mangled stalk and broken petals and sod, I hurried outside and dumped it all into the dead stone fountain atop some dried brittle leaves. My palms were stained yellow, brown in the cracks and under my fingernails. Whimpering, I scrubbed my hands on my trousers, averting my gaze from the stone angel posed atop the fountain, its decaying face and open mouth. A shadow was casting over the yard, and I stared up at the sky as a cloud eclipsed the sun, turning black at heart and blazing at its silvered edges. I cringed, expecting some kind of celestial rebuke: a torrent of rain, spike of lightning. I almost yearned for it, a swift punishment. I let my eyes close. Get it over with! Then sunshine flooded the yard.

By the next day I felt rather better. A convalescent relief, as if I had purged myself after a horrible binge. I had done the right thing, sending the girls away from me. Maybe they would even return home. After all, Jeannie's story had been a lie. Their da had not tried to sell them into slavery. I had looked into his eyes. Jeannie had simply run away, as she would have run from me if I hadn't chased her off first.

But her imprint upon the house was hard to erase. I stripped off my black satin bedclothes and carried them to a laundry, but the squashy feather pillow she'd liked to use had to be hurled off the verandah — it would not give up her scent. In the kitchen, scrounging for a loaf of bread I'd bought that had apparently vanished, I came across a teacup Jeannie had dinged with her plate one morning at breakfast, producing a chip in the rim, a pointy flaw that I now fingered bitterly. Yet quickly I put it back on the draining board, almost blushing, for I felt myself being watched by some sardonic spy suppressing a snicker. I turned and, indeed, there was Mrs. Deaker in the doorway, head tilted, gazing at me as if I were a huge scavenging rodent. Her silver hair was pinned up, her eyes clear and cold. Master is — hungry? she said, mockingly servile. Try the second drawer from the bottom. Go on, she encouraged when I hesitated. I eased the drawer open and regarded the shriveled turd inside. An apple, brown and soft. She chuckled, but when I looked up again, the doorway was empty.

She seemed to be daring me to give her the sack. She had stopped cooking my breakfast and no longer cleaned or did chores from what I could tell. She just lived in my house, wandering the rooms like the ghost of someone I'd accidentally killed. Yet I refused to give her the satisfaction, to validate this pose as the poor old victim by evicting her — even though I was beginning to suspect the old witch of gossip, of spreading rumours about me. For I could swear that the locals were looking at me oddly, observing me askance on the street. When I'd first moved into Ghyll, months before, I had received some attention, speculative assessment. *There he goes*, I'd imagined them murmuring to each other, *took that old house on Ghyll Road, the whole lot*. But now the local gazes felt different, less curious, edged with menace. It was not overt; I didn't often catch anyone actually glaring at me. The sliding eyes of a woman with a baby on her hip, the way that pair of charwomen in kerchiefs both shifted their heads away from my glance at the very same moment. Little things in which I could detect an unmistakably hostile glint. And there persisted still that sense of something or someone spying on me while repressing a snort of laughter.

I stopped before a pawnshop window one day, my attention snagged by a set of painted wooden dolls. They had been designed to nest one inside the other, all fitting within the largest oblong doll, but in the window they were arrayed in a line, ten or so, all wearing kerchiefs like Russian peasants, arranged from the largest to the smallest, which was the size of a bullet. The display unsettled me. This one dummy with so many replicas stored inside. I thought of Emile Verlaine. That third, unknown entity, L'inconnu. Jekyll said Emile had no awareness of the others. But could he sense their autonomous desires? Was three the limit or could the multiplicity go on and on, like these dolls with their cryptic, replicated smiles?

I glanced uneasily over my shoulder. Strange. The light had changed. The shadows had grown. A chestnut vendor who had been stationed on the far corner was gone. How long had I been standing here?

I had noticed this effect before. As if the clock had skipped ahead with a soundless click. Those lapses I had experienced, when I had jumped from one present moment to another with no sense of how I had arrived. I had assumed that Jekyll was the cause of such lapses, that he was reaching into the body, directing its animation. Except this time I had not moved from the pawnshop window. It was like instantaneous transportation into the future with a blankness in between. As if Jekyll had taken control of the body and gone for a stroll and then returned to the exact same place and posture I had occupied before.

As I stood there frowning at the street, the door of the neighbouring shop opened and a corpulent man with fiery red hair waddled out. I glanced at him; our eyes met, and I recognised him. The agent from the leasing office who had found Ghyll for me. He looked at me once and then quickly again and broke into an awkward smile, nodding at me. Before he could move on, I leant over and extended my hand. This gesture I'd seen men perform every day, this emblem of civilisation, I had made only once, with this very man, after I'd signed the contract. Naked and white and raw at the knuckles, my hand hovered between us. The fat man stared at it for a slowed-down second, so drawn out that I could observe the glisten of copper splinters on his flabby cheek, a droplet of sweat standing from his wispy orange muttonchop. Then his eyes jerked up and he let out a queasy, twittering laugh and cried, Ah, yes, Mr. Hyde! Very good!

My hand faltered. The man nodded again, jowls wobbling,

showing me his small, childlike teeth as he backed away. Then he turned and hastened down the lane.

My name had rolled off his tongue so readily. It had been months since I'd seen him last. Was it just his special talent, remembering names? Or did he have some reason to remember mine? And why would he not take my hand? By the time I veered into Ghyll's courtyard it was nearing dusk, and the drawing-room window mirrored the violet streak of sky. Yet behind the stained glass a figure seemed to be standing, motionless, gazing out. I lifted my hand. The shape did not respond.

The air in the entrance hall felt electrically charged. I crossed to the drawing room and peered round the door frame. No one stood at the windows. I stepped in and looked at the wingback against the wall where Mrs. Deaker liked to sit and surprise me, but the chair was empty. My eye moved again to the window, then fell to the round table beneath it, where the flowerpot had sat. Something lay upon it now, a ring of silver, a whiteness. A tarnished silver plate with a white envelope on it. And scratched in a cramped, spiky line of ink across its face was my name:

Mr. Hyde

Never in my months of residence here had I received a single letter. I reached for the envelope, hesitated, then snatched it up. With my thumb I tore open its seam and drew out a square inch of crudely folded paper. It was folded five or six times; I almost ripped it in my impatient fumbling before finally turning the page right-side up:

> *you be hide and I play seek*
> *tho I know where you've hid, you see,*
> *so I play hide and you play hide*
> *and see who's found out first!*

I read it again. But it made no more sense the second time. Was this a threat? A warning? The writing itself, awkward chicken scratch, looked bizarrely familiar. Could it be —? Could it be from Jeannie? For a pathetic second, hope surged in my breast. Then it fled, leaving me flustered, and with a stifled chortling in my ears. I narrowed my eyes and whirled around and found Mrs. Deaker in the doorway, watching me. I lifted the paper, resisting the urge to clear my throat. *When did this come?* Mrs. Deaker shrugged. Perhaps an hour ago. Slipped into the letterbox. *The letterbox?* I repeated dumbly. Indeed, the old lady said. It is a letter, is it not, Master? I pray it isn't bad news.

She gave me a wintry smile and withdrew from the doorway. I gaped after her. Could *she* have written it? I examined the queer poem again, the cheap foolscap crackling in my hands. *You be hide and I play seek.* Hide and seek. Of course. Of course it was her! Who else could it be? Was it a coincidence the letter had been left where her precious flowerpot once sat?

I crossed the room and went into the entrance hall, refolding the paper and thrusting it into my pocket. At the front door I hunkered down, pushed my hand through the letterbox, lifting the brass trap, and peered through the slot at the portico and the purpling courtyard and the black iron spears of the fence and beyond that the cobbled road. I had never liked this letterbox. I had been leery of it back when I was inspecting the house for security. It was a peephole, a chink in my fortress. Should I nail it shut? I withdrew my hand. The trap dropped with a *clack*, and I squatted there in the dark, certain the old witch must be watching me, gloating in the depths of the corridor. I rose and opened the front door, as if simply checking the weather, and stepped out onto the portico. I did not want to be in this house. I wanted to be elsewhere, anywhere but here. And with a sudden pang of amazement I remembered the Castle Street door.

The cabinet! How long had we been away? Weeks, it seemed. I had almost forgotten about it, as a dreamer forgets his bed, and his body slumbering in it. The prospect now opened before me like an avenue of retreat. I cast a glance back into the entrance hall, the coagulating shadows. Then I drew the door shut behind me.

Ten minutes later I stood below the Castle Street door, panting from my hasty pace. A lamp shed its light across the pitted face of the surgery block and the cement stoop, which, I saw now, was spattered with crusted bird droppings. The door too had suffered in my absence. People had been carving into the wood, as lovers inscribe their initials — except these marks were strange, indecipherable hieroglyphs. There was one that resembled an open eye inside a triangle, slashed vertically through. By the knob, little bits of paint were chipped away, stab marks. Welcome home. Key in hand, I climbed the steps, droppings crunching like chalk underfoot.

Jekyll exited the Castle Street door, carrying a battered leather travelling satchel he had removed from the wardrobe after dressing himself. He picked his way down the soiled steps and walked south on Castle to the corner, where he turned toward Leicester Square. His keys clanked in his pocket, but when he reached Big House, he rang the doorbell, and Poole ushered him in. *How excellent to see you again, sir. I trust you had a pleasant holiday?*

Jekyll strolled past him into the main hall. *Pleasant? You might say it was pleasant, yes. Good for you, sir. You are looking very well.*

This was a lie. His clean-shaven face was ashen, bruised under the eyes. His clothes smelt faintly of mould, which didn't mask the body's sour, garlicky odour. *Thank you. All the same, I think I'll have a bath.*

At breakfast the following morning I stared through him in shock at the date on the freshly ironed paper. It was 1 April 1885. We had been away nearly a month. Upstairs, we found a collection of letters and calling cards arranged on the desk in order of their arrival. Jekyll stood over the green leather blotter, two fingers at the desk edge, scanning the array, while I braced myself, almost expecting to see the crabbed, spiky handwriting leap out. But there was nothing of interest. Except for the last calling card. Danvers X. Carew, MP. Jekyll tapped it twice, then withdrew from his pocket the square of crudely folded paper which he had removed from my own pocket last night. He unfolded the coarse, brittle foolscap and gently smoothed it flat on the blotter. His lips moved as he read again the four lines of spidery ink scratch: *you be hide and I play seek, tho I know where you've hid, you see, so I play hide and you play hide, and see who's found out first!*

Jekyll's pulse was light and quick. *Found out first*, he repeated in a whisper. That line disturbed me too. Found out about what? What did she mean, *I know where you've hid?* Jekyll's thoughts whirred, a vast machine beyond the membrane of my cell. Yet I could feel his anticipation, his fear, and something more obscure, a kind of pride. He was going to send me back soon. This letter was merely the beginning. And Jekyll didn't intend to hide from it. He reached out and ran his fingertips over the spiky script indenting the page as if it were written in a Braille only he could read. At last he folded the letter, slid open a desk drawer, and dropped it inside.

By the following evening I was in the body again. Nowhere to go but home. Holding my breath, I clicked my key into Ghyll's front door and let it creak inward. The stage was just as I had left it, shadows pooling at the edges of the entrance hall. A rapt expectancy crackled in the air as I crossed the boards to the drawing-room doorway and peered round the frame at the table under the window. It was empty.

I awoke the next morning frantically brushing at my face. I'd had a dream, nastily vivid: spiders and centipedes spilling out of a book onto my hands. I scrambled out of bed and wrapped myself in my gown, then stole down the stairs, feeling queerly like a child on Christmas morning, hopeful and apprehensive. On the last step I stopped. An envelope was trapped in the letterbox, as I had somehow known it would be. Back in my bedroom, I struggled to pierce the slit with my newly manicured thumbnail but my hands were shaking. I eviscerated the envelope and dropped it to the floor. The letter was folded into a square as before. Four crooked lines of ink stamped the page:

> *hidey hide, holy hole*
> *kiss the girls, make them go*
> *but when the boys come to play*
> *hidey hide will run away*

I paced the upstairs landing until I heard Mrs. Deaker's footsteps cross the hall below and the front door close. I scurried downstairs and immediately tried the door to her room off the kitchen. Locked. I stuck my house key into the keyhole and screwed it around, but it wouldn't catch. I scoured the kitchen, yanking open drawers and cupboards, and was at last rewarded with a twisted scrap of charred paper that had been used to light the stove. Upon peeling it open I discovered the remains of an old grocery list, presumably from when the girls had been here: lamb, turnips, potatoes, bread . . . Upstairs, I laid it on top of the second letter for comparison, to confirm what I could already see. The writing did not match. The grocery list was composed in a refined, flowing hand with a finesse to the loops. The letter was exactly the opposite: crabbed, spiky stitches of ink.

Lightly I ran my fingers over the lines, as Jekyll had done. Opposite. Could the woman have written the letter with her opposite hand, her left hand? The calligraphy leant in opposing directions, the grocery list to the left, and the letter to the right. Was this meant to be some kind of disguise? If so, it was pretty transparent. Who else could have written these lines? *Kiss the girls, make them go?* It was even more apparent than the hide-and-seek reference. What was her game? And what did she mean, *when the boys come to play?*

It was just a piece of nursery rhyme. Yet there was a prophetic certainty to that word *when*, which proved itself that very afternoon. I was wandering the lanes when seemingly out of thin air a gang of dirty urchins descended upon me and scrabbled through my pockets with a hundred coordinated hands. Before I could swat them off, the mob dissolved all together. Disheveled and plundered, I stood in the middle of the road. I had wet my trousers in a spurt of surprise. People were looking at me. They had paused, these witnesses, in their passing business, an elaborate tableau of street life now frozen in place, all eyes upon me: complicit, amused, suppressing their smirks. For a second I was convinced they had all assembled at this spot, like an audience, to revel in my humiliation. Then time clicked back into place and the bustle continued around me, and I pulled my hat brim low and slunk away with their silent laughter burning the rims of my ears.

A day or two later, a bird dropped its filth on my shoulder, a runny green-and-white splatter. There was no one around to witness this time. The lane was nearly empty. Yet that made it all the more astounding. The bird had chosen me as its target. I remembered the stoop of the Castle Street door, encrusted in droppings. The door itself carved with those symbols, like a witch's curse . . .

Something was happening to me, something terrible and yet also sly and grand, for which the help of numerous small elements seemed to have been enlisted. It was almost flattering. To be selected and persecuted with such care. But how far would it go? That night I lay awake in my bed, wide-eyed, racing with insomnia, while below my verandah that tabby beggar yowled out its lonesome meow. Over and over came the plaintive mewl, as if the animal were trying to pronounce some word of warning I would never understand. I crushed my pillow to my ears, but the sound was in my head now, a maddening imitation, until at last I leapt out of bed and strode onto the balcony and roared like a crazed king, *Silence! Silence!*

The echo rippled off over the rooftops. I wiped my lips, panting. The yowling began again from below.

> *here kitty kitty*
> *here hidey hide*
> *kittys hiding, what a pity*
> *where the pretty flower died*

I'd returned from my rambles several days later to find the third letter stuck through the brass trap. I pulled it free and ripped it open there on the portico. Then I turned and stared at the stone fountain in the centre of the courtyard. On numb legs I clumped down the steps.

The cat had been dead a day or two. I had caught a certain scent as I entered the yard, a sweet, rancid odour. It lay on its side in the dried leaves, teeth bared, dirty fur matted to its ribs. The eyes were closed, or gone; a line of black ants explored the sunken lids. Had the animal just — died? Was that what I'd been hearing the other night, its death cries? Or had Mrs. Deaker —?

In the entrance hall, I could hear sounds from the kitchen. The old woman was frying an egg at the stove. I watched her from the doorway until she glanced over with a gratifying little gasp. Her letter was crumpled in my pocket; I could hear it crackle as I stepped into the room, affecting nonchalance. *Have you noticed any funny smells, Mrs. Deaker — coming from the courtyard, that is?* Funny smells? she said. No, I don't believe so. But then I don't have much sense of smell these days. Her acting was perfect, innocent, bemused. She scraped the spatula under her egg and flipped it; the grease sizzled and spat. What does it smell of, Master?

I eyed the cunning old witch, almost convinced by her performance. Could she have caught and killed a feral cat with her bare hands? Yet who else knew about the flower, its resting place in the fountain? She *had* to be writing these letters — even if she was merely a pawn in the complex design, she had to know something! I took another step forward. *Listen.* My voice had gone husky. *Listen to me. You know they couldn't have stayed here. You know that. You must know we couldn't have just kept them.*

She had gone still, was not looking at me. And why is that?

Because. Because of — of what I am.

Now she turned, holding the twisted spatula, and fixed me with her cold accusing eyes. And what are you, Master?

I'm — I'm, I stammered, wanting suddenly, alarmingly, to confess, to tell the woman everything, everything. What sweet, forbidden relief it would be! But I clenched my jaw against it, crushed the urge into anger. I would not reveal myself to this ill-meaning hag. *What've you been saying to people?* I demanded.

A wry smile brushed her lips. She turned back to the stove. I don't need to tell anyone anything about *you*, Master.

For a second I had a vision of myself striding up and grabbing her hand and pressing it to the frying pan: the hiss of searing flesh. I flinched from the sound and stepped back toward the door with a ghastly little laugh. *You're right, old girl. No smell out there at all.*

In the morning, I donned my leather gloves and went down to the courtyard, planning to drag out the cat and dispose of it. I could smell it as I approached, riper than before. Holding a gloved hand over my mouth, I peeked over the rim of the fountain at the corpse, blue around the lips and tongue. But it was not alone. A small, grey-brown shape lay in the dried leaves alongside it. I blinked, not trusting my eyes, certain I was hallucinating the thing. It was a bird, a swallow, dead. I looked around and found a stick on the cobblestones and tentatively extended it into the fountain to poke the bird, but I drew back before I touched it. I craned my neck up at the pale morning sky. It was like the bird had just dropped dead from the air, a tiny Icarus.

The next day brought another bird, and the day after that another. Exhilarated with horror, I watched the grey-brown shapes accumulate around the rotting cat, which a mix of superstition and curiosity forbade me to remove, or even touch. The birds appeared unharmed, simply limp and dead, as if struck down in flight. Or as if they had come to my fountain specifically to die. I knuckled my eyes and peered closer, hoping the brown bodies would resolve into harmless leaves. From the drawing-room window I watched the yard and the fountain, hoping I might actually see one tumbling from the sky. Once I did see a bird alight on the stone angel's head and hop down to the fountain rim to peck around. Breathless, I waited for it to keel over. But it flitted off. I went out to examine the rim, to see if anything was sprinkled there, crumbs, rat poison ... From the window of a bare front room on the second floor I also watched Mrs. Deaker's movements to and from the house. But she never so much as glanced at the fountain, never once peeped inside on her way past.

Was I actually cursed? One day I passed a doorway with a sign above it. *Tarot*, the sign read, and below the word a symbol I recognised at once: a triangle with a staring eye inside. The glyph had been carved into the blistered wood of the Castle Street door. I climbed the flight of rackety steps to a garret reeking of incense. The tarot witch had wild white hair and cataract-covered eyes. She sat me down at a table. Her cards were gilt-edged, well worn, bearing faded, unsettling pictures. She laid the first three down on a velvet cloth between us. *What's that one?* I asked, pointing at the middle card, a man dangling upside down from a tree, arms tied around his chest. She touched the picture with her long curving fingernail. The Hanged Man, she croaked. *And that one?* I pointed at the card to its right, a robed and bearded figure holding a scepter or a bubbling glass phial in the air. The Magician, the witch replied, and then she moved her claw to the card on the left, a horned beast with goatish legs crouched upon a golden throne. The Devil. She paused, beholding the display with her milky, blinded eyes. From the slanted attic ceiling hung a family of peculiar scarecrow figures made of bundled twigs and twine, slowly revolving amidst the rising wraiths of incense. *Voodoo.* The word appeared in my head, though I did not know what it meant. I looked down at the three cards, my throat dry. *Which am I?* The witch made a clucking sound with her tongue and laid two more cards below the line of three. All, she murmured, all is you.

She arranged a dozen cards in the shape of an H, pronouncing each one's name in her sibilant accent. The last card was placed at the bottom left, closest to me, and displayed a tall white monolith against a black churning sky. Flames poured from the single window at the top, where a body was framed, arms outspread in rapture. Other people stood on the rocky ground below looking upward, one holding a torch. The witch let out a whispery sigh at the sight of it, caressing the edge with her raptor's nail. The Tower. Her smoked-glass eyes moved up to me. Chaos, she crooned. Transformation. I clasped my hands under the table to keep from grabbing her fragile claw. *When?* I demanded. *How?* Her lips drew back, revealing smooth, toothless gums. The Hanged Man must wait, she said. Her nail moved to a card on the other side and tapped twice: a gold compass in a blue sky. Wheel of Fortune, she whispered. The hooked fingernail lifted and began to circle in the air, stirring the smoke into a spiral. You will see.

I stood up, frightened. I had to stoop to avoid the low ceiling. One of the voodoo scarecrows dangled near my face, arms and legs stiffly extended, its head an empty circle with a twine cross within. I dug a coin from my pocket and tossed it down on the velvet. The witch was smiling, pink and toothless, nodding her frazzled luminescent head. Beware the Fool, she purred.

◆ ◆ ◆

Beware the fool? I did not need Jekyll's sneering disdain to know it was just mystic babble. Yet for days I could not get those pictures out of my head. I could not help feeling that in the configuration of cards, the witch had seen my destiny plotted out, past and future, one as ineluctable as the other. In my dreams I laid the cards out across the floor in fiendishly complex patterns that I had to stand on a chair to see, for there were hundreds of them, and millions of possible permutations, and I would wake with a suffocated cry. Sometimes I'd find scratches across my chest and throat, as if I'd clawed myself with my raggedy nails in the midst of these night terrors.

The weather turned. For days rain sputtered from the gutters, and the whole house smelt of mouldy furniture. Claustrophobic, I paced the many rooms, remembering those afternoons of hide-and-seek silence, the unbreathable pressure of the air. I was scrounging loudly in the barren kitchen one day, hoping more to draw Mrs. Deaker out of hiding than to find anything edible, when I stopped before the sink and hunkered down again by the drain cupboard door. It was swollen shut; I had to tug the black knob before it popped open with a squeak. The hanging loop of pipe, the steel bucket and scrub brush, the tarry reek of carbolic. What was I looking for? I squatted there at a loss, my mind a blank. Then I blinked and jerked back to myself. I had heard something: a metallic *clack*. I rose and walked from the kitchen, down the corridor to the entrance hall. The day had darkened; the hall was deep in gloom. I turned to the front door and saw the envelope sticking through the letterbox, a square of whiteness.

hide hide hide hide hide hide hide hide hide hide hide hide
hide hide hide hide hide hide hide hide hide hide hide
hide hide hide hide hide hide hide hide hide hide hide hide

I almost dropped the paper in shock. The word was scribbled spiky and hectic, breaking down at the bottom into illegible marks that in one place had ripped through the page, like a peeling flap of skin. An insectile tickle raced over my hands, as if the paper were covered in beetles and spiders, and I hurried with it into the drawing room and dropped it onto the cold grate. I tried to strike a match and snapped it in half; I scratched another alight, touched the flame to the page. It curled and buckled as it burned, collapsing into ash.

In the hall I snatched my hat and stick and then plunged into the lashing rain. I hastened past the fountain without looking; I did not want to think of those bloated, floating corpses inside. I sloshed through the runnel gushing down the road and ten minutes later pushed into the Pig and Gibbet.

I stood dripping inside the door, my heart welling with relief. I had not been to the Pig in a fortnight at least. I'd been avoiding my regular haunts. Nothing had changed, of course: the half a dozen regulars were stooped on their stools; Vic mumbled over his daily rag. My old seat at the far end was even empty. I squelched down the length of the bar and clambered onto my stool. Vic did not look over at me. No one did, in fact. There was an unpleasant tension to the silence. I wiped my face, drummed my fingers on the bar, then worked a sovereign from my sodden pocket and snapped it onto the blackwood plank with a loud *clack* that made me flinch along with the old men down the line nursing their sudsy bitters. I cleared my throat. *Vic.* He fetched a heavy sigh, flipped his paper over. My skin was shrinking. I slid off my stool and sloshed to where Vic leant against the back counter. I said his name again. He lowered the rag and lifted his weak, sullen eyes, trapped in that porcine mask. His gaze was almost cool, aloof, yet I could see fear glinting at the edges. He licked his pulpy lips. Go on, he said. Go on with you.

Droplets of water were tapping from my coat to the floorboards. A thin creaking came from my open mouth. Vic's hand, I saw, was inching downward to the shelf below the bar where he kept a wooden axe handle — fer emergencies, he'd told me once.

You've got some bollocks, Vic said now, coming in here again. I told you last time, didn't I, we don't need yer business, Mr. *Hyde*. His voice was getting louder, gaining confidence. Everyone was watching; I could feel the eyes. Last time? I could not speak. Vic's pudgy hand closed around the axe handle. He did not draw it out, he just gripped it. What did I tell you? Vic said, emboldened, eyes flicking to his audience. Eh? Didn't I tell you we don't need nothing you've got? I fell back a step and threw a desperate glance down the bar. Indeed, all the old phlegmy eyes were fast upon me, eager with malice, more alive than I'd ever seen them. Lips peeling back from their tarnished teeth, nostrils distended, eyes swimming in rheumy venom, like people suffering from some bloodthirsty plague. I stepped back from them in dismay. The Pig was infected too. Vic had drawn out the handle now, a sleek club of blond wood, the heavy end laid in his palm. I had seen it somewhere before, not just here, but elsewhere. My lower eyelid was starting to twitch. I had the sense that something was open-ing behind me, that doorway again, widening into an unknown dimension. I did not turn round. Pressing my eyelid to contain its rapid pulse, I scuffled backward to the door.

Up the rear stairwell of the surgery block I stumbled. I lurched into the cabinet, dropping my keys. The room whirled; I could not stand, so I crawled across the floor to the glazed press and groped for the box and the tourniquet. Slumped against the bench, I wrapped the tubing around my arm and took up the syringe, but I was too drunk to see it straight. The barrel and beaded needle split into two syringes, and I could not tell which was real un-til I squinched one eye shut. The wavering needle veered toward my forearm until it touched the skin, and I sank it in and hit the plunger and flipped gratefully back into blackness.

Morning. Jekyll woke sprawled on the cabinet floor. Piercing headache. Shielding his eyes, he sat up, surveyed the bright, hor-rid world. The rear door was ajar. A pool of vomit glistened on the boards by the stove. He was still wearing my wet clothes, with sick stains on the shirt front and cuffs. Safe inside, I stared blearily out, unable to remember even how I'd returned here. The rain had stopped. A white, soundless haze suffused the windows.

Jekyll climbed carefully to his feet, as if standing up in a boat. He poured a glass of water, then removed from the press a small bottle. He dipped a glass pipette into it and drew up a portion of brown nectar. Drop, drop, drop; he tapped it into the water glass, each droplet exploding into amber curlicues. He swirled the cocktail and drank it.

He stripped off my clothes, dressed in his own. He snipped the rusty beard growth and shaved to the grain. He used my shirt to mop up the vomit. The morphia was taking effect, his actions acquiring a dreamy steadiness, the pain and nausea ebbing away. He seemed to move through a rich, silky medium as he smoothed his hair before the mirror, gave the room a final review, and then descended the front stairs and went through the theatre. The gravel yard was steaming, the conservatory greenhouse humid. But the dining room was cool. Jekyll sat in his place at the table, blissfully numbed. Poole entered with a polished silver urn and did not see his master until he'd set it on the sideboard and turned. Goodness, he said, straightening, Dr. Jekyll, forgive me, I was not aware you had returned. I'll have your breakfast straightaway. Jekyll waved a hand, a kingly, languid pardon. *Just tea, Poole,* he murmured with elastic lips, *tea and toast would be lovely.*

He spent the morning and afternoon adrift on the sofa in his study. By evening, the hangover he'd kept at bay was beginning to ebb back into the body. His eyeballs felt gritty; his temples throbbed. He wanted another dose of morphia. I too wanted to continue floating weightless, thoughtless. Instead he bathed and dressed for dinner, forgoing a tie. He felt lightheaded as he sat down at the table. He could not eat; his bowels gurgled at the sight of his veal chop bleeding oil onto the plate. Is it not to your liking, sir? Poole asked. Shall I bring you something different?

No, Jekyll said faintly, turning his head from the smell, *no, I have no appetite, I'm afraid. Working too hard, I expect.* Indeed, sir. Your character studies, is it? Jekyll looked up at him. *Precisely.*

At that moment the front doorbell rang, chiming in the main hall. Jekyll stiffened. I'll see who it is, sir. *I'm not home,* Jekyll said quickly. *Whoever it is, I'm not home. Unless —* The word dissolved off his tongue into suggestive silence. Poole held his gaze a moment, then bowed. Very good, sir.

Georgiana was standing in the main hall removing her gloves when Jekyll entered from the corridor. Of course she would come back to us now. As she looked up, I saw a flash of Jeannie, a russet halo round her head, and my gorge rose in misery. Georgiana extended an icy hand. You're having dinner, aren't you? I can leave right now if I'm a disturbance. Jekyll repressed a shiver at her touch. *Have you eaten?* Oh, she said, I'm not hungry. I'll sit with you, though, if I'm interrupting. *I'm not hungry either. Come.*

In the cabinet he knelt before the stove, struck a match, and lit the coals. Georgiana, a white shawl around her shoulders, was looking at Father's portrait again. Her belly was swelling now; one of her small hands rested absently upon it. Her eyes caught Jekyll watching, and he glanced away. I would have written you, Georgiana said, to ask if I could visit. But I didn't know I'd be left alone in the house tonight. I saw an opening and I took it. She paused. How have you been, Henry? *Oh, busy.* Yes? Is that good? He lifted a shoulder. *It keeps things interesting.*

I could feel her gaze as Jekyll strolled to the windows with a hand in his pocket. I could picture Jeannie's narrowed examining eyes, the half-amused little smile, the vermilion forelock falling to her naked white shoulder. Jekyll was breathing hard through his nostrils. Henry, Georgiana said. Do you want me to leave? Jekyll looked at her, wearing a yellow dress let out at the seams for the ripening. *You look well.* She brought her other hand to her belly and glanced down. I am well. I'm feeling very — optimistic.

Her ear was flushed, beneath a stray white-blond whorl. *That's the whole trick, isn't it.* She nodded. Yes, as a matter of fact, I think it is. She looked up, coyly. You know, I took your advice. When you said I should surprise myself. Take a souvenir. *Oh?* Yes, and I think you were right. It was very liberating. She hesitated. Would you like to see it? *See what?* The souvenir. What I took. I carry it with me sometimes, like a charm.

Jekyll nodded. Georgiana reached into a pocket of her dress as she swished around the table toward the windows. With a mischievous grin she brought from her pocket something thin and silver, held it up. It was a tiny silver fork. A wave of queasiness swelled from our heart. *What is that?* I heard Jekyll say. It's an oyster fork, Georgiana replied with a laugh, then looked concerned. Henry, are you all right? *I'm fine, I simply — where did you get that?* Well, it's rather a long story. Do you really want me to tell you? Wouldn't that, I don't know, spoil it somehow? Jekyll stared at the fork and I through him: the minuscule beaded design around the rim, the three tapered tines. I could see Jeannie plunge it into a snail and twist. Jekyll's hand lifted toward the fork, but before he could touch it, an electric twinge seized the fingers and he drew back. *Yes, perhaps it's best if you don't.* Chilled, sick, he turned to the window, reflecting the room. Henry, Georgiana said softly. Is there — anything I can do?

Do. Do to what?

To help you.

To help me. He laughed, a harsh bark. *Tell me, why is it you people think that I need your help?* He moved his eyes to hers, widening, bewildered. *What makes you think you can do anything for me, Georgiana?* Oh, but I didn't — she said. Henry, I didn't mean to suggest — *That I am some invalid? In need of care? Of rescue?* No, of course not. Henry, you're the least invalid person I know. But you seem — you seem so alone. He was sneering now. *I'm not alone. Believe me, I am not alone. So understand this: You cannot help me. No one can help me. And I can't help you. I have never been able to help you* — But that's not true! she cut in, that's what I'm trying to tell you! You have helped me. A great deal. Do you think you had to make love — to become my husband to help me? *We're not going to talk about that,* Jekyll said. He began to turn away, but she reached out and touched the back of his hand. He froze, half turned, her fingers lightly on his skin. You are a good doctor. And you have been a good friend.

A good doctor, Jekyll repeated. *My patient in Paris killed himself. He hanged himself. Haven't you heard?* But that's not your fault, she protested. *How do you know that? You don't know, so don't say that you do.* He moved his hand from her touch. *You don't know me, Georgiana. You don't know what I am, what I've done. And I don't know you either. What do you imagine we are anymore? Why did you come back here?*

She was shaking her head in slow vehemence, her widened eyes starting to shine. I don't — I don't know what I've done to you. *Of course you don't. You just come and go at your convenience.* At my convenience? she cried. Henry, nothing about my situation is convenient. I thought you understood. But I came anyway, because I wanted to see you. To say thank you.

Well, you've done both. Now you can go again.

We could hear her tripping down the stairs and across the theatre, then crunching over the gravel yard. Jekyll stood rigid by the windows, eyes glazing with heat. He pressed the back of his fist to his lips, shutting his eyes. Then he turned and went to the press for the little brown bottle. He poured a glass of water and dripped in the amber droplets, each unravelling in the depths. He held up the tincture — and then his heart crushed into itself and he spun and whipped the glass at the wall, where it burst. *You get nothing,* he whispered through his teeth, *you get nothing!*

No morphia, no food: for the following two days he indeed took almost nothing. He confined himself to his study, accepting only tea and otherwise lying with rumbling stomach on the sofa navigating a fine, hairline crack in the ceiling overhead. I could not access him; his thoughts seemed as distant as the grumbling of his hunger. What were we going to do? It struck even me as a futile, pathetic question. What could we do? My life was contaminated. This plot against me had polluted every aspect of my existence. Look how the Pig had been turned against me! They had never liked me in there, I'd known that, but they had taken my money, they had suffered my patronage until now. So what had changed? It was like the whole place had been bewitched. My life as Edward Hyde was finished. My name itself was tainted. How clearly I could hear Vic say, We don't need yer business, Mr. *Hyde* — like the very echo of that final, terrifying letter I had burned! Where could I go with a tainted name? What could I look forward to? Lurking about my haunted house and waiting for the letterbox to clack with my tormentor's latest riddle? I would never learn its author's identity, assuming there even was an *identity* to be learned. The mystery would simply keep chipping away at my sanity until I'd been reduced to a paranoid wreck.

Such was my turmoil that I hardly noticed when Jekyll at last left his study and descended the stairs. Only when he stepped from the conservatory into a blinding, balmy afternoon did I perk up, squint about. He crossed the courtyard, climbed up to the cabinet. For a moment, I thought he might be going for the morphia after all. But then he slid the E drawer from its slot in the press, set it on the table, shed his dressing gown, and rolled up his sleeve.

He was setting me loose? Why? I was wary. Yet I could feel the heart unclenching from its stubborn fist as he drew the serum from the phial and flicked the glass barrel, then pushed out a glittery jet of palest green. Did he have a solution? I was quaking as the needle zeroed in on the vein. Oh, Jekyll, I prayed, don't lead me wrong.

Ten minutes later I stepped from the Castle Street door onto the crusty stoop. I wore a clean shirt. My jacket and trousers smelt musty but were dry. I had nearly fifty pounds in my various pockets. From under my brim I sucked a noseful of the day's late bouquet: coal smoke, horse dung, bread, sun on the stones. The light along the upper house fronts had started to thicken into a golden, yolky hue. A warm breeze moved up the lane, flapping my coattails. I had to lean on my stick for a moment, weak-kneed with delight. Then I pitched down the cement steps and the cobbled lane. South I was headed, not north toward Soho but south toward—I did not know what. But I was not going back to Ghyll. At Trafalgar Square I turned east, strolled along the Strand. The theatre crowd congested the pavement, all of them milling about in their stoles and silk scarves and cloying perfumes, and I slipped through them with a kind of increasing revelation. No one looked at me. No one noticed me. I was nobody to them. The light became denser as I continued east, the sky darkening to royal blue above the black rooflines, and hours later, the evening found me strolling along a dilapidated road in the light cast by shuddering gas lamps somewhere in the maze of Whitechapel. A dog was woofing, a man and woman shrieking at each other in one of the ragged tenements looming over the lane. Tipsy laughter cackled from a swollen-legged dolly sprawled drunk against a wall. Another girl staggered up and pawed my chest, cooing with rotten breath. At a corner stood a shriveled ancient who edged away from me and snarled, I 'aven't got any! I 'aven't got any, I tell you, don't even ask! I marvelled at these mad, anonymous characters as if they had been invented solely to amuse me. I came to a pub, and went in.

Low-ceilinged and a cosy sulphurous glow. The barman was bald with a giant glossy moustache. He poured me a brimming glass of gin and pushed it over with a friendly nod. Three bristly heavies stood farther down the bar, watching me. Heart in my gullet, I raised my glass to them. After a pause, they lifted their beers and turned back to their talk.

I felt like bursting into laughter. How foolish I had been!

How hidebound and narrow! Here I was, imagining my life as Edward Hyde was finished, when there was all this undiscovered country to be explored. Soho was not my life, and Ghyll was not my *home*. It was just a rotting old house I'd leased for thirty lousy quid. I could lease a hundred houses at that rate — what did it matter? Even my poor tainted name — it was just a name! I hadn't even chosen it; Jekyll had given it to me when he'd given me the five thousand pounds and a world of problems to go with it. I had existed for months without a name, without a house and without so much money, and I had been perfectly happy. Happy! I had lost track of something since those early days, something I had known innately when Jekyll first let me loose, more than half a year ago. This was my life. I carried it with me wherever I went. This was my home. Right here.

I spent the night in a rundown hotel by the river. From the caving bed, I could smell the water lapping the pylons, its fishy, womanish stink. I could feel Jekyll inside me, branching through my blood, stiffening from the root of my groin. Shivering as if with cold, I unbuttoned my flies and worked delicately toward the crest. I had never done it like that before, drawing it out like torture, nearing the burning brink and then ebbing back, over and over, its sensitivity toward the end so exquisite that I held our rigid life at the lowermost stem, kept in excruciating limbo, like that paradox of halving and halving forever without ever reaching the mark — and when I crushed out the climax at last, the whole body bucked in rapture. I could not open my eyes; a brilliant grid of phosphorescence cast its tracery across the darkness. Jekyll was fused to my every nerve, welded to me. Oh God. I did not need a house, a canopy bed, satin sheets. I did not need servants, dolly, neighbours, friends. I did not need a bank account; I did not need a name. All I needed was this.

In the morning, I continued east, strolling along the river, watching the ragpickers wade in the mucky banks and feel about the bottom for bits of sunken treasure. An androgynous scrap of muddy child straightened with something that it put in its mouth, sucked on, and then removed, clean for inspection. A gull careened down and landed on a wooden mooring post filmed green with algae. A low-slung boat piled with netting skimmed by, leaving in its wake ripples like silk on the oily water. By dusk I had reached the inlet and docks of the Isle of Dogs and joined a rowdy crowd of workers shouting and cursing at two men fighting shirtless for money. Later on, in a clapboard shanty groaning over the water, pitch-black but for knotholes gleaming here and there, I felt my way into a low-cushioned berth, and a frail Chinese boy lit the long slender pipe extending from my lips. A bright ball of opium burned in the gloom as I drew in its milky, mesmerising smoke.

Yes, Jekyll urged me toward the opium. The miraculous black, sticky tar was kin to his laudanum in the brown bottle in the press — yet so much more potent when drawn into the lungs and absorbed into the alveoli. I imagined I could actually feel the smoke dispersing through my capillaries like a healing milk, a magical balm, anointing my nerves. My fingertips were especially affected. I could spend hours caressing my splintery beard, enthralled by its electric crackling, or rubbing my fingertips together and deciphering the secret contained in their whorls. An opium hour is infinitely elastic, and when the wan pink dawn pierced the shanty walls, it would seem to me — goggle-eyed, transported — that the night had lasted for days. I did not always keep to my wooden berth, though. Often I would wake in the queerest places — a broad rubble lot by the railroad tracks, an empty trough in a muddy pen where pigs sprawled in a pile asleep and snoring, the tumbled bed of a middle-aged wench — with no recollection of how I'd arrived there. I didn't particularly care if I could not remember these hallucinatory tours. We were on an adventure! I was not Edward Hyde; I was the dark, nameless hero travelling incognito far from my troubles at home, where I was a hunted man, unjustly pursued. I was a fugitive playing the tramp, and it gave me crafty pleasure to move amongst the citizens and vagabonds of the slummy east-side warrens as though I were one of them.

Of course, I was not. I had almost fifty pounds tucked into my various pockets, as I said. The large banknotes, the fivers and tenners, were in a sense worthless, for no one could change them. Everything was too impossibly cheap; I could hardly keep track of the insignificant coins required to actually pay for things. By the time the honeyed moon had made its complete cycle, I had spent less than a single pound. I could have lived for years on fifty pounds in the East End and south of the river. But, inevitably, I was robbed.

One night in foul-smelling Bermondsey, I stumbled upon a tiny den with a gypsy proprietress, wild-haired and, it seemed, blind in one pale blue clouded eye. I had an uneasy feeling about the place, which was empty except for the gypsy, who reminded me of someone I could not place. She ushered me into a bunk and lit the pipe for me herself, and when I drew in the first draught, it struck me with a cold jolt: of course, the witch who had read my cards back in my other life. The two women could have been sisters! I stared at her hooked fingernail as the gypsy traced a corkscrew pattern into the swirling smoke, whispering something to herself, and like an echo I heard the other croon in my ear: *Wheel of Fortune*. It was a bad omen, this reincarnation, this empty shack — I wanted to leave. But her drugs were quick; already my limbs, my eyelids, were leaden.

When I swam back to consciousness with a dragging gasp, I found myself alone in the bare room with a single window at the back ablaze with menacing sunshine. I staggered out into the harsh morning, into the bustle of commerce, shielding my eyes. The overwhelming stench of turpentine and leather tanning sharpened my wits as I blundered along, smacking my mouth, absently patting my pockets. Then I stopped and dug through my jacket, my trousers, my waistcoat in bafflement. Where was all—? My eyes widened. I turned and reeled back the way I'd come, shoving through the busy masses, but the lanes were labyrinthine, and all the hovels looked the same—scrap metal and spare lumber—and I couldn't remember how I'd found the gypsy's den to begin with. Disoriented, bathed in icy sweat, I came to a halt and plunged through my pockets again. But in vain. I had been picked clean.

My boots were falling apart, the heels run down and one sole flapping loose. My blisters hurt. My back was stiff and my neck tweaked from assorted hard lodgings. An itchy rash had invaded my anus, and I could swear I had lice crawling around my scalp. All at once I was tired of tramping, tired of playing fugitive. I missed my bed. I wanted to go home.

I hobbled northwest all day, crutching with my stick. (It had clung to me, that stick! I should've lost it dozens of times, befuddled and dumb as I'd been, but the trusty stick had kept by my side, waiting to satisfy its terrible destiny.) By the time I reached Ghyll a ragged lid of cloud was clamping over the last silvery light in the sky. I stood across the street, not quite believing the house was still here, unburned by a mob and as I had left it. I edged across the road into the courtyard and, bracing myself, peered over the rim of the fountain. I frowned in astonishment, then poked around with the cleat of my stick. The basin was empty. No birds, no cat, no bones, just the stone hollow and some dried leaves. In the entrance hall, I leant my stick against the wainscoting and eased off my boots, then limped to the drawing-room doorway. I stood just within the room, staring at the round table agleam under the window. It too was empty. Very still I stood, waiting to wake up with a lurch in that wooden berth all over again to find the whole day had been a dream.

Mrs. Deaker found me the following morning in the lavatory on the third floor. I had been sitting in a brown tepid bath examining my face in a shard of broken mirror I'd extracted from a mysterious pile of such slivers in the sink when the knob squeaked and the door swung inward. The lady was holding a fireplace poker and wore a grimace that was almost comical; I had to gulp back a giddy laugh. *Hello, old girl,* I cried with a surge of fondness. The sound of my own voice startled me — I felt as if I hadn't spoken in weeks. Mrs. Deaker sighed, poorly disguising her relief, and thumped the hooked poker down on the tile. She regarded me with a shrewd well-well-well playing upon her wrinkled lips. *Master returns, eh?* I offered. *Home from his long travels.* She was silent. The leaky tap went *plink, plink, plink.* I cleared my throat, glancing down at the rusty water. *Look. I'm sorry. Plink, plink* from the spigot. You're sorry, Mrs. Deaker said at last, musingly, as if she had never heard the expression before. It was the first time I'd ever uttered it. The old lady shrugged one bony shoulder. Well, then.

Downstairs, I found on the kitchen table a lukewarm chop on a plate, like an offering. I sat down and devoured it, eyes roaming in disbelief around the dreary room. No more bodies in the fountain, no more letters — and a veal chop for breakfast. It seemed too good to be true. Could I trust it? Could I let myself believe it was over, that the curse had simply vanished in my absence? All day I waited in a state of high anticipation, certain that something would happen — some response to my homecoming. Yet by the next morning, there had been nothing still, no *clack* of the letterbox, no birds in the stone basin. The weather was sunny and clear. I could not believe it. I wouldn't be allowed to escape so easily, to resume a life of careless freedom. No, I was chary as I strolled through the old streets of Soho, alert to people's expressions, eying the windows, ready for anything. I passed a newspaper stand and made myself stop and read at last the date below the black header. It was early June.

Behind my own thoughts, I could feel Jekyll's flow, closer now than before, like a running murmur. We had been away for over a

month, our longest absence from Big House yet. Poole was bound
to be concerned. Jekyll had said nothing before he'd left. Poole
would have to be assured of Jekyll's well-being. Yet how could we
return to Big House now, when everything was going so suspiciously, ominously well on my end?

That afternoon I hardly recognised Leicester Square. The
pavement was crowded with pedestrians, couples linking elbows, and the central park was busy with parasols and toppers
and people milling about the salt-white statue of old Shakespeare
at its heart. Nervously I sidled through them, perspiring in my
black winter suit. Perhaps, I thought absently (and with insane
optimism), it was time to order a summer wardrobe. I wiped my
streaming cheek with my sleeve as I paused below Big House's
front door, which was gleaming black, as if newly painted. I swallowed and pressed the button. I could hear the distant chiming
from inside, then clicking footsteps.

The sun hung behind me, and when the door opened, it
blared full on Poole's face, which could not quite conceal its eagerness and worry. Mr. Hyde, he said, with something expectant,
almost welcoming, in his tone. Do come in. He moved aside, and
I stepped up into the cool, dim hall. You are aware that Dr. Jekyll
is not presently at home? *I am. I have a message from him.* I kept
my eyes averted. I wanted badly to remove my topper and drag
my hands through my damp, tangled hair. But I didn't dare, even
with the beard, reveal myself completely to Poole's inspection. My
eye caught the cabinetry opposite the hearth: the pebbled-glass
panels, a row of murky jars displayed within. John Hunter's specimens. *Jekyll has been travelling,* I heard myself say. *We've been travelling together. I had to return to this side of town, take care of some
business. He asked me to tell you that he's well, that there is no cause
for concern.* Poole's gaze was like a fierce circlet of sunlight reflected onto my cheek. Travelling where? he demanded, and then
added courteously: If I may ask? *East End, mostly. But all round
London, really. A research expedition, Jekyll calls it.* Do you have

any notion when he'll return? *Hard to say, hard to say,* I replied breezily, beginning to enjoy taunting him. I snuck a glance at the man, nursing a smirk. *Didn't tell you he was leaving, did he? Isn't that Jekyll for you?*

His eyes held mine, the whites so clear and sharp, they were almost blue in the gloom. Then his gaze faltered and flicked to the left, down the length of the entrance hall. In the far illumined doorway to the main hall stood a female figure, obviously eavesdropping; she froze as we stared at her. Thank you, Lizzie, Poole called to her, that will be all. With a start she came to life; she dipped her head, curtseyed, and hurried on. Poole continued to regard the bright empty portal, his jawline stiff. *Will you be returning to the doctor,* he asked tightly, *when your business is attended to?* My tongue came unstuck from my palate with a wet click. *Perhaps.* Then perhaps you will tell him, Poole said, and then he stopped and flicked his eyes back to me. Did I detect a flash of uncertainty behind the serene façade? He cleared his throat. Perhaps you'll tell him he is eagerly awaited at home. *I should hope so. Is that all?* He did not look away. Yes, that is all. Unless you have something further to add to your enlightening report?

Something rose in my gullet — a bubble of laughter. I clamped my lips against it, mutely shook my head.

In that case, I wish you good day, Mr. Hyde.

Back at Ghyll I found Mrs. Deaker on the drawing-room sofa, drinking sherry. I sidled in, plucked a glass from the sideboard, and eased down onto the other end of the sofa. She sat upright, staring ahead. After a moment she lifted the crystal decanter from the floor and without quite looking at me poured a ruby splash into my outstretched glass. I settled back and we watched the light in the front windows fade to a dusk that suffused the baroque old room and made it beautiful once again, as it must have been many years ago when that noble happy family had lived here. What had happened to them? What had befallen this place? I swung my head to Mrs. Deaker and realised how dark it had become. I could see her profile like a marble effigy, a silver glint round the rim of her glass. I wanted to ask her something, something terribly important, yet I couldn't remember what it was. The question welled up in me and I cracked my lips to speak. Ssshh, she said.

I dreamt I was back in the entrance hall. I was staring at the pebbled-glass cabinetry, at the jars of Hunter's pickled specimens which moved and writhed in the murky liquid like captive eels, and meanwhile I was trying to explain to Poole what Jekyll was up to. But all my features — lips, nose, ears, cheeks — felt rubbery and unattached, liable to slough off at any second and reveal to Poole what was underneath. Not Jekyll, but someone I didn't know, slimy and nascent beneath the leprous rind of my face. My teeth were wobbling as I spoke, and I was covering my mouth to keep from spitting them out, and when I woke I was holding my nose in place.

I was still in the drawing room, sprawled on the sofa. I could not remember falling asleep here. Dry-mouthed, head thudding, I pulled tentatively at my earlobe, making sure it was firmly affixed, then pushed on my teeth with my tongue. My hand felt tacky and smelt odd, and I found, stuck to the webbing of my thumb, a long, dark, curly hair. I pulled it free and shook the sticky thing away and scrambled from the room, hurrying across the shadowy hall and out the front door.

I paced the lanes, muddled and nauseated as if hungover, though I couldn't remember drinking anything aside from the sherry. Gradually the sun rose and the streets became thronged with my neighbours. I could smell my rough, sour armpits and crotch. Something was about to happen, I could feel it: this tremulous quality to the atmosphere. That old tic was tapping in my eyelid again, like inscrutable Morse code. I downed a scalding pint of coffee at a stall and made for home.

A man was leaning against the fence of my house as I approached, lounging with his arms crossed and one boot propped on the iron rail. Nondescript, bearded, looking off the other way. I stopped before him and glared until he swiveled his head and gave me a calm, insolent once-over. He glanced over his shoulder at my house, showing a hint of canine tooth. Then he pushed off the fence and sauntered down the road. I stood watching him recede, a fuzzy roar in my ears. I shut my eyes, squeezed them tight, and gripped the square-cut iron railing as if for balance, the stones under my feet feeling loose, like my teeth in their sockets in that dream. Then I opened my eyes. The twitch in my lower lid had stopped. I could hear a carriage horse clopping nearby. Everything was fine. I exhaled, tossed my head, then turned into the courtyard. At the fountain I paused to peer inside — empty, again — but at the sagging front steps I stopped short.

A white square was sticking crookedly from the letterbox.

I mounted the porch as if it were a gallows. I pinched the envelope and pulled it from the brass trap. The barbed, spiky stitching across its face: *Mr. Hyde.* The cheap granular texture of the paper. I turned the envelope over. The front door was cautiously opened. Mrs. Deaker beheld me, surprised. Master, she said, I thought — did you? Her narrowed eyes fell to the envelope in my hand. I heard the letterbox not a minute ago, she said.

I looked down at the envelope too, then turned and squinted at the fence where that man had been standing. Had he been waiting for me, like a lookout? Should I —? I took a bewildered step forward, stopped, and looked at the envelope again. I stuck my thumb into its throat and ripped it open:

> *hide, says seek, and hidey hides*
> *and thinks the play is done*

but i've been counting, one two three,
now ready or not, here I come!

I braced myself for an explosion, a white evaporating flash. I waited, shoulders hunched, the letter crackling in my hands. I peeked upward: the world was still here. People were passing obliviously back and forth beyond the fence. I seemed to hear laughter, aquiver in the air. I swung around to Mrs. Deaker, who was regarding me with guarded curiosity, as if I were some unpredictable lunatic on her doorstep. I thrust the letter at her. After a hesitation, she accepted it. She brought it toward her face to read, then lowered it and looked at me, confused, disconcerted, almost fearful. Her rimpled lips pursed, as if she were about to ask a question. I plucked the letter from her fingers. She was not pretending. Oh no, I could see quite clearly now, as if a film had fallen from my eyes. This was no performance. She had not written any of the letters. She was innocent.

Innocent! What did that even mean? Who was guilty, then — that lone man lounging against my fence? He was, if anything, a mere scout, watching for my arrival so the messenger could deliver the letter at the perfect moment. Yet surely *he* wasn't the true letter writer either; he was just a messenger, another pawn!

Part of me was feverishly relieved. It wouldn't be long now. I had known it was not finished. I'd known it would start again, and now it had, it was coming — *ready or not, here I come!* In preparation I made another inspection of the house, checking the bare floors and the windows and the rear cellar door. The heavy chest was still pushed against it, but when I tried the rusted knob, to my surprise, the rear door opened. I was certain I had left it locked; it had always been locked. Had Mrs. Deaker been down here?

The next day I left the house early and looped around the block to position myself inside a recess across the road from Ghyll, with a view of the gate and the fountain and the front door. All morning and all afternoon I stood there, nervous and bored and needing to urinate, watching the bodies bumbling back and forth and thinking of Utterson staking out the Castle Street door night after night, patient, imperturbable. The next day I tried watching the rear cellar door in the alley out back, and the day after that . . .

But soon I gave it up; the tedium was too nerve-racking. My tormentor was too cunning to strike while I was watching. I had to be cunning too, then — I had to feign laxity, heedlessness. I tried frequenting some of my old haunts again, not the Pig, of course, but the Toad, the Gullet — and, once, even the Black Shop Pub, where Cornelius Luce had led me to Carew that night, ages ago. The bar was again packed with Irishmen, and I stood at the balustrade with a glass of black beer, staring at the table where Carew had sat with his back to me. I retraced his route up that steep spindly lane, climbed those steps to the top where he'd stood and shouted my name: Mr. Hyde! The echo of his triumphant cry returned to me. Could Carew be connected to all this? I scanned the lane below, the shadows where I'd pressed myself, and I scanned the rooflines above, almost hoping to see a figure up there, framed like an archangel against the shifting sky. But there was no one.

June was passing. An intricate machinery within Ghyll was winching tighter click by click, a palpable tautening that even Mrs. Deaker perceived. One evening I slumped at the kitchen table slugging glumly from a bottle of cheap hock while behind me the old lady puttered at the stove, fixing her supper. The homey sounds of sizzle and scrape comforted me; a lull had settled over my mind. I plonked the bottle down on the table and hit the edge, and the bottle toppled off and struck the stone floor a second later with a sharp crack. Mrs. Deaker screamed: a chicken squawk of surprise. I spun around in my chair, my blood like ice water, and she goggled at me with a hand dramatically at her breast. We both looked down at the broken bottle and the spill of crimson wine. She let out a fluttery laugh, and I chuckled awkwardly. But that note of terror hung in the air. Neither of us moved as the puddle bled across the flagstone. That confessional urge was taking hold of me again, the desire to break myself open like that bottle and bleed out my secret. This old woman I had invited into my life, into my chaos, as a kind of witness — she had questions for me too, I could tell, seething in her withered heart. So why could we not speak? I stared at the spotted hand upon her chest, its silky livered skin. I wanted to feel it on my brow. As if she sensed this, her hand moved to the stove, where she drew a dishrag from the handle of the door. She offered it to me, like a grey, ragged flag of truce.

The last days of June it stormed: lashing rain and spasms of lightning followed by tumbling, buckling thunder. It cheered me up immensely, the electrifying violence of it. I ventured onto my verandah and clutched the rail as if it were the prow of a ship in tempestuous seas and whooped and dared the lightning to strike me, dared the gods to wrench the whole terrace from its flimsy moorings and whisk it away like a chariot of Hades. I hoped the storm would last for weeks and weeks, a biblical flood washing clean my trivial concerns — all trivial concerns everywhere! *Ready or not*, I screamed into the swooping wind, *here I come!* But after several days, it drizzled out. The streets steamed under the misted sun, strewn with tidal patterns of leaves and debris, roof shingles, mangled umbrellas, sodden paper, the wreckage of a baby pram. People emerged, peering at the sky. The sun sharpened to a crisp blaze, and all at once, without any warning, it was July. Summertime in Soho, the roads choked with bustle; food sellers on every corner calling out their wares, flavoured ices, grilled meats, boiled eggs; a festival for out-of-towners, ladies with lacy parasols and men in cream suits. I pushed my way through the cattle of tourists, annoyed by the world's hearty continuance. I hardly recognised my seedy old Soho, bright and gay as a seaside resort. All the production seemed suspiciously theatrical, a grand-scale diversion to confound me. Absolutely anything could happen in a crowd, after all. Someone could steal the hat right off your head.

For a few steps I did not even feel it was gone. Disoriented, knocked about by passing traffic, I was aware at first only of the heightened brightness, the air moving over my ears. Then, with a spike of panic, I clapped a hand to my head and discovered it bare. My topper! I swiveled around, elbowed my way back a few paces. It wasn't on the stones under the trampling feet. It wasn't on anyone's head. I halted, heart gone cold. This was 6 July.

What street was this? I could not get my bearings, could not remember where I'd been going. The sun seemed hotter and higher in the sky than it had been just seconds ago. Bareheaded and exposed to the blinding glare, I groped along until I came to a corner I knew and then set a hasty course for Ghyll. This had been no theft or prank; it was too precise, too deliberate. And, damn it, I had *liked* that hat, it screwed perfectly to the groove of my brow. Addled by the direct sun I laboured up Ghyll Road, which was so busy with overflow from the main streets that I could not see my front gate until I had nearly reached it. I dragged a sleeve across my eyes and then stopped in my tracks.

My hat hung on the wooden gatepost as if by a hook.

But not a hook. The topper was nailed into the wood through the brim. A fat rusty iron nail. The nail would not budge, was buried too deep. I glanced over my shoulder at the moving herd, then worked the brim of my hat over the nail head. That is when I saw the newspaper behind it, pinned to the post through the nail as well. The *Pall Mall Gazette*. I half expected my fingers to pass through the apparition. But the news sheet was shockingly solid and grainy. I ripped it free.

Up in my bedroom, I shut one eye and peered through the neat hole punched in my hat brim. Then I threw the ruined topper on my bed and turned to the newspaper, which had a jagged tear just above its headline:

THE MAIDEN TRIBUTE OF MODERN BABYLON
WE BID YOU BE OF HOPE

The Report of our Secret Commission will be read today with a shuddering horror that will thrill throughout the world. After this awful picture of the crimes at present committed as it were under the very aegis of the law has been fully unfolded before the eyes of the public, we need not doubt that the House of Commons will find time to raise the age during which English girls are protected from expiable wrong.

I read faster and faster. *English girls, the sale of English girls, the sale and purchase and violation of children, the procuration of virgins.* Soon I was just scanning the crossheads in capitals scattered throughout the article: *The Violation of Virgins, Virgins Willing and Unwilling, Buying Girls at the East End, Strapping Girls Down, The London Slave Market, A Child of Thirteen Bought for £5.* Practically the whole paper was given over to the hysterical article. Hectically I tore through the pages, hands smeared in ink, scouring the lines almost instinctively for, yes, my name, convinced at any moment it would leap out from the columns of dense type. What in hell was this? What was this Secret Commission? Why had this been nailed to my gate? I looked up, flushed, my face seized with a petrified smile as I listened to the walloping silence of the house. Then I read the thing over from the beginning.

It was a campaign, a railing diatribe. In ancient Greece, the writer cried, the Athenians paid tribute to King Minos by sending virgin youths, seven boys and seven maidens, to be devoured by the Minotaur in his foul labyrinth once every nine years. And yet in London, this same beastly transaction was made every night, English girls sacrificed into the maw of the monster. *Maidens they were when this morning dawned, but tonight their ruin will be accomplished, and tomorrow they will find themselves within the portals of the maze of London brotheldom.* Padded, soundproofed underground rooms for the gentlemen who wanted to make them scream. Leather straps on the four-poster beds. Midwives in the East End to certify their virginity beforehand and patch up the damages afterward. Gruesome stuff. And this London Society for the Protection of Young Females — where had I heard of that before? I backed away from the bed where the newspaper lay. Movement caught my eye; I glanced left into the gigantic mirror, where a bearded, leering stranger eyeballed me as he crouched, wiping his hands compulsively on his trousers. I crept closer, entranced by the feral reflection, and cautiously extended my inky hand toward the hand on the nether side. Instantly I jerked back, alarmed at the contact — not glass, it seemed, but a silken, liquid force. I spun around to my bedroom. The deceptively haphazard furnishings all hoarded their secrets.

That night I hurled my topper from the verandah and watched it wheel in a wide arc over the tiles and gables and then sink from sight. The hat was no good anymore. It had been changed by its sinister ordeal. This was the closest I had yet come to my tormentor. Hide and Seek, Hide and Seek. He was real. He had actually touched me, from the midst of that crowd, reached up and tipped the hat off my head, exposing my face to the people. *Ready or not, here I come . . .*

Thrilling with defiant dread, I sidled through the throngs the next day in search of a hat shop. I found one on Wardour Street and dove into its musty twilight. The mole-like proprietor would not let me alone until I snapped my teeth at him, and then I was allowed to pass a soothing hour alone amongst the stacks of dusty hats, trying on one after another in front of the crooked look-ing glass. At last I came upon a pale grey rounded bowler with a satin lavender band, fairly louche, not my style at all, yet when I twisted it down, the fit to my cranium was perfect. I grinned to the gums at myself, tilting my head down till the brim covered all but my glistening shark teeth. It could be like a disguise, this hat, so opposite from my other. Back on the street, I blended into the carnival, keeping my brim low, my red-rimmed eyes darting about. The sun splintered off windows and bits of mica buried in the brickwork, giving me a headache. I passed the doorway of a pub and ducked inside. But it was packed in here too, men shout-ing their orders down the line. I stood in their rowdy clamour, blinking away the black cigarette hole scorched into my vision. I felt parched, headache like a spike in my orbital socket. I shut my eyes and for a blissful moment leant my weight onto the bodies behind me, a heartbeat or two of sweet, utter blankness. Then I lurched, staggered back, and caught myself from falling with a ringing backward stamp on the floor. As if awoken from a split-second nap, I gazed about, befuddled yet refreshed, my eyesight back to normal, even my thirst somewhat abated. I touched my face, my hat brim, assuring myself that all was still in order. Then I turned and walked out to the street.

I could not put my finger on it, the odd feel of everything, as I wandered down Wardour. The architecture looming above me seemed off — something in the angles, the shadows, as if the whole streetscape had been dismantled and replaced by two-di-mensional backdrops. There was the sense of an immense practi-cal joke, stifled laughter in the passing faces of all the background actors. No one was looking at me directly. There was, in fact, something strained and deliberate in the way they *weren't* look-ing at me. Except for a sooty-faced urchin who stood at the cor-ner and stared as I strolled by, his eyes red and hot as cinders, his head turning to follow my progress. I thought of that ur-chin gang, that coordinated pickpocketing. Had this boy been amongst them? He knew me, and he was afraid of me, for when I made an indecisive move in his direction, he flashed off into the crowds and vanished.

Up Ghyll Road I panted, certain that, as yesterday, something had been arranged in my absence. As I approached, I could see a group of people gathered around the front gate. They were reading newspapers. A man was strolling my way down the road, perusing one. Others were standing with their news sheets spread open, heads inclined. I sauntered up with wretched casualness. A paper was nailed to the gatepost again, and a pile of *Pall Mall Gazettes* that had been tied with twine were cut loose and strewn across the stones, allowing people to pick up their free issues. I reached for the copy nailed to the post — it had been punched through the old rusted nail — and with a whimpering grunt, I ripped it free.

THE MAIDEN TRIBUTE OF MODERN BABYLON II
THE REPORT OF OUR SECRET COMMISSION

For a second, I considered grabbing up the remaining papers and bolting for the house. Instead, I stepped into the courtyard clutching my own copy and made for the door, feeling like a rifle was aimed from the road at the point between my shoulder blades. It took a fumbling moment to get the key in the lock, and when I slammed the door shut behind me, I found Mrs. Deaker in the drawing-room doorway. She had been watching the spectacle from the window. Her brow was creased and her mouth parted as if to speak. The paper crackled in my grip. I dashed past her up the stairs.

I described yesterday, the article began, *a scene which took place last Derby day, in a well-known house, within a quarter mile of Oxford-circus. It is by no means one of the worst instances of the crimes that are constantly perpetrated in London or even in that very house. The victims of the rapes are almost always very young children be-*

tween thirteen and fifteen. The reason for that is very simple. The law at present almost specially marks out such children as the fair game of dissolute men. The moment a child is thirteen she is a woman in the eye of the law, with absolute right to dispose of her person to anyone who by force or fraud can bully or cajole her into parting with her virtue.

As before I slapped through the pages, appalled: *Procuration in the West End, A Firm of Procuresses, "You Want a Maid, Do You?," An Interview with the Firm, I Order Five Virgins, The Virgins Certified, Delivered for Seduction.* I could hardly comprehend it — here was the crusading newspaperman himself at the firm of Madame X attempting to order five certified virgins to distribute amongst his friends. What kind of lunatic story was this?

I opened the slender letter drawer in the antique desk where I had stored two of my tormentor's poems in their envelopes. From the slit, I extracted one and read it once again: *hidey hide, holy hole, kiss the girls, make them go, but when the boys come to play, hidey hide will run away.*

Kiss the girls.

The spidery words now assumed a new menace. Had the letters all along been leading to this insane campaign, this underhanded accusation? What was the implication? That *I* was one of these dissolute monsters, these girlie-shop patrons? Because I'd harboured two girls in my home? I could feel a maddening bulge just beyond the meniscus of my memory, unable to break the skin. I grasped my hair at the roots, gritting my teeth. What was the connection? Where was this all leading? The game was getting bigger and more public with each move. Exposure. No more hiding in my anonymous house, nestled in my secret life. Yes. That had been the message all along, from the first taunting letter. *I play hide and you play hide and see who's found out first!*

The next day I determined to watch the front gate. I dragged a wingback to the drawing-room window and settled down to wait.

It grew stuffy as the morning bloomed, but I would not open the window, as if some contagion were loose in the air. A thick fly bumped at the glass with its stumbling drone. On the windowsill a dead fly lay on its back, minuscule legs bristling. I could smell myself: my unchanged clothes, my unbathed body, pungent, becalming. The fly dawdled at the glass. My eyelids began to leaden.

Father was sitting beside me in his wheelchair. His wasted yet still shapely hands with their yellowed nails hung off the chair's wooden arms. His ash-white hair fell to his shoulders as he tilted his head to regard me, giving me a small, encouraging smile. Those naked, shaven lips. He nodded at the window as if to say, *Let us watch together.* I wanted to tell him something, urgently, but I couldn't remember what it was.

My eyes flicked open.

There was movement out in the courtyard, a flurry in the air. For a second I could not breathe, then I hitched a delayed, strangled gasp and lurched upright in the chair. People were gathered at the gate again. As if drugged, I staggered to my feet and out to the entrance hall, where I flung open the door. Sheets of newspaper were tumbling and skittering across the courtyard, and I could hear shouting, or chanting, like the taunting singsong of schoolchildren. I rubbed at my eyes, and from the gathering at the gate I distinguished a number of boys throwing news sheets into the air and jumping up and down as they chanted. The words — it sounded almost like my name. Mis-ter Hyde! Mis-ter Hyde! Mis-ter Hyde! I lunged down the steps and over the cobbled yard, batting windblown paper from my path. I charged through the gate and skidded onto the pavement. Two of the boys saw me — little scamps, like the one I'd seen yesterday — and they dropped their newspapers and scooted off. There was another boy who was too absorbed in his jumping and joyful yelling of what I swore was my name to see me, but as I windmilled my arms for balance and started for him, he turned and pulled a comical popeyed expression and pelted off. I stood there, chest heaving, glaring at the gathered crowd clustered in the road like an impromptu audience. They considered my arrival on the scene with curious expectation, as if I were a new character in whatever performance they had been watching. Newspaper sheets lay flat on the stones or flapped away; one was impaled on the fence rails. I spun to the gatepost: a single torn-off news sheet was skewered through the nail, aflutter in the breeze. I whirled back on the crowd. My eye caught a fop in front; he wore a white hat and a flower in his buttonhole and was arm in arm with a pretty number in purple — both of them were watching me with eager distaste. Mocking laughter echoed all around me. I yearned to barrel into the crowd and trample them under my hooves, bellowing. But I stepped back, snatched the news sheet off the nail, and strode toward the house with a kind of furious dignity.

Mrs. Deaker opened the door for me and I stamped across the hall and slumped down at the bottom of the stairs. The old lady clicked up in her boots until she was gazing down on me from a few paces away. I lifted a soiled, scowling eye. The adrenaline was draining away; I felt spent and woozy. Mrs. Deaker returned my weary glower from a pitying distance, looking at me as if I were some deformed wretch on a doorstep. A wave of bitterness swamped my heart. *You old cunt. Are you happy? This what you wanted, was it?*

Happy, she repeated with a soft, scornful laugh. No, Master. I am not happy.

You cursed me. Admit it, you put a curse on me. Because of the girls. This is all your doing, am I right? Am I right? I was pleading. Her pity deepened. She smiled, a stricken twitch. You've done this to yourself, Mr. Hyde. She turned and swished from the hall.

The news sheet was crunched in my fist. I forced the fingers to unflex and smoothed the page flat on my knee. It had been torn out from the middle — and marked, I noticed now, with a heavy pencil or a piece of coal, a rough circling around the lower-right column where the crosshead read *The London Minotaur:*

As in the labyrinth of Crete there was a monster known as the Minotaur who devoured the maidens who were cast into the mazes of that evil place, so in London there is at least one monster who may be said to be an absolute incarnation of brutal lust. Here in London, moving about clad as respectably in broadcloth and fine linen as any bishop, with no foul shape or semblance of brute beast to mark him from his fellows, is Dr. ——, now retired from his profession and free to devote his fortune and leisure to the ruin of maids. This is the "gentleman" whose quantum of virgins from his procuresses is three per fortnight — all girls who have not previously been seduced. But his devastating passion sinks into insignificance compared with Mr. ——, another wealthy man, whose whole life is dedicated to the gratification of lust. During my investigations in the subterranean realm I was constantly coming across his name.

It is no part of my commission, the writer promised, *to hold up individuals to popular execration, and the name and address of this creature will not appear in these columns.* The name and address of this creature! Up in my bedroom, I scoured the passage again. I knew it couldn't be referring to me — I hadn't bought any virgins or ruined any maids. And yet that did not matter. My tormentor had ripped out *this* particular page and circled *this* particular column. Dr. Blank and Mr. Blank. *Now retired from his profession and free to devote his fortune and leisure to the ruin of maids . . .* Mr. Seek, whoever he was, had selected this page to nail to my front gate. Its message was undeniable. Seek knew. About me, about Jekyll. About us.

We couldn't stay here. Exposure, public exposure to the masses, our secret unmasked. That was the endgame of all this. We had to run, to disappear. We had done it before, could do it again. Leave the house, leave this identity behind. It would be . . . What was the word?

Forfeit. It flew contemptuously into my head. At once I was filled with Jekyll's disdain and derision. Run? Run where? The East End again? For how long? What about Big House — would we *forfeit* that too? Cowardly! Pathetic! His thoughts boomed in my mind with an underwatery warble and then subsided, leaving me shaken and ashamed. *What, then?* I asked the stubborn silence. *Tell me! Tell me what to do!*

There was no response. The sky beyond the greyed tumble of rooftops was turning a watercolour tangerine with ribbons of uncoiling lilac. Where had the hours gone? The aroma of roasting chicken wafted upward from the lanes below, making saliva spring into my mouth. I had not eaten all day. I shut my burning eyes, rested my temple against the frame of the open verandah.

Then I stiffened, ears flattening to my scalp: a dim but distinct knocking had come from downstairs. I listened, breathless. It came again: *knock-knock-knock-knock!* I opened my eyes and stared across the bedroom. Someone was here. I could not move a muscle, was frozen like an animal at the sound of a snapping twig. Then a new, sharper noise began, a quick, repetitive *clack*. I knew that noise. The letterbox.

I crept downstairs and halted, crouching, at the second-to-last step up from the entrance hall. I could see the letterbox winking orange light as if the door — the house itself — were trying to tell me something in a frantic sputter. I should have listened.

I opened the door. Somehow I was not surprised by the sight of the two big men in tweed suits on my front porch. The taller had a sandy moustache, and the shorter a ruddy complexion with ice-blue eyes. Evening, sir, said Moustache politely. Would you be Edward Hyde, then? I could not speak. They exchanged sidelong glances. Sir, I'm Inspector Blank, said Moustache, and this is Inspector Blank. Scotland Yard, Mr. Hyde. May we come in?

I did not absorb their names. My eardrums were roaring like conch shells. Yet I could hear my own voice, oddly calm, saying, *Gentlemen, good evening. May I see your identification?* Each inspector produced a leather billfold, flipped it open: two silver stars, *Metropolitan Police* stamped in a blue ring around the centre. I opened the door wider and stepped aside, and they clumped into my home. *This way, please*, I heard myself say, almost briskly, as I led them across the entrance hall and then up the first flight of stairs. I was astonished at my steadiness. On the second floor I turned into the empty parlour. A carpet of dust lay over the floorboards, undisturbed since the girls had gone. The only place to sit was the sagging velvet sofa coated in mousy fluff. The inspectors were surveying the room dubiously; Moustache peered at the dead chandelier hook in the ceiling. Mr. Hyde, is this your primary residence?

My eye caught on the opposite wall, the picture hanging there. That silvery beachscape with that solitary black figure wavering mirage-like down the glistening shingle. A pang of longing pierced me. How I yearned to be transported into that picture, that alternate dimension, on that forever moon-silvered beach . . .

I jerked my eye back to Inspector Moustache, who was watching me with a cautious, puzzled curiosity. *My primary residence*, I heard myself murmur, *yes, yes, it is.* Heard you had some kind of disturbance this morning, said Inspector Ice-Blue. He reached into his breast pocket and pulled out, as I knew he would, a folded news sheet. He glanced at the type and for a moment I thought he might begin reading aloud. *Yes, that,* I said. *Just kids. Bit of mischief, is all.* Well, you'd know about that, wouldn't you, said Inspector Moustache. Mischief, that is. I gulped and tried to smile, toothy and crazed, anxiously blinking. Was I being arrested? Could they do that? They were the police, they could march me out of my house and throw me into an iron-barred coach and haul me off to a cell if they wanted. Who would stop them? I took a step backward. *Gentlemen,* I cried. *How rude of me. I'll let my woman know you're here. I for one could use a drink.* I backed out of the parlour, eyes swivelling between Inspector Moustache and Inspector Ice-Blue, waiting for one of them to hold up his hand and say Whoa, sir, to charge and wrestle me down to the floor and clip shackles round my wrists. But they simply stood and watched me retreat, impassive, unconcerned. I backed onto the landing and descended the stairs. The entrance hall was empty. My new grey bowler hung on the banister knob, and I reached out to take it, startled by the thing's actuality, the stiff dry felt of its brim. My stick leant against the wainscoting by the drawing-room doorway, the brass warm and accommodating to my grasp. The doorknob revolved smoothly in my palm. Across the yard and the road, the neighbouring brick held the marmalade light. I stepped onto the porch in a daze of wonderment. How easy it was. I turned and looked back through the open doorway into Ghyll's entrance hall.

Forfeit. Yes, that's the word.

DAY THREE

From behind the oval mirror, I slide out the black leather violin case and carry it to the table. The silver buckles easily unsnap and I draw the lid open. In its blue velvet bed, the instrument lies quiet, larger than I remembered. Maybe because it always looked small in his loose, sprawling hand. I am not sure why I felt the urge to see it just now — this old witness, Father's old friend. He adored this bloody violin. He could have donated it to a museum or a music academy, somewhere worthy, for indeed it is beautiful, with its slender neck and bronze skin, its lacquered frailty. Instead he left it to us, to stand untuned and neglected against the wall. Why? Atonement? What did he imagine he would prove by leaving us these beloved things?

I turn my head to the blank northern wall where his portrait used to hang. There is no faded rectangle on the wood panelling, no sign the picture was ever there at all; the wall is just — bare. My face is starting to prickle beneath my beard, as if from shame. But why should I feel ashamed?

I look again at the instrument and brush the strings with my thumb, touching off a husky, vibrant chord. I shiver and abruptly shut the case, snap the clasps. For a moment I stand with fingers on the leather, feeling something slip through me, some fleeting kind of understanding, about relinquishment, and Father, and

Ghyll, and everything . . . Yet the pattern dissolves as I attempt to grasp it. I haul the case off the table and slide it again behind the mirror, the cheval glass swiveled around to look at the wall, as Jekyll left it.

Better this way, the mirror turned to the wall. Better not to look at myself, to see what I've become, this caged, pacing animal waiting to be put out of its misery. He is toying with me, surely, Poole is! How can he detect nothing? How can he think that Jekyll is still up here? What if this *does* continue indefinitely, what if that is to be my punishment? No axe, no cyanide, no moment of glory. Instead, death by atrophy.

Ha. Must not delude myself. I should be so lucky.

This pricking of shame. It's for Ghyll, of course. The way I relinquished it to those supposed inspectors and ran. Craven, pathetic, I abandoned my fortress to a pair of strangers, and after all the precautions I'd taken to guard against infiltration. Yet it wasn't merely myself I was preserving. As I scurried south toward Castle Street, I could feel Jekyll's frightened elation at our narrow escape. He had not wanted to stick around to see what the inspectors would say any more than I had. I lunged through the Castle Street door and up the rear stairwell into the safety of the cabinet, practically whimpering with gratitude at the sight of it. I had been gone a long, long time. More than two months, my longest stretch in the body yet. The lower syringe in the Milward box was still loaded, of course, but as I slipped my fingers into the steel loops, a prophetic thought struck me. Could the serum go stale — become inert — enclosed in the glass barrel all that time? What if the needle failed?

It didn't, at first. Jekyll tottered to the mirror and stared at his estranged reflection. A rust-blond beard camouflaged the face from cheekbone to throat, and a grungy mane hung before his gaunt blue eyes. He took out scissors and razor, poured some water into a bowl, snipped the beard down, and scraped off the bristle. He wet his hair and combed the knotted locks back as best he could, then dressed in his own clothes. He was recognisable again, but hollowed, white where the beard had been, with a haggard intensity to his gaze. He turned away, descended the stairs, and crossed the courtyard to Big House.

From the dining room, he could hear a voice speaking, precisely, continuously, a muted intonation emerging from the arched passageway. Jekyll followed it to the parlour doorway. Poole was sitting in the emerald velvet chair reading from a book to the whole assembled staff, about a dozen seated around the room in attentive repose. The maids and the cook sat on the long sofa with the cook's little boy at their feet, and Bradshaw the footman perched on the sofa's rolled arm, one shoe dangling, hands crossed on his knee, his copper hair agleam. The footman's gaze slid to the arching doorway and focused upon Jekyll, leaning there. All eyes in the room then moved simultaneously, and Poole paused midsentence and turned in his chair. A blank, spooky moment of unrecognition, as if he had strolled into the wrong house. Dr. Jekyll, Poole exclaimed. My goodness, what a surprise. Swiftly he stood, slipping the book behind his back. Please excuse us, sir, and welcome home, it's so very good to see you. He cleared his throat. All of them began rising to their feet from the sofa and chairs, with a certain begrudging air, like obedient but disgruntled children told it's time for bed. Sir, said the fat blowsy cook, fixing her skirts, will you be wanting yer dinner, then? Poole shot her a glance, and she looked down at the floor. Forgive us, sir, Poole said. Will you be dining tonight?

Something cold will do.

Poole served him cold roast beef and vinegar-dressed potatoes in the dining room. I hope you will pardon my liberty in the parlour, sir, he said. Jekyll's cheek was full of beef. He swallowed the cold lump and dabbed his lips. *What were you reading?* Just a spot of Dickens, sir. Your research expedition. I trust it was fruitful? Jekyll sucked a strand of meat from his molars. *There was fruit, all right.*

When Poole left, Jekyll dispatched the rest of the food and went upstairs to his bedroom, where he ran a bath. He sat on the edge of the crashing tub, his heart clenched like a cramping muscle. That scene in the parlour, everyone gathered together listening to Dickens. As if he were standing outside a brightly lit window, spying on a large contented family at their cheery hearth, with the ragged darkness at his back and the chilly pane of glass dividing him from that warmth. The way they had looked at him, with mild alarm and consternation, as if he were indeed an intruder in his own home. What had happened in his absence?

He sank into the scalding water to hang suspended beneath the surface. We throbbed in seeming unison. His thoughts were an underwater warble but I did not need to hear them clearly. Of course something was happening. Nothing definable, a mere penumbra of trouble to come, but the mantle of Dr. Henry Jekyll could not protect us anymore. If Mr. Seek knew about Jekyll and the link between us, if he was determined to expose us, then he would not stop at chasing me out of my home. He would come for us at Big House as well. We had to be ready. Jekyll could not continue to keep his own infuriating counsel. He had to accept me into the sanctum of his reasoning.

Jekyll padded, dripping, into his dressing room, struggled into his gown. He threw open the windows in his bedroom and slumped on the edge of the bed, streaming sweat. I could feel the silk sticking to the burning skin, the refreshing air wafting in from the square, the pulsing of the room, its expanding and contracting. We lay back woozily on the bed, the ceiling awhirl like a fan.

The surgical theatre. The dissection table. White sunshine poured through the cupola. Surgeons were working on us with scalpels and forceps while students we could not see watched from the ring of benches. John Hunter, the great father of Big House, was lecturing as he sliced a section of flesh from our biceps. We raised our arm and marvelled at the sleek, purplish fascia under the skin. We put our fingers into the incision and began to pull it wider, and as if the whole forearm and hand were a rubbery glove, we peeled the flesh down from the braided tissue and ripped the entire sloppy thing off, strands of clear integumental membrane stretching from the webbing of the fingers before snapping loose. The surgeons were trying to hold us down, but we fought them off and sat up, hooked our fingers into the rims of our eyes and tugged till the eyeholes popped and the whole suffocating mask of the face was sloughing free —

Then awake: eyes flicked open.

On the belly, face crushed to the bed. Morning light like a magnesium flare. Head pounding, beastly thirst, but couldn't even lift the face from the rough silk cover. Eye slipped shut into a blissful second of sleep, then jerked open again, staring at the hand that lay on the bed before me. Dead, disembodied hand: I tried to move the thumb, and to my surprise, it twitched. The fingers fluttered to life too, arachnoid. I curled them into a fist, released them, fascinated by the simple action of my hand.

My hand.

I scrambled to my knees, heart galloping. Jekyll had gone to sleep — and yet here I was, waking in the body. I leapt from the bed and stumbled into his dressing room, approached the oval mirror and tipped it down. Oh God. Wild-haired and bleared with sleep, my reflection gaped back; I could feel Jekyll recoil. I reached toward the glass, then peered down and experimentally pinched my nipple, a sharp tweak. Pain. It was firmly attached. This was no dream.

I spun from the mirror. I had to get to the cabinet. With Jekyll jumping like a frantic candle flame in the mind, I fumbled into his clothes and crept to the bedroom door. I peeked down the corridor. Poole might be anywhere at this hour. I slipped from the bedroom and slid along the wall to the stairs. I peered over the railing and down the spiraling steps to the marble parquet of the main hall, listening. From the main hall I ducked into the narrow hallway leading down to the dining room. The dining room was the greatest danger; Poole always appeared within a minute of Jekyll's sitting down for breakfast. I tiptoed rapidly past the dining table and skipped down the two steps into the conservatory. I was reaching for the steel handle of the door when my eyes jogged left, and I froze. Bradshaw and Lizzie stood by the hanging plants ten paces away, quietly watching me.

Lizzie was watering a ferny plant while Bradshaw stood close behind her, hands clasped behind his back, as if surveying her work. A suave little smirk lay stranded on his lips. The girl was flushed, a guilty sparkle in her startled eyes. Clutching Jekyll's trousers at the waist, shirttails billowing and the buttons askew, a sneaky lover escaping out the back door, I snatched at the handle and hobbled barefoot across the gravel yard. They did not matter; all that mattered was bringing Jekyll back. Up the stairs I scurried, to the red-baize door, where with a spasm of panic I thought: The keys! But they were in his trouser pocket, and then I was inside the cabinet. The key clattered into the glazed press; I pulled open the doors and slid E drawer from its slot.

I had never prepared the needle. This was Jekyll's domain. And yet I could feel him guiding my hands, suddenly dexterous. I watched them operate: pluck down an Erlenmeyer, pour the crimson liquor into the flask, scoop out a spoonful of powder. When it fizzled down to pale green, I transferred it to the phial and jabbed the needle through the rubber plug, at last pushing a thin jet of serum from the hypodermic. I pumped my fist, pulling the tourniquet tight with my teeth. And as I steered the needle home I did not let myself wonder what would happen if it failed.

◆ ◆ ◆

Twenty minutes later Jekyll sat down for breakfast. He pretended to read the paper as Poole poured his coffee. When the cup was full, Poole idled at attention behind the paper until Jekyll lowered the top half and looked him resolutely in the eye. Poole dipped his glossy head. I merely wanted to say, sir, that it is good to have you home. *Thank you, Poole,* Jekyll replied cagily. *Good to be home.* Poole bowed again and turned with the urn, then paused and said, Might we expect you to stay for some time, sir? Jekyll shrugged, shamming indifference, and gave his paper a shake. *Yes, I expect so.*

When Poole left, Jekyll set his newspaper aside and carried his coffee upstairs, moving very deliberately, as if the cup were brimming full and he did not want to spill a drop. But it was the body that felt precarious, as if a sudden gesture might pitch me back into it without warning. I was scared, and baffled, and could not help feeling somehow responsible, like a bad dog who had done something rash and stupid — even though of course I had not *done* anything. If I did not understand the laws of nature and science it was no matter, they existed, immutable, reliable, and the central one of my existence was that the needle was my key, my passport into and out of the world of the senses. Yet now it seemed the laws were breaking down. The façade of Henry Jekyll was no longer an absolute protection.

Jekyll held himself tensely against the intrusion of my thoughts as he paced his study. From a shelf he had pulled down a collection of cloth- and leather-bound books that he piled on his desk and consulted sporadically, scanning the lines of ornamental fluid scrawl — his own, I recognised — before shoving the books aside with an exasperated hiss. By that evening he was sprawled on his leather sofa, brooding at the reddish stain of sunset upon the ceiling. When Poole rapped on the door, he was silent. When Poole rapped again he called out testily, *What is it?* Poole opened the door. Mr. Utterson to see you, sir.

Jekyll sat bolt upright. *What,* he cried, *now?* We had not even heard the doorbell. Yes, sir. Mr. Utterson is downstairs.

Jekyll dragged a hand through his hair. Utterson! I had almost forgotten about the man, with all our other worries. We could not see him, of course, not now, not like this . . . Poole cleared his throat. Sir, I took a small liberty, I hope you don't mind. I told Mr. Utterson that you had been slightly under the weather and that I would see if your circumstances had improved. Jekyll lifted his finger in the air, nodding. *Yes, yes, that was very good thinking, Poole. You know, I am still recovering from my travels, in fact. Perhaps you would tell Mr. Utterson I'll come to see him soon, in the next few days.*

As soon as Poole left, Jekyll leapt up and crossed the room, pressed himself flat to the wall beside the window. He could see the front steps and the walk, and after a minute, Utterson emerged and descended to the front gate. There, as if feeling our hidden gaze, he turned and looked directly up at the study window. Jekyll moved his head at the last moment and stood rigid, waiting. When he peeped out again, Utterson was stalking away down the pavement.

That night Jekyll prepared another injection of the serum in the cabinet and carried it back to his bedroom. He tucked it into his bedside drawer and then settled down fully clothed in the armchair before the windows. He was keeping a vigil against me, steeling himself against sleep. As if I would usurp the body again the moment his eyes slipped shut. As if I even *wanted* the body now, under these circumstances. How was I to blame? How could he know so much and seem to understand so bloody little?

At dawn we snapped awake. Jekyll quickly looked at his hands, front and back, and clasped his gritty face, touching all the features as if to make certain they were still attached. He dropped his chin to his chest with a relieved sigh and murmured, *Thank God.*

Thank God? I had never heard him say such a thing before. And I wouldn't ever again.

We heard the doorbell this time. Jekyll was in his study, where he'd spent the morning and afternoon poring over his old journals. They were his journals from France on the case of Emile Verlaine. I tried to read along, but it was like trying to read over his shoulder or within a dream. Yet I could tell he was reading about the powder, the chemical injection. Emile Verlaine had not required any needle to change into Pierre, and the Other, not at first. The transformation had occurred involuntarily. Jekyll had simply manipulated, tamed, this natural process. Our case was different; I needed the injection. Was this because Jekyll had better control of himself than had Emile? Or because I was more obedient than Emile's interdependent personalities?

The doorbell's three notes knelled. Within a minute, Poole was knocking on the study door. Forgive me, sir. Sir Danvers is downstairs. I explained that you were indisposed but he was very insistent. He asked that I deliver this.

Poole held a white envelope in his hand. He came forward and Jekyll reached out automatically to accept it. Together we stared at the sinuous line looping over its face:

Dr. Jekyll

Our heart was frozen in a block of blood. The hands flipped the envelope over and tore the flap apart, drew out the slip of pale green paper. Jekyll's bank cheque. Made out to Bearer, for ninety pounds, on December 12, 1884. His signature — my fishy forgery — scrawled across the lower line. A red bank stamp impressed on the corner. Jekyll was turned toward the windows, not breathing. There was something else in the envelope. His fingers picked out the familiar calling card: Danvers X. Carew, MP. He turned it over.

You must see me

Poole was waiting. Sir? he ventured. If you are unwell, I will tell him to leave.

No. No, send him up.

Poole departed. Jekyll set the envelope down near the journals spilt across the desk. Something had happened to the air — it was thick as water. Footsteps began to click across the main hall. Jekyll opened his desk drawer and swept the journals inside. He smoothed his hair and wrung his hands, exhaling three sharp gusts, as he did before a fencing match. When Poole entered with Carew, Jekyll was gazing out the window, hands in his trouser pockets. Sir, Poole murmured, shutting the door on his way out.

Electric silence. Jekyll did not move. He was composing his face: a bland lift to the brow, a nonchalant little moue of distraction. He turned and presented it to Carew. The man wore a grey suit with a lavender bow tie; his beautiful, brushed ivory hair hung in wings to his shoulders. Good evening, Doctor, he said. Jekyll made no response. Carew gestured to the leather chair across from the desk. May I? Jekyll nodded, and Carew sat down, crossed his long thin legs. He had removed something from behind his back. A folded newspaper. He frowned at it, then leant forward and placed it on the desk. The *Pall Mall Gazette*.

Today was Stead's last report, he said. I thought you might be interested.

A blaring chromatic chord was sliding into harmony in our head. Carew settled back, gave an almost apologetic smile. I confess, I'm quite pleasantly surprised by all the attention the piece has received. When Stead originally told me what he intended to write, I rather assumed it would all be dismissed as the hysterical ranting of a radical. People don't want to hear what really goes on out there, they don't want to be hectored by some angry newspaperman. But Stead knows the public better than I do, it seems. Cables of support and interest from America, from the Continent, an endorsement from the *British Medical Journal*. People are outraged, at long last. Something might actually be done. I find it almost incredible. Carew paused and gave again that slight smile, almost a grimace. Of course, Stead's methods were — there will be questions he'll have to answer. Goodness, buying a child, even if it's only to prove that one can. He went too far for his own good in this crusade. But I suppose a man must go too far, sometimes, to get something done. Wouldn't you agree?

Jekyll stood perfectly still behind the desk. Tiny sparks were starting to pop at the edges of the eyes. Without looking away from Carew, he lowered himself into his reclining chair. What I am trying to tell you, Carew said, is that this Maiden Tribute campaign, in spite of everything, is going to produce some substantial measure of action. Mr. Stead has wisely restrained himself from levelling specific accusations, but everyone knows the corruption is rampant, all the way to the top, to the lords themselves. And there are certain committees that will now make it their business to expose, indict — humiliate, at the very least — the perceived dirty parties. It will be a circus; mud will spatter. Of course, power and money protects its own. No lord is going to stand trial for this. But there will be trials. Sacrifices; scapegoats, perhaps. I'm in a position to say so — I am on one of the committees, you see. Two of them, in fact, the London Committee for the Suppression of Traffic in Young English Girls and the London Society for the Protection of Young Females. I like the full perspective . . .

Carew's eyes drifted down to the desk, to the envelope. Maybe it's best if I speak more plainly. I have no intention of hurting you, Doctor, of harming your reputation. Quite the opposite. I would like to help you. To provide what protection I am able to offer, if you are willing to accept it. It would be a terrible waste if you were to be mixed up in this circus. A waste to science. To our common aim.

Our common aim.

That's right, Carew said. Understanding, Doctor. Understanding the nature of the human mind, and all its miraculous potential. Is this not your goal? Is this not why you do — what it is that you do? To explore the limits of what is possible? He paused, eyebrows lifted theatrically. Or is this not about science or understanding at all? Is it merely a matter of — pleasure? Jekyll said nothing. I stared out from behind his cool, contemptuous shell. You may decide not to speak to me, Carew said. It's your choice. But if you won't speak to me, then I am unable to protect you in what is to come. That is not a threat, it's simply a fact. Investigations will be carried out, and names will be dragged through the mire. A man's name, Dr. Jekyll, is his legacy, as I'm sure you must agree. And I fear that yours will not survive another scandal. All your progress, all your work, will be tarnished, dismissed by the scientific community and by history. You will be remembered, if at all, as a criminal freak. Is this what you want? Tell me, if it is, and I will sadly leave you to it.

God, he was good. He sat across the desk with an earnest plea in his eyes, his bluff all but impenetrable. Jekyll spoke calmly. *You said something about speaking plainly. I would like to hear, plainly, what crime you believe I've committed.*

Carew's eyes settled again upon the envelope with the pale green cheque edging out the tattered slit. How about association with a known pedophile? he began. A patron of establishments that imprison children as concubines. A man who kept a fourteen-year-old mistress in his house, a man who could be charged with multiple crimes: assaults on innocent persons, petty larceny, evading the police . . .

He let the word fade off with a snakelike hiss.

Association. If I happen to know a man, that is a crime?

Carew pursed his lips in a one-sided smile. Oh, very well, if you insist. On the twelfth of December of last year, a certain man entered your property at three in the morning via the door off Castle Street that leads into the surgery block at the rear of this property. He emerged less than five minutes later with a cheque for ninety pounds, in your name, signed in your hand. Hush money, for the father of a girl he'd tried to abduct on the street. The very next day you opened an account in this man's name and deposited five thousand pounds. Shortly thereafter, Edward Hyde took up residence at seven Ghyll Road in Soho and employed one Eudora Deaker to keep house. Do you know, incidentally, what is truly extraordinary? I met Eudora Deaker, many years ago. Her husband was the Great Lazaar. The magician. He was quite famous in the forties and fifties. Eudora was his assistant. His grand trick was to make her vanish from a standing wardrobe that was lifted off the floor. Stunning woman, back then. Carew shook his head. And now she reappears in the house of Edward Hyde. Extraordinary. A coincidence? There's a design to our lives, I think, a great elaborate design we can just discern, if we know how to look.

And you've been looking.

I make no secret of it, Carew said. Edward Hyde has fascinated me from the moment I first heard of him. *From Cornelius Luce.* That's right. Mr. Luce mentioned it to me as a peculiarity, but something about the story — especially after I'd confirmed that Mrs. Horace Waller was not, in fact, deceased, much less in the manner described — well, it intrigued me. It is instinct, by now, a nose for the unusual. So, yes, I began to poke around. And what should I find?

You tell me.

Carew held Jekyll's eyes. I find you, Doctor. I find the inescapable conclusion that Edward Hyde is you.

Jekyll almost broke into laughter. He tightened the edges of his mouth and swiveled around in his chair to the windows. The sky was indecently lovely, gauzy as a lilac scarf above the rooflines.

You are wrong. Edward Hyde is not me. That is the whole point.

What is the whole point?

To shed yourself. To become someone else. Exactly, Carew said. And how does one do that? Shed oneself? Jekyll gazed musingly out the window. *What is it you want from me? You protect me in exchange for what, precisely?*

There was soft amazement in Carew's voice: Don't you know by now? I have wanted only one thing from the start. I want to understand. To understand how it works. How the mind can create a personality — how it can give birth to a person, a wholly distinct individual. This is what you have done, is it not? You have created this other self inside yourself. I have observed Hyde. Certain physical characteristics cannot change. Your colouring is the same. Your hairline. Your facial-bone structure. The shape of your ears. But otherwise your body, in his possession, is unrecognisable. His spine. He seems half a foot shorter than you, at least. He moves quicker too, but like someone crippled, like his pelvis is deformed in some way. And his face is — all twisted. I very much agree, he is not you. But, then, who is he?

Jekyll did not turn from the window. There was power in this pose; I could feel the shifting in advantage. He raised his hands and enmeshed the fingers together. *I don't believe I'm going to say anything further this evening.*

A long pause. Carew sighed. Well, as I said, that is your choice. If you wish me to leave, I will leave. But I suggest you consider this situation carefully. If you are capable of doing so.

Now Jekyll turned in his chair. *I strike you as being incapable?* You strike me as being in considerably over your head. This Hyde — can you control him? Are you fully aware of what he does — what you do when you are him? Do you have any notion what has been going on in that house you leased for him? Because what the people of Soho are willing to say about this man is quite far from flattering. Now the police are aware of his existence. You cannot create a man, give him a name and a bank account and a lease on a house, and still pretend that he is imaginary. That he does not leave evidence, legal evidence, everywhere he goes. If his young mistress could be made to testify, for example, do you have any idea what she might say? Or if a warrant were procured to search that house on Ghyll Road —? Carew exhaled through his nose. I'm sorry, but I must say this. You have made yourself into a Dr. Frankenstein, and Edward Hyde is your monster. And he will destroy you, along with everything you value, if you do not accept my help.

You mean, if I do not accept the terms of your blackmail.

Blackmail? Carew repeated, as if genuinely astonished. Blackmail? Doctor, these terms are entirely of your own making. You think I want to see you exposed — to see this miraculous science reduced to a piece of infamy? How many times can I say that I want to *help* you, help you see this properly through? You are on the brink of a revolutionary discovery, I have no doubt, but you cannot continue solely on your own — the whole experiment will implode. It is imploding. You need counsel, and you need protection under which we can work together to harness your science, to make it palatable to the public and thus of practical use to humankind. Is that not what science is for?

Oh, I marvelled at the man: his bright imploring eyes, his impeccable performance. Jekyll swiveled back to the window. The sky had lost its tender colour above the blackening line of the square. He touched his steepled fingers to his lips. *I must consider all this. You must give me time.* Take all the time you like. But the courts and committees do not wait on you. I hope for your sake that you consider it quickly, and wisely.

Jekyll nodded once. *Thank you for dropping by, Sir Danvers. Always a pleasure.*

Jekyll continued to sit as Carew's footsteps clicked away on the pavement below. He lifted the edge of the newspaper Carew had brought; its headline: *Of Good Cheer Indeed.*

In one sense I wasn't surprised. I had known Carew was dangerous, known there was something wrong in his triumphant cry that night outside the Black Shop. And yet, I still could not wrap my mind around it. Carew was my tormentor? The letters, the newspapers, the police inspectors; it was Carew? How could one man have orchestrated such a grand-scale persecution? Then again, Carew was not the only man involved, was he? Those letters — he could have hired underlings to deliver them. And those two inspectors — obviously, Carew had influence with the police. He had mentioned something about a warrant to search my house. My Ghyll. Abandoned to those two goons, offered up to them on a platter. Carew wouldn't want to search my house unless he knew he would find something incriminating. Evidence — *legal evidence* — he could be planting things to find when he arrived with his warrant. And he had said something about Jeannie too. My mistress. But how could he make her testify unless he knew where she was? Had he helped her escape? Was he keeping her somewhere?

Jekyll had sealed me off again; the membrane hardening like cement. He did not want to hear my thoughts and did not want me to hear his. What was he hiding from me? Some crucial element was eluding me, and Jekyll was harbouring it like some crafty, snickering stowaway in the outer reaches of his mind. I pressed myself to the barrier and squirmed, searching for an opening, but I could not escape my rigid cell.

At least Jekyll could not escape his either. All that night, he lay awake on the study sofa, his mind racing and sleepless behind the deceptive closed eyelids. He ate breakfast at his desk in the morning — pushed it around the plate, rather — and then spent the afternoon slumped in his chair gazing blankly out the window. He had rolled up his left shirtsleeve, and now and then he examined the arm, smoothing his thumb down the pockmarked cephalic vein, inspecting the abscess budding like a blood blister in the crook of his elbow. He clicked his tongue disapprovingly, as if at a rambunctious child's scrape, and then rolled down his sleeve, pushed up from his chair, and absently stamped his dead foot on the floor. Then he went to Gaunt Street.

It did not seem at first that he had any destination in mind.

He merely rambled through the humid sunset until he came, as if by chance, to Utterson's grey wooden house, looming sombrely above a patch of balding grass. The scuffling, stooped old manservant opened the door and led Jekyll upstairs to the study, the hunting-lodge-like room, with the carven ceiling and the portrait glowering down from the mantel, where Jekyll had first mentioned his will. Utterson sat wilted in a wingback chair, tie loosened, hair frowzy in the heat. He considered Jekyll with a rueful, sour frown. You look awful, Harry. Jekyll sniffed a laugh. *Same to you, old man.* He remained on his feet, jingling his keys in his pocket. His pulse ticked, distinct and steady as a second hand. *I've come to tell you something. I've made a decision. It's finished between Hyde and me. It's done. I won't be seeing him again.*

Jekyll met Utterson's eyes — those basset-hound eyes, rolling upward with pitiful hope. Utterson pressed his fist to his lips and sucked in through his flaring nostrils. I want to believe you, Harry. God, how I want to believe you. *Then believe me.* And what about him? Utterson asked. What happens to Hyde? He'll simply disappear?

Hyde will return to Edinburgh, Jekyll said. *Into good care. He knows he can't stay here. He is — fracturing. Becoming a threat to himself. And, yes, to me.*

I did not react, did not give him the satisfaction. Utterson was nodding like a proud, mawkish uncle. I am glad to hear you say it, Harry. This is good news. Utterson rose, went to the sideboard, and returned with two dainty glasses of amber liqueur. He gave one to Jekyll and held up his own, a meaningful gleam in his sagging eyes. Let's drink to it, he commanded. To its end, Harry.

Jekyll raised his glass; they clinked crystal rims. *To its end, John.*

To its end? Nonsense. He couldn't just order me to go away, and he knew it. What was this about fracturing, becoming a threat? Did he really believe I had grabbed control of the body that night?

That I was to blame for the disintegrating barrier between us? If this was another of his symbolic gestures, it wasn't very convincing. If he'd wanted to make a convincing gesture, he'd have gone up to the cabinet and dumped all the remaining powder out the window.

Instead, he took a cool bath, shaved, dressed in lightweight twill, and went to the Grampian for dinner. What was I meant to do — crawl off and die? Go to sleep? Return to that dreamless void wherein I had lived for almost all of his life? No, I wasn't going back there, however he pushed and stamped me down. How would that even solve our problem? How would my disappearance satisfy Carew?

In amazement, I watched him attempt to slip back into the part of blasé Dr. Jekyll. He went to his barber on Bond Street. He dropped by his tailor and ordered an ecru summer-linen suit. He returned to his fencing club and then retired to the Grampian lounge for a soda water in the circle of gossipy old boys. He wasn't fooling me, and he was not fooling himself either; he could surely feel me writhing with outrage at this idiotic pretence. There he would sit in his club chair, smiling mildly at the blather, meanwhile gripping and releasing his toes inside his tight, tailored shoes. He did look awful. He had not slept for days; his vigilant guard against me kept him awake. In the shaving glass, his face was drawn, peaky. One morning he nicked his chin with the razor, and a line of red trickled vivid through the cream. Later, at Lobb's, he was being fitted for a pair of oxford brogues to match his new linen suit when the clerk discreetly cleared his throat and tapped a finger to his chin. Jekyll touched his own chin, and then stared at the bright daub of blood on his fingertips. He wiped his chin and caught sight of himself in the standing mirror, his eyes stark with alarm and blood smeared beneath his open lips. Are you all right, Doctor? the clerk asked uneasily.

He was not. At the fencing club that afternoon, he panted inside the cage of mesh helmet. His legs were sluggard, and his feet stumbled over each other as his opponent backed him up across the floor, flicking his blade and smacking Jekyll's wrist precisely on the bone. White-hot pain slithered up the arm, and Jekyll ripped off his mask and hurled it behind him, then drew back his sword and advanced as if to deliver a backhand slash. Then he stopped. The helmet had bowled into some clattering equipment. Men in their whites watched, startled, from the sidelines. Jekyll's opponent had removed his own helmet and gaped in appalled indignation. Jekyll's glove creaked, as he gripped his sabre tighter.

He turned and stalked from the silent hall, and by the time he reached Big House, he was drenched and seeing whizzing spots of colour. He took a few unsteady steps past Poole into the entrance hall before his vision greyed and the room pitched like a ship and Poole cried, Sir! We were on the floor, staring dazedly at the andirons in the dead fireplace. It's happened again, I thought, with disconnected horror. I've fallen into the body again. Poole turned us onto our back to loosen the collar and tie, smoothed the damp hair from our forehead and asked in a ringing voice, Can you hear me, sir? Can you hear my voice?

Thrashing in bed, throwing off the muggy sheets while Poole and Bradshaw held us down by the shoulders. It wasn't the bedclothes but the body we were trying to thrash off, this fevered thing smothering us; if only we could get it off, we would feel immediately better. But Poole kept forcing us back into it, and eventually we were too weak to fight him. Soon we were freezing, locked with shudders under heaps of quilts, and then roasting again, rolling a haunted eye at the gigantic scorching sun making steam rise from our sizzling skin. The body was dying. I could smell its meaty rankness. It was dying and we would die trapped inside it. *There has to be a way out!* I'd think in claustrophobic panic, dreaming myself lost inside the torchlit labyrinth of the body with its nightmarishly intricate system of capillaries and alleyways, millions and millions of coiling miles. As I plunged through, I would find myself in familiar rooms. My garret bedroom at Ghyll appeared often, and I would think, quite lucidly, that while here, I ought to check around and see if Carew and his goons had planted anything incriminating. Odd, nasty things turned up. Handfuls of hair. A drawstring bag filled with teeth. Alien-looking coins that slipped greasily between my fingers. From the walls, I would tear away the bloated silk paper and find burlap sacking nailed up in a thick layer, as if to soundproof the place. I seemed to conduct these monstrous searches over and over, for I kept coming upon my bedroom in the replicating labyrinth.

Gradually the delusion dissipated, and I began to accept that there was no escape from the body. If the body died, then we would die. This notion was increasingly comforting. Already the world of Jekyll's bedroom seemed pleasantly distant: the people moving blurrily through, ministering to the body, lifting it, rolling it, wiping it down. None of it seemed to relate to us. It was like peering upward from a deep sheltered well. Sometimes the bedroom appeared to be swarming with people, all jostling to peer down into the well shaft where we lolled at the bottom, a tombal darkness through which we drifted together like shipwrecked sailors on a raft. There was no resistance at this stage. We were beyond conflict, floating serene toward death, our well-earned respite.

When we opened our eyes, I thought we really were dead. The room glowed, shining glorious whiteness. We shut our eyes, and woke later to cooler, clearer light. A man stood at the window, a nimbus about his head. He turned and approached the bedside, his red elfin face coming into focus. Lanyon. He touched our forehead with the back of his hand, then our cheek. Deliciously sensitive, the skin. Harry, he was saying, Harry, can you hear me? Blink if you can hear me. We dipped the eyelids shut, pulled them open. Good! Lanyon said. That's very good, Harry.

He lifted our hand from the bed. It did not seem attached to us, the dumb appendage. He gave it a squeeze and bent to kiss the knuckles. You made it, Harry. You made it back.

Soon we could sit up and sip tea from a cup Poole held to our lips. We could squeeze Lanyon's hand until he patted our wrist and laughed, saying, That's enough, that's enough, very good. But we did not feel *back*. The bedroom still seemed illusory, as if this were not life but its hovering reproduction, its afterimage. Lanyon was elated by our progress, and even stoic Poole could not suppress his tender relief as he served us tea and lukewarm soup. Utterson came to visit too, and he stood at the foot of the bed with a sheepish smile, shaking his shaggy head. Damn it, Harry, must you always be so dramatic? Lanyon laughed and grasped our shoulder, and Utterson chuckled, and a dry, coughing sound rattled from our throat. But we did not yet speak. Lanyon gently pressed us to respond to his questions so he could determine if we could indeed still talk. We knew we could talk. But silence was tranquillity. To speak was to answer questions. Our left elbow, we had noticed, was wrapped with a white bandage, a wad of padding in the inner crook, where the abscess had budded. One day Lanyon rolled up our pajama sleeve and began to unwind the wrapping, keeping his eyes briskly down on his work. The arm was stained yellow from the tincture of iodine, but the abscess had drained and deflated, and the purpling vein looked better, the pockmarks fainter. In silence we watched Lanyon dab on more gluey unguent and wrap the arm in fresh bandage. His eyes flicked upward, pale blue, with a little vein burst in the white. He gave a shadow of a smile, reassuring and sad.

Lanyon seemed to be staying at the house. Every morning he came in and checked our vital signs, fed us spoonfuls of medicine from the litter of bottles on the bedside. While we dozed during the day, he often read a book in the armchair. One afternoon we woke and watched him awhile, a hard ache in our throat. His flaxen hair was aglow in the crisp lemon light; his studious profile was stamped in radiance. Jekyll wet his lips. *Hastie*. Lanyon set his book aside and came to the bed. He took our hand. Harry. Good Harry. Tell me something, tell me anything.

Hastie. What's the day?

Lanyon's brow creased with sympathy. It's a Thursday, I believe. September tenth, Harry.

September tenth. It had been ... July, last we knew. Two months, we had lost.

Harry, Lanyon said, I'd like to tell you something. His faded eyes were clear, unwavering. I'd like to tell you that I'm sorry. About Winnie. I should have let her see you. Let you talk to her. You wanted only to help, and I should have seen that, and instead I insulted you. We have wasted so much time with our stubbornness, our principles. And I'm damned sorry for it. A new leaf, now, yes? A new leaf for us both?

Lanyon laid his hand upon our left arm and gave us again that sad, consoling smile.

Agreed?

Within days, Jekyll was sitting up by the open window, wrapped in shawls. He could sip tea and spoon soup for himself. Poole carried Jekyll's razor and scissors from the dressing room on a folded towel, like religious implements. He draped Jekyll with a cloth and set about clipping the beard down to stubble. He lathered the cheeks and throat and meticulously scraped them clean, grimacing with concentration. He combed the long tangled hair and snipped with the scissors, his fingers cool and light, with a trace of caress. Then he produced a hand mirror, and Jekyll regarded his reflection, gravely awed. His face was stretched tight across the sharp cheekbones and brow, luminously pale. His blond hair was silvered almost entirely through with fine, glinting strands of sterling. His eyes burned like core ice from hollowed sockets. He looked as if he'd survived an Arctic winter locked within a ship frozen fast in the wastes. He could not put the mirror down:

a rapt, ravaged Narcissus. *Quite the improvement,* he murmured hoarsely. By the end of the week, he was limping up and down the corridor with a walking stick. Lanyon had reluctantly returned home, leaving Poole with a catalogue of instructions as to diet and continued treatment, which Poole enforced with strict rigour, watching Jekyll take his odious medicines as if he were a child who might try to trick his old uncle. The bandage on Jekyll's arm, he did not touch. Jekyll unwound it himself one afternoon and let the arm breathe. He did not cover it again, and by the next day the once-open sore was reduced to a raised bruise in the cleft, and the punctures down the vein had faded to crimson pinholes.

I noted the arm's improvement with neutrality, a sign of the body's healing. But it did not mean anything. At some point Jekyll would need me again. We had not died. Our troubles had not vanished. Yet as September chilled the windowpanes and left a fragile overnight frost on the grass in the square, I found that I was not afraid. That illusory quality still clung to the world, the relativity of everything. We felt only a placid expectancy, a readiness for the inevitable.

At last the doorbell chimed below.

You have a visitor, sir, Poole said. *Carew,* Jekyll replied, without turning from the windows. Yes, sir. I will turn him out directly, but he asked me to deliver a message first. The message is: If he leaves now, he will not be returning.

Well. We wouldn't want that, would we. Show him up. He won't stay long.

In a royal-blue dressing gown and embroidered slippers, we sat listening to two sets of footsteps cross the main hall and climb the carpeted stairs. The window was partly ajar, and I could smell a tang of autumn smoke on the air. Jekyll drew it in through his nostrils and held it as Poole entered with our visitor. Sir, he murmured, and pulled the door shut on his way out. Carew stood behind us in silence. I could hear the rusting leaves in the square rustling in the light breeze. Jekyll turned in his chair.

Carew wore a yellow checkered waistcoat and a chocolate velvet jacket. He strolled toward the desk with his hands behind his back and that apologetic grimace on his bloodless lips. I see that Mr. Poole wasn't exaggerating. You have been through the wars, haven't you, Doctor.

He seemed to be holding something behind his back, but when he reached the chair across from the desk, he laid one hand atop the back of it and slid the other into his pocket. He regarded Jekyll almost contritely, head tilted. I don't wish to tax you or impede your convalescence in any way. But it is necessary that we speak, I'm afraid.

So speak.

Carew drummed the top of the leather chair with his fingers. You know, I almost envy you. I'd rather have spent the last two months sick in bed than wrangling with committees and petitions and recalcitrant Tory opposition. It has been a circus, all right; I shall have a nice nervous collapse myself at the end of it. You might be interested to hear that Mr. Stead will likely be facing charges for abduction, as will his conspirators. Those in charge wish to make an example of him. Buying a young girl is buying a young girl, even if one does it only to prove that one can. Mr. Stead is quite keen about the prospect, actually, of grandstanding in court. Though I don't imagine his accomplices will share his enthusiasm. Prison is nothing to look forward to. I've made a study of them, English prisons. Horrifying places, like dog kennels. No one in his right mind would care to spend even a night.

Carew lifted the leg of his trousers and lowered his lean haunch onto the edge of the desk, crossing his hands on his thigh. His eyes moved cautiously up. You should not think, he said in a new, lower tone, that because I did not receive your agreement last time we spoke, I have been neglecting the protection I offered.

If the papers contain no mention of Edward Hyde, I can tell you
that this is due in no small part to me. On behalf of the committees I serve, I have taken on the investigation of certain claims
that reach our attention. Mr. Hyde's name was submitted to us
in August by a lady of some influence who maintains social con-
nections in Soho. People have been talking, speculating, about
their illustrious neighbour Mr. Hyde. It's the common Londoners
whom this story has affected most. It has them riled and in an up-
roar — for these are *their* children, their maidens being devoured
by Stead's Minotaur. They are angry and eager to lay blame, and
Mr. Hyde in his castle makes for a very tempting target. Much of
what I am hearing on my interviews is fourth- or fifth-hand and
possibly fabricated at the source, but there is a general consistency
that is difficult to ignore. It has been ignored, but only because I
am suppressing it, thereby committing a crime and opening myself to liability. I have been doing this, perhaps incredibly fool-
ishly, to protect you. To protect what I think you are capable of.
Tell me, am I mad?

   Yes.

   Carew made a tolerant smile, which gradually faded as Jekyll
said nothing more. And you, Doctor? Do you believe yourself to
be a healthy man? Jekyll said nothing. Carew was close enough for
him to touch. Carew's eyelids grew hooded, reptilian. I wonder if
you would do something for me. It is a small thing next to what I
have done for you. Would you mind if I asked you to roll up the
sleeve of your robe to the elbow?

   The left hand gripped the chair by reflex. Carew lifted his
eyebrows, waited. No? Is that too much to ask? To roll up your
sleeve?

   He held the innocently incredulous look another moment.
As I thought, he said quietly. As I thought. I haven't been devot-
ing the entirety of my time to this Maiden Tribute business, you
see. Two weeks ago I took a little holiday to Paris. Dr. Petit had
agreed to meet with me at the hospital. He put up a decent pre-

tence of a struggle, you should know, refusing at first to speak about you and Mr. Verlaine, honouring whatever pact of silence you established with the board before you left. But even silence can be instructive, don't you agree? And in the end, people always talk. They yearn to talk. We all long to tell our secrets. We simply must wait for someone to come along and ask the right questions.

Carew swiveled round on his perch and peered across the study at the fireplace mantel and the black, ghoulish painting. That picture, for instance, he said. Dr. Petit showed me the others. But do you know, I think I like this one best. The violence is so — palpable. Dr. Petit said that L'inconnu mixed his own feces into the paint. Hardly something a man would choose to display in his study. Yet there it hangs, for all to see. Does anyone ever ask what it is?

No.

Of course they don't ask. And that is the problem. Here we are, all of us dying to reveal our secrets, yet no one asks the right questions. Carew turned back and fixed his eyes on us with languorous, cunning inspection. You will not find a better audience than me. I am the very man you have been waiting for all this time. Are you willing to let me help you?

Jekyll forced the left hand to relax, release the arm of the chair.

Where would you like to begin?

Carew settled back on his bony haunch on the desk. He lifted his chin, victory playing upon his lips. The injections, he said carefully. The injections you were administering to Mr. Verlaine. Dr. Petit did not see the system in your method. He chose to believe you were experimenting with a haphazard range of narcotics over the course of that year. It is the way of mediocre men, to blind themselves to the brilliance of their betters. My presumption is that you had two distinct injections. The first turned Emile into Pierre, and the second transformed him into L'inconnu. They would have acted as triggers, these injections, summoning whichever personality you wished to access at whatever time you chose. Am I correct thus far?

You are.

Carew held his speculative pose. The second injection, he continued, would have been a modification of the first. The core chemical ingredient would have been altered, perhaps to encourage a more aggressive effect befitting the third's hostile personality. You would have had to induce Emile to associate this effect with L'inconnu, like a reflexive, conditioned response. If Emile believed that the injection would change him, then it would do exactly that. The personalities would willingly switch places. It is an ingenious theory. Mr. Verlaine, unfortunately, was simply not strong enough, and the experiment was cut short. So you continued it on yourself. The result, I can only assume, was this being you have named Edward Hyde. This is how you shed yourself. How you become him.

Bravo. Jekyll lifted his hands from the armrests and clapped, a dry and hollow sound.

If that is the case, Carew said, then I want to watch it happen. Watch you self-administer the injection and become Mr. Hyde. We may begin our collaboration there. Does that suit you?

Jekyll nearly smiled. *Splendidly. But I will need a little more time. It would kill me, weak as I am, to become Edward Hyde at the moment. I'll need my strength.*

Would a week be sufficient? Jekyll lifted his shoulder. *A week, then. We do it here?* Carew glanced around the study. No, not here. Somewhere more . . . neutral. I was thinking, as a matter of fact, we might meet at Cornelius Luce's house. *Surely you're joking.* Carew frowned. Why would I be joking? Forgive me, but you can't expect me to meet your Mr. Hyde entirely on my own. He is too unpredictable. Mr. Luce does not need to be in the room, but his presence in the house will assure me of some security. He needn't know anything more than that you and I require a private room in which to talk.

Jekyll moved his eyes to the window, pretending to consider the terms. I knew we weren't actually going to go through with any of it. But I understood we needed the time. A gust of wind leant into the glass. *All right,* Jekyll said wearily, as if worn down. *At Luce's. In a week.*

Carew's expression was strange as he gazed down at us: a veiled pride, laced with pity, as if Jekyll were some brave soul confined to a wheelchair. I'll send word as to the details, he said gently. I am glad, Dr. Jekyll, very glad indeed that you have decided to save yourself. I will not fail you. He stood up and extended his hand. Jekyll weakly slipped into his grip, and a flicker crossed Carew's face, a stricken twinge of realisation. Mr. Hyde can't — he blurted. I mean, he can't — He paused, mouth parted. *Hear us?* Jekyll suggested. *Right now, you mean?* Jekyll's grip closed tighter around the man's hand. *No. He can't hear us. He goes to sleep when I don't need him.* He released the hand, and Carew withdrew it to his chest. That's good. *It is good,* Jekyll said, *for you.* He let a beat go by, then chuckled amiably, a joke. Carew gave a halfhearted smile, gingerly holding his own hand. Yes, he murmured. I'll send word.

Oh, Carew, you should have heeded that premonition. I could see it on your face as the shadow of your destiny slipped over you. You should have listened, should have left us alone. Jekyll sat by the window, his breathing steady. He knew what we had to do. So did I. It hovered just beyond our acknowledgement. Jekyll pushed up from his chair and spread his wings in a grunting stretch, rotating his wrists. Then he went into the corridor and called down the stairs for Poole, who appeared at once. *I'll take my dinner downstairs tonight,* Jekyll said airily, then he strolled to his bedroom and drew a bath. He dressed in the cream linen suit he had ordered before his sickness; it hung loose on his atrophied frame. He cinched his belt and buttoned the double-breasted jacket and threw back his shoulders, raising a debonair eyebrow at himself in the mirror.

Jekyll eased down the stairs and found the entire staff of Big House gathered in the main hall. They all held flutes of champagne. Poole stood at the banister with the bottle, a linen towel draped over his arm. He handed Jekyll a sparkling flute, and in unison the staff lifted their glasses and called, To your health, Dr. Jekyll! Poole bowed and said, To your health, sir.

Jekyll stood supporting himself on the railing, his eyes travelling over the upturned, eager, inquisitive faces. He lingered on Bradshaw, standing a full head above everyone else, his copper comb-tracked hair agleam. Again I saw him across the conservatory with that suave, stranded smirk on his lips. The footman tipped his master a covert nod, raising his flute a bit higher.

Jekyll only picked at his chop and boiled vegetables. At last Poole carried the plate away, and Lizzie came forward with a silver urn. Tea, sir? Jekyll nodded, watched her pour a steaming stream into the cup. Her pale, averted profile beneath the mass of tied-back hair, a trace of dusky shadow down her cheek. Glad to see yer better, sir, she said, and turned away with the urn. Jekyll said quietly, *Lizzie*, and she paused. *Are you happy here, in this house?* Her eyes rose, coal-black, fierce in their shyness. Yes, sir. Very happy, sir.

That night we dreamt we were back in Father's room at Bagclaw Hospital, kneeling by his wheelchair and rolling up his sleeve, a syringe on the little table nearby. Lizzie sat beside Father patting his other arm. The needle, for some reason, would not slide properly into the vein; it seemed as if it was hitting something hard, the steel point scraping off. Father watched us working on his arm with a graceful mien of forbearance.

I knew the dream's origin. I remembered Father regarding us from his wheelchair, yellow-nailed hands dangling. *Didn't bring me anything, did you?* he had asked in his ruined voice. *Finish me off? Clever doctor like you could mix something up in a trice. Make it look natural.*

Make it look natural.

We lay awake as morning paled the room.

After breakfast the next morning, Jekyll went to Maw's. We had been here the previous summer, after returning from our trip north to see Father in the hospital, and then to see Pent Manor, that final time. The old tiny chemist's shop was cluttered with bottles and jars and tiers of shelving, a sharp, vinegary tang to the atmosphere. Maw himself came clumping from the back to greet Jekyll, taking his hand in his knurled, knowing grip, worn smooth and strong as wood. His watery eyes, bespectacled and magnified, swam over Jekyll's face. You are thin, Dr. Jekyll, he crooned, you are working too hard.

Jekyll ordered four powders and a tincture, all in small, precise amounts. Maw edged around behind the counter and squinted at the labels of the bottles crowding the shelves. He eased down each one he wanted, scooped a measure of its contents onto a silver scale, then tipped the powder into a brown-paper sachet. At last he put all the sachets into a thick brown envelope and handed it over the counter to Jekyll as though it contained a precious, seditious manuscript. You have rats, Dr. Jekyll? he asked with a sly lift of his eyebrow. Jekyll chuckled grimly. *With a vengeance.*

At home Jekyll went straight back to the cabinet. He separated the powders into two round-bottomed flasks partially filled with colourless liquid. He arranged a Bunsen burner beneath each flask, each connected to a condenser, the delicate lip suspended just above a graduated glass to catch the distillate drip of the vapourised powders. The two distillations he combined in a phial, and then he dropped in three beads of the tincture. He stoppered it with a rubber plug and turned the phial upside down several times, then held it to the light from the window. The fluid was perfectly clear, slightly more viscous than water. Once the solution was administered, the heart would stop pumping blood within ten seconds, and within twenty seconds the body would be dead. I marvelled at the crystalline serum. All at once, it was no longer hypothetical. We could kill him. Draw the serum into a hypodermic, wait for him at Luce's front gate, stick the needle in his neck, and walk away. Old man dies. Happens every day. Who would suspect different? Luce? What proof would he have?

The next morning at breakfast the doorbell rang, and Poole entered a moment later with an envelope, which he set at Jekyll's elbow. Jekyll pretended to ignore it for a few minutes. Finally he wiped his mouth and slit the envelope's throat with his yolky knife. The note was brief:

Friday, 2 October
Midnight

Midnight! How dramatic. But the street would be deserted at midnight. All we had to do was catch Carew approaching the house and take care of him outside. Once he entered Luce's house, everything became far too complicated. Jekyll would have to get there early, watch for Carew's arrival, then try to appear as if he were arriving at the same time. A handshake at the gate, then the needle in the neck. All in the timing.

We worked it over and over on the long walks Jekyll took in those last days of September. Restless, exhilarating days, the leaves flattening in swooping gusts of wind. I yearned to be out in the body and the billowing smoky air. But I did not expect release. I understood that my way back to the world was through Carew; it was as if he were blocking the entrance. He had made it impossible for me to continue with my life. He had spied on me, taunted and tormented me. He had taken Jeannie, taken Ghyll, and would take over Jekyll's life as well. The rationale was the easy part. But the *doing*. Sticking the needle into his neck, pressing the plunger, marking him as little as possible. Could we perform such a cold-blooded act? Carew might be wearing an overcoat with the collar turned up. He might be stronger than anticipated; he might put up a struggle, escape. Or he might wait inside Luce's house from early evening. What then? Could Jekyll kill him inside, in private, claim Carew had suffered some sort of sudden illness? It would be fishy; they would conduct a careful autopsy, with such a high-profile corpse. No, it had to happen outside the house. Over and over we turned it, the plan, as Jekyll stalked the city, building up his legs and heart and appetite.

At mealtime he cleared his plate. He found a heavy crate in the surgical theatre and lifted it rhythmically above his head, carried it up and down the stairs. In his drawers he stood before his dressing room mirror, examining his scrawny shanks, his concave abdomen and emaciated chest, tensing the sinewy muscles. He combed his fingers through his silvered hair, from the well-seasoned temples to the glittering strands strung through the long forelock. Twice a day he climbed to the cabinet and removed the glass phial of lucid fluid from the press, held it up to the light to check for change, impurity. From A drawer he took down another Milward box, this one with a single syringe embedded in purple velvet, and with his left fingers through the loops, he practised, holding it behind his back or in his coat pocket and then whipping it out and into an imaginary jugular. Five seconds, that was all it would take. Five crucial seconds, and then we could walk away, free. We deserved our freedom. We had to win. It was justice.

That was Utterson's word: *justice*. He and Lanyon dropped by unexpectedly on that Thursday evening of 1 October, inviting themselves to dinner. The meal was interminable. Jekyll's appetite had vanished. He was acting weaker than he truly felt, as if he were still in the midst of convalescence. Yet he had to attend the conversation and put in the occasional comment, for Lanyon was watching him soberly beneath his ruddy good cheer and chatter. By dessert I had stopped listening and began to pay attention again only when I realised the talk had turned to W. T. Stead and his Maiden Tribute campaign. Lanyon was saying it was outlandish, the notion of pressing charges against the man. He was the reason they were conducting investigations to begin with; he'd brought the issue into the open. My goodness, Lanyon exclaimed, have we lost all perspective? The man deserves praise, not prison! Utterson, stirring his coffee, gave an exasperated sigh and set down his spoon. Hastie, the man purchased a thirteen-year-old girl. Without consent of the father, and by misleading the mother. He had her examined and certified by a midwife and then drugged with chloroform and arranged in a bed in a strange room. He entered that room; she woke; she was frightened. He deserves praise, you say. Perhaps. But if he serves a spell in prison, well, in my mind that is justice.

Lanyon opened his mouth to protest, then flicked his eyes at Jekyll. Something in his watchfulness made Lanyon pause and then look down at his custard, blushing. There was silence. Utterson lifted his droll, mournful gaze up to Jekyll. And I heard, like an echo, the clinking rims of their glasses, their toast:

To its end, Harry. To its end.

Friday morning, a matrix of frost rimed the bedroom windows. Jekyll stood in a trance as clouds raced across the sun and shadows swung through the room. By dinner, this dreamy calm had dissolved. Jekyll managed to swallow an overboiled Brussels sprout and then ran upstairs to his bathroom and released a burning watery torrent from the bowels. His stomach was rippling as he later paced the cabinet, round and round the laboratory table. By ten o'clock I was growing concerned. Jekyll was trying to draw the clear serum from the phial but the needle tip was wavering and wouldn't punch smoothly through the rubber plug. *Easy, easy,* I soothed, and the needle sank through and sucked the serum into its glass barrel, to the full white line. Jekyll fit a rubber nipple over the tip, then he set the syringe back into its velvet bed. He shut his eyes. His pocket watch ticked its tiny heartbeat.

We had to leave. The plan was to arrive at Luce's no later than eleven o'clock. Jekyll was shaking his head, beginning to breathe strangely. *I can't.* He moaned aloud. *I can't.* I pressed myself forward in the mind, frightened now, but angry and impatient too. We didn't have any choice; there wasn't another way, unless Jekyll wanted simply to surrender, mix up the other injection and trot it along to Luce's to become Carew's laboratory rat. It *had* to be done. Jekyll shook his head faster, moaned again. *I can't.* He panted. *You do it.*

You do it. I didn't waste a second. I yanked him around to E drawer and watched the hands go to work, suddenly competent, pouring the red liquor and tipping in the powder and plunging the hypodermic through the plug. Jekyll stripped. I could almost see our breath as he gripped the chilly tourniquet in his teeth. I teetered on the brink, wheeling my arms, and when the steel slid into the bruise, I leapt into the sickening whipping free fall and hit the body and the floor with a bark.

I sprang to my feet and staggered dead-legged into the table, sending the Erlenmeyer spinning away to the edge — it dropped off and bounced with an improbable *bong.* I laughed. The air tickled my lungs. I laughed harder, scratching my chest and raking my fingers through my hair. From the wardrobe I pulled out my clothes and shuddered at the luscious feel of the fabric, my old familiar costume, its welcoming odour. I took down my pale grey bowler from the high shelf. It had never really felt like *my* hat. But gravely I set it on my head and swiveled it down to the groove of my brow. Last, I removed my stick from the wardrobe, curled my hand around its always warm, willing knob. I stared at my face in the mirror, hairless and gaunt, eyes aglow like sapphires through the shadow of the brim. I plucked up the loaded syringe, dropped it into my overcoat pocket. Then I clattered down the back stairs and plunged onto Castle Street.

The night! It smelt of burning leaves, and the sky was a royal black embedded with scattered stars. Fresh air whisked into my clothes as I stumbled south, slapping the stone wall now and then for the ringing smack of life against my palm. Everything was impossibly vivid. The cobbles under the lamps looked like worn lumps of gold, and the stones in the shadows like greasy pewter. A riotous band of leaves tumbled down the lane and through my legs. We were going to kill a man. Suddenly that seemed incidental, merely an excuse to be outside and alive on such an exquisite evening. I was barely watching where I was going, the mind a rainbow blaze of colour and texture and scent. Only on crossing Regent Street did it register that we had reached St. James's Square, that we still had a job to do. I hurried across the expanse of crunchy frosted grass, fingering the syringe in my pocket and wondering what time it could be. At the far end of the square I darted up King Street and moved under the lee of Luce's gigantic brick house looming to my right. I struck the spears of wrought-iron fence wrapping the mansion's perimetre and turned the corner onto Dury Street.

And there he was. In his tall topper, Carew was striding up the pavement from the other direction, toward the gateposts between us. My momentum carried me a few steps, but when he raised his head and saw me, we both came to a halt. The timing was perfect. I was not surprised. My hand was in my pocket, lightly touching the glass barrel. Carew stood twenty paces away, rigid. He knew it was not Jekyll. He knew my hunched, steaming silhouette. I slipped my fingers through the steel loops and began to approach, showing no urgency or malice, and as he watched me, he slowly lifted a splayed hand like a warning. Mr. Hyde! he called out. Not like before, when he stood above me in triumph. Now the cry broke at the end, which turned it into a question. Mr. Hyde, we had an agreement, Carew cried, Jekyll and I had an agreement! I kept approaching. He seemed shackled to the spot. Hand raised, he glanced at the barren street behind him and then cried out, Jekyll! Jekyll, can you hear me? Are you in there? Control yourself and stop this! I have a gun! His voice was shrill, and he groped with his other hand in his overcoat pocket. His eyes shone like a cat's. I kept coming, in a kind of trance. Carew was tugging frantically at something trapped in his pocket. I have a gun! he shouted again. Don't be a fool, I tell you I'm armed! He looked down at his pocket and then up again, mouth agape, eyes wild and spellbound, as he watched me close the last steps.

A delayed epiphany: *Beware the fool*, I whispered.

The brass cleat of my stick cracked his right ear, pitching him into the fence. He bounced off and staggered but remained upright. In my hand, the oaken stick quivered up the shaft with the ring of his skull. I stared down its wooden sheen, my arm growing weirdly warm, then up at Carew. His legs buckled; he fell to one knee, gripping the fence. I lifted the stick in both hands and as if it were an axe chopped it down on his wrist. With a snap, his hand flew open and he shrieked like a fox, falling onto his back. His hat toppled off and his gorgeous white hair fanned the walk, splashed with a streak of black that dribbled from his ear and along his jawline. He clutched his arm, the hand jutting off at an upsetting angle, the fingers hooked. He rolled his head from side to side. Wait, he said thickly. Wait, please, please wait. A queasy despair seized me — there was so much of him left, so much life still to break. With a groan I raised the stick above my head and shut my eyes. The blow made a hollow *whunk* on his chest and I felt a rib crack like a twig underfoot, a sickly gratifying sensation. I hit him three or four more times in the torso with a wood-chopping swing, then stepped up and punted the ribs he'd left exposed to cover his head with his arms. He rolled onto his side, coughing. I kicked him desperately in the back. How much more? The feel of his frail breakable bones vibrated in my palms like the stick itself was abuzz. Carew was rolling onto his front, clawing at the pavement and scraping his boots. He was trying to get up, I realised with a squeamish thrill. I wound back the stick and then paused,

aghast, watching him writhe like a limbless wretch I'd once seen
worming along in the gutter. Up on one elbow, broken hand dangling, Carew turned a crazed yet comprehending eye to me. The
other eye blinked uncontrollably. His black-matted hair stuck to
his cheek. His mouth opened and closed. A hoarse whine came
out, like something was wrong with his voice box. I looked at my
stick, tapering to its brass cleat, and with dreadful clarity watched
myself take hold of the slimmer end in both hands and wind the
heavy knob over my shoulder like the head of a golf club. Carew
seemed to be trying to say my name. I shut my eyes and swung
for his face — a splintering *crack* and the weight of the stick disappeared as something boomeranged off into the dark and then,
seconds later, clattered to the stones and rolled fast with a rattle
before coming to rest.

I stared at the stick. It had snapped. I held less than half, a
jagged stake. Then I looked down at Carew.

He lay on his back with his head in the street, his limbs
twitching. I stepped up and peered at his face. I almost recoiled,
then forced myself to look. The nose and upper teeth were
crushed in, but the lower teeth were intact and the jaw moved as
he gurgled on the black glistening oil that seemed to well up from
his throat. One eye was punctured, leaking down the cheek.

I tore my gaze up to the street, expecting to see jumping lan-
terns and people running toward me. But there was no one. I
wanted to drop the end of my stick but instead gripped it tighter.
I stepped over Carew's spasming legs to his other side, where the
eye was open and unbroken, examining the sky. There was a dark
fecal odour as I hunkered down and poked his overcoat pocket
with the splintered stake. My hand reached for his pocket and
slipped inside, and I winced, certain I'd find a wriggling mass of
insects in there. Instead I felt a cold heavy thing, and I eased out
the revolver, gleaming like lubricated lead. I hefted it in my palm,
turning the snub barrel around and peering, mesmerised, down

the hole. Then I jerked to my senses and stood up, thrusting the revolver in my own coat pocket.

The stick. I had to find the other half of my stick, it was — it was — I couldn't even think of the word *evidence*. I wheeled around in the middle of the street like a drunk, lunging at stick-shaped shadows between the cobblestones. I pricked up my ears, walleyed, certain I had heard a sound, a snicker of mockery. Yet there was nothing. Carew had stopped kicking and twitching, and I stumbled a few steps toward him. Should I check his pulse? Was there something else I was supposed to do? *Just go!* a voice rang in my head, and I reeled around and pitched off down the lane.

I don't remember the route I took. I don't remember deciding to go back to Ghyll. Only when I drew to a halt across the road from my house, saw it deep in its crevice and framed against the ragged stars, did I realise where I was and what I was supposed to do. They would come looking for me here. They would search the house.

The entrance hall smelt stale, had a hint of putridity, like rotting fruit. I almost expected the floor to be sticky, a tacky layer of slime. I ascended the stairs to my bedroom. Gripping the stake like a knife, I tipped the door open. I stepped inside. It seemed almost exactly as I had left it when I'd gone down to let the inspectors in: the rumpled bed, the verandah doors ajar. I could even see the sheet of newspaper I'd left lying on the floor by the bedpost. Yet I did not trust it. It all seemed too carefully arranged, as if this were not my house but a perfect full-scale replica, down to the last impossible detail. Warily I crossed the room, wondering where to start. At the antique desk with the curlicued legs, I opened the slender letter drawer, regarded the two envelopes stored inside, my tormentor's riddling poems. I ran the drawer shut, opened the larger file drawer next to it, and flinched in surprise.

A big, battered, wood-handled hammer lay inside.

A few thick, mismatching nails rolled alongside it. I blinked, then reached in and lifted out the hammer by the scarred handle. It was very heavy, the huge dented claw and head; I hefted it, mystified. This was not mine. I set it down on the desk and opened the middle file drawer. It was packed with newspapers, like a rubbish bin that had been stamped down by a foot. *Pall Mall Gazettes*. Except I hadn't kept the copies in here, I'd — what *had* I done with them? I slammed the drawer shut and yanked out the bottom one, too hard, ripping it free of the slot and sending it crashing to the floor. Treasure spilt out. Coins, a heavy landslide of them, mixed with crumpled banknotes. I plucked a note out: blue, foreign. The coins rolled unevenly over the floor. I dropped the bill, wiped my hand on my trousers. I turned and swept the room with my eyes, a hysterical giggle bubbling on my lips. To the wardrobe I scurried and flung the doors wide. I plunged in with both hands and pulled out my folded clothes and found myself clutching a brown-paper sack. It made a tinny jingling. I stuffed my hand in and brought out a fistful of rings and trinkets; a silver-link chain dangled from my fingers. I rummaged further, hurling clothes over my shoulder, and emerged with another paper sack, something soft inside. I shook it onto the floor. Coils and tresses of hair tumbled out, of all colours, yellow and chestnut and brown and black, like a motley animal. I backed away in terror. Why did all this seem so nastily familiar? What dream was this? I threw open the sideboard. A large parcel was jammed against the rear. I pulled it out and tore at the butcher's twine and brown paper. A flash of iridescent green inside. An emerald waistcoat. *The* emerald waistcoat. I held it up before me like a fantastic dragon skin. In the wrapping was more clothing, folded as if from the laundry: a loud yellow checkered jacket that looked disturbingly familiar; a nightshirt from which fell a white frilly article. I hooked up this thing with my stake: a pair of girl's drawers stained crimson brown along the under seam.

I surveyed the bedroom in a frenzy of disbelief. Had Carew

really done this? Had his goons planted these things here? I had to get rid of it, as much of it as I could. At the fireplace, I groped inside the filthy hole and tipped open the flue, then I wadded up all the sheets of newspaper that had been crammed into that drawer and struck the ball aflame. As it burned, I crawled under the bed, then ripped off the sheets, and finally found under the mattress a pasteboard-bound ledger, its pages filled with crabbed scribble, crowded with spiders of a familiar spiky scrawl — a demented manifesto. I slapped through it, catching glimpses of its manic snarling sense: *fishhooked the blokes cheeks* and *break it off in the cunt* and *glug glug glug goes it down the hole* and then a whole page filled with nothing but *hide hide hide hide hide hide hide hide hide*, like that letter I had burned. I clapped the ledger shut, wild-eyed, heart hammering. I dashed to the fire and threw the book on the smouldering grate. I tore the satin casing from a pillow, then snatched up the bundle of hair, stuffed it inside, and followed it with the paper sack of rings and trinkets and the parcel of clothing. I thrust the hammer into the pillowcase and then scooped up as much of the pile of pirate's treasure as I could, though many of the coins were oily and impossible to pry up from the floorboards. That fecal stink from Carew was still in my nostrils as I squatted, shovelling coins into my sack, and I could sense that stifled mirth in the air, like I was blundering through some comic burlesque for an unseen, malicious audience. Smoke was seething through the room. I toed the ledger into the back of the grate and threw in my tormentor's letters in their envelopes and slapped at my clothes, my pockets. From the inner lining of my greatcoat, I produced a green leather booklet. My cheque book. I had not used it once, of course. I tossed it on the flame, watched the leather blister and cheques curl.

I gave my ransacked room a final, hopeless survey, then twisted up the pillowcase and hastened down the stairs. Halfway across the entrance hall, however, I stopped, pulsing in the dark. I was not alone. I could feel it along the nape of my neck. I turned, peered into the teeming shadows of the passageway alongside the stairs. I licked my lips. *Mrs. Deaker?* I took a step, and the floorboard creaked an intricate response that made me stiffen. Was she there? *Mrs. Deaker?* I repeated, almost urgently. *You shouldn't stay here, they're going to come, they're going to* — the words dried in my throat. It was not Mrs. Deaker watching from the shadows. It was not anyone.

Mr. Seek? I whispered.

The floor groaned beneath me, as if I were standing on a trapdoor. I shuffled back, putting up my hand. *It's yours. It's all yours.*

I raced south with my satin sack through the deserted streets as light grained the sky. Soon I could smell the river. I crossed a park to Waterloo Bridge, bounded up the steps, and at what felt like the centre I stopped. Eastward the river curved, picking up the paling colour in the sky, bridges strung in fine-spun silhouette across the mountainous pile of translucent clouds on the farthest horizon, the City etched in dove grey against it, spires and domes and threads of spindly smoke. The view shivered, prismatic. I dragged my hand across my eyes and gulped down a sob. Then I swung to the railing and looked at the river below, its shifting obsidian slabs flecked with foam. I hung the weighted satin bag over, let it go. Heart in my throat, I listened a second, two, for the *ploosh!* I hauled the revolver from my pocket, curled my fingers round the grip and trigger, yearning to squeeze, to feel it kick and clap thunder. My fingers tightened, the hammer drew slightly back, and then I opened my hand. Made hardly a splash. From another pocket in the overcoat, I withdrew the syringe, holding it by its steel loops, the ridiculous thing. I pushed my thumb to the plunger and watched the silvery chain of serum arc from its tip. I let it swing from my finger and fall.

Halfway back across the bridge I took off my hat, the pale grey bowler, and flung it in a spinning ellipse over the water. Moments later, I watched it bobbing along the current and under the bridge.

Back in the cabinet I surveyed the mess we had left: E drawer unpacked on the table and the Erlenmeyer flask on the floor, a single Milward box open with its empty indentation. I felt on the verge of euphoric collapse. I had done it. It had gone horribly, horribly wrong, but I had done it. He was dead. We were free. Numbly, I picked at my buttons, dragged off my sticking clothes. I pulled down my trousers and drawers and stared at the filthy streaks down my legs, a blast of stench making me cover my mouth and cough. I had soiled myself. The notion was peculiarly liberating, arousing even. My thing was starting to thicken and stand from its thatch of hair, and I shut my eyes as my knowing fingers closed around it. Soon it seemed that the cabinet was in raging flames all around me. They had set the whole surgery block on fire and were standing in the courtyard with torches, waiting for me to stagger out, gasping for mercy. The heat beat against me, wavering the air, as undulant flames licked the walls. You fools, I thought in rapture, you fools! Let it burn! All of it burn!

Jekyll stepped into the courtyard. Low mist lay over the gravel; it parted as he crunched toward the alleyway leading out to Castle Street. He carried my dirty clothes bundled and tied up in my coat, which he held by the sleeve. The alley ran along the limestone wall and emerged onto Castle Street. Jekyll looked up and down and walked south a little ways. Then, with his whole arm, he spun the bundle around and around as if for a hammer throw and let it go. It flew in a high arc and bounced to the stones, rolled into shadow. Children would find it and untie it, of course. Jekyll brushed his palms together and turned back to the alley.

DAY THREE

Night

What am I meant to feel? Remorse? What does that even mean, *remorse?* That I'm sorry I killed him? I'm not sorry. Killing Carew ruined everything, certainly. But he hadn't left us any choice. Even if I did have it all wrong — how could I have known that? Jekyll saw to it that I knew and understood nothing! *He* was the one who'd cooked up the poison in the first place and then thrust me forth to do the dirty work, knowing I could not possibly use the needle as we'd planned. I was meant to use that stick after all. I had taken it from Big House for the very purpose; a murder weapon can never elude its predestined —

Hush. What was that?

A creak.

Now another creak, from the stairs outside the cabinet door. Footsteps, climbing the wooden staircase. Poole? Where did he come from? Is it dinnertime already? I did not hear him — how can he just appear soundlessly? I stand at the head of the cabinet not three paces from the door. Slow and deliberate as ever, Poole clumps up to the middle step. A silvery *cling* as he sets the dinner tray down. I hold my breath. Silence wells up like water. Now another creaking step, and another — but not downward. He is coming up. He is coming to the door.

I don't move a hair, lest the groaning floorboards give me away.

Poole halts on the other side of the door. Now comes the gentle rap of his knuckle on the wooden frame. Sir? His voice is muffled by the baize-insulated door. I tense my diaphragm against the slightest exhalation. Sir? Dr. Jekyll? Won't you answer me? I shut my eyes. I feel dizzy. I am not prepared for this. I need more time. I can imagine him out there: his crooked fingers raised to knock again, his head cocked as he listens to the skin-crawling void. He knows. Jekyll would answer; Jekyll would say something. Should I try to mimic his voice?

But Poole backs down a step, a crepitating scrape. He retreats another. Now the swivel of his sole as he turns, descends to the bottom. Still, I do not move a muscle, not until his crunching over the gravel courtyard takes him to the conservatory door, which squeaks as he opens and closes it.

How did I not hear all *that*? The squeaky hinge, the stony crunch, the wrench of the surgery door, his footsteps over the theatre boards. How can he just noiselessly appear at the foot of the stairs? Does he know some secret, soundless way into the surgery block?

He must know by now. He knows *someone* is up here — someone who will not respond. He will go to Utterson. Tonight? Christ, the two of them could be pounding again at that door within the hour!

At the press, I pull open E drawer. The glass phial of cyanide lies on its side. I lift it out and hold it, loosely, in my palm. I am not ready for this. I haven't finished yet.

Over an hour has passed, and still nothing.

Perhaps Poole will sleep on it. Cautious Poole. In the morning he will do something, go to Utterson. But tonight is still mine. I cannot waste it. I must keep on.

Jekyll's room, the morning after Carew. Golden seam of light searing through the curtains and dappling the polished bedpost. Jekyll drew his hands from under the covers, inspected the backs of them, touched his face. I almost suspected that it was Friday morning all over again, that we had dreamt the whole demented thing. Jekyll slid from his bed and drew back the curtains, shielding his eyes from the late-morning sun. He pushed open a window, and a crisp breeze bent into the room. A high thin voice was singing somewhere below, rising and falling. Jekyll went into his dressing room and ran cold water into the white basin, examining himself in the shaving glass. He frowned slightly, turned toward his profile. Then he cupped his hands under the stream and bent to splash his face, rubbing the cold water into his gritty cheeks. A flash of pain — he straightened, staring at his palm.

A flap of skin had peeled loose on the pad below the pointer finger. He pried the flap gently back with his other thumb, and Carew rolled up his crazed imploring eye before the stick broke across his face, the weightless, delightful follow-through. Jekyll shuddered, shutting his eyes, and then the singing voice out on the square became suddenly clear: a newsboy calling out the headlines. Murder! he was crying in his pure voice. Murder of an MP! Shocking Murder! MP Murdered!

Downstairs in the dining room, the newspaper was waiting at Jekyll's place, flat and warm as always from Poole's iron. Jekyll made himself sit down and cross his legs before reaching for the paper. The letters were half an inch high and black as his blood had been:

BELOVED MEMBER OF PARLIAMENT
BRUTALLY SLAIN

Last evening, popular Member of Parliament Danvers Xavier Carew, DCL, FRS, GCMG, and Knight of the Realm, was beaten to death outside the house of renowned hypnotist and spiritual adviser Cornelius Luce. The contemptible attack occurred slightly before midnight and was carried out with a stout oaken walking stick, a broken por-

*tion of which was recovered by the police from a nearby gut-
ter this morning. The perpetrator of this foul crime has been
identified by a witness, who had been positioned at a window
in the Luce residence at the time, as one Edward Hyde, who
had called upon Mr. Luce in his home several months before.
Mr. Hyde's connection to Sir Danvers Carew is as yet unde-
termined.*

Jekyll ripped his eyes upward as Poole came in with breakfast. *Have you read this, Poole? Have you seen what they're saying?*
Poole set the plate down, gaze averted. I have, sir. Jekyll shook his
head, speechless. *I — I swear to you, I hadn't the slightest idea Mr.
Hyde was capable* — Poole removed the silver cover and looked at
his master with black, measuring eyes. Sir, I know nothing of this
matter. And neither does anyone in this house. I give you my assurance of that.

He turned to go and Jekyll reached out and took the man's
wrist in his grip. Poole went still. We could nearly feel his pulse
through the twill sleeve. Jekyll squeezed, and released him. Poole
cleared his throat, sketched a bow, and left the dining room.

Up in the cabinet, Jekyll and I pored over the newspaper with
damp, inky hands. I was not surprised to see my name. I had been
expecting to see it in newsprint for months and now here it was,
indisputable at last. Yet so quickly! Who was this witness? Had
Luce himself been watching from a window? Jekyll threw the paper down and plunged about the room, then snatched the pages
up again, as if the words might have changed, metamorphosed
into his own name. At last he collapsed into a chair by the windows. He was not in the clear yet. This was only the beginning.
Utterson would come today; Jekyll would have to deflect him as
well. After a few minutes he jumped up again, went around to the
writing desk, removed some paper from a drawer, and sat down,
flexing his left hand open and shut. He removed Father's fountain

pen from his pocket. Exhaling, he hunched over the desk and began to write with the left hand, an awkward script scratching out
from the nib. *To my Loyal Benefactor, Dr. Henry Jekyll:*

> *For your thousand generosities, I have repaid you most
> poorly. Myself I've proven unworthy of your tutelage and sup-
> port, of the civilised company you wished me to keep. There
> is no civility in me, as I showed the world last night. That my
> deed might besmirch you causes me such pain and disgust I
> cannot bear to see your reproach and disavowal, and so I will
> do the job for you. You needn't worry, I have sure means of
> escape. You shan't ever see me again. Please forgive your un-
> worthy pupil,*
>
> > *Edward Hyde*

It was strange. As with Jekyll's journals, I could gather its
sense but just barely read the scribble, as if he were blurring it or
veiling it from me somehow. The moment he was finished, Jekyll
waved the confession dry and folded it crudely in thirds. He took
an empty envelope from the drawer and carried it to the stove,
struck a match to its edge, and used the flame to light the coals.
He watched the envelope curl and blacken, then stuffed the letter
into his breast pocket and scanned the cabinet. He turned back
the bolt of the cabinet door and sat again by the windows to wait
for Utterson.

He came in the afternoon. Fog lay thick over the courtyard.
We could hear Utterson crunching over the gravel, alone. He
clumped across the theatre and up the stairs and knocked once on
the wooden frame. Jekyll composed his face a final second, then
called out, *It's unlocked, John.* He did not turn as Utterson entered and approached in his clunking boots, did not turn until the
solicitor stood above him, breathing audibly through his nostrils.
Jekyll twisted to show his tortured expression to Utterson — the

solicitor stern, weary, unshaven, lips pressed shut. Jekyll smiled brokenly. *Will you tell me now, John, I told you so?*

No point, Utterson said, is there. I don't need to tell you anything, do I, Harry? *No, you don't. John, listen to me. I have not seen Edward Hyde since you and I last spoke. I had no knowledge of his actions until this morning.* Utterson nodded, as if he'd expected Jekyll to say that. And you have no notion of where he might be, I presume? Jekyll held his sceptical scrutiny, then glanced away at the windows. *I think he is dead. Or will be soon, if he's not already.*

Dead? Utterson repeated. What makes you think so? *This.* Jekyll drew the letter from his breast pocket and offered it between two fingers. Utterson plucked it free. His sinuses whistled as he read. How was this delivered? he asked. *Slipped under the door, down there. The Castle Street door.* And the envelope? *It was blank. I burned it.* Jekyll looked up again, eyes wide and fraught. *It's a suicide note, John.* Or so he wants us to think. Wouldn't that be convenient, if everyone believed he was dead? *Well,* Jekyll said, faltering, *perhaps. I don't know. You may keep it. I leave it to you to decide if it's necessary to share it with the police.*

The police! Utterson said with a derisory laugh. The police do not seem to need much help in this matter, Harry. They have a witness, and they have a murder weapon, or rather two halves of a murder weapon, one half recovered at the scene of the crime and the other half from Mr. Hyde's bedroom. He made the job very easy for them. *His bedroom? How do you know this?* Because I was there, Utterson said. I was there with the police when they found it. And before that, I was at the police station identifying Sir Danvers's corpse. I have seen some things, but that man on the slab was, it was — he was unidentifiable but for the hair. After I had a good look at that, I was shown the murder weapon, the half they'd recovered from the street. And that I recognised at once. Are you aware which walking stick he used? Jekyll shook his head, blanching under Utterson's glare. Damn it, Harry, I gave you that walking stick. Ten years ago, it was a present, when you were made a fellow. Why did he have it? Did you give it to him? *I — I didn't know; he had free rein of the house, he might've taken it from the stand at any time. John, forgive me, but why did the police come to you? Why were you asked to identify the body?*

Utterson clucked his tongue in vexation and glanced away, breathing hard. Because, he said, reaching into his breast pocket and pulling out a folded white envelope. The police found this in Carew's pocket.

He flapped the envelope open in Jekyll's face.

> *Gabriel John Utterson*
> *13 Gaunt Street*

The seam was torn neatly along the top.

Jekyll's mouth had gone dry. Carew had written Utterson a letter. It had been in his pocket. Jekyll slid his eyes up to Utterson's, who was watching his friend's reaction very carefully. Why Carew? Utterson asked. Why did Hyde go after him? *I'm not certain. Jealousy, maybe. He'd always been threatened by my acquaintance with Carew. Hyde had bones to pick with nearly everyone. And he was coming apart, as I told you.* What you told me was that he was being remanded into good care, Utterson said. A hospital in Edinburgh, you led me to believe. *Yes, I know. He was meant to voluntarily commit himself. I put him on a train. I made a mistake. John — what did Carew write to you? Did he mention Hyde by name?*

Utterson kept his cardsharp's gaze on Jekyll another moment, then folded the envelope, slipped it back into his breast pocket. No, he does not mention Hyde by name. He does not mention either of you by name. But your name, Harry, is all over this ghastly business as it is, and if it ever comes to trial, you will be dragged into it without a doubt. Do you really expect me to show Hyde's

supposed suicide note to the police? With your name on it? Of
course you don't; you expect me to stow it away in my safe. You
have already made me an accomplice, an accomplice to crimes of
which I do not know the extent. But not anymore. Do you understand what I'm saying? As far as we are concerned, Mr. Hyde
is dead. We shall not speak of him again, because he shall never
be seen again, by anyone. And if I should learn that this is not the
case, if I should learn that you and he are — in communication,
then you are on your own. You are without my protection. And
I do not think you fully realise how much you depend upon my
protection. This is the end of it, right here. Utterson came forward, extending his hand. Take it, Harry. Jekyll did, in a kind of
awe. Say it, Utterson commanded. This is the end.

This is the end.

That evening Jekyll went out and bought four newspapers and
carried them back to the cabinet. All featured the same drawing
of me, that troglodytic pencil sketch I was to see over and over in
the following weeks: the snarling face of an ape with hairy chops
and gnarled brow and tiny needlelike teeth. They had been busy,
those newspapermen. They knew where I lived. *A decrepit palazzo,* one writer called it, *tucked amidst the dingy back roads of Soho.*
They knew what the police had found in my bedroom, *ransacked
by the villain in a futilely pathetic attempt to erase in an hour the
whole of a sordid career culminating in murder, the primary evidence
of which, the missing half of the shattered walking stick, was left in
plain sight on the floor.* They knew how much money I had in my
Blackhaven bank account, an amount just shy of forty-five hundred pounds, which, they assured the public, was *but a per diem
pittance set aside from the monster's fortune to facilitate his foul pleasures.* And of course they knew about the witness. Not Luce, but
a *servant in Mr. Luce's household.* The maid, I realised at once, the
pretty thing with the green mistrustful glare, who reported that

the victim was merely asking me for directions when I *set upon him like a madman.* Who had instructed her to say that? Was Luce trying to distance himself, deny involvement?

Alongside these diatribes unfurled the eulogies for Sir Danvers Carew. They produced a photograph of him, partly in profile, hair flowing in platinum wings and eyes incandescent. Carew was a *national hero, an impeccable gentleman, a white knight, a champion of progress and science, a crusader against the vile criminality infecting this city. Every hour his killer roams free,* one writer cried, *chalks yet another blackened mark upon the tally of outrages scratched across English virtue and character.* They had a field day, those newspapermen. I imagined a pack of them storming about, a fledgling revolution, shaking farming tools and chanting anti-Hyde slogans. By the second day after the crime, however, some were beginning to suggest that the murder was deliberate. That I had *eliminated the distinguished gentleman not in blind hot rage but in cold-blooded calculation.* They were conducting interviews with my neighbours, my *unwitting associates.* Here was Victor Fleming, proprietor and barkeeper of the Pig and Gibbet public house — old Vic, I realised with a pang of betrayal — calling me a *rightly perturbing character, flashing his tin about and boasting of the pretty polly he'd dossed afore dropping in.* Sometimes, it was said by the *establishment's regular clientele,* I brought my girls in with me and bought them gin, offered them for sale to anyone with *a fiver to spare* and then laughed as if it were a good joke. I was suspected, furthermore, of being a *frequent visitor to the houses of horror so recently brought to light, wherein gentlemen of means may purchase the abducted maidenhood of unfortunate innocents.* It was known, one paper suggested, that before his untimely death, Sir Danvers was investigating on behalf of the LSPYF the claims that a ring of such houses were *operating within the anonymity of Soho.* Was it possible that Carew's murder — or, rather, his *assassination* — was Mr. Hyde's fiendish solution to the problem of his own imminent exposure as a purchaser and purveyor of English maidenhood?

During the days of the Maiden Tribute campaign, there were reported disturbances at the front gates of Mr. Hyde's *palazzo*, and rumours circulated as to what precisely went on in the *dilapidated seventeenth-century manse*. From the street was plucked *a nameless denizen* who said it was commonly known that Edward Hyde kept *a pair of girls at a time, chucking the old ones out when the fresh ones came in*. In agreement was *a mother of six*, who said she tried to stop her nippers running free about the streets, *but if he has his eye on them, who can really stop him, living up there in his castle?* Who could stop him, indeed, the writer cried, when men like Edward Hyde *operated with impunity behind their piles of money*, and Samaritans like Sir Danvers were *executed in cold blood whenever they approached too near the uncomfortable truth?*

It was all happening just as Carew had promised it would, as if his death were the trigger to a complex trap he had rigged. I seemed to watch myself dangling before the masses, with their jeers and poles and rotting vegetables, and my sole consolation was that Mrs. Deaker's voice was not amongst them. I kept waiting to see her name, her denunciations against the master who had practically enslaved her in the house, et cetera. But she had slipped away into the crowd, and I said a private prayer of gratitude every day the old lady remained out of print. The final vanishing act of Eudora Deaker.

Jekyll was more concerned with his own absence from the expanding story. Every day, I knew, he expected to hear the doorbell ring, to find a clamour of reporters on the front stoop, to see his name stamped at last on the newspaper page. Surely some enterprising investigator could sniff out the source of those pounds in my bank account. Surely the story of the Night of the Little Girl would leak out and someone would start poking about the Castle Street door. I waited for it too, tense as a spring wound for a celebratory burst. Not that I wanted Jekyll to be caught, of course. He was my hideout, my sanctuary. Nonetheless, it rankled me to take all the blame, all the jabs and ranting spittle in my face. I didn't care for Jekyll's increasingly exuberant attitude, either, his incredulous relief. He ventured out to the Grampian at the end of that first week, engaged in the usual banter with the barman who served up his soda water, then eased down with a few of the old boys by the fire. They were talking about me. What's your bet, Doctor? Percy asked. Osgood here thinks he's headed for Shanghai, and Bertie said — what was it, Bangalore? My guess is South Africa. What's yours?

They were all merry and red from drink and the hearth. Jekyll looked off, pretending to think. *What about America?* Percy's eyebrows shot up and he nodded approvingly. America, yes, I hadn't thought of that. He'd fit right in with the Yanks, wouldn't he?

Jekyll sipped his soda water, smacking his lips at the fizzle.

The next afternoon, he went up to the cabinet with a valise. One of my suits hung inside the wardrobe, along with a spare overcoat. He went through the pockets, folded the clothes. He found a rumpled shirt in the drawer and folded that too, then packed the articles into the valise. This he carried to a pawnbroker off the Strand. The clothes had belonged to his dead brother, he said, he didn't want to sell them, he just couldn't look at them anymore. Back in the cabinet he removed my chain of keys from the wardrobe drawer. There were three — to Ghyll, to Castle Street, and to the cabinet. Jekyll pocketed the cabinet key and put the two others into a glass dish and poured in a clear, acidic solution. Several hours later, he plucked the keys out with a tweezers, rusted and bitten through. They snapped between his fingers like tinder. The pieces he threw down the rear stairs, and that was that.

I watched him do these things in silence. When I did not react, when I did not think or do anything at all, I found that I could hear the flow of Jekyll's thoughts beyond the tissue-thin membrane far clearer than ever before. It was as if Jekyll had relaxed in his concentration against me, as if he wanted me to know his reasoning, to appreciate that he did not have a choice. Hyde, after all, had become an impossibility. There was no point in keeping the keys or the clothes; it was finished. We had eliminated Carew and gotten away with it. If I had not smashed the man to death, if I had administered the needle like we had planned, then perhaps things would be different, but I couldn't expect Jekyll to let me out into the body again. I did not plan to argue. I did not want the body back. But I wasn't simply going to evaporate within the mind. He would have to let me out eventually. For now, however, it was better for us both to have a calm inconspicuous façade to hide behind until everything simmered down.

Jekyll returned to his fencing club, found his former opponent in the bar, and apologised. He accepted an invitation to a gala at the British Museum. He wrote cheques. Five hundred pounds to the Royal Geographical Society. Five hundred to the LSPYF. Five hundred to the Ladies National Association. Five hundred to the Committee of Investigation into the Deplorable Condition of London's Slums. The last sent Jekyll a letter inviting him to join an excursion into the East End, and a few days later he trooped with a dozen men and ladies out to Whitechapel to inspect lodging houses and tenements and to interrogate the wretches and distribute pamphlets. The company was passing a dripping archway when I spotted a peeling poster of my apish mug slapped to the bricks: WANTED, EDWARD HYDE — 5,000 POUNDS. Alongside Jekyll, a gentleman snorted and said quietly, They could make it a million for all the good it would do. The man must be halfway to the moon by now.

There was a consensus to these stray remarks. No one believed I was still in London. After all, why would I remain when there was a world out there to hide in? Did we have to stay in London? The idea bloomed inside me over the course of that October: leaving the city, escaping England altogether. We could go anywhere! Perhaps not Bangalore or Shanghai . . . but what *about* America? Jekyll had suggested it himself. The New World. Was that not exactly what we needed now, a new world to explore?

I nourished the idea quietly in my cell, for by now I had learned that hectoring Jekyll would not accomplish anything. Ideally, Jekyll should come to the idea as if by his own inspiration. It was Utterson who, inadvertently, provided the catalyst. At the beginning of November he invited Jekyll to dinner at his house, where we found another guest already waiting. Jekyll vaguely knew him, Dr. Church, a spritely old man in tweeds and owlish spectacles who reminded me of someone. Halfway through dinner it struck me: Dr. Pinter. He looked like Dr. Pinter, Father's doctor at Bagclaw Hospital. I remembered the doctor standing on the steps of the massive stone castle as our carriage crunched into the drive; remembered his knuckly grip and sly admiring searching smile. This Dr. Church was speaking of his own hospital, St. Bartholomew's, with that same meekly crafty smile, humbly boasting of the medical college and its interest in developing a department of psychological medicine. Utterson listened, chewing, and when Jekyll caught his gaze, he lifted his eyebrows innocently. Utterson had arranged this, of course. This job offer, or whatever it was. I can imagine, Church was saying in his tweedy voice, you have many demands on your time, Dr. Jekyll; we would not expect anything more than you are able to commit to. Perhaps a short series of lectures to begin with?

I saw Dr. Pinter again, knuckles raised to knock on the door to Father's room. You understand, Pinter said quietly, he does not expect your forgiveness.

After Church had gone, Jekyll and Utterson sat in the study. Jekyll pondered the snapping coals, fingers steepled before his chin. Utterson lounged with his longs legs stretched and ankles crossed, nursing a glass of burgundy. At last he said, Is the offer really so insulting? Jekyll roused himself. *I'm sorry. No, it's not insulting at all. It's quite flattering, in fact.* You might even enjoy it, Utterson suggested. Teaching. Fresh minds to mentor. A new protégé, perhaps ... Jekyll glanced over at his friend, who was frowning into his wineglass. I think, Utterson said, that you should do something, Harry. You have been given an opportunity to make a new start. You should use it.

You should use it. Jekyll mulled the words over on his walk home. A new start. This was true. He had been spared, miraculously. But teaching? Professor Henry Jekyll? The idea had a certain allure, a muted dignity. Yet it was also a kind of retirement. He would be turning fifty-one in January. Was that too old for a new adventure? He was a Jekyll, after all; the line of Jekylls ran back to Nordland, to the Vikings, shipbuilders, explorers, adventurers to the very end, to the flaming pyre set adrift on the sea. Was he not an explorer himself? He had braved the outermost limit and returned home alive, in private victory. Now to teach, to retire, for the rest of his life on this gloomy island, in its safe familiar heart?

In his study Jekyll strolled up to the globe in its wooden stand near the far window. The Earth was slanted on its axis, the landmasses lumpy with mountainous texture in their dun-coloured oceans. He put his hand upon Russia and spun the world with a fast, rattling whir, then stopped it abruptly, his fingers in the middle of the Atlantic. He walked them over to England, and then with his index finger traced a route across the Atlantic Ocean to the twin Americas connected by a tapering umbilical cord, which he crossed at the slenderest point and turned north along that gnarly root up the coast to California.

California. San Francisco, California, on the Pacific Ocean. The city shimmered in our mind, built into the mossy-green hills and bathed in blue haze. I had heard of San Francisco on my travels in the East End; some loony old salt was crooning on about it in the opium berth above mine one night, and as I listened, the city rose from the smoke, impossibly exotic, with its turquoise coast and snaking hills and tramcars clanging, its clapboard bars where men paid for whisky with dirty nuggets of gold. Jekyll tapped his index finger on the spot, the gigantic rounded rump of the United States. I could feel the fantasy starting to spark like fresh coals before they begin to truly burn, their flammable dust dancing and crackling in the air above the flames. I hovered, beating my wings, awaiting the invitation to plunge.

Yet there were practicalities Jekyll had to consider. If we *were* going to immigrate to America, he wasn't going to sever himself from London entirely. He had no intention of selling Big House, for example. But if he closed up the house, what would he do with all the staff? He didn't like the idea of dismissing them, releasing them into other scattered households, where they might gossip, spreading rumour like contagion amongst the serving class. And what about Poole? Obviously, we wouldn't bring Poole with us to America, that would defeat the whole purpose of starting anew. Hypothetically, Jekyll determined, he could put all the staff on paid, indefinite holidays, on retainer, as it were, and as for Poole, perhaps he would be able to stay on at Big House as caretaker, selecting one or two underlings to keep him company.

I listened to these calculations in stifled, torturous anticipation, restraining myself from attempting to influence his decision in any way. He would come around. He didn't want to teach, to waste away in retirement. I tried to soothe myself with fantasies and plans for our life in the New World. We would be wise, this time; we would learn from our mistakes. No big conspicuous house for Mr. Hyde, no servants, no steady dolly, no bank account, and no name. I would be an unofficial phantom in a foreign land with no traceable connection whatsoever to the eminent English doctor. We would not settle down in San Francisco either — we would keep on the move, roving through all that enormous, anonymous country at our wondrous disposal. Jekyll drew from his shelf a coloured atlas and perused the ruggedly geometrical shapes of the states and the territories and read their marvellous names: Oregon, Idaho, Wyoming, Montana. *Montana,* Jekyll whispered, covering the glossy page with his hand, and I conjured a picture of him standing atop a mountain in leather boots with a red kerchief tied round his throat, sunburnt and tousle-haired, surveying the expanse of timbered wilderness.

I could not really imagine Jekyll climbing mountains and camping outdoors and so forth. But the vision tickled his vanity: Jekyll the explorer, the rugged pioneer. And the next morning, he went to the offices of the Cunard Steamship Company and was escorted to a private chamber with paintings of ships displayed around the wood-paneled walls. Jekyll sat down across the desk from a gentleman in pinstripes wearing a monocle. *I've been thinking about America,* he said breezily.

Half an hour later he strolled out, having purchased a first-class ticket aboard the almost brand-new RMS *Umbria,* which would sail from Liverpool on 25 January 1886 and arrive approximately a week later in New York. From New York, the monocled gentleman assured Jekyll, he could travel all the way to the western coast by railroad.

I contained my jubilation, superstitious at the suddenness of it all; 25 January was more than two months away, and Jekyll had arrived at the decision so abruptly that he might just as quickly change his mind. Yet the following afternoon he went to Lobb's and was fitted for a pair of flexible travelling boots. At home he inspected his wardrobe and then paid a visit to his tailor, where he ordered three suits of durable Harris tweed and two paisley waistcoats, one double-breasted and the other a low-slung, five-button affair. He dropped by Louis Vuitton on Oxford Street and ordered a set of cream-canvas flat-topped trunks, a valise, and a carrying satchel with monogrammed buckles and caramel leather straps. At Coutts he spoke with a bank manager about the conversion rate to dollars and liquidity and railroad bonds.

He was actually going to do it. They were tangible commitments to the plan, these accessories, and I watched his preparations with increasing elation. There was only one detail we were both overlooking. It was the most crucial detail, the only one that really mattered. The powder. Jekyll would need to resupply the powder. He would have to bring along all the chemical apparatus and ingredients. Yet it did not even occur to me. I was agitated and overeager, and the powder was never my province — nonetheless, it was at the core of my ability to exist, in London, California, anywhere. How could I have forgotten this? It seems impossible to believe that Jekyll could have forgotten this too. Did he never intend for us to leave? In spite of all his expenditure, did he never expect us to truly escape? Did he know that it was no use resupplying the powder, that any effort to avert our fate was useless?

If he did know, deep beneath his surface thoughts, I could not detect it. I did not want to detect it. I was blissfully lost in my fantasy, my yearning for time to *pass*. Which it did. One night it began to snow outside the latticework windows of the Grampian lounge. Then it was Christmas. Like the year before, Jekyll dressed in his whites and sat down in the dining room with the whole staff at the long table. Silver, candlelight, wine, the works. The mood felt constrained at first. No one seemed to be drinking the wine. When Poole wheeled out the roast, Jekyll stood at the head of the table, took charge of the two-pronged fork and carving knife, and began to dissect the dripping joint, serving the slices onto the plates that were solemnly passed around. When the carving was done, Jekyll remained on his feet and lifted his wineglass.

This has been an unusual year. Both for me and for you, for my life affects each of yours. I hope you do not think I am unaware of that. I have been absent. I have been unwell. And I have made poor choices in the company I keep. Let us say his name. It was my mistake inviting Edward Hyde into this house. I was trying to help him, to introduce him into a warm, stable household such as you all maintain. I misjudged his character, however. We are all perhaps capable of this, but my misjudgement had terrible consequences. Consequences that you have all been asked to overlook, to dismiss from your thoughts. Well, I can tell none of you what to think. All I can do is observe that every one of you has remained in my house, making it a warm and stable home, and for that I am sincerely, humbly grateful. Thank you. And happy Christmas.

Looking across the table, Jekyll met Poole's eyes, shimmering like oil in the candlelight. There was a silence, and the little flames down the line all staggered to one side, as if a door had whooshed shut. For half an instant I thought they would all be snuffed out, a foul omen, as a shadow swooped over the table. Then the flames jerked upright, and Poole lifted his wineglass and said, Happy Christmas, sir, and everyone called the cheery echo: Happy Christmas!

I knew that Jekyll had decided on his birthday party as the occasion to announce his departure. He didn't want his farewell to arouse any suspicion, but neither did he want to explain his plans individually to every person in his life. His birthday presented the perfect opportunity for him to make a gracious speech and then sail away with a unified bon voyage behind him.

On January 8 he was up at dawn, watching the pink light catch in the frosted windowpanes. Fifty-one years old. An exciting number. The start of a second half. Bradshaw was the first to wish him happy birthday. The footman was sitting on the mahogany bench in the main hall buffing Jekyll's black evening slippers with a brush strapped to his hand. He looked up as Jekyll descended the stairs, tipped his copper head, and flashed his roguish, younger-brother smile, shrewd and faintly complicit. Happy birthday, sir, he said, buffing the shoe back and forth.

A load of deliveries for the party arrived at noon. Poole directed them in through the alley from Castle Street and across the courtyard to the servants' door. Jekyll stood in the conservatory watching the men carry crates of wine and butcher-paper-wrapped packages. In the late afternoon he shaved again, combed his silvery hair, then dressed slowly and meticulously, as if for a duel, in the double-breasted paisley waistcoat of emerald and claret, which he paired with a claret bow tie. He drew on his midnight-black tailcoat and posed before the long mirror, one hand idle at his hip, as if a revolver were slung there, a pearl-handled silver Colt. Every American carried a revolver, after all. Perhaps he would grow a curling moustache too. There was a light knock on the bedroom door.

Jekyll stepped from the dressing room and called out, *Come in.* The door inched open, and Lizzie inserted her head with a hesitant *Sir? I'm perfectly decent, Lizzie,* Jekyll said. He touched his lapels and parted his patent-leather slippers. *What do you think, my dear?* She stood half inside the door holding the edge in one hand, wearing an intent, studious expression. She nodded approvingly. Very spruce, sir. Jekyll chuckled. *Spruce. I like that. Was there something else, Lizzie, or did you drop by merely to admire my waistcoat?* She smiled and ducked her head. No, sir, Mr. Poole sent me, sir. Dr. Lanyon's just come.

Lanyon. He was in the parlour by the fire, small and trim and elfin-haired. I hope I'm not too early, he said, I thought I'd have a few minutes of you for myself. Happy birthday, Harry. His faded blue eyes were clear and sober, twinkling as Jekyll shook his firm little hand. His gaze drifted down and he gave a delighted laugh. Look at that waistcoat! he cried. Look at the pair of us! He opened his lapels to reveal his own double-breasted waistcoat of Scotch plaid. *That's a shame, Hastie,* Jekyll said, *because as the man of the hour, I'm going to have to insist you take it off. My waistcoat won't stand for any detraction. Go on, off with it now.* Lanyon sighed resignedly and reached for the top button, then laughed again, and Jekyll clapped his shoulder. *Can I get you something?* he said, moving off toward the sideboard. No, thank you, Lanyon replied. When Jekyll glanced back, he shrugged with shy pride. A new leaf, he said.

They sat together by the fire in silence. Now was the time to tell Lanyon, to say it aloud to someone and make it real: we were going to America. Jekyll's throat was dry. He cleared it, and the doorbell chimed from the entrance hall.

Jekyll and Lanyon stood as Utterson strolled into the parlour, one hand behind his back. Beaten me to the punch, I see, he said to Lanyon. Well, I'll be the second, then. Happy birthday, old friend. An awkward quiet fell amongst the three men, before Jekyll said, *So is that a birthday present behind your back, or are you going to stand around like the crown prince all evening?* Utterson and Lanyon exchanged a glance. A moth fluttered suddenly in our stomach. Utterson cautiously drew from behind his back a long, thin object wrapped in white paper.

Jekyll accepted it with two fingers of each hand, held it balanced like a sword. His heart was thumping in his temples. He peeled off the wrapping and beheld a walking stick: slim and yellowish white, like ivory or bone, with a curve to its tapering length. The handle was hooked and carved into a whale with a wide mouth of teeth and curling waves along its flank. Below the grip was a golden ring, engraved:

> For Harry, for strength and grace
> With love, H and J

It's baleen, Utterson said. Whalebone. Quite strong, but fragile as well. Jekyll nodded. *It's beautiful.* He forced himself to meet Utterson's grave, hangdog gaze, with its wrinkled lift of hope. *Thank you.* He looked at red-faced Lanyon, boyishly pleased and eager. *Thank you both. This is — very considerate.* Another spell of silence. The wrapping on the floor crackled uncertainly.

Poole came around the parlour with a silver tray of whiskies when everyone had arrived. Ten men milling about in their tailcoats, Lanyon's plaid chest flashing like a robin amongst the penguins. Jekyll accepted a whisky. He let the liquor run to his lips and then opened his throat and took the fire down. His eyes watered up, and Father said in our ear, *Good boy, down the hatch.* Soon the sharp, dark edge of it started to bite in, like a superfine film of graphite dust filtering into the room. Everyone else trooped through the archway passage into the dining room, but Jekyll lagged behind to splash a hasty refill into his glass from the decanter. He tipped it back, baring his teeth as Father whispered again into our ear, *Good lad.* Jekyll wiped his eyes and jerked his lapels and strode grandly through the passageway onto the stage.

The silver and crystal rang overbright in the air, every edge aglint. Yet the dining room otherwise seemed too dim, the faces in shadow. Jekyll sat at the centre of the table, Lanyon to his left and Utterson directly across. He couldn't eat the food. The quiver of lobster claw in crème, the pastry topped with a glistening pile of black caviar, like minuscule beetles. But the wine he drank. His head swam. Everyone seemed to be talking at once, at a very loud volume. Jekyll and I sat inside this shell of noise, in the midst of these people we might never see again. Now was the time to speak the words and make it a reality. In two weeks he was sailing away and he could not say if or when he would be back.

Jekyll stood up. The floor teetered alarmingly and wine sloshed in his glass before the room settled right again. Everyone was looking at him, all the faces paused in midconversation. The flood of noise drizzled out to a hanging bead of silence.

Jekyll opened his mouth. He had rehearsed his speech before his dressing room mirror. But now the words seemed distant, submerged. His mouth remained open; the silence gained weight. *Gentlemen,* he said at last. *Good evening. This has been an unusual year.* He stopped, swayed on his feet. *But today I'm fifty-one. A long time to be alive. The human animal lives a long time, compared to most of its lesser cousins. Decades and decades to be filled with activity, now that we've mastered the problem of basic survival. Now we must do things to make it all seem meaningful. But I will tell you something. Something they don't want you to know. There is no meaning. None of this means anything.* Jekyll gestured at the room with his wine, which splashed over the rim. *Do you understand what I'm telling you?* Knuckles dripping, he stared at his guests. A dull blood anger had begun to beat in his face. He let out a bitter laugh. *Of course you don't understand. How could you? What have you people done with your lives, anyhow? What've any of you actually done?* He stopped again. The floor was starting to roll. He shut his eyes and gripped his wineglass as if it would steady him. His other hand found the back of Lanyon's chair. *This isn't what I wanted to say,* he muttered, *I'm getting this all wrong. Forgive me.* Jekyll raised his eyes to Utterson, a doming shadow across the table beyond the leaping candle flames. *Forgive me,* Jekyll said, and sank into his chair.

A long, awful silence. I could hear the candles sucking at the oxygen. Then Utterson said, Hip-hip for Harry, in a toneless voice, and everyone responded in unison: Hurrah.

For dessert, Poole wheeled out a gigantic chocolate cake and served Jekyll a thick black slice. Beneath the table Jekyll was pressing his thumb to the tines of a fork just hard enough not to break the skin. Everyone watched him lift a morsel to his mouth, where it turned to paste. He nodded and tried to smile with it stuck to his teeth. After the meal the company retired to the parlour. But a pall of restless discomfort had fallen over the group. They all accepted snifters of brandy from Poole but none pulled out cigars, and soon they all began to shuffle about, eying each other. Jekyll stood with his elbow resting on the mantel and his back to the mirror in which we had seen a glimpse of our face: redly congested, with that squiggly vessel bulging at the temple. A sneer was moulded to the lips as he glared around the room, blood pounding in his eyeballs. What did it matter if he told them or not, if he never saw these people again? Why should he have to explain himself to *them?*

Percy started the exodus, setting down his snifter and approaching with a tight smile. Happy birthday, then, old boy, he said, not quite meeting Jekyll's eyes. Then everyone was shaking hands and herding into the main hall. Jekyll leant in the parlour doorway watching them go. At last it was just Utterson and Lanyon left standing uncomfortably in the main hall. The slim whalebone walking stick leant against the mahogany bench, and Jekyll nodded his chin at the thing. *Thank you for that, gents, I'll put it to good use.* He pushed off the door frame and crossed the canted floor, offered his hand to Lanyon, who took it with an upward glance of concern. Jekyll clapped Lanyon's shoulder and moved him toward the entrance hall, and Utterson followed. *My old friends*, Jekyll said, *what would I do without my old friends, eh?* He opened the front door and clapped Lanyon's shoulder again, making him almost stumble. Lanyon looked back at Utterson, and gave a compressed, pained little smile before stepping out. Utterson eyed Jekyll from under his shaggy brows, holding his topper by the brim. Perhaps, he said, we overdid it on the Scottish, a trifle. Jekyll shrugged impatiently, still holding the door open. Utterson reached a hand into his overcoat. Harry, he said reluctantly, I have something for you.

From an inner pocket he withdrew a white envelope. This isn't from me, he said, I'm just an intermediary. Between two fingers, the envelope was extended toward us.

I watched it come like a rush of sickness, watched Jekyll's hand rise and accept the envelope. This was not possible. I stared at the spiky scratching of ink across the white face. *Hyde.* A crescendo was rising in the air. I was certain the entrance hall was going to explode. Jekyll looked up at Utterson. He was buttoning his overcoat, glancing down discreetly. I received it yesterday, he said. She asked if I would convey it to you in person.

Jekyll's eyes dropped to the envelope again, and he blinked. It had changed; the line of ink had reconfigured itself. *Henry*, it read now, in elegant feminine script. Jekyll flipped it over, looked at the red drop of sealing wax, then flipped it back to squint at the name: *Henry.* How could —? Utterson was saying something. He caught sight of Jekyll's face and paused, his expression widening in alarm. Harry, goodness, I'm — are you all right? He reached and grasped Jekyll's forearm. I'm sorry; this was foolish of me, I shouldn't have involved myself. Jekyll pulled his arm from Utterson's grip and looked out the open door at Lanyon standing as if miles away on the front stoop, gazing up at the sky, the swarming immensity.

Well, Utterson said. I guess I'll leave you to it, then. Good night, Harry.

Jekyll shut the door and sleepwalked into the parlour, holding the envelope rigidly at his side. Burn it, I was thinking. At the fire he lifted it again, ran his thumb across the line of flowing script. *Henry.* He turned it around and popped the seal and drew out the folded letter.

> *Dear Henry,*
>
> *Happy birthday. I'm sorry to use Mr. Utterson as a messenger like this, but I wanted someone you know to hand this to you, if I could not. I'm a mother now. Her name is Hermione. She has grey eyes and no hair and ten fingers and toes — ten of each, of course. I count them sometimes in disbelief. As I'm writing, this very moment, she is lying on her back staring up at me, quite solemn, grabbing with her chubby fingers at the air. You said that you have never been able to help me, and here is proof that you are wrong. I have a profound certainty of this. You were the deciding difference this time. Seeing you in that restaurant. I'm sure you don't believe in fate, but I do, and that, as you said yourself, is the whole trick. I love you, Henry. That does not require you to do anything or make any response. I just want you to know that I love you.*

The letter swooned in flame and curled on the coals. Jekyll's vision was fractured like cut glass as he turned to stare half blindly at the parlour. Poole stood holding something silver stocked with crystals that winked and stabbed. Sir? he said, stepping forward, and Jekyll cried, *Get away from me, Poole. Get out of here, get away from me!* Poole turned and left the room. Jekyll grabbed for a glass on the low table and slugged the brandy down, then ground the heel of his hand into his eye socket. He careened from the room and across the main hall. He wrenched open the front door and staggered down the steps and into the square.

The fresh icy air sharpened his senses. Jekyll dragged a sleeve across his eyes and smacked himself hard in the face. At the top of the square, he flagged a cab and called up to the driver, *Berkeley Square!* The cab clipped west through the traffic, and we huddled sweating and freezing on the creaking seat. There was a rip in the leather, which his fingers found, and he probed the hole, tearing it wider, twisting the straw stuffing. The cab swung off Piccadilly onto Berkeley, the houses fused together on one side of the park and the barren trees standing on the other. Jekyll hunched at the small window watching the houses roll by, then he punched the canvas ceiling, and the cab crunched to a halt. The white-brick house was tall and narrow, with a green door and pairs of arch-shaped windows on each floor, up to the tiled mansard roof, where chimney stacks released twin spindles of smoke. The windows were filled with gauzy, lemony light. On the second floor, a figure was passing from one frame to the other, pacing back and forth, slowly, dreamily, like a dance. Georgiana. She was pacing with her baby, it seemed, soothing it to sleep. Through the cab window Jekyll mooned up at her, throat thickening with a voluptuous grief. *I love you.* How could that not require any response? From one painted archway to other she strolled, head down, singing that high sweet humming song — God, I could hear it — drifting out of that night, a lifetime ago, when Jeannie had walked beside me back to Ghyll in her raggedy coat and insufficient shoes. The windows blurred into one melting glow, and against it I saw Jeannie place a hand upon her belly and look down and murmur, I have to tell you something. That doll, that naked orphaned thing with a single button for an eye — why did it come back to me now? Jekyll crushed his eyes shut, clutching the cold metal rim of the window. He whipped his head and then punched the canvas roof and called out, *Greek Street! Go!*

He had flayed the whole seat apart by the time we turned off Shaftesbury into the tight bounds of Soho. He hopped down, thrust a banknote at the driver, and set off down the icy crowded lane in his evening shoes. The lamps swam like lights underwater. Everyone seemed to be moving against us, as if we were on the wrong side of the human tide. Jekyll blundered and pushed through the shoulders. At the corner of Old Compton he hooked left and then right at the next crossing and came to the wooden sign on its crooked chains jutting from the brick: a bloated, peeling toad painted half a century ago. He pitched down the rackety stairs into the deafening subterranean lounge. The Toad. Jekyll edged through the crowd in his tails and paisley waistcoat, just another gentleman slummer. *Whisky*, he shouted at the barman. He tipped back the brimming shot, then slammed the glass on the wood plank. Right down there. That was where I had first seen her, my little Jeannie, throwing her head back and laughing as some lucky bloke cupped his mouth and spoke into her ear. Where had she gone? Was I really never going to see her again? The gaping painted mouths around the room all roared out noise, and as we scanned without hope, an obese dolly beside us hacked out a coarse guffaw, baring her throat and wobbling bosom. We stared at the monstrous parody, then reeled from the bar, stumbling through the smoky haze for the stairs.

The Gullet was just down the snaking lane; we plunged through the humid crush toward the back where the ramshackle stairs dove down into the grotto. Jekyll paused on the last step. There too Jeannie had stood, at the bar, one foot curled around the other ankle, gesturing at the barman as he rag-cleaned a glass. *And one more for the lady*. It was the same beefy barman, grizzle bristling from his lardy face. Eyes fishy and measuring as Jekyll approached. What'll it be, then? *I'm looking for a girl*, Jekyll said. *Her name is Jeannie. Red hair, chatty. Have you seen her?* The barman's lips parted, a big dented gold tooth in front. Lotta girls in through here, *sir*. Jekyll pulled off a banknote and slapped it on the tacky plank. I remember Jeannie, the barman allowed, peeling up the note. But I haven't seen that one in ages. Heard she fell in with some, like, unsavoury company and that.

Glancing over the barman's shoulder, we caught our unexpected reflection in the warped mirror: a bulging mass of flesh with eyes goggling on the distended forehead and an octopus mouth. Jekyll backed away.

On the lane outside, yanking at the bow tie noosed around the throat. Clothes plastered to the skin. He leant against a brick wall. Sir! a lady cried in mock alarm. A pair of hefty dollies arm in arm, looking like Siamese twins, both their curly-wigged heads tipped to one side. Sir, you look downright peaky. Don't he, Lorrie? The other nodded. He do, he'll catch his death out here, the poor man. They came closer, and I could smell their perfume and meaty pungency. Sir, why don't you let Lorrie and Dorie take you someplace nice and warm, eh? Each had taken one of Jekyll's arms and were pulling him from the wall. Their mammal smell was making him harden. Jekyll let himself be dragged along a few steps before he jerked his arms away, and the ladies teetered back, off balance. Lorrie clapped a hand to her wig. Fucking poof! she screeched. Fucking cock-sucking poof! Dorie shrieked laughter and grabbed her crotch. Jekyll turned and ran down the lane, skidding in his ballroom shoes onto Greek Street, where a cab was clopping at a trot and nearly bowled him over. Horses stamped and screamed, the driver yelled, and Jekyll threw himself at the door. *Leicester Square!*

He pressed his thighs together, teeth locked in chatter.

His hands were shaking so bad he could barely separate out a banknote when the cab pulled up before Big House, and he dropped his keys on the stoop before managing to crunch the right one into the hole. The entrance hall blasted us with godly warmth, rippling from the log fire. Jekyll ripped off the bow tie and sank to his knees on the flagstones. He stripped off his tails and then his waistcoat, held his hands toward the heat until they stopped trembling. He rose and limped across the main hall, kicking off his shoes as he climbed the carpeted stairs.

In his bathroom he twisted the taps and eased down on the edge of the tub as hot water roared from the swan-necked spigot. The thing still thudded with blood below, pulsing a sick ache into the belly. Jekyll unbuckled his trousers and reluctantly drew back the hem of his drawers. The flesh was almost purple, the sheathing peeled back at the angry knob. Jekyll swallowed and wrapped his fingers round, and Father whispered in our roaring ear, *That's it, boy, go on.* Immediately Jekyll stood, yanked up his trousers, and twisted off the bath. *Plink, plink, plink.*

He strode to the far end of the upstairs corridor, gripping his hands, then he paced back and went down the stairs. The cinders in the parlour were almost dead. He continued into the darkened side parlour and up to the hidden panel in the wall. He pushed the partition until it clicked and dropped open an inch, then he slipped into the servants' pantry. Heart was beating like a rabbit's. Was he letting me loose? He turned left down the narrow corridor. The gas was tuned very low. Shadows ebbed like scampering spiders toward the darkness of the big courtyard door at the far end. Half a dozen smaller doors on either side, behind each one a servant asleep. Jekyll's weight creaked on the wooden floor. A crack of light appeared to the right, five paces ahead.

He froze. The crack widened, and someone peered out. Hello? she whispered. Weak light from the room within touched the side of her face; a braided rope of hair hung below the white nightcap. Sir?

Jekyll pushed her into the room and shut the door. Lizzie's hair was caught in his fingers as he grasped for her face. She was trying to shake loose his grip on her nightdress. She jerked her shoulder free and backed away, crouching. Little box of a room, a desk and a bed and four pulsating walls. Lizzie's fingers were splayed and her eyes wide in the white face, her nightcap askew. No, she was whispering, sir, no, please just wait, sir, please. Jekyll reached out and she stumbled back against the bed. He caught her slender forearm, spun her in a rough pirouette, slipped his arm around her throat. *You little whore*, he breathed into her ear, grinding the thing into her hip. His other hand was fumbling with the buckle, and then the trousers dropped to his ankles. She kept whimpering, Please, sir, not like this, oh God, please wait. Jekyll took the collar of her cotton nightdress and tore it with a gratifying *rrrip*. He pressed her down at the edge of the bed; her knees buckled, and she collapsed onto her belly. Dizzy with urgency, he peeled off her drawers; her slim white buttocks were clamped. He drooled a glob of saliva into his fingers and then felt into her cleft for the seam. I watched him work in his thumb and smear her petals apart as Father had taught us. By the hair, Father had held us tight, a haze of whisky in our ear whispering what to do, Jekyll obediently fitting the bell of his thing into her seam and beginning to push. It was like Father was here in the room behind us, his fingers twisting our hair from our scalp, his goading whisper on our cheek. *That's it, boy, all the way in, now, to the hilt.* Jekyll shut his eyes and turned his head aside and suddenly groaned out, *Hide!* The spasming began, a bucking from the core as the grip on our hair tightened in climax and then gradually, almost tenderly, released, his fingers fading like a ghost's.

Trying to stand up, Jekyll staggered into the bedside table and knocked something off. He put a hand to the wall until the floor stopped rocking. He pulled up his trousers and tucked in his shirt, averting his eyes from the girl on the bed. At the door he stopped. His face burned with a kind of boyish pride. He turned and looked back at her, sitting in the bed's corner, hugging her knees and staring at the wall. Her face was hard and pale as bone.

Thank you, he said.

He stood in the servants' corridor as if he did not remember where he was. This was his house, this bare dingy hallway? Where was everyone? Why were they not crowded in the doorways? He returned to the pantry and pushed through the partition into the side parlour, where a portrait of a wigged gentleman in riding breeches gazed tranquilly down in the gloom. Upstairs, Jekyll peeled back the covers and climbed in his clothes into bed.

We were lying on the dissecting table in the surgery again. Except this time it was us alone, operating on our own torso. Head lifted and fingers probing the slimy piles of our intestines, searching for something, like a tumour, to cut out. A cure.

We woke together: pink light in the windowpanes, like the morning before. And like before, it seemed that maybe the evening had been just a dream, and it was 8 January, Jekyll's birthday, all over again. From beneath the covers, Jekyll withdrew his hands, shapely and white and stained, the right one with a brownish smudge in the fork between his thumb and finger. He brought the hand to his face, sniffed, and caught the metallic trace of her. He flung the covers back and yanked his tucked-in shirt from the trousers, expecting to see it caked in blood. There was just a splotch down the shirttails that flaked like rust when he rubbed it. Not a dream.

From the window we looked down on the square, everything — trees, ground, pavement — frosted in a frail lamina of pink snow. Jekyll pulled on his overcoat and stamped into a pair of boots, and a minute later he was striding north along the square in the pure sharp morning air, bareheaded, collar unfastened, blowing out plumes of breath. Each fresh step left a perfect print in the gritty crunch of hoarfrost. On the main road, the early cabs had cut twin lines into the pink, veering and intersecting and pocked with the clop of hooves. We passed a horse pulled up to the kerb who lifted his tail and ejected a pile of green droppings that steamed like hot food. As we neared, a clutch of pigeons pecking at the ground took off in explosive unison, banking together over the rooflines where the sky was turning from coral to palest blue. Soon men started blooming from the Underground, and little boys appeared on the corners selling hot chestnuts wrapped in newspaper. Jekyll walked and walked, bringing a film of sweat to the skin that cooled instantly around the ears and throat. We were heading north. On a street lined with white stone houses, he came to a path that led to a gated enclosure of barren trees. Jekyll opened the gate door and strolled down the gravel aisle, hemmed on both sides with hedges. Mist clung to the ground, making phantoms of the trees and the equestrian statue rearing in triumph ahead. At a black slatted bench, Jekyll sat down.

The trees dripped as the sun burned through. We sat listening to the pattering of droplets. Inside Jekyll's trousers the thing was thickening as in our mind Lizzie whimpered into the bedding. Why hadn't she screamed? Why hadn't anyone stopped him? How could Jekyll be sitting here in this park, and I inside him, on this flawless morning? Jekyll removed the hand from his pocket and again pressed the palm to his face, and I could smell her too, as if it were my own hand. How simple it had been! All this time, convinced of his impotence. All the trouble he'd taken to hide inside while I discharged his desire.

He tipped back his head and gaped at the sky through the interwoven branches. We could hear birds scattered in the trees chattering like old friends returned from long travels apart. The oblivious birds. What did they care about us? What did it matter to them what we had done? Our adventures meant no more to them than their little adventures meant to us. It did not matter what we had done. It dawned, this cautious, glorious revelation. There was no curse, no plot to destroy us. There was only the chaos of the world. And the world did not care. The world didn't care! The branches overhead shook with a squirrel and shivered down drops of silver sunlight. One struck our brow with a cold miraculous *plop*. Then the black gnarled branches all flashed white as lightning forked against the greenish sky. The earth lurched around in a roll to flip us upside down. Ecstatic with terror, we gripped the slats of the bench to keep from dropping and smashing through the tree limbs into the ocean of outer space. Blood filled our head and we groaned in the suction of gravity, and then everything flipped upright again.

Stars and dazzles danced in the eyes. I clutched the bench for life. The gorge of sickness went down in my throat, and the park shimmered into place. In a flood of relief, I clasped myself, panting laughter. Then I stopped, and looked down at my hand.

My hand.

I could feel the air passing over the fine hairs. The cricking in the joints as I flexed and relaxed. I watched the action in wonder, then looked up, heart booming. It had happened again. I was back in the body. Jekyll was paralysed, a block of ice behind my sternum. I glanced up the path and saw with a jolt two men ambling down the path toward me. I jumped to my feet, flipped up the collar of Jekyll's overcoat, and scurried the other way, toward the statue.

I had forgotten how huge and unwieldy Jekyll's clothes felt. His trouser cuffs scuffed the ground as I hurried along, and his overcoat banged against the backs of my ankles. I turned the collar up to cover my face as I swept through a gateway at the far end and emerged onto a mirror street of white stone houses. A cab was clipping up toward me, and I turned away as it rattled by. My mind felt like rats in a sack. I had to slow it down, I had to *think*. I was nowhere near Big House. I couldn't knock on Big House's front door anyway; I was a wanted murderer. And Jekyll had destroyed my key to the Castle Street door, and his own key ring for some reason was not in his roomy pockets. I had to get off the street. At the next corner I peered around for a sign, then found a tile embedded in the brick: Howland Street. Howland, Howland — did this sound familiar? I reached inward for Jekyll, to draw him into the moment. *Pay attention; where could we go?* Another cab was clopping up toward me, and then with a leap of epiphany I hailed it and flung myself inside.

It was an open two-seat affair with the driver in front. He turned, his skin pitted with pimples. *Donne Hotel.* I panted. *You know it?* The ugly gnome just glimmed at me. I had to control the urge to lean back and kick him into action. *Donne Hotel,* I said again through my teeth, *do you know it?* His lashless eyes slid down to my clothes and then back to my twitching face; then he turned around and flicked the reins. I gripped my hands into a shaking lump. Was it possible he had recognised me? Did I really look like that grinning baboon on the posters? I scanned the passing street, poised to spring down at the slightest hint of suspicion. When he stopped a minute later I almost pounced from the cab, certain the bastard was up to something — but then I glanced at the crimson awning with the words in white across it: Donne Hotel.

The name seemed vaguely familiar, and so did the garishly decrepit lobby when I pushed my way in. A chandelier at a crooked angle. The walls papered in stripy crimson silk and peeling near the top, bloated. It smelt like fried food. Why would Jekyll know this place? At the front desk, a man was sprawled on his arm, asleep. I approached and smacked the brass bell beside the man's elbow. He jerked awake with a snort. He was just a boy, dusky and dark-eyed, with a crop of cowlicked black hair and wearing an oversize maroon jacket. *I want a room.* He tipped his head to one side and his neck gave a *crack.* I snapped my fingers. *A room, oi, let's go.* I hit the bell again. *Speak English? English? We're in England, yes?* Then a woman stepped through the doorway behind him, toadish and squat with a ripe mole budding within her left nostril. Christ, who were these people? Yes, how may we help?

she said, heavy Slav in her manly voice. A room you would like, my sir? *A room, yes.* She pruned her lightly moustachioed upper lip. Just you? I gave an exasperated sigh, spread my hands. Then I said, out of nowhere, *One with a writing desk.*

She laboured ahead of me on the stairs. The fusty odour of her underclothes wafted back at me as we clomped up like some appalling quadruped. At a door on the second floor, at the end of a deserted corridor, she worked a key into a lock. Once the door opened, I stepped past her into a sitting room.

Jaundiced wallpaper, cheap wingbacks by the poky fireplace, two muslin-draped windows brimming with daylight. Again I was struck by a weird familiarity. Without turning round I said, *This will do.* But Madame Toad stood wheezing in the doorway behind me. I glanced over my shoulder, despising her with a sudden passion, and she said, My sir, you will please to leave deposit, for the room? I slapped at Jekyll's clothes for his billfold, snapped out a banknote, and handed it over with my face twisted away. She pointed at a bell rope by the fireplace, pantomimed yanking at it. If anything you should need, my sir. Then I was finally alone.

The windows looked down on Portland Street. Tobacconist, jeweller, cheese shop, pedestrians and cabs, a mass of droppings stamped and spread about in the road. I turned back to the room. I could feel Jekyll absorbing its details. Georgiana. He had been here with Georgiana, once, many years ago. I laid a hand on the wingback and caught a sudden vision of her standing here by the chair, young and bright with a pained, puzzled smile. A white door stood at each end of the main room. I crossed to one and opened it, expecting the bedroom. It was an empty closet, with a yellowed lacy dress hanging alone from the bar. The bedroom was behind the opposite door, dwarfed by a monster of a canopied bed that no one had slept in for months, it seemed. I shut the door, shook my head quickly. We needed a plan! I narrowed my eyes at the writing desk near the fireplace.

An antique, with slender curling legs, rather like the traitorous one from my bedroom at Ghyll, which I did not want to think about. But I had asked for a writing desk for a reason. If I couldn't get into the cabinet myself, then I had to have someone transport the contents of E drawer to me. Someone had to bring it here. Or if not here, then somewhere I could access. So whom could we trust? Poole? Poole might be persuaded to bring the chemicals to us here at the hotel, but he wasn't going to simply drop them off outside the door. He would insist on seeing Jekyll, on speaking to him, at least. The same went for Utterson. Neither of them would simply play delivery boy and then retreat. We needed someone trustworthy and loyal and yet innocent of Jekyll's connection to me, to Hyde —

Lanyon, of course. Lanyon had never seen my face, never heard Jekyll mention my name. And Lanyon lived on Cavendish Square, not a mile from here. Lanyon could get the chemicals from the cabinet and bring them to his home, where I could retrieve them at nightfall.

But that was the easy part. I would have to write to him, and to Poole, explaining everything in exact detail, and I would have to do it in Jekyll's hand. I had never written anything with the right hand, in Jekyll's flourishy style, unless one counted the signature I had signed on that blasted cheque a lifetime ago. I slipped my hand into Jekyll's baggy pocket and felt the polished weight of Father's fountain pen. I drew it out, the lethal implement. Dark red mahogany with a brass ring and a clip on the rounded cap. It was a more modern, expensive kind of pen than the one Father had trained us with, binding my right arm tight to my body and leaving my left hand free. *The hand of art*, Father would explain. The pen he had inserted into my fingers then was longer and lighter, with a spade-shaped blackened nib that squeaked and scratched at the paper as I contorted my tongue in Father's watching shadow.

I dragged the chair from the desk, threw off Jekyll's overcoat, set the pen on the blotter, and pulled open the top drawer. Three sheets of foolscap paper, a few unmatching envelopes. I squared a page on the blotter. My temples were thumping. I shut my eyes. I would need Jekyll closer than ever, in the body with me, the right arm, the right hand. His hand. The fingers moved, reached for the pen and picked it up. I cuffed up the hanging sleeve, and glanced at the ticking clock on the mantel: 9:15.

The arm was glowing warm with his guidance, and the instant the nib touched the paper, it started scribbling away, seemingly of its own volition. We wrote to Poole first, to set the plan straight. Everything would have been easier if I'd had Jekyll's keys — we could have sent them with the letter. But I didn't have his keys. So Poole was to find a skilled locksmith and wait for Lanyon. The locksmith would pick the cabinet lock and then the lock on the glazed press. Lanyon would remove E drawer and be permitted to carry it away. That was all Poole needed to know. A short letter, but I was drenched in sweat by the end, a suffocating sensation in my chest at the strain of concentration. I examined the damp paper, impressed. It was Jekyll's penmanship, all right. Slightly frantic, but maybe that was good. Our letter to Lanyon would have to be longer, however, to make certain he did everything right. I slumped in the chair. I needed a drink.

In the bedroom, half a decanter of ruby liquid stood on the bedside table. It smelt sour. I took a glugging slug and gasped at the rancid burn. I carried it to the desk and sat down again.

It was nearly eleven when we finished. I sat trembling, right arm sprawled dead on the desk, a tremour in the thumb. The decanter was drained, and some minuscule flies hovered over the lip, imbibing its fumes. The two remaining sheets of paper had been filled with flowing scrawl, dented and smudged and torn where the nib had jerked from my control. But on the whole, it was a masterpiece.

Dear Lanyon,

You are one of my oldest friends; and although we may have differed at times on scientific questions, I cannot remember, at least on my side, any break in our affection. There was never a day when, if you had said to me, Harry, my life, my honour, my reason, depend upon you, I would not have sacrificed my left hand to help you. Lanyon, my life, my honour, my reason, are all at your mercy; if you fail me to-night, I am lost. You might suppose, after this preface, that I am going to ask you for something dishonourable to grant. Judge for yourself.

Bring this letter, I told him, and go to Big House, where Poole would be waiting with a locksmith. Break into the cabinet and the glazed press and remove E drawer, *with all its contents as they stand. Letter E,* I emphasised, *on the left hand, the fourth drawer from the top or (which is the same thing) the third from the bottom. This drawer I beg of you to carry back with you to Cavendish Square exactly as it stands.* There he would wait alone in his consulting room. *At midnight, then, I have to ask you to be alone in your consulting room, to admit with your own hand into the house a man who will present himself in my name, and to place in his hands the drawer that you will have brought with you from my cabinet. Five minutes afterwards, if you insist upon an explanation, you will have understood that these arrangements are of capital importance; and that by the neglect of one of them, fantastic as they must appear, you might have charged your conscience with my death or the shipwreck of my reason.*

Think of me, I implored him at the end, *at this hour, in a strange place, labouring under a blackness of distress that no fancy can exaggerate, and yet well aware that, if you will but punctually serve me, my troubles will roll away like a story that is told. Serve me, my dear Lanyon, and save*

Your friend, H.J.

I read it through as the ink dried. *Save me.* Lanyon, our saviour. I laughed, and it broke out like a sob. I rooted in the drawer again and pulled out two envelopes, addressed the first to Big House and the second to Cavendish Square. Then I stood up — too quickly, swooning a second — and lurched to the bell rope.

The boy stood in the corridor in his drooping maroon jacket, mooning at me with somnolent, yet observant eyes. I held the envelopes in his face. *I want these posted, and I want them registered. You know what that means,* registered? He gave a nodding drop of his head. I flicked a sovereign at him and he caught it. Then I showed him another, fat and gold. *For the receipt. Hop along, now.*

An hour later he returned, and by that time I was in a near hysteria, convinced that he had gone for the police. I opened the door a crack, then forced myself to draw it wider like a normal person with nothing to hide. He was holding the postal receipt. I flicked him the other quid and shut the door and immediately regretted not having asked for something more to drink. I was cold. Jekyll's shirt clung to my skin. I knelt before the fireplace and soon had the coals sparking, then I dragged a wingback over and huddled before the warmth.

I could see I had the whole looming day with nothing to do but wait. The clock on the mantel was ticking its mechanical heart out, and I had to tamp down the urge to hurl it out the window. What was happening to us? We had just been sitting there on that bench, gloating because the world did not care about what Jekyll or I had done, and right then we'd been struck as if by a bolt of lightning. It almost seemed like a kind of retribution for our presumption in imagining there was no plot against us. As if someone had *heard* our thoughts. As if someone had been listening inside our head. Biding his time, waiting for the perfect opportunity to strike, to begin again his tormenting games. Hide and Seek, Hide and Seek, *you be hide and I play seek.*

I felt like a red-eyed rat in a maze, furtive, persecuted, my right paw twitching. I held up the hand, staring at the tapping

nerve beneath the skin. Those letters I had just written. That Jekyll had written. How had we done that, exactly? Jekyll had written those letters *through* my hand. As if he had reached through
the membrane between us and into the right arm. That membrane was evidently more permeable than we had thought. This
was the second time I had pitched through it and into the body
without the aid of the needle. And what about those lapses, those
unaccountable spells of blankness? Hadn't that been Jekyll, reaching through me into the body? In which case, was the needle absolutely necessary to switch back and forth? Could we do it on
our own, like Emile Verlaine?

Jekyll was hardly listening. As I expanded in the mind toward
him, imploring, I found myself tumbling into an open tunnel of
memory, over a decade in the past. I was looking into this room,
or its nearly identical double: the windows suffused with mus-
lin-filtered sunlight, Georgiana moving slowly toward them. She
wore a summery yellow dress and a wide-brimmed white sun-
hat, which she was unfastening from her hair. Then, bareheaded,
she turned and gave a small, nervous smile. This liaison had not
been planned. They had been strolling down the street from the
park and seen the crimson hotel awning and, as if obeying a grave,
compulsory pact, they had pushed into the lobby together. Now
Jekyll watched her, his innards constricting. To the right stood
the open, darkened doorway of the bedroom. Henry, Georgiana
said, you are pale. She stepped toward him. He felt pale. Drained.
He made himself move forward, a numbed somnambulant, until he had almost reached her, and could smell her sweet, somehow antiseptic scent. Her face tilted up, nostrils flared, the sharp
blue eyes alive with fright and that same reckless excitement I had
seen in Jeannie's eyes on our first night together. Jekyll raised his
hand, intending to take her chin with the crook of his finger as
he'd seen a man do in a French painting. Yet his finger stopped,
as if held back by some form of inverse magnetism. Her thin lips
were pressed together and looked dry. It seemed suddenly impos-

sible that he could ever kiss them, those finely shaped, sterile lips. He could not even touch her, let alone lead her into that darkened bedroom. He had known the moment he entered the lobby that it was a mistake, impossible. Between his legs, the flesh was inert. He could feel its absolute lack of response. He had willed himself this way, desireless and thus invulnerable, triumphant over failure, over Father and his lessons. But he was starting to feel suffocated by her proximity. Her lips moved, inviting. He lowered his hand and stepped past her, toward the windows, freedom. Pushing the muslin aside, he peered down onto the street, wishing he could evaporate into the air. His face was cold and hot, and frustration choked in his throat. *I can't,* he said to the window. *I'm sorry, I can't.*

He turned and found her standing a few steps closer, by the wingback chair. *Why can't you?* she asked, soft, yet insistent. *You can tell me, Henry, it's all right.* He shook his head. *I'm not,* he struggled, *I'm not like other men. I'm not — whole. My father . . .* That spark of recklessness still shone in her eyes, yet her brow was creased with concern, as if he had only minutes to live. *Henry,* she said gently, very close now. *What did he do to you?* Her hand was rising, and with a spasm, Jekyll jerked from her touch —

I blinked as the memory popped. I was alone in the sitting room, in the wingback. My ears were on fire with Jekyll's rage. I hadn't been meant to see that.

You simpleton, he hissed. *You fool. Is the needle necessary? Do you really think I could emerge out of you, like a mushroom from shit? Are you so revoltingly stupid?*

His rebuke stung my cheeks. So he had been listening after all. But it was not my fault I had seen this particular memory; *he* had been the one reminiscing, the one to bring us to this nearly defunct hotel out of his precious, protected past! The coals seethed and snapped, and a red-hot chunk dislodged itself with a rattle and tumbled out of the grate. It lay smoking on the hearth rug, dying from orange to an ashen black, and without thinking

I bent down and with my right hand picked it up. It felt cold at first, then a second later white-hot. I held the amplifying pain, counting one, two, three, before tossing the coal back on the pile. My thumb and first two fingers were blistering already. Inside I could sense Jekyll's shock as we stared at the raw shiny finger pads. With a grimace of satisfaction I stood up and stalked to the windows.

Daylight was draining from the sky. The lamps along the far side of the street were already lit. In an hour, it would be fully dark, and I could quit this miserable room. I yanked the bell rope, and when Madame Toad knocked, I told her I wanted dinner and drink. She carried it up not long after, whipped a spotted table-cloth over the writing desk, and set down the tray, perspiration on her fluffy moustache. I had a banknote ready, to get rid of her, and she gave me a pale-gummed smile. My sir, she announced, it is to our very great honour we have you stay, a gentleman as such as you. I shooed her out and fell on the food. Meat stew with cream, a leg of chicken, a pastry dumpling, and even a slice of apple cake for dessert. I bolted it down, guzzling from the bottle of acerbic hock.

It was by now full dark. I threw on Jekyll's overcoat and scanned the sitting room, then crept down the corridor and the stairs to the empty lobby, my stomach sloshing. I pushed through the front door into the delectably fresh night air. The lamps sparkled out lunar haloes against the velvety blueness. People strolled in pairs along the pavement, their arms linked. I kept my face buried in the overcoat collar, clutching my blistered fist in my pocket like an amulet. I peeled off the main road into the emptier side streets, where I shuffled back and forth, up and down, killing time.

I kept waiting for a church bell somewhere to toll the hour. At last I found a giant iron street clock on Regent with hands like the nibs on Father's fountain pen, and with a jolt I saw it was after eleven thirty. Cavendish Square was only two blocks west, a

square of barren trees and earth bounded on four sides by graceful buildings, scattered with yellow-lit windows. Lanyon's was on
the northwest side. I cut through the park to the far end, where
I crouched in the shadows, looking at the slim six-storey brown-
brick house with the gateposts and twin blazing lamps. Jekyll had
not been here in some time. At the sight of Lanyon's home, we
felt a burn of guilty nostalgia biting into our heart. I slunk across
the street. A brass plaque was embedded in the gatepost: *Hasting
Lanyon, MD, DCL. Consulting Room Directly Ahead.* A flagstone
path led to the white-pillared portico and the red door with brass
fittings and a rose-glowing lamp, grown all around with deadened
ivy vines.

There was something sweet and pathetically innocent in this
little professional setup, this little life of Lanyon's that we were
about to tip over the edge. I approached the door, raised my fist
to knock. Just then, a distant bell began to dong, dong, dong. I remained motionless, fist lifted. I could feel Lanyon on the other
side, lips quivering, counting the knells until midnight. When the
twelfth one echoed away, I stood another moment, poised on the
brink. Then I rapped on the door.

Lanyon wrenched it open at once. His face was purplish and his
eyes swimming. When he saw me, his brow crumpled and his
mouth flew open as if he were about to cry out something, but it
died in his throat. He stank of whisky. *Lanyon,* I said sharply, *have
you got it? Did you get the drawer?* He couldn't seem to answer. He
could only inspect my face, my clothes. I leant in and grasped him
by the upper arm. *Lanyon, tell me you have the drawer!*

He swayed a step back and shrugged off my hand. Excuse
me, he said blearily, I — I don't believe I know you. I held up
the offending hand. *I come for Dr. Jekyll. May I enter?* The re-
quest came out loaded with sarcastically elaborate politeness.
Poor Lanyon stared at me through his boozy haze. It would have
started with a rationalisation, just a small whisky, to steady his

nerves, and then . . . Lanyon drew back, and I stepped into the consulting room. Spacious, comfortable, with a cosily low ceiling. The walls were striped emerald silk, the desk and cabinets and bookshelves dark walnut, the floorboards worn and varnished. A white fur rug lay before the flickering fire near a curvaceous leather sofa. I did not see the drawer anywhere. Lanyon was leaning against the door, one hand thrust into his black smoking jacket pocket, and I wondered if he too could possibly have a gun. Without taking his eyes off me, he sidled to his desk and felt for the chair. He waved vaguely at the two emerald chairs across the desk. I clenched my jaw and forced myself to sit. In the shaded lamplight I could see the broken veins in his cheeks and nostrils, a white crust along his jawline. The tips of his ears were translucent crimson. I tried to grin. *Dr. Lanyon, let's not be coy. As you know, I've been sent here by Dr. Jekyll. There was a drawer you were to retrieve, I understand. A drawer, from the press in his cabinet — did you get the bloody thing or not?* My voice quavered. Lanyon's eyes fell to his fingertips, which he had arranged on the edge of his desk. He lifted his left hand. It's there, he said.

I spun to examine the bookshelves, the cabinets, the small laboratory table — and then I saw the white drop cloth on the floor under the table. I sprang to it, giddy with the sick thud of my pulse. I hunkered down and drew the sheet away. The drawer, with the stoppered powder bottle and the flask of red liquor and the Milward box and the black rubber tourniquet. It was all here. We were all right. Carefully I lifted the drawer and set it on the laboratory table. Lanyon was watching me with hooded curiosity, like a beaten dog looking on from its corner. *A glass,* I heard myself say, *I need a graduated glass.* He nodded at the cabinets behind me, and I took down the one we needed. My hands felt very deft all the sudden; Jekyll was in them now. I poured the red liquor into the glass to the third bold line, popped open the stoppered bottle, and scooped out the last dose of the powder with the silver spoon. This I tipped into the liquor, which frothed and bubbled to royal violet and then fizzled out to the pale transparent green. Yet as the reaction settled to its proper colour, I felt an unexpected pang of loss. I was going back inside, and I did not know when I'd be coming out again. No time to savour the moment, however; the hands were already removing a syringe from the Milward box. I tilted the graduated glass and dipped the needle in and drew the plunger out with my thumb, sucking up the serum to the three-quarter line.

Lanyon was still watching, transfixed, mouth open. I held up the syringe by its steel loops. *This is what I came for. You've done your bit, Lanyon. Now the choice is yours. Do I take my things and leave, or do I stay and show you the end of it?* My voice sounded distant now, as if my ears were plugged with blood. Lanyon was nodding, helplessly. His lips moved; he swallowed. Go on. I will see it to the end.

I threw off Jekyll's overcoat. Rolled up the left sleeve and wrapped the rubber tubing around the biceps, yanked it tight with my teeth. Lanyon was staring at my arm. *Hastie*, I said, and his watery eyes jerked to mine. *You deny everything you cannot see. And your sight is so very narrow. But no more blinders now, old friend.*

Down on the floor, sprawled against the cabinets. The needle was still inserted into the arm. Groggily, Jekyll drew it out, opened and closed the left hand. He groped for the table and hauled himself to his feet.

Lanyon was pressed to the wall, covering his mouth with one hand. His glossy eyes trembled; he shook his head back and forth. Oh God, he sputtered, oh God, Harry, it is you — it is you! That was you?

Jekyll tossed the tourniquet back in the drawer, where it coiled up like an obedient snake. His head was crashing; I squinted out through his wince. *Yes, Hastie, it's me.* I thought it was you! Lanyon cried in a kind of wretched triumph. I thought it the moment

I opened the door! But what — what have you done to yourself? Harry, what've you been doing to yourself?

Jekyll edged toward the chair where I'd been sitting. *Sit down, Hastie. Let us sit.* Lanyon reached for his leather chair and shuffled into it like an invalid, and Jekyll sank down as well. *You should have a drink,* he said, almost tenderly. Lanyon's expression hardened into a beady, defiant glare. He glanced down, breathing through his nose. Then he yanked open a desk drawer and pulled out a whisky bottle and a glass and thumped them on the blotter. Have a drink, he muttered, splashing into his glass. Six months, I'll have you know, Harry. Six bloody months until today I'd been without a drop. A new leaf, remember? He scowled at the brimming glass, then slugged half of it down and showed his neat white teeth. So that was Mr. Hyde, was it? That was Mr. Hyde knocked on my door?

Jekyll blinked, surprised. Lanyon lifted a tearing baleful eye. D'you think I'm a child, Harry? That I'm a child sitting obliviously by while the big people talk? That's why you wrote me, isn't it, and not John, because you think I don't know anything. You thought I'd just do as you asked, none the wiser, is that it? Well?

More or less.

Lanyon slumped back in his seat with satisfaction. That's what you've been shooting in your arm, then? That — that junk? How does it work? You shoot that junk into your arm and what — you become this, this other person? This Mr. Hyde? *Yes,* Jekyll said, *that's how it works. Except I don't really become him. I am him.* You are him, Lanyon repeated. I've known you all my life and I've never seen you — act like that, talk like that. It was like — someone else, someone deformed, and horrible. *Yet he is me,* Jekyll said. *I created him, from my own mind. A long time ago, when I was a boy, I needed him. I needed someone to protect me, and so I created him inside my head.* That isn't — Lanyon began, and paused. Possible? *It's very possible, Hastie. The conditions must be right. There must be a powerful need. But where there is need, and the urgency to survive, anything is possible. I have told you this before. It is nature. When threatened, we either die or evolve. I evolved.*

Lanyon shook his head incredulously. Nature? You're going to make this about evolution? That old rubbish? That's your explanation? So your father beat you, Harry, is that it? You think my father didn't beat me? You think you're the only one with a bastard for an old man?

Jekyll sighed and for a moment examined the burn blisters on the right thumb and fingertips, which were swollen tight with fluid. *In the end, Hastie, it does not make any difference if you understand what I'm telling you, or if you believe me. I promised only to explain. My father did not beat me. He hardly touched me, in fact. He would take me by the scruff of the neck, sometimes, or by the hair . . . Once or twice he chopped all my hair off. But he didn't have to use his hands. I obeyed him. I had no choice. It was like school. He was teaching me what he thought I needed to learn. He collected spiders, all around the old manor. He would make me lie still on the floor while he shook them onto me. I wasn't allowed to shut my eyes . . . Then there was a maid, a servant girl. Alice. He would tell me what he wanted me to do. To her, to myself. He forced me to drink whisky. Injected cocaine into my arm. He made me crawl into a tiny cupboard in his study, drunk and racing. Curled up in the dark, for hours and hours, while he played his violin. It was all part of his education, you see. It's taken me many years to realise it, but he wasn't trying to torture me. Not out of meanness. My father knew what the world was like. Indifferent to suffering. A pitiless competition. He believed he was shaping me into something unusually resilient, something extraordinary. He was deranged, of course. But in his way, he succeeded.*

Jekyll looked at Lanyon and gave him a small smile.

Lanyon stared back. And is that what you were doing to that poor young man in Paris? Making him into something extraordinary, Harry?

Jekyll's smile went cold. Lanyon gave his own, humourless. You think I don't know about that either. You really think I don't know a thing. I'm a doctor, in case you've forgotten, I know other doctors, we have doctor conversations. People talk; I don't know if you realise that. You were experimenting on that Frenchman, weren't you. Whatever you're doing to yourself with that stuff, you were doing to him. Trying to make him — evolve, like you say. Because that is nature, isn't it, Harry?

No, Jekyll said. His lips were numb. *That was not natural.* No, Lanyon echoed, it wasn't. You were shooting that junk into his arm, weren't you. The same stuff you're giving yourself. *Not exactly. The core is the same, the powder at the core. The rest is — it must be individualised. Each mind is distinct —* Details, Lanyon interrupted. Details. You were experimenting on him with drugs, and he killed himself because of it. Because he could not take it. Isn't that right. *Yes*, Jekyll said, his painful fingers clenched in a fist, his eyes beginning to sting. *You're right. He hanged himself. All those voices in his head, all those yearnings pulling him apart, turning on each other, in the end. The demon, he started terrorising the child. Ripping up his things, leaving his nasty paintings in places around the room only Pierre would find. And there was Emile in between, trying to hold the centre together. It was extraordinary. Except Emile didn't want to be extraordinary, he just wanted them gone. He wanted to be cured. He thought I could cure him. But there isn't any cure. You can't just cut it out. It's too deep for that. It's in the system. You can only marvel at it, its ruinous multiplicity. I had to see. I couldn't stop. He asked me to stop, and — and I couldn't stop.*

Jekyll's face contorted; he pressed a whitened knuckle to his lips. Lanyon was nodding, a triumphant glint in his blurry gaze. For shame, he said with vehemence. For shame, Doctor.

Because you are so blameless, Hastie?

Lanyon cocked his head as if perplexed. He was slumped in his chair, holding the drink on his desk. I'm sorry? For what am I to blame? Eh? I want to hear you say it, Harry, what am I to blame for? *You couldn't treat her on your own. You wanted to believe you could, but you couldn't. She needed a proper doctor, she needed care,* and you denied her those things, because you did not want to see that she was sick. Lanyon's face was darkening to a livid bruise. How dare you? How dare you judge me, how dare you say anything to me about treatment and care? Lanyon slammed his whisky glass on the desk. How dare you! he shouted, a vein forking under his eye. What care? What proper doctor? You? I should've let you treat her? Are you out of your mind? Keeping Winnie away from you was the best thing I could've possibly done for her!

It didn't have to be me. I told you that from the beginning. I could have recommended any psychiatrist in Europe. But you didn't want to hear it. You didn't want to acknowledge her illness, you wanted to pretend that she was merely unhappy. You were content to lock her in the bedroom when she was in one of her moods, as you would put it. One of her moods. That is what she told me, at any rate, when she came to see me. Jekyll paused. Lanyon pressed his spittled lips together. *You know she came to see me; I know that she told you. I can see it in your face. But perhaps she didn't tell you everything that she told me. That you locked her up in her bedroom when she misbehaved. That was your treatment. Far more effective, I'm sure, than a professional could have provided.* That's a lie! Lanyon shouted. That is a lie, goddamn you, I did not lock her up for misbehaviour, I — I confined her to her room so she wouldn't make a spectacle of herself, diminish herself. She would say things when she was — when she was — she would weep and say unimaginable things, make ridiculous accusations, in front of Collins, the staff. I would find her on the drawing-room sofa with the maid, clutching the girl by the wrist and saying the most astounding things. I just wanted to show her you cannot just — you cannot just give in to yourself! You cannot just indulge in every whim and emotion, you have to — you have to — Lanyon had risen from his chair and stood trembling over the desk, grasping the edge. What should I have done? Tell me! Send her away to live in a hospital like a lunatic? Send my own wife away from me?

His voice cracked and he looked off, streaming tears. To hell with you, he croaked. He took a step from the desk and stumbled, fell to his knees. Jekyll sighed, shut his aching eyes. He rose and went around the desk, gripped Lanyon under the armpit, and hauled him up. *All right, all right.* Lanyon was limp, Jekyll guided him over to the leather sofa by the fire and eased him down. Lanyon dropped his head back and peered up, the firelight flickering over his wet cheek and the veiny hollow under his eye. Jekyll turned and crossed to the cabinets, where he poured a glass of water and added two brownish drops of morphia from a bottle he plucked from the collection. He carried it back and took Lanyon's hand, curled the fingers round the glass. *Drink, Hastie,* he said, guiding the glass toward Lanyon's lips. Lanyon jerked his hand away, sloshing the cocktail. He squinted into the glass and sniffed, then raised it and pointed a finger. It all would've ended just the same, he said, slurring. Jekyll stood over him. *Perhaps. Now drink.* Lanyon held the wavering glass another moment, then tipped its contents back at a swallow. His hand slumped to the sofa, the fingers released, and the glass rolled off to the white fur rug. He sat blinking into his lap. A minute later his chin dropped to his chest, his flaxen hair hanging. Jekyll lifted him under the knees and laid him on the sofa, arranged a cushion under his head. Lanyon's crimson face gradually relaxed, and a light snore began to whisper from his lips.

At the laboratory table Jekyll packed everything back into E drawer and wrapped it up in the sheet. He took it under his arm and crossed to the door. Hand on the knob, he turned and looked back at his friend, sleeping deep and calm as a child.

Good night, Hastie, he murmured.

Goodbye.

DAY FOUR

Sunrise

I bolt awake with a scream, embracing myself. I am in the chair by the windows, a blaze of orange light in my eyes. I shut them, quaking. Just a dream, then. Just a dream: Tied to the cabinet floor with ropes run through iron hooks in the boards, all my limbs spread. Poole and Utterson and Lanyon above me, and Lanyon holding the axe. He lifted it high and chopped down on my elbow; I rolled away spurting from the cross-section of arm and bone. Utterson took the axe and whacked through my knee. I felt the heavy steel bite into the floor, and blood fanned from the stump in a fine high-pressure spray — I can still hear that *whunk* of the axe head.

I climb aching from the chair and stamp my dead foot as it needles into sensation again. That axe, that axe. Is the dream a prophecy, a message? What am I meant to do — go down there and find it? Will that stop them? Of course it won't stop them. So what am I doing? I am limping across the cabinet and sneaking back the bolt of the door and drawing it open. The sunrise behind me slices down the steps and the railing and meets the impenetrable blackness of the theatre beyond. I draw the door wider and my shadow rears down the rough brick wall. My palms are damp. I wipe them on my trousers and then steal down in my stockings to the middle step, the twelfth step, and stop.

This is madness. I have been safe all this time; why test the boundary line? Because of a dream? And yet at the same time I know that the spell of protection — whatever has been keeping me and the cabinet secure — is weakening, eroding. Poole himself broke bravely through it last night when he knocked on the door. There is no more refuge for me, no more asylum. Today all that ends. I lower my foot onto the thirteenth stair, easing my weight into its hair-raising creak. I wait, and my shadow self waits, reflected beneath my feet, in that sinister inverse world below where he is me. I take the fourteenth step, the fifteenth. At last I touch the floorboards of the theatre. I wriggle my toes, allowing my pupils to dilate to the darkness. The glass cupola high overhead filters a snowfall of light onto the dissection table, cluttered with crates and clustered bottles. I shuffle toward it, crackling over the packing straw strewn across the floor, until I can lay my hand on the startlingly cool marble. A smooth runnel grooves along the edge as a drain. I can see my exhalations chilling in the air. I hunker down and peek underneath the table, pat around with my hands. My fingers close over a wooden slat, splintered like a stake. I toss it aside and make out a slim suggestive shape propped against the farther edge. I hurry over and pick it up — a cold, heavy rod of iron. The jimmy bar, with its clawed hook at one end. Jekyll was using it to pry the crates open before smashing them apart. I heft it in one hand, comforted by its balance. Beneath the stairwell are the rings of wooden benches where students once sat to watch the horror show. I take a step toward them and then swivel around, cocking the jimmy bar, certain I heard something from there. I edge around to the other side of the table, not wanting to turn my back on the mob of shadows in the theatre depths. Then my eye falls on something, a shape, just beyond the circumference of light.

An optical trick: it looks like a person sitting in a chair. It does not move, and neither do I. I inch closer, squinting. It looks like a man sitting there; I can see a head atop the shoulders.

What the hell is that thing? I take another step toward it. Then it moves, there's a sudden scratch and sizzling flare, a leap of yellow light. A match. A face and widened eyes hover behind the swaying flame — it's Poole. It's Poole! I stand rooted to the spot. The flame whiffs out, and pitch-darkness rushes into the void. A croak escapes my throat. Then panic storms like a horde of bats in my chest and I break free and run, bashing into the table and reeling off toward the stairs, clumping up and kicking the under steps and tripping, scrambling to the top. I reach for the open door and the glaring daybreak, and then I am in the cabinet, throwing myself against the door and slithering to the floor.

I breathe in hitching gulps, a shrill ringing in my ears, as if from an explosion. I swallow and try to listen, pressing my face to the wood. At last I hear something — crunching — footsteps over the gravel. I crawl to the windows and press my cheek to the glass. Poole is crossing the courtyard back to Big House. I watch him enter the conservatory and then I slump against the lower wall.

So this is it. All at once, this is it. Poole saw me. He knows it is me up here and not Jekyll, once and for all. It's over, it's done. God! Was he down there the whole night long, just sitting in that chair? What is his secret, soundless way in? Will I even hear them coming, or will they simply appear out of the air at the bottom of the stairs? I try to climb to my feet and cry out, my hip and right foot shrieking pain. I grab my ankle as if to choke off the throb. I can't even wiggle the big toe, the pulsing mass. I must have broken it in my mad scramble up here. I grip the arm of the chair and groan up into it from the floor. I had to go looking for that ludicrous axe, didn't I? I just had to go down there where the man was waiting for me! Well, he won't wait anymore. He'll go to Utterson for certain now, and within an hour or maybe two, they'll be at the cabinet door together, banging away. I have to ready myself. I push up from the chair and hobble around the table to the glazed press, where I pull out E drawer and gaze lovingly, gratefully at the glass phial of cyanide lying on its side. Hello, pretty. I hold it in my palm again, loosely curling my fingers over it and feeling the solace kindle through my arm. My escape. My smouldering hole in the world, with me at its scorching centre. Whatever is coming, I will have this. I bring the phial to my lips and kiss the warmed, silky glass, then slip it into my pocket.

With the last of the coals snapping, I sit in the chair I've dragged before the stove, holding the crook of my left arm. The vein is aching now, in rhythm with my pulsing toe. Tentatively I cuff the sleeve and stare at the gouged and pockmarked arm, the black weeping pustule in the cleft. The vein is dark and hard as piano wire under the skin, obviously infected. Under ordinary circumstances, I bet they'd amputate the arm from the elbow down. An appalling sight. There was no need to do this, to keep testing all those powders, when it was obvious even to me that none were going to work. But Jekyll kept pushing, demanding I sample every one. Mystifying business, the powder. Jekyll knew we were down to our last brick of the stuff. He had removed the silver-wrapped rectangular cake from H drawer and transferred the white crumbly brick to the empty bottle the night he returned home from Lanyon's consulting room. And yet he waited over a month — well into February — before even attempting to order more of it from Maw's. We were burning through the supply — I was taking four, sometimes five, injections a day by that point to bring him back into the body. And yet it didn't seem to occur to him that we were running dangerously low on the last of the stock. Though it *must* have occurred to him. Perhaps he knew it didn't matter, that nothing else would work. So why did he make me do this to my arm?

Remember it. Concentrate; take your mind off the pain.

From Lanyon's house that night, Jekyll went home, up to the cabinet. The red-baize door hung open. The lock on the glazed press had been broken. Jekyll slid E drawer into its empty slot, and then slept on the table. Woke at dawn; stood wrapped in his overcoat by the red-stained windows. He crossed to the cabinet door and turned back the bolt, and it slid open with its well-oiled *snick*. That locksmith had picked it cleanly. Jekyll went through the theatre and crunched out into the frosted gravel courtyard. Big House soared against the flushing daybreak. We would have to leave it, of course. We had no choice now. After Lizzie, after Lanyon, we could not stay. We would go to Liverpool and wait for 25 January and then leave England, possibly forever. Jekyll dragged the back of his hand across his eyes. Then he took a step toward the house, and it struck: the house flashed white, and the sky turned that odious greenish black and the earth lurched and spun upside down. Waving our arms to grab at something to keep from plunging into all that immensity, we groaned in the suck of gravity, before the world flipped upright. I staggered forward and fell to the stones, which bit into my knee and my palm. I stared at my hand, the skin indented and a white chunk of pepper-flecked gravel sticking to it. I gaped at the house, the crimson sky. Then scrabbled to my feet and loped back to the surgery block, the cabinet, and E drawer.

I was eager to give the body back to him — to make certain that I could still disappear inside it and hide. By the end of that first day of confinement, however, I had taken three or four injections to bring Jekyll back. He couldn't hold on to the body for more than a few straight hours. As if he were clenching a constant muscle with his conscious mind, clasping the body to him. When his concentration slipped, the floor would lurch in a sickening spin and pitch me out, queasy and increasingly desperate. Poole knocked on the cabinet door that evening, and Jekyll spoke to him through a two-inch crack, bracing the bottom edge with his foot. *Poole*, he said with a moan, *I've — I've made myself rather sick. You can't help me, I'm afraid. No one can help me, except by leaving me in peace so I can work on — on a cure. I'm trying to fix what I've done, to make myself better — but you must let me work, you mustn't disturb me, however long it takes. Is that clear?* Poole's eyes glimmered through the crack. *I have to close this door now,* Jekyll said. *I'm sorry, Poole. Please just let me be.*

A cure. It was a clever excuse and provided us time. Yet for weeks, Jekyll did nothing, certainly nothing by way of *curing* us. It wasn't until February that he finally wrote to Maw's for more powder. He passed the days pacing, muttering, mentally thickening the membrane that divided us, and when I pressed to this permeable barrier to try to hear his thoughts he would jerk his head, as if away from a fly. On the desk he kept a collection of books, and one leather volume in particular he pored over constantly, running his raggedy fingernail along the dense print, tapping and nodding vigourously. *The Descent of Man*, by Charles Darwin. There was one underlined passage that Jekyll returned to again and again: *The inquirer would next come to the important point whether man tends to increase at so rapid a rate as to lead to occasional severe struggles for existence; and consequently to beneficial variations, whether in body or mind, being preserved, and injurious ones eliminated. Do the races or species of men, whichever term may be applied, encroach on and replace one another, so that some finally become extinct?*

I wanted to understand this — variation, extinction. It was crucial. But Jekyll had sealed me off and would just read his book, using Utterson's folded note to mark his place. Utterson had sent two notes. This bookmark was the second. His first letter arrived about a week into our confinement. Poole set it on the dinner tray, which he was by then leaving on the stairs. Utterson had been to see Lanyon. *Our friend is badly changed,* he wrote. *He looks ruined. He is drinking again, very heavily. I know that you are involved, that you know the cause of this. Yesterday I called at your house and was told that you aren't seeing anyone. What has happened? Harry, for God's sake, what is happening?*

The second letter came a week later, and this was the one

Jekyll used for a bookmark. There was only one line, across the middle of the page: *Hastie is dead.*

Jekyll would unfold it often and gaze at the words. There was something mesmerising about them, a kind of perfect truth. Anytime we read them, those words, they were true, and always would be. The line of ink swam with a kind of power. *Hastie is dead.*

Day after day, it was the same, except worse, pitching into the body and quelling the nausea, possessing the body and not *wanting it*. This was the worst part: I could feel no pleasure in physical existence anymore, no animal joy in having the body. It was just this aching, foul-smelling encumbrance. The instant I had control of it, Jekyll withdrew to the outer reaches beyond the barrier, and it was lonely and cold and frightening. For it felt like existence was being imposed upon me. Like I was being ejected helplessly into the body and the world for some specially prepared punishment. Which, of course, I was.

Jekyll waited until the last brick of the powder in the stoppered bottle was almost half gone, then he wrote to Maw's. He was reading his Darwin book, that passage again, murmuring to himself the phrase *encroach on and replace*. He rose and went to the glazed press and opened E drawer, lifted out the bottle of powder, and tilted its remaining contents. He made a contemplative ticking sound with his tongue as he regarded all that was left of the six foil bricks he had shipped back from Paris. He carried the bottle to his writing desk and set it on the edge of the blotter, then sat and squared a sheet of paper and at last dashed off the letter to Maw's that he should have written months before. It came out oddly cryptic. In March of 1883, he wrote, he had ordered a large quantity of a *certain salt compound*, of which he now wished a new supply. Would Messrs. Maw please send him a *testable sample of the salt compound to be sure it is of the same efficacy?*

Jekyll crept down and set the letter on the stairs, and that evening there was a brown envelope included on the dinner tray.

From the envelope, he slid a brown-paper sachet and a note of compliments from Maw. Jekyll tipped the white powder from the sachet into the silver spoon until it was full, and then he overturned the spoon into a glass of the crimson liquor, which at once began to froth and boil. When it fizzled out, Jekyll held it to the light and frowned. I could see for myself: the colour did not look exactly right. The fluid was pale green and transparent — yet, while I couldn't say if it was too light or too dark, it seemed a shade off. Jekyll sucked the serum into a syringe, which he set in the Milward box in the upper groove pointing left. Then he prepared the other needle with the old powder in the stoppered bottle. The two syringes lay in their beds pointing in opposite directions, and for a while Jekyll scrutinised the glass barrels, comparing their colour.

He had fallen asleep, his head on his arms, at the table, and I banged awake, almost tipping backward off the bench. I fisted my gummy eyes and saw the open Milward box. I rolled up Jekyll's hanging sleeve and reached for the syringe pointing left, loaded with the compliments of Messrs. Maw. I had been working the curling vein that branched off the main and wrapped around the forearm, and now I flexed it up and slid the needle in and pressed the plunger.

I sat there as the stuff flowed through the arm. I wiggled my fingers, then eased the steel from the vein. My heart thudded dully. Nothing was happening. I was not surprised. I had known it would not work. That subtle contrast in colour: this new compound from Maw's was different from the old. I waited for Jekyll to react, to tell me what to do. Yet from within, there was only inscrutable silence, a palpable muteness. What else *was* there to do? I took up the other needle and punched it into the abscess and pressed the plunger.

Early the next morning, Jekyll wrote again to Maw's. The sample, he said, did not achieve the same effect as the original stock. *Thus it is quite useless to my present purpose. It is the old, orig-*

*inal stock I require, not merely the same compound but the same exact
stock from which my supply was taken. I cannot exaggerate the importance of this. Anything other than the old is worthless to me.*

A reply from Maw's arrived with lunch. The original stock,
it explained, had been depleted almost entirely by Jekyll's first order. The sample compound he had been sent was *chemically identical to the original. There is no formulaic difference between them.
Perhaps the failure in efficacy resides, with all due respect, in some
other factor. We have included another sample of the same compound
for your examination.*

Jekyll picked up the brown-paper sachet by its edge.

Some other factor, he whispered.

All at once I could see the inevitable end. We were going to run
out of the powder — there was no more of it to be had — and I
would be left alone. The original supply was the powder Jekyll
had used on Emile Verlaine to release L'inconnu, this precise,
unique compound. It was the key Jekyll had used to unlock his
own mind, and now no other key would fit. A dead boy's medicine, we had been taking. Emile, who had hanged himself. From
the wrought-iron bars of his window, with a bedsheet, in his pa-
jamas, face purple and eyes bulging, his bare toes dangling inches
from the floor.

That night Jekyll cooked up the cyanide. Into a clear corrosive
acid, he mixed a dab of dark blue unguent, and then fired the co-
balt froth over the Bunsen in a round-bottomed flask attached at
the top to a condenser. The colourless, lethal distillate dripped
into a glass, infusing the cabinet with the pleasant scent of almonds. Jekyll poured the poison into a glass phial, plugged it, and
held it to the light, turning it, as if to check for imperfection.

But it is perfect. From my pocket I remove the phial again and
hold the glass column as tightly as I dare. My amulet, my cure.

◆ ◆ ◆

Jekyll was sitting on the windowsill a day or two later, the middle window pushed open to let in some air. The courtyard lay dank with mist that seemed to swirl in through the alleyway leading out to Castle Street. The effect was oddly hypnotic and calming, the mist oozing from the bottleneck. Then, without warning, two men walked through the alley into the yard. Jekyll started, half rising from the sill. The man in the tall topper saw the movement and looked up at the windows. It was Utterson. Harry! he called out before Jekyll could duck down. He strolled across the gravel and the other man followed slightly behind. Harry! he called up again with a forced cheerfulness, and then he seemed to truly see his friend and stopped.

Jekyll was still attempting to shave every few days. But his hair was long and matted, and he had been wearing the same clothes for over a month. Utterson's expression faltered as he glanced down from the window and along the limestone wall to the splashed gravel at the bottom. Jekyll had been pouring the chamber pot out the window onto the stones below. Utterson appeared to take this in before yanking his gaze upward again. The other man, wearing a grey bowler at a rakish tilt, was standing at his side looking up at the windows as well. Harry, Utterson said, you — you seem unwell. Jekyll gave a hollow laugh. *I'm low, John. I'm very low.* Perhaps a little air would do you good, Utterson called, a little exercise! Whip up the circulation a bit. It's quite pleasant out, despite appearances. What do you say, Harry? A little stroll with Enfield and me. You remember my cousin, by the way, Richard Enfield?

Enfield. From under the cocked grey bowler he peered steadily up at us, and his mild, insolent face clicked at last into place. Enfield. His grip on my collar, the speck of spittle hitting my cheek as he snarled, One hundred pounds.

You — you are very good, John, Jekyll stammered, *I'd like to, but — it's not possible, I'm afraid, I'm not well at the moment.* Well, Utterson said, well, perhaps we might stand here and chat from where we are? Would that be agreeable to you, my friend? But the sky was black and the rooflines white, and I had the sudden presentiment of standing on a gallows above an eager crowd of uplifted faces. Jekyll twisted from the windows. The cabinet rolled and the floor disappeared, and for a sick second I pitched into free fall, clawing at my throat as if swinging from the rope, kicking to a roar of applause. Then the room rose to meet me with a smash, and I found myself on the floor. Seasick, I shut my eyes and heard the sound of footsteps crunching across the courtyard, fading into the alleyway.

Soon I was regularly taking two injections to bring Jekyll back to the body. I watched him draw up a list of all the chemists in London and begin to send out his missives, each with his maniacally specific instructions on the formulation of the powder, the precise percentages of the compound. Each sample arrived in its tiny sachet with its maker's compliments, and each was drawn into a syringe and set into the box for the laboratory rat to test. We both knew none of it would work. Only our own rapidly diminishing supply could bring him back. I could have tried to resist his experiments. But I was too tired and ill and frightened to fight him. These were Jekyll's final, futile moves against the inevitable — his extinction. I could not refuse him that. For when the last dose was gone, I would *replace* him, as Darwin had said. Jekyll would be no more.

Sometimes in the dead of night I'd jerk awake in the body. Left arm pounding down to my fingertips, I would pace around the table, to put off the needle. When I paced quickly I found I could keep just ahead of the terrorising notions that trailed behind like an evil odour, waiting to catch up and envelop me in nauseous dread. All night sometimes I would patrol the long perimetre of the table, until dear morning began to grain the cabinet in pink-grey dust, and I could at last face the prospect of creeping back into our decomposing head. I was on the final turns of my haunted march one such early dawn when I passed Jekyll's writing desk and noticed that his precious leather-bound Darwin had been left lying open. One page stood up like a stray hair. I came to a halt and found myself extending a hand to lay upon the open page. As if direct skin contact might help me to understand its awful concepts. On the blotter alongside the book lay Father's fountain pen, a gleam along its polished wood, and I picked it up and unscrewed the cap, and with my fingertip I touched the needle-pointed nib: like a flash I saw Father punch his wasted throat, and for a horrific second there was no blood, just a black startling hole, before he punched again and the two bright red geysers hissed at high pressure and he spastically blinked, eying us still — I jerked my head, breathing fast. Then I bent over the book and scratched the nib across the page, puncturing the paper on the last furious stroke. I drew back and stared at the black, spiky scrawl:

> *Jekyll*
> *please!*

Slowly I looked to the pen in my hand, my left hand.

I knew this spidery scribble by heart.

You be hide and I play seek.

The witch's tarot cards: the Magician, the Hanged Man, the Devil.

All is you.

I was nodding, a choking suffocation in my throat, as if I were about to scream or laugh or both. I released the pen, which rolled from my fingers onto the blotter, and I backed away, clamping a hand to my mouth. I looked down at my feet, half expecting to find the floor like a pane of glass and the shadow world reflected upside down below, my own demonic double stemming from my soles, his pupils dilated and black above his hand clapped to his own mouth, mocking my horror. Hide and Seek.

Mrs. Deaker had been right.

You've done this to yourself, Mr. Hyde.

Later that morning, Jekyll stood over the desk. He had waited hours to approach the Darwin book. As if he did not know what I'd done to it, or did not care. But his heart was slamming as he stared at the open page. He reached out, and with his fingertips traced the ink indentations, as he had done to that first letter, as if reading Braille.

He had known, all along. He had been able to read what I couldn't. He had said it to Utterson: Hyde is fracturing. He'd known we were not alone.

*Jekyll
please!*

Please? What did I think he could do? He had wanted this to happen. Wanted to watch it happen. *There isn't any cure,* he'd said. *It's in the system. You can only marvel at it, its ruinous multiplicity.*

Jekyll's eyes were blurring. He reached out and slapped the book shut. He almost turned away but then seized the volume from the desk and carried it over to the chamber pot in the far corner by Father's portrait. He dropped the book into the pot, then turned and unbuckled his trousers, hunkered down, and strained out a dry painful curl of movement. He stood and looked woozily down at the soiled book. Father was watching from the wall. Jekyll buckled his trousers and then looked up and met Father's imprisoned stare. He drew in a breath, as if on the brink of shouting something, then stepped up and gripped the gnarled wooden frame in both hands. He leant his face toward Father until their foreheads nearly touched, their eyes an inch apart, and with a groan, Jekyll stepped back, wrenching the picture from the wall — a tug, then a snap of wire, and he staggered backward with the heavy thing. He lifted it over his head and smacked it down on the table with a splintering crack. He smacked it down again, the frame snapping and canvas buckling; he threw it to the floor and stamped, stamped, roaring something I couldn't understand, spittle flying from our lips as we jumped up and down like an ape, grinding our heel into Father's face and feeling the canvas shred apart as we grated it into the floorboards. We snatched up the broken sagging thing and dragged it to the stove, began ripping it apart and feeding the pieces to the coals, wadding up the canvas and stuffing it into the hell and watching the paint blister and hiss. I dragged a hand across my mouth, then stared at my hand. A sliver of wood was embedded in the meat of my palm, like a mark of stigmata.

Jekyll would write later that I'd done this on my own. That I played *apelike tricks, scrawling blasphemies on the pages of my books, destroying the portrait of my father.* And by the time he wrote those words, he seemed to fully believe that this version of events was the truth. He had to believe it. He was going to die. And it seemed he did not want to face what he had done. He did not want to know the truth anymore, and he didn't want anyone else to know it either. He began to write his *Full Statement of the Case* when there were perhaps ten doses left in the bottle. He managed to make them last for a week. He started the document in the middle of the night, after pacing around the table for hours as if working himself up to it. At last he sat down at his desk, squared a sheet of clean paper before him, and carefully unscrewed the cap of Father's fountain pen.

I was born in the year 1835, he began, *to a large fortune, endowed besides with excellent parts, inclined by nature to industry, fond of the respect of the wise and good amongst my fellowmen, and thus, as might have been supposed, with every guarantee of an honourable and distinguished future.* I watched as this peculiar confession grew over the page in this roundabout, concealing style, admitting nothing, confessing to nothing except an *imperious desire to carry my head high, and wear a more than commonly grave countenance before the public.* After three hours hunched over the desk he glanced up, ears pricked. He drew the lower desk drawer open and removed a dusty sheaf of forgotten files, inserted his finger into a sly hole in the bare wood, and lifted out the false bottom. In the coffin of space underneath, he stored the crumpled, inky pages and then fit the false bottom back into place and put the portfolio in the drawer again. I could hardly believe it. He was hiding it from me. Was he demented? Did he actually think I couldn't read every word he had written? Yet the bizarre ritual continued over the course of that final week. Discreetly he would remove the false bottom and extract the expanding pile of pages and scribble away for several hours before tucking the document back into its hiding place. It was our story, *of the two natures that contended in the field of my consciousness. If each,* he wrote, *could be housed in separate identities, life would be relieved of all that was unbearable.* And yet it was all abstruse and misleading nonsense. There was nothing of Father or the childhood. Nothing of his work on Emile Verlaine. Nothing of the letters, the newspapers, Carew, Mr. Seek, any of it. There was nothing even of the syringes. According to his confession we *drank* the magic serum — *compounded the elements, watched them boil and smoke together in the glass, and when the ebullition had subsided, with a strong glow of courage, drank off the potion.*

I have observed, he wrote, *that when I wore the semblance of Edward Hyde, none could come near to me at first without a visible misgiving of the flesh. This, as I take it, was because all human beings, as we meet them, are commingled out of good and evil: and Edward Hyde, alone in the ranks of mankind, was pure evil.* Pure evil! Me! His protestations were becoming pathetically transparent: *It was Hyde, after all, and Hyde alone, that was guilty.* I was the *devil,* I was *that child of Hell — not only hellish but inorganic.* I was *despised and friendless.* He had to say such things, I told myself, he had to invert everything against me, insist that it was I *alone* who'd destroyed us. He had to delude himself before he could die. And it wouldn't be long. The stoppered bottle was draining day by day like an hourglass. I did not know him anymore, this paranoid, muttering, desperate wretch who had stopped shaving and trimming his nails, who kept the long mirror swiveled around to face the wall so he could not catch sight of himself, who wept, curled up on the table at night like a man in the straw of his execution cell, moon-barred and cold. *The powers of Hyde,* he wrote, *seem to have grown with the sickliness of Jekyll. And the hate that now divides them is equal on each side.* Hate? I did not hate him. I pitied him. For his own incurable sake, I wished him dead. I wished us all dead. With a broken heart I pushed the last dose of the powder into my blighted arm at dawn. Coughing, shivering, Jekyll shuffled to his desk and scratched out the final page of his confession. Father's fountain pen was nearly dry, and his scrawl grew fainter and fainter as he coaxed out the last of its black blood:

Will Hyde die upon the scaffold? or will he find courage to release himself at the last moment? God knows; I am careless; this is my true hour of death, and what is to follow concerns another than myself. Here then, as I lay down the pen and proceed to seal up my confession, I bring the life of that unhappy Henry Jekyll to an end.

I stand over the desk, over the white envelope propped against the bell-glass lamp. Do you see? Jekyll, you lunatic, do you see? I have not destroyed it, I have not touched it. I have left it absolutely intact, your precious manifesto, your revised will and testament, with Utterson's name in my place. I have not laid a single foul finger upon it. Utterson will see through all your lies and it will have been for nothing that you deluded yourself and maligned me, who never wanted anything but to serve you, to protect you!

My hand feels fuzzy at my side, weighted with blood. And yet, strangely enough, I find that my hand is rising, magnetised, toward the envelope. I try briefly to resist before my fingers close around the thick paper, and I wince, half expecting it to sear my flesh like something baptised. But it lifts freely from the desk in my hand, the buckled pages crackling lightly inside. I lick my lips, heart hammering. Then I turn the envelope around to the flap at the back.

hide hide hide hide hide hide hide hide hide hide hide hide hide hide hide hide hide hide hide hide hide hide hide hide hide hide hide hide hide hide hide hide hide hide hide hide hide hide hide hide hide hide hide hide hide hide hide hide hide hide hide hide hide hide hide hide

The inky spiders scrabble back and forth and up and down over the boundaries, intersecting and crawling over one another; I drop it on the desk, stagger back a step. Impossible. Impossible! Yet I am grinning uncontrollably even as I shake my head in denial, a grin like a rictus of recognition. He's been here all along. Watching, waiting. Hide and Seek, Hide and Seek. The Hanged Man and the Devil, together at the end. I stumble into the table behind me, bumping my hip, which shoots a white flare of pain up my side. I spin around to the gathering blue dark in the windows. So dark! Where's the day gone? I hobble round the table and gape out at the sky, burning royal blue with a fingernail cut of moon on its back shredded across with cloud. How is it nighttime already? Why haven't they come for me?

On cue, I hear something and go rigid: distinctive metal squeak across the courtyard. The conservatory door. Now the crunch of gravel. I duck down and smash my face to the glass and catch the pair of tall shadows walking toward me, one behind the other, before they disappear from my view. I stand up, the whole cabinet rippling with my pulse. It's here. Thank God, they're here. My hand slides into my pocket, gropes around. I plunge into my other pocket. Empty. The phial, it was — it was just here. My eyes peel wide. The cyanide. He took it. Seek. He's hidden it. My escape. From downstairs comes the *woof* of air and clang of the surgery-block door, then the pair of footsteps clumping over the theatre boards. I stand paralysed by the windows. There is silence as they pause at the foot of the stairs. Then they start to climb: a scuffling echoing stamp up the bowed old steps. The crack beneath the door flickers with an unstable candle flame.

A rapping on the door frame. Sir? Poole says, his voice muffled. Sir? Dr. Jekyll?

I cannot breathe.

Dr. Jekyll? Mr. Utterson is here to see you, sir.

I shut my eyes.

Dr. Jekyll! Poole calls like a threat, and suddenly I bellow out: *I can't see him!*

It rings in the air as I hunch, amazed. It half sounded like Jekyll, in fact. In the awful quiet I watch the flickering crack of the door, waiting for the axe blow to fall. Then Poole says, Thank you, sir, very good. The scuffling footsteps descend; the crack grows dark again as they cross the theatre floor and I listen to the crunch-crunch-crunch over the courtyard.

I didn't fool them, of course. I heard that triumphant note in Poole's voice. They are in Big House now, planning their attack. The storming of the cabinet! Where is the phial? I need the cyanide, I can't let them take me out of here alive. I can't have this go on! Seek! There is only that smothered silence, the devil with a hand clapped over his mouth, containing his mirth. He wants to see me dragged out of here alive, publically exposed and punished. It's what he's wanted all along. What Jekyll has wanted, in his secret heart, all along. To be found out. Stripped naked. Mortified. Scourged clean. Oh God, what's he done with the phial? I must know where it is, the knowledge is in my head! Where would I hide it? At Jekyll's desk, I wrench out the lower drawer, pull up the false bottom. The space is empty. I paw through the papers in the upper drawer and slam it shut. At the glazed press, I yank out each drawer in turn — nothing, nothing — I scan the shelves, fumble through a rack of clattering glass phials, all of which are empty. I scamper to the wardrobe, fling open the doors. Am I to keep repeating everything over and over in a hellish cycle? I pull out the wardrobe drawer and angrily run it shut again. I stand panting at the wooden back of the oval mirror, facing the wall, and I take hold of the top and spin the glass back around. Bearded, pallid, starved, mad-eyed, I stare at the nerve jerking in the veiny cave of the socket. My head buzzes with a sound of stumbling flies. I reach out to touch the glass, the tapping spot beneath my skin. Then my gaze clicks down, to the wall behind the mirror frame. The black leather violin case, leaning behind the wardrobe. Yes. Recognition leaps from my groin. *Yes.* I reach behind the mirror and grasp the thing by its head and slide it out, with a twang of strings from inside. My eyelid's twitching faster, and that spike is piercing my oculus as I throw the case up onto the table, unsnap the clasps, draw the lid open.

The instrument is shattered. As if it had been held by its throat and smashed, the lacquered bronze body is crumpled inward, the face splintered, revealing the coarse, unvarnished innards. The ebony fingerboard juts awry, a compound fracture, and the tailpiece is broken free; the strings are coiled in a twanging farrago. The neck is snapped like a bird's and the scrolled peg box is twisted to the side. The wooden wreck lies in its blue velvet deathbed. I brush the knotted strings, touching off a rough resonance as my fingers slide toward the top and stop at the flap to the compartment where the resin is stored. Oh, please. Oh, Jekyll. I pull open the flap. Nestled sideward in the niche is the phial, still filled with my salvation.

I press it to my lips, gulping out a sob of laughter. Spearing pain in my eyeball—oh, he is livid!—but I squinch the eyelid shut and hobble to the windows. I push the middle one open and thrust my head out into the rushing blue-black night. Flecks of rain spittle my face, racks of clouds race across the sickle moon. I want to scream in victorious defiance—I win! I win! But there is a sound, and I draw back. Footsteps over the gravel, moving fast and nimble. A slim shadow slides over the rear wall and vanishes into the alleyway. I catch a gleam of copper before it disappears. Bradshaw. I pull my head inside, clutching the phial as tight as I can without breaking the glass. Very clever, John, cutting off the Castle Street door, the rear escape. Except I won't be using that door, will I. I take the rubber plug of the phial between my knuckle and thumb.

Now the creak of the conservatory door again, and two sets of footsteps crunching over the gravel. I don't bother to peer down this time: Poole will carry the axe, and Utterson will wield something else, a poker, the jimmy bar I dropped. I work the rubber plug from the glass lip with a faint celebratory *pop*, lift it to my nostrils, and sniff: acidic tickle in my sinus, that sweet smell of almonds. It will burn as it goes down, scorch and smoke and suffocate as it sears through this world and opens up the blackness beyond. Am I ready? Am I ready for extinction? How is it possible that everything will keep on running after I'm reduced to nothing — all those lives out there continuing unchanged? Surely *she* will feel it, wherever she is. Surely out of all those oblivious people, Jeannie will register the impact of my absence like — like some minuscule yet necessary element removed from the air. She will stop what she is doing and look up, with that adorable, quizzical furrow between her brows, and she will turn to her sister or whoever is there beside her and say — what will she say? What will be my eulogy?

The surgery door downstairs *woofs* open, and now they clump back across the floorboards to the steps. The stamping climb, the door crack filling again with that trembling yellow light. A pause.

Rapping on the door frame. Harry! Utterson shouts. Harry, open the door! I demand to see you!

I shut my other eye, squeeze against the spiking pain. Rhythmic, as if he is throwing himself up against the wall of me, stabbing with a shard of light again and again, trying to get out, to get into the body and stop me from ending everything. He is not ready. He hasn't finished with his game. My terrible story could yet go on.

Harry! Utterson shouts. Open this door or we will smash it down! Do you hear me? We will break down this bloody door, I promise you!

For a last second, with my eyes closed, I can almost hear them, that other mutiny from years and years ago. Carlton and all the men pounding at the door of Father's study as we clasp our knees inside the chokey, listening to the muffled sounds of our deliverance, our father bellowing from far away, *Hen-ryyy! Hen-ryyy!*

I cover the lip of the phial with my thumb and suck in a breath to roar: *John! No mercy, John! No mercy! Bring on the axe!* A second of undulant silence, then a crashing *whunk* that makes the door jump in its frame. Yes! It's the axe! The axe! It's happening exactly as I knew it would. There was never any escaping it. It was written. Another bash against the door as the axe bites it, a squeaking crack as Poole tears it loose and winds back and whacks it into the wood: the door rebounds and a chip splinters out near the knob. Yes, that's it, clever Poole. He's going for the lock, he'll chop through the lock and the door will spring inward and I will hold the phial grandly up toward them, like one of Jekyll's toasts. Utterson is shouting behind the door, and it sounds like my name with each blow of the axe — Hyde! Hyde! — like there are innocent people down in the theatre and he is waving his arm wildly, telling them to run, to escape. A white sliver of wood splinters outward again near the lock, and I lift the shaking phial into the air, half blinded by the frantic stabbing pain. Seek! Devil! You lose, do you see? You lose! Ready or not, here I come! No more hiding!

To its end!

INTRODUCTION

to *The Strange Case of
Dr. Jekyll and Mr. Hyde*

The inspiration for *The Strange Case of Dr. Jekyll and Mr. Hyde* famously came to Robert Louis Stevenson in a dream. According to his wife, when she woke him from what seemed to be a dreadful nightmare, he snapped, "Why did you wake me? I was dreaming a fine bogey tale."*

This was in 1885; Stevenson was thirty-five years old. He had written a substantial number of stories, poems, essays, and plays, including his second-most-enduring novella, *Treasure Island*. He was weeks away from publishing a novel he had been laboring over for several years, which was, he imagined, to be his masterpiece — the melodramatic *Prince Otto*, which almost no one has heard of today. It is tempting, in fact, to speculate that Stevenson's impressive corpus of witty, elegant prose would be all but unknown to most modern readers if not for that dream in which, by the writer's description, "one man was being pressed into a cabinet, when he swallowed a drug and changed into another being."

Sitting up in bed, chain-smoking in his usual fashion, he dashed out a draft in three days and then read it aloud to his step-

---

* Quotations from Robert Louis Stevenson and Fanny Stevenson in this introduction were taken from Claire Harman's biography *Myself and the Other Fellow: A Life of Robert Louis Stevenson* (New York: Harper Perennial, 2005).

son and wife. Fanny Stevenson criticized it heavily, insisting that he was missing an opportunity for a "great moral allegory" (in her words). The wounded Stevenson petulantly threw the manuscript into the fire and then submitted to his wife's advice and banged out a second version in just three more days. Like a man possessed — like Jekyll himself scribbling out his desperate Statement of the Case — Stevenson composed the most famous moral parable of modern life in under a week. "Practically it came to me as a gift."

Dreams span universal across human consciousness, evoking the primal fantasies and neuroses that define our peculiar species. *Jekyll and Hyde*'s extraordinary success can be linked not so much to its clever artistry as to its conjuration of our most nightmarish fascination: the horror of self-transformation. Horror not at changing from I into Other, but at changing from I into something repulsive and alien that the unfortunate transformer must admit is also I. Just as Gregor Samsa reluctantly begins to enjoy clambering on sticky insect legs about his walls and ceiling, Jekyll concedes to feeling the "leap of welcome" at the sight of his base, hidden self. Stevenson has truly tapped into the timeless dilemma of human self-awareness. Here is "me," walking around, wearing my clothes, speaking words, interacting with society. Yet somewhere inside this civilized shell is another me, watching and evaluating all this posturing, harboring thoughts that are often directly contrary to what is being externally expressed. Is this the real me or yet another construction? And why are the impulses of this other me so frequently — gratifyingly — inappropriate, misanthropic, and, indeed, self-destructive?

The moral allegory Fanny Stevenson was pushing for is very clear: Jekyll is good, Hyde is bad. Victorian sensibilities did not care for shades of grey; sympathy for the devil wasn't culturally popular, the way it is today. Yet Stevenson was hardly the stuffy Victorian, and despite his characters' insistence on Hyde's unredeemed depravity, there are little hints of a nuanced human being in Hyde's artfully appointed rooms, the tea things laid out in the cabinet at the end. More important, if you look beyond the biased emphasis on Jekyll's goodness, you will see the actions of a calculating, self-loathing egomaniac who makes conspicuous mention of his secret to his lawyer and butler, who lies to his friends, who places poor Hastie Lanyon in a position from which he can't recover, and who leaves himself no choice but suicide in the end. Jekyll is no more a saint than Hyde is pure evil. The story is a veil masquerading as truth, stiffened into a simplified metaphor of human duality. But the dream lives behind it, complex and primeval, the untold tale of the inner man, the sociopath, the other I.

I must have brushed that dream myself. One morning several years ago I woke on my stomach and found myself staring at my own hand, and I suddenly remembered the scene in *Jekyll and Hyde* when Hyde awakes unexpectedly in Jekyll's bed, having transformed overnight, and recognizes first his "lean, corded, knuckly" hand. I had been searching for a project and all at once here it was — a gift: *Hyde.*

There have been many *Jekyll and Hyde* retellings over the years — stage plays, films, television series, musicals starring David Hasselhoff. My interest was not in reconfiguring the premise but in returning to the original, exploring the inconsistencies of character and crafting a convincing psychological model to explain Jekyll's plunge into self-annihilation. The original, too, is a murder mystery; why does Hyde kill Sir Danvers Carew? The story says it is coincidence. Yet the murder is witnessed by a maid in an upstairs window who recognizes Hyde, "who had once visited her master." Who is this master, and why should Hyde visit him? Questions yearn for their answers. For nearly 130 years *Dr. Jekyll and Mr. Hyde* has remained immovably on the fickle (and often unfair) shelves of classical literature, an endurance no doubt due to these suggestive ripples in its surface, the tantalizing hints of an underworld calling out for discovery.

If the plot points of Stevenson's story were graphed on one

sheet of tracing paper and the points of my own version graphed on another, it is my hope that the two, held together to the light, would overlap in a harmonious, albeit rocky, landscape. I am deeply indebted to Robert Louis Stevenson, romantic, bohemian, adventurer, consummate stylist, and fellow soul, for the use of his haunting yarn and his fantastic dream, which belongs, in the end, to us all.

THE STRANGE CASE OF

DR. JEKYLL

AND

MR. HYDE

by

ROBERT LOUIS STEVENSON

1

Story of the Door

Mr. Utterson the lawyer was a man of a rugged countenance that was never lighted by a smile; cold, scanty and embarrassed in discourse; backward in sentiment; lean, long, dusty, dreary and yet somehow lovable. At friendly meetings, and when the wine was to his taste, something eminently human beaconed from his eye; something indeed which never found its way into his talk, but which spoke not only in these silent symbols of the after-dinner face, but more often and loudly in the acts of his life. He was austere with himself; drank gin when he was alone, to mortify a taste for vintages; and though he enjoyed the theatre, had not crossed the doors of one for twenty years. But he had an approved tolerance for others; sometimes wondering, almost with envy, at the high pressure of spirits involved in their misdeeds; and in any extremity inclined to help rather than to reprove. "I incline to Cain's heresy," he used to say quaintly: "I let my brother go to the devil in his own way." In this character, it was frequently his fortune to be the last reputable acquaintance and the last good influence in the lives of downgoing men. And to such as these, so long as they came about his chambers, he never marked a shade of change in his demeanour.

No doubt the feat was easy to Mr. Utterson; for he was undemonstrative at the best, and even his friendship seemed to be founded in a similar catholicity of good-nature. It is the mark of a modest man to accept his friendly circle ready-made from the hands of opportunity; and that was the lawyer's way. His friends were those of his own blood or those whom he had known the longest; his affections, like ivy, were the growth of time, they implied no aptness in the object. Hence, no doubt the bond that united him to Mr. Richard Enfield, his distant kinsman, the well-known man about town. It was a nut to crack for many, what these two could see in each other, or what subject they could find in common. It was reported by those who encountered them in their Sunday walks, that they said nothing, looked singularly dull and would hail with obvious relief the appearance of a friend. For all that, the two men put the greatest store by these excursions, counted them the chief jewel of each week, and not only set aside occasions of pleasure, but even resisted the calls of business, that they might enjoy them uninterrupted.

It chanced on one of these rambles that their way led them down a by-street in a busy quarter of London. The street was small and what is called quiet, but it drove a thriving trade on the weekdays. The inhabitants were all doing well, it seemed and all emulously hoping to do better still, and laying out the surplus of their grains in coquetry; so that the shop fronts stood along that thoroughfare with an air of invitation, like rows of smiling saleswomen. Even on Sunday, when it veiled its more florid charms and lay comparatively empty of passage, the street shone out in contrast to its dingy neighbourhood, like a fire in a forest; and with its freshly painted shutters, well-polished brasses, and general cleanliness and gaiety of note, instantly caught and pleased the eye of the passenger.

Two doors from one corner, on the left hand going east the line was broken by the entry of a court; and just at that point a certain sinister block of building thrust forward its gable on the street. It was two storeys high; showed no window, nothing but a door on the lower storey and a blind forehead of discoloured wall on the upper; and bore in every feature, the marks of prolonged and sordid negligence. The door, which was equipped with neither bell nor knocker, was blistered and distained. Tramps slouched into the recess and struck matches on the panels; children kept shop upon the steps; the schoolboy had tried his knife on the mouldings; and for close on a generation, no one had appeared to drive away these random visitors or to repair their ravages.

Mr. Enfield and the lawyer were on the other side of the by-street; but when they came abreast of the entry, the former lifted up his cane and pointed.

"Did you ever remark that door?" he asked; and when his companion had replied in the affirmative. "It is connected in my mind," added he, "with a very odd story."

"Indeed?" said Mr. Utterson, with a slight change of voice, "and what was that?"

"Well, it was this way," returned Mr. Enfield: "I was coming home from some place at the end of the world, about three o'clock of a black winter morning, and my way lay through a part of town where there was literally nothing to be seen but lamps. Street after street and all the folks asleep — street after street, all lighted up as if for a procession and all as empty as a church — till at last I got into that state of mind when a man listens and listens and begins to long for the sight of a policeman. All at once, I saw two figures: one a little man who was stumping along eastward at a good walk, and the other a girl of maybe eight or ten who was running as hard as she was able down a cross street. Well, sir, the two ran into one another naturally enough at the corner; and then came the horrible part of the thing; for the man trampled calmly over the child's body and left her screaming on the ground. It sounds nothing to hear, but it was hellish to see. It wasn't like a man; it was like some damned Juggernaut. I gave a view halloa, took to my heels, collared my gentleman, and brought him back to where there was already quite a group about the screaming child. He was perfectly cool and made no resistance, but gave me one look, so ugly that it brought out the sweat on me like running. The people who had turned out were the girl's own family; and pretty soon, the doctor, for whom she had been sent put in his appearance. Well, the child was not much the worse, more frightened, according to the Sawbones; and there you might have supposed would be an end to it. But there was one curious circumstance. I had taken a loathing to my gentleman at first sight. So had the child's family, which was only natural. But the doctor's case was what struck me. He was the usual cut and dry apothecary, of no particular age and colour, with a strong Edinburgh accent and about as emotional as a bagpipe. Well, sir, he was like the rest of us; every time he looked at my prisoner, I saw that Sawbones turn sick and white with desire to kill him. I knew what was in his mind, just as he knew what was in mine; and killing being out of the question, we did the next best. We told the man we could and would make such a scandal out of this as should make his name stink from one end of London to the other. If he had any friends or any credit, we undertook that he should lose them. And all the time, as we were pitching it in red hot, we were keeping the women off him as best we could for they were as wild as harpies. I never saw a circle of such hateful faces; and there was the man in the middle, with a kind of black sneering coolness — frightened too, I could see that — but carrying it off, sir, really like Satan. 'If you choose to make capital out of this accident,' said he, 'I am naturally helpless. No gentleman but wishes to avoid a scene,' says he. 'Name your figure.' Well, we screwed him up to a hundred pounds for the child's family; he would have clearly liked to stick out; but there was something about the lot of us that meant mischief, and at last he struck. The next thing was to get the money; and where do you think he carried us but to that place with the door? — whipped out a key, went in, and presently came back with the matter of ten pounds in gold and a cheque for the balance on Coutts's, drawn payable to bearer and signed with a name that I can't mention, though it's one of the points of my story, but it was a name at least very well known and often printed. The figure was stiff; but the signature was good for more than that if it was only genuine. I took the liberty of pointing out to my gentleman that the whole business looked apocryphal, and that a man does not, in real life, walk into a cellar door at four in the morning and come out with another man's cheque for close upon a hundred pounds. But he was quite easy and sneering. 'Set your mind at rest,' says he, 'I will stay with you till the banks open and cash the cheque myself.' So we all set of, the doctor, and the child's father, and our friend and myself, and passed the rest of the night in my chambers; and next day, when we had breakfasted, went in a body to the bank. I gave in the cheque myself, and said I had every reason to believe it was a forgery. Not a bit of it. The cheque was genuine."

"Tut-tut," said Mr. Utterson.

"I see you feel as I do," said Mr. Enfield. "Yes, it's a bad story. For my man was a fellow that nobody could have to do with, a really damnable man; and the person that drew the cheque is the very pink of the proprieties, celebrated too, and (what makes it worse) one of your fellows who do what they call good. Black mail, I suppose; an honest man paying through the nose for some of the capers of his youth. Black Mail House is what I call the place with the door, in consequence. Though even that, you know, is far from explaining all," he added, and with the words fell into a vein of musing.

From this he was recalled by Mr. Utterson asking rather suddenly: "And you don't know if the drawer of the cheque lives there?"

"A likely place, isn't it?" returned Mr. Enfield. "But I happen to have noticed his address; he lives in some square or other."

"And you never asked about the — place with the door?" said Mr. Utterson.

"No, sir: I had a delicacy," was the reply. "I feel very strongly about putting questions; it partakes too much of the style of the day of judgement. You start a question, and it's like starting a stone. You sit quietly on the top of a hill; and away the stone goes, starting others; and presently some bland old bird (the last you would have thought of) is knocked on the head in his own back garden and the family have to change their name. No sir, I make it a rule of mine: the more it looks like Queer Street, the less I ask."

"A very good rule, too," said the lawyer.

"But I have studied the place for myself," continued Mr. Enfield. "It seems scarcely a house. There is no other door, and nobody goes in or out of that one but, once in a great while, the gentleman of my adventure. There are three windows looking on the court on the first floor; none below; the windows are always shut but they're clean. And then there is a chimney which is generally smoking; so somebody must live there. And yet it's not so sure; for the buildings are so packed together about the court, that it's hard to say where one ends and another begins."

The pair walked on again for a while in silence; and then "En-field," said Mr. Utterson, "that's a good rule of yours."

"Yes, I think it is," returned Enfield.

"But for all that," continued the lawyer, "there's one point I want to ask: I want to ask the name of that man who walked over the child."

"Well," said Mr. Enfield, "I can't see what harm it would do. It was a man of the name of Hyde."

"Hm," said Mr. Utterson. "What sort of a man is he to see?"

"He is not easy to describe. There is something wrong with his appearance; something displeasing, something downright de-testable. I never saw a man I so disliked, and yet I scarce know why. He must be deformed somewhere; he gives a strong feeling of deformity, although I couldn't specify the point. He's an ex-traordinary looking man, and yet I really can name nothing out of the way. No, sir; I can make no hand of it; I can't describe him. And it's not want of memory; for I declare I can see him this mo-ment."

Mr. Utterson again walked some way in silence and obviously under a weight of consideration. "You are sure he used a key?" he inquired at last.

"My dear sir . . ." began Enfield, surprised out of himself.

"Yes, I know," said Utterson; "I know it must seem strange. The fact is, if I do not ask you the name of the other party, it is because I know it already. You see, Richard, your tale has gone home. If you have been inexact in any point you had better correct it."

"I think you might have warned me," returned the other with a touch of sullenness. "But I have been pedantically exact, as you call it. The fellow had a key; and what's more, he has it still. I saw him use it not a week ago."

Mr. Utterson sighed deeply but said never a word; and the young man presently resumed. "Here is another lesson to say nothing," said he. "I am ashamed of my long tongue. Let us make a bargain never to refer to this again."

"With all my heart," said the lawyer. "I shake hands on that, Richard."

2

That evening Mr. Utterson came home to his bachelor house in sombre spirits and sat down to dinner without relish. It was his custom of a Sunday, when this meal was over, to sit close by the fire, a volume of some dry divinity on his reading desk, until the clock of the neighbouring church rang out the hour of twelve, when he would go soberly and gratefully to bed. On this night however, as soon as the cloth was taken away, he took up a candle and went into his business room. There he opened his safe, took from the most private part of it a document endorsed on the envelope as Dr. Jekyll's Will and sat down with a clouded brow to study its contents. The will was holograph, for Mr. Utterson though he took charge of it now that it was made, had refused to lend the least assistance in the making of it; it provided not only that, in case of the decease of Henry Jekyll, M.D., D.C.L., LL.D., F.R.S., etc., all his possessions were to pass into the hands of his "friend and benefactor Edward Hyde," but that in case of Dr. Jekyll's "disappearance or unexplained absence for any period exceeding three calendar months," the said Edward Hyde should step into the said Henry Jekyll's shoes without further delay and free from any burthen or obligation beyond the payment of a few small sums to the members of the doctor's household. This document had long been the lawyer's eyesore. It offended him both as a lawyer and as a lover of the sane and customary sides of life, to whom the fanciful was the immodest. And hitherto it was his ignorance of Mr. Hyde that had swelled his indignation; now, by a sudden turn, it was his knowledge. It was already bad enough when the name was but a name of which he could learn no more. It was worse when it began to be clothed upon with detestable attributes; and out of the shifting, insubstantial mists that had so long baffled his eye, there leapt up the sudden, definite presentment of a fiend.

"I thought it was madness," he said, as he replaced the obnoxious paper in the safe, "and now I begin to fear it is disgrace."

With that he blew out his candle, put on a greatcoat, and set forth in the direction of Cavendish Square, that citadel of medicine, where his friend, the great Dr. Lanyon, had his house and received his crowding patients. "If anyone knows, it will be Lanyon," he had thought.

The solemn butler knew and welcomed him; he was subjected to no stage of delay, but ushered direct from the door to the dining-room where Dr. Lanyon sat alone over his wine. This was a hearty, healthy, dapper, red-faced gentleman, with a shock of hair prematurely white, and a boisterous and decided manner. At sight of Mr. Utterson, he sprang up from his chair and welcomed him with both hands. The geniality, as was the way of the man, was somewhat theatrical to the eye; but it reposed on genuine feeling. For these two were old friends, old mates both at school and college, both thorough respectors of themselves and of each other, and what does not always follow, men who thoroughly enjoyed each other's company.

After a little rambling talk, the lawyer led up to the subject which so disagreeably preoccupied his mind.

"I suppose, Lanyon," said he, "you and I must be the two oldest friends that Henry Jekyll has?"

"I wish the friends were younger," chuckled Dr. Lanyon. "But I suppose we are. And what of that? I see little of him now."

"Indeed?" said Utterson. "I thought you had a bond of common interest."

"We had," was the reply. "But it is more than ten years since Henry Jekyll became too fanciful for me. He began to go wrong, wrong in mind; and though of course I continue to take an interest in him for old sake's sake, as they say, I see and I have seen devilish little of the man. Such unscientific balderdash," added the doctor, flushing suddenly purple, "would have estranged Damon and Pythias."

This little spirit of temper was somewhat of a relief to Mr. Utterson. "They have only differed on some point of science," he thought; and being a man of no scientific passions (except in the matter of conveyancing), he even added: "It is nothing worse than that!" He gave his friend a few seconds to recover his composure, and then approached the question he had come to put. "Did you ever come across a protégé of his—one Hyde?" he asked.

"Hyde?" repeated Lanyon. "No. Never heard of him. Since my time."

That was the amount of information that the lawyer carried back with him to the great, dark bed on which he tossed to and fro, until the small hours of the morning began to grow large. It was a night of little ease to his toiling mind, toiling in mere darkness and besieged by questions.

Six o'clock struck on the bells of the church that was so conveniently near to Mr. Utterson's dwelling, and still he was digging at the problem. Hitherto it had touched him on the intellectual side alone; but now his imagination also was engaged, or rather enslaved; and as he lay and tossed in the gross darkness of the night and the curtained room, Mr. Enfield's tale went by before his mind in a scroll of lighted pictures. He would be aware of the great field of lamps of a nocturnal city; then of the figure of a man walking swiftly; then of a child running from the doctor's; and then these met, and that human Juggernaut trod the child down and passed on regardless of her screams. Or else he would see a room in a rich house, where his friend lay asleep, dreaming and smiling at his dreams; and then the door of that room would be opened, the curtains of the bed plucked apart, the sleeper recalled, and lo! there would stand by his side a figure to whom power was given, and even at that dead hour, he must rise and do its bidding. The figure in these two phases haunted the lawyer all night; and if at any time he dozed over, it was but to see it glide more stealthily through sleeping houses, or move the more swiftly and still the more swiftly, even to dizziness, through wider labyrinths of lamplighted city, and at every street corner crush a child and leave her screaming. And still the figure had no face by which he might know it; even in his dreams, it had no face, or one that baffled him and melted before his eyes; and thus it was that there sprang up and grew apace in the lawyer's mind a singularly strong, almost an inordinate, curiosity to behold the features of the real Mr. Hyde. If he could but once set eyes on him, he thought the mystery would lighten and perhaps roll altogether away, as was the habit of mysterious things when well examined. He might see a reason for his friend's strange preference or bondage (call it which you please) and even for the startling clause of the will. At least it would be a face worth seeing: the face of a man who was without bowels of mercy: a face which had but to show itself to raise up, in the mind of the unimpressionable Enfield, a spirit of enduring hatred.

From that time forward, Mr. Utterson began to haunt the door in the by-street of shops. In the morning before office hours, at noon when business was plenty, and time scarce, at night under the face of the fogged city moon, by all lights and at all hours of solitude or concourse, the lawyer was to be found on his chosen post.

"If he be Mr. Hyde," he had thought, "I shall be Mr. Seek."

And at last his patience was rewarded. It was a fine dry night; frost in the air; the streets as clean as a ballroom floor; the lamps, unshaken by any wind, drawing a regular pattern of light and shadow. By ten o'clock, when the shops were closed, the by-street was very solitary and, in spite of the low growl of London from all round, very silent. Small sounds carried far; domestic sounds out of the houses were clearly audible on either side of the roadway; and the rumour of the approach of any passenger preceded him by a long time. Mr. Utterson had been some minutes at his post, when he was aware of an odd light footstep drawing near. In the course of his nightly patrols, he had long grown accustomed to the quaint effect with which the footfalls of a single person, while he is still a great way off, suddenly spring out distinct from the vast hum and clatter of the city. Yet his attention had never before been so sharply and decisively arrested; and it was with a strong, superstitious prevision of success that he withdrew into the entry of the court.

The steps drew swiftly nearer, and swelled out suddenly louder as they turned the end of the street. The lawyer, looking forth from the entry, could soon see what manner of man he had to deal with. He was small and very plainly dressed, and the look of him, even at that distance, went somehow strongly against the watcher's inclination. But he made straight for the door, crossing the roadway to save time; and as he came, he drew a key from his pocket like one approaching home.

Mr. Utterson stepped out and touched him on the shoulder as he passed. "Mr. Hyde, I think?"

Mr. Hyde shrank back with a hissing intake of the breath. But his fear was only momentary; and though he did not look the lawyer in the face, he answered coolly enough: "That is my name. What do you want?"

"I see you are going in," returned the lawyer. "I am an old friend of Dr. Jekyll's — Mr. Utterson of Gaunt Street — you must have heard of my name; and meeting you so conveniently, I thought you might admit me."

"You will not find Dr. Jekyll; he is from home," replied Mr. Hyde, blowing in the key. And then suddenly, but still without looking up, "How did you know me?" he asked.

"On your side," said Mr. Utterson, "will you do me a favour?"

"With pleasure," replied the other. "What shall it be?"

"Will you let me see your face?" asked the lawyer.

Mr. Hyde appeared to hesitate, and then, as if upon some sudden reflection, fronted about with an air of defiance; and the pair stared at each other pretty fixedly for a few seconds. "Now I shall know you again," said Mr. Utterson. "It may be useful."

"Yes," returned Mr. Hyde, "it is as well we have met; and *à propos*, you should have my address." And he gave a number of a street in Soho.

"Good God!" thought Mr. Utterson, "can he, too, have been thinking of the will?" But he kept his feelings to himself and only grunted in acknowledgement of the address.

"And now," said the other, "how did you know me?"

"By description," was the reply.

"Whose description?"

"We have common friends," said Mr. Utterson.

"Common friends," echoed Mr. Hyde, a little hoarsely. "Who are they?"

"Jekyll, for instance," said the lawyer.

"He never told you," cried Mr. Hyde, with a flush of anger. "I did not think you would have lied."

"Come," said Mr. Utterson, "that is not fitting language."

The other snarled aloud into a savage laugh; and the next moment, with extraordinary quickness, he had unlocked the door and disappeared into the house.

The lawyer stood awhile when Mr. Hyde had left him, the picture of disquietude. Then he began slowly to mount the street, pausing every step or two and putting his hand to his brow like a man in mental perplexity. The problem he was thus debating as he walked, was one of a class that is rarely solved. Mr. Hyde was pale and dwarfish, he gave an impression of deformity without any nameable malformation, he had a displeasing smile, he had borne himself to the lawyer with a sort of murderous mixture of timidity and boldness, and he spoke with a husky, whispering and somewhat broken voice; all these were points against him, but not all of these together could explain the hitherto unknown disgust, loathing and fear with which Mr. Utterson regarded him. "There must be something else," said the perplexed gentleman. "There *is* something more, if I could find a name for it. God bless me, the man seems hardly human! Something troglodytic, shall we say? or can it be the old story of Dr. Fell? or is it the mere radiance of a foul soul that thus transpires through, and transfigures, its clay continent? The last, I think; for, O my poor old Harry Jekyll, if ever I read Satan's signature upon a face, it is on that of your new friend."

Round the corner from the by-street, there was a square of ancient, handsome houses, now for the most part decayed from their high estate and let in flats and chambers to all sorts and conditions of men: map-engravers, architects, shady lawyers and the agents of obscure enterprises. One house, however, second from the corner, was still occupied entire; and at the door of this, which wore a great air of wealth and comfort, though it was now plunged in darkness except for the fanlight, Mr. Utterson stopped and knocked. A well-dressed, elderly servant opened the door.

"Is Dr. Jekyll at home, Poole?" asked the lawyer.

"I will see, Mr. Utterson," said Poole, admitting the visitor, as he spoke, into a large, low-roofed, comfortable hall paved with flags, warmed (after the fashion of a country house) by a bright, open fire, and furnished with costly cabinets of oak. "Will you wait here by the fire, sir? or shall I give you a light in the dining-room?"

"Here, thank you," said the lawyer, and he drew near and leant on the tall fender. This hall, in which he was now left alone, was a pet fancy of his friend the doctor's; and Utterson himself was wont to speak of it as the pleasantest room in London. But tonight there was a shudder in his blood; the face of Hyde sat heavy on his memory; he felt (what was rare with him) a nausea and distaste of life; and in the gloom of his spirits, he seemed to read a menace in the flickering of the firelight on the polished cabinets and the uneasy starting of the shadow on the roof. He was ashamed of his relief, when Poole presently returned to announce that Dr. Jekyll was gone out.

"I saw Mr. Hyde go in by the old dissecting-room door, Poole," he said. "Is that right, when Dr. Jekyll is from home?"

"Quite right, Mr. Utterson, sir," replied the servant. "Mr. Hyde has a key."

"Your master seems to repose a great deal of trust in that young man, Poole," resumed the other musingly.

"Yes, sir, he does indeed," said Poole. "We have all orders to obey him."

"I do not think I ever met Mr. Hyde?" asked Utterson.

"O, dear no, sir. He never *dines* here," replied the butler. "Indeed we see very little of him on this side of the house; he mostly comes and goes by the laboratory."

"Well, good-night, Poole."

"Good-night, Mr. Utterson."

And the lawyer set out homeward with a very heavy heart. "Poor Harry Jekyll," he thought, "my mind misgives me he is in deep waters! He was wild when he was young; a long while ago to be sure; but in the law of God, there is no statute of limitations. Ay, it must be that; the ghost of some old sin, the cancer of some concealed disgrace: punishment coming, *pede claudo*, years after memory has forgotten and self-love condoned the fault." And the lawyer, scared by the thought, brooded awhile on his own past, groping in all the corners of memory, lest by chance some Jack-in-the-Box of an old iniquity should leap to light there. His past was fairly blameless; few men could read the rolls of their life with less apprehension; yet he was humbled to the dust by the many ill things he had done, and raised up again into a sober and fearful gratitude by the many he had come so near to doing yet avoided. And then by a return on his former subject, he conceived a spark of hope. "This Master Hyde, if he were studied," thought he, "must have secrets of his own; black secrets, by the look of him; secrets compared to which poor Jekyll's worst would be like sunshine. Things cannot continue as they are. It turns me cold to think of this creature stealing like a thief to Harry's bedside; poor Harry, what a wakening! And the danger of it; for if this Hyde suspects the existence of the will, he may grow impatient to inherit. Ay, I must put my shoulders to the wheel — if Jekyll will but let me," he added, "if Jekyll will only let me." For once more he saw before his mind's eye, as clear as a transparency, the strange clauses of the will.

3

Dr. Jekyll Was Quite at Ease

A fortnight later, by excellent good fortune, the doctor gave one of his pleasant dinners to some five or six old cronies, all intelligent, reputable men and all judges of good wine; and Mr. Utterson so contrived that he remained behind after the others had departed. This was no new arrangement, but a thing that had befallen many scores of times. Where Utterson was liked, he was liked well. Hosts loved to detain the dry lawyer, when the light-hearted and loose-tongued had already their foot on the threshold; they liked to sit awhile in his unobtrusive company, practising for solitude, sobering their minds in the man's rich silence after the expense and strain of gaiety. To this rule, Dr. Jekyll was no exception; and as he now sat on the opposite side of the fire — a large, well-made, smooth-faced man of fifty, with something of a slyish cast perhaps, but every mark of capacity and kindness — you could see by his looks that he cherished for Mr. Utterson a sincere and warm affection.

"I have been wanting to speak to you, Jekyll," began the latter. "You know that will of yours?"

A close observer might have gathered that the topic was distasteful; but the doctor carried it off gaily. "My poor Utterson," said he, "you are unfortunate in such a client. I never saw a man so distressed as you were by my will; unless it were that hide-bound pedant, Lanyon, at what he called my scientific heresies. O, I know he's a good fellow — you needn't frown — an excellent fellow, and I always mean to see more of him; but a hide-bound pedant for all that; an ignorant, blatant pedant. I was never more disappointed in any man than Lanyon."

"You know I never approved of it," pursued Utterson, ruthlessly disregarding the fresh topic.

"My will? Yes, certainly, I know that," said the doctor, a trifle sharply. "You have told me so."

"Well, I tell you so again," continued the lawyer. "I have been learning something of young Hyde."

The large handsome face of Dr. Jekyll grew pale to the very lips, and there came a blackness about his eyes. "I do not care to hear more," said he. "This is a matter I thought we had agreed to drop."

"What I heard was abominable," said Utterson.

"It can make no change. You do not understand my position," returned the doctor, with a certain incoherency of manner. "I am painfully situated, Utterson; my position is a very strange — a very strange one. It is one of those affairs that cannot be mended by talking."

"Jekyll," said Utterson, "you know me: I am a man to be trusted. Make a clean breast of this in confidence; and I make no doubt I can get you out of it."

"My good Utterson," said the doctor, "this is very good of you, this is downright good of you, and I cannot find words to thank you in. I believe you fully; I would trust you before any man alive, ay, before myself, if I could make the choice; but indeed it isn't what you fancy; it is not as bad as that; and just to put your good heart at rest, I will tell you one thing: the moment I choose, I can be rid of Mr. Hyde. I give you my hand upon that; and I thank you again and again; and I will just add one little word, Utterson, that I'm sure you'll take in good part: this is a private matter, and I beg of you to let it sleep."

Utterson reflected a little, looking in the fire.

"I have no doubt you are perfectly right," he said at last, getting to his feet.

"Well, but since we have touched upon this business, and for the last time I hope," continued the doctor, "there is one point I should like you to understand. I have really a very great interest in poor Hyde. I know you have seen him; he told me so; and I fear he was rude. But I do sincerely take a great, a very great interest in that young man; and if I am taken away, Utterson, I wish you to promise me that you will bear with him and get his rights for him. I think you would, if you knew all; and it would be a weight off my mind if you would promise."

"I can't pretend that I shall ever like him," said the lawyer.

"I don't ask that," pleaded Jekyll, laying his hand upon the other's arm; "I only ask for justice; I only ask you to help him for my sake, when I am no longer here."

Utterson heaved an irrepressible sigh. "Well," said he, "I promise."

4

The Carew Murder Case

Nearly a year later, in the month of October, 18 —, London was startled by a crime of singular ferocity and rendered all the more notable by the high position of the victim. The details were few and startling. A maid servant living alone in a house not far from the river, had gone upstairs to bed about eleven. Although a fog rolled over the city in the small hours, the early part of the night was cloudless, and the lane, which the maid's window overlooked, was brilliantly lit by the full moon. It seems she was romantically given, for she sat down upon her box, which stood immediately under the window, and fell into a dream of musing. Never (she used to say, with streaming tears, when she narrated that experience), never had she felt more at peace with all men or thought more kindly of the world. And as she so sat she became aware of an aged beautiful gentleman with white hair, drawing near along the lane; and advancing to meet him, another and very small gentleman, to whom at first she paid less attention. When they had come within speech (which was just under the maid's eyes) the older man bowed and accosted the other with a very pretty manner of politeness. It did not seem as if the subject of his address were of great importance; indeed, from his pointing, it sometimes appeared as if he were only inquiring his way; but the moon shone on his face as he spoke, and the girl was pleased to watch it, it seemed to breathe such an innocent and old-world kindness of disposition, yet with something high too, as of a well-founded self-content. Presently her eye wandered to the other, and she was surprised to recognise in him a certain Mr. Hyde, who had once visited her master and for whom she had conceived a dislike. He had in his hand a heavy cane, with which he was trifling; but he answered never a word, and seemed to listen with an ill-contained impatience. And then all of a sudden he broke out in a great flame of anger, stamping with his foot, brandishing the cane, and carrying on (as the maid described it) like a madman. The old gentleman took a step back, with the air of one very much surprised and a trifle hurt; and at that Mr. Hyde broke out of all bounds and clubbed him to the earth. And next moment, with ape-like fury, he was trampling his victim under foot and hailing down a storm of blows, under which the bones were audibly shattered and the body jumped upon the roadway. At the horror of these sights and sounds, the maid fainted.

It was two o'clock when she came to herself and called for the police. The murderer was gone long ago; but there lay his victim in the middle of the lane, incredibly mangled. The stick with which the deed had been done, although it was of some rare and very tough and heavy wood, had broken in the middle under the stress of this insensate cruelty; and one splintered half had rolled in the neighbouring gutter — the other, without doubt, had been carried away by the murderer. A purse and gold watch were found upon the victim: but no cards or papers, except a sealed and stamped envelope, which he had been probably carrying to the post, and which bore the name and address of Mr. Utterson.

This was brought to the lawyer the next morning, before he was out of bed; and he had no sooner seen it, and been told the circumstances, than he shot out a solemn lip. "I shall say nothing till I have seen the body," said he; "this may be very serious. Have the kindness to wait while I dress." And with the same grave countenance he hurried through his breakfast and drove to the police station, whither the body had been carried. As soon as he came into the cell, he nodded.

"Yes," said he, "I recognise him. I am sorry to say that this is Sir Danvers Carew."

"Good God, sir," exclaimed the officer, "is it possible?" And the next moment his eye lighted up with professional ambition. "This will make a deal of noise," he said. "And perhaps you can help us to the man." And he briefly narrated what the maid had seen, and showed the broken stick.

Mr. Utterson had already quailed at the name of Hyde; but when the stick was laid before him, he could doubt no longer; broken and battered as it was, he recognised it for one that he had himself presented many years before to Henry Jekyll.

"Is this Mr. Hyde a person of small stature?" he inquired.

"Particularly small and particularly wicked-looking, is what the maid calls him," said the officer.

Mr. Utterson reflected; and then, raising his head, "If you will come with me in my cab," he said, "I think I can take you to his house."

It was by this time about nine in the morning, and the first fog of the season. A great chocolate-coloured pall lowered over heaven, but the wind was continually charging and routing these embattled vapours; so that as the cab crawled from street to street, Mr. Utterson beheld a marvellous number of degrees and hues of twilight; for here it would be dark like the back-end of evening; and there would be a glow of a rich, lurid brown, like the light of some strange conflagration; and here, for a moment, the fog would be quite broken up, and a haggard shaft of daylight would glance in between the swirling wreaths. The dismal quarter of Soho seen under these changing glimpses, with its muddy ways, and slatternly passengers, and its lamps, which had never been extinguished or had been kindled afresh to combat this mournful reinvasion of darkness, seemed, in the lawyer's eyes, like a district of some city in a nightmare. The thoughts of his mind, besides, were of the gloomiest dye; and when he glanced at the companion of his drive, he was conscious of some touch of that terror of the law and the law's officers, which may at times assail the most honest.

As the cab drew up before the address indicated, the fog lifted a little and showed him a dingy street, a gin palace, a low French eating house, a shop for the retail of penny numbers and two-penny salads, many ragged children huddled in the doorways, and many women of many different nationalities passing out, key in hand, to have a morning glass; and the next moment the fog settled down again upon that part, as brown as umber, and cut him off from his blackguardly surroundings. This was the home of Henry Jekyll's favourite; of a man who was heir to a quarter of a million sterling.

An ivory-faced and silvery-haired old woman opened the door. She had an evil face, smoothed by hypocrisy; but her manners were excellent. Yes, she said, this was Mr. Hyde's, but he was not at home; he had been in that night very late, but he had gone away again in less than an hour; there was nothing strange in that; his habits were very irregular, and he was often absent; for instance, it was nearly two months since she had seen him till yesterday.

"Very well, then, we wish to see his rooms," said the lawyer; and when the woman began to declare it was impossible, "I had better tell you who this person is," he added. "This is Inspector Newcomen of Scotland Yard."

A flash of odious joy appeared upon the woman's face. "Ah!" said she, "he is in trouble! What has he done?"

Mr. Utterson and the inspector exchanged glances. "He don't seem a very popular character," observed the latter. "And now, my good woman, just let me and this gentleman have a look about us."

In the whole extent of the house, which but for the old woman remained otherwise empty, Mr. Hyde had only used a couple of rooms; but these were furnished with luxury and good taste. A closet was filled with wine; the plate was of silver, the napery elegant; a good picture hung upon the walls, a gift (as Utterson supposed) from Henry Jekyll, who was much of a connoisseur; and the carpets were of many plies and agreeable in colour. At this moment, however, the rooms bore every mark of having been recently and hurriedly ransacked; clothes lay about the floor, with their pockets inside out; lock-fast drawers stood open; and on the hearth there lay a pile of grey ashes, as though many papers had been burned. From these embers the inspector disinterred the butt end of a green cheque book, which had resisted the action of the fire; the other half of the stick was found behind the door; and as this clinched his suspicions, the officer declared himself delighted. A visit to the bank, where several thousand pounds were found to be lying to the murderer's credit, completed his gratification.

"You may depend upon it, sir," he told Mr. Utterson: "I have him in my hand. He must have lost his head, or he never would have left the stick or, above all, burned the cheque book. Why, money's life to the man. We have nothing to do but wait for him at the bank, and get out the handbills."

This last, however, was not so easy of accomplishment; for Mr. Hyde had numbered few familiars — even the master of the servant maid had only seen him twice; his family could nowhere be traced; he had never been photographed; and the few who could describe him differed widely, as common observers will. Only on one point were they agreed; and that was the haunting sense of unexpressed deformity with which the fugitive impressed his beholders.

5

Incident of the Letter

It was late in the afternoon, when Mr. Utterson found his way to Dr. Jekyll's door, where he was at once admitted by Poole, and carried down by the kitchen offices and across a yard which had once been a garden, to the building which was indifferently known as the laboratory or the dissecting rooms. The doctor had bought the house from the heirs of a celebrated surgeon; and his own tastes being rather chemical than anatomical, had changed the destination of the block at the bottom of the garden. It was the first time that the lawyer had been received in that part of his friend's quarters; and he eyed the dingy, windowless structure with curiosity, and gazed round with a distasteful sense of strangeness as he crossed the theatre, once crowded with eager students and now lying gaunt and silent, the tables laden with chemical apparatus, the floor strewn with crates and littered with packing straw, and the light falling dimly through the foggy cupola. At the further end, a flight of stairs mounted to a door covered with red baize; and through this, Mr. Utterson was at last received into the doctor's cabinet. It was a large room fitted round with glass presses, furnished, among other things, with a cheval-glass and a business table, and looking out upon the court by three dusty windows barred with iron. The fire burned in the grate; a lamp was set lighted on the chimney shelf, for even in the houses the fog began to lie thickly; and there, close up to the warmth, sat Dr. Jekyll, looking deathly sick. He did not rise to meet his visitor, but held out a cold hand and bade him welcome in a changed voice.

"And now," said Mr. Utterson, as soon as Poole had left them, "you have heard the news?"

The doctor shuddered. "They were crying it in the square," he said. "I heard them in my dining-room."

"One word," said the lawyer. "Carew was my client, but so are you, and I want to know what I am doing. You have not been mad enough to hide this fellow?"

"Utterson, I swear to God," cried the doctor, "I swear to God I will never set eyes on him again. I bind my honour to you that I am done with him in this world. It is all at an end. And indeed he does not want my help; you do not know him as I do; he is safe, he is quite safe; mark my words, he will never more be heard of."

The lawyer listened gloomily; he did not like his friend's feverish manner. "You seem pretty sure of him," said he; "and for your sake, I hope you may be right. If it came to a trial, your name might appear."

"I am quite sure of him," replied Jekyll; "I have grounds for certainty that I cannot share with anyone. But there is one thing on which you may advise me. I have — I have received a letter; and I am at a loss whether I should show it to the police. I should like to leave it in your hands, Utterson; you would judge wisely, I am sure; I have so great a trust in you."

"You fear, I suppose, that it might lead to his detection?" asked the lawyer.

"No," said the other. "I cannot say that I care what becomes of Hyde; I am quite done with him. I was thinking of my own character, which this hateful business has rather exposed."

Utterson ruminated awhile; he was surprised at his friend's selfishness, and yet relieved by it. "Well," said he, at last, "let me see the letter."

The letter was written in an odd, upright hand and signed "Edward Hyde": and it signified, briefly enough, that the writer's benefactor, Dr. Jekyll, whom he had long so unworthily repaid for a thousand generosities, need labour under no alarm for his safety, as he had means of escape on which he placed a sure dependence. The lawyer liked this letter well enough; it put a better colour on the intimacy than he had looked for; and he blamed himself for some of his past suspicions.

"Have you the envelope?" he asked.

"I burned it," replied Jekyll, "before I thought what I was about. But it bore no postmark. The note was handed in."

"Shall I keep this and sleep upon it?" asked Utterson.

"I wish you to judge for me entirely," was the reply. "I have lost confidence in myself."

"Well, I shall consider," returned the lawyer. "And now one word more: it was Hyde who dictated the terms in your will about that disappearance?"

The doctor seemed seized with a qualm of faintness; he shut his mouth tight and nodded.

"I knew it," said Utterson. "He meant to murder you. You had a fine escape."

"I have had what is far more to the purpose," returned the doctor solemnly: "I have had a lesson — O God, Utterson, what a lesson I have had!" And he covered his face for a moment with his hands.

On his way out, the lawyer stopped and had a word or two with Poole. "By the bye," said he, "there was a letter handed in to-day: what was the messenger like?" But Poole was positive nothing had come except by post; "and only circulars by that," he added.

This news sent off the visitor with his fears renewed. Plainly the letter had come by the laboratory door; possibly, indeed, it had been written in the cabinet; and if that were so, it must be differently judged, and handled with the more caution. The newsboys, as he went, were crying themselves hoarse along the footways: "Special edition. Shocking murder of an M.P." That was the funeral oration of one friend and client; and he could not help a certain apprehension lest the good name of another should be sucked down in the eddy of the scandal. It was, at least, a ticklish decision that he had to make; and self-reliant as he was by habit, he began to cherish a longing for advice. It was not to be had directly; but perhaps, he thought, it might be fished for.

Presently after, he sat on one side of his own hearth, with Mr. Guest, his head clerk, upon the other, and midway between, at a nicely calculated distance from the fire, a bottle of a particular old wine that had long dwelt unsunned in the foundations of his house. The fog still slept on the wing above the drowned city, where the lamps glimmered like carbuncles; and through the muffle and smother of these fallen clouds, the procession of the town's life was still rolling in through the great arteries with a sound as of a mighty wind. But the room was gay with firelight. In the bottle the acids were long ago resolved; the imperial dye had softened with time, as the colour grows richer in stained windows; and the glow of hot autumn afternoons on hillside vineyards, was ready to be set free and to disperse the fogs of London. Insensibly the lawyer melted. There was no man from whom he kept fewer secrets than Mr. Guest; and he was not always sure that he kept as many as he meant. Guest had often been on business to the doctor's; he knew Poole; he could scarce have failed to hear of Mr. Hyde's familiarity about the house; he might draw conclusions: was it not as well, then, that he should see a letter which put that mystery to rights? and above all since Guest, being a great student and critic of handwriting, would consider the step natural and obliging? The clerk, besides, was a man of counsel; he could scarce read so strange a document without dropping a remark; and by that remark Mr. Utterson might shape his future course.

"This is a sad business about Sir Danvers," he said.

"Yes, sir, indeed. It has elicited a great deal of public feeling," returned Guest. "The man, of course, was mad."

"I should like to hear your views on that," replied Utterson. "I have a document here in his handwriting; it is between ourselves, for I scarce know what to do about it; it is an ugly business at the best. But there it is; quite in your way: a murderer's autograph."

Guest's eyes brightened, and he sat down at once and studied it with passion. "No sir," he said: "not mad; but it is an odd hand."

"And by all accounts a very odd writer," added the lawyer.

Just then the servant entered with a note.

"Is that from Dr. Jekyll, sir?" inquired the clerk. "I thought I knew the writing. Anything private, Mr. Utterson?"

"Only an invitation to dinner. Why? Do you want to see it?"

"One moment. I thank you, sir"; and the clerk laid the two sheets of paper alongside and sedulously compared their contents. "Thank you, sir," he said at last, returning both; "it's a very interesting autograph."

There was a pause, during which Mr. Utterson struggled with himself. "Why did you compare them, Guest?" he inquired suddenly.

"Well, sir," returned the clerk, "there's a rather singular resemblance; the two hands are in many points identical: only differently sloped."

"Rather quaint," said Utterson.

"It is, as you say, rather quaint," returned Guest.

"I wouldn't speak of this note, you know," said the master.

"No, sir," said the clerk. "I understand."

But no sooner was Mr. Utterson alone that night, than he locked the note into his safe, where it reposed from that time forward. "What!" he thought. "Henry Jekyll forge for a murderer!" And his blood ran cold in his veins.

6

Remarkable Incident of Dr. Lanyon

Time ran on; thousands of pounds were offered in reward, for the death of Sir Danvers was resented as a public injury; but Mr. Hyde had disappeared out of the ken of the police as though he had never existed. Much of his past was unearthed, indeed, and all disreputable: tales came out of the man's cruelty, at once so callous and violent; of his vile life, of his strange associates, of the hatred that seemed to have surrounded his career; but of his present whereabouts, not a whisper. From the time he had left the house in Soho on the morning of the murder, he was simply blotted out; and gradually, as time drew on, Mr. Utterson began to recover from the hotness of his alarm, and to grow more at quiet with himself. The death of Sir Danvers was, to his way of thinking, more than paid for by the disappearance of Mr. Hyde. Now that that evil influence had been withdrawn, a new life began for Dr. Jekyll. He came out of his seclusion, renewed relations with his friends, became once more their familiar guest and entertainer; and whilst he had always been known for charities, he was now no less distinguished for religion. He was busy, he was much in the open air, he did good; his face seemed to open and brighten, as if with an inward consciousness of service; and for more than two months, the doctor was at peace.

On the 8th of January Utterson had dined at the doctor's with a small party; Lanyon had been there; and the face of the host had looked from one to the other as in the old days when the trio were inseparable friends. On the 12th, and again on the 14th, the door was shut against the lawyer. "The doctor was confined to the house," Poole said, "and saw no one." On the 15th, he tried again, and was again refused; and having now been used for the last two months to see his friend almost daily, he found this return of solitude to weigh upon his spirits. The fifth night he had in Guest to dine with him; and the sixth he betook himself to Dr. Lanyon's.

There at least he was not denied admittance; but when he came in, he was shocked at the change which had taken place in the doctor's appearance. He had his death-warrant written legibly upon his face. The rosy man had grown pale; his flesh had fallen away; he was visibly balder and older; and yet it was not so much these tokens of a swift physical decay that arrested the lawyer's notice, as a look in the eye and quality of manner that seemed to testify to some deep-seated terror of the mind. It was unlikely that the doctor should fear death; and yet that was what Utterson was tempted to suspect. "Yes," he thought; "he is a doctor, he must know his own state and that his days are counted; and the knowledge is more than he can bear." And yet when Utterson remarked on his ill-looks, it was with an air of great firmness that Lanyon declared himself a doomed man.

"I have had a shock," he said, "and I shall never recover. It is a question of weeks. Well, life has been pleasant; I liked it; yes, sir, I used to like it. I sometimes think if we knew all, we should be more glad to get away."

"Jekyll is ill, too," observed Utterson. "Have you seen him?"

But Lanyon's face changed, and he held up a trembling hand. "I wish to see or hear no more of Dr. Jekyll," he said in a loud, unsteady voice. "I am quite done with that person; and I beg that you will spare me any allusion to one whom I regard as dead."

"Tut-tut," said Mr. Utterson; and then after a considerable pause, "Can't I do anything?" he inquired. "We are three very old friends, Lanyon; we shall not live to make others."

"Nothing can be done," returned Lanyon; "ask himself."

"He will not see me," said the lawyer.

"I am not surprised at that," was the reply. "Some day, Utterson, after I am dead, you may perhaps come to learn the right and wrong of this. I cannot tell you. And in the meantime, if you can sit and talk with me of other things, for God's sake, stay and do so; but if you cannot keep clear of this accursed topic, then in God's name, go, for I cannot bear it."

As soon as he got home, Utterson sat down and wrote to Jekyll, complaining of his exclusion from the house, and asking the cause of this unhappy break with Lanyon; and the next day brought him a long answer, often very pathetically worded, and sometimes darkly mysterious in drift. The quarrel with Lanyon was incurable. "I do not blame our old friend," Jekyll wrote, "but I share his view that we must never meet. I mean from henceforth to lead a life of extreme seclusion; you must not be surprised, nor must you doubt my friendship, if my door is often shut even to you. You must suffer me to go my own dark way. I have brought on myself a punishment and a danger that I cannot name. If I am the chief of sinners, I am the chief of sufferers also. I could not think that this earth contained a place for sufferings and terrors so unmanning; and you can do but one thing, Utterson, to lighten this destiny, and that is to respect my silence." Utterson was amazed; the dark influence of Hyde had been withdrawn, the doctor had returned to his old tasks and amities; a week ago, the prospect had smiled with every promise of a cheerful and an honoured age; and now in a moment, friendship, and peace of mind, and the whole tenor of his life were wrecked. So great and unprepared a change pointed to madness; but in view of Lanyon's manner and words, there must lie for it some deeper ground.

A week afterwards Dr. Lanyon took to his bed, and in something less than a fortnight he was dead. The night after the funeral, at which he had been sadly affected, Utterson locked the door of his business room, and sitting there by the light of a melancholy candle, drew out and set before him an envelope addressed by the hand and sealed with the seal of his dead friend. "PRIVATE: for the hands of G. J. Utterson ALONE, and in case of his predecease *to be destroyed unread*," so it was emphatically superscribed; and the lawyer dreaded to behold the contents. "I have buried one friend to-day," he thought: "what if this should cost me another?" And then he condemned the fear as a disloyalty, and broke the seal. Within there was another enclosure, likewise sealed, and marked upon the cover as "not to be opened till the death or disappearance of Dr. Henry Jekyll." Utterson could not trust his eyes. Yes, it was disappearance; here again, as in the mad will which he had long ago restored to its author, here again were the idea of a disappearance and the name of Henry Jekyll bracketted. But in the will, that idea had sprung from the sinister suggestion of the man Hyde; it was set there with a purpose all too plain and horrible. Written by the hand of Lanyon, what should it mean? A great curiosity came on the trustee, to disregard the prohibition and dive at once to the bottom of these mysteries; but professional honour and faith to his dead friend were stringent obligations; and the packet slept in the inmost corner of his private safe.

It is one thing to mortify curiosity, another to conquer it; and it may be doubted if, from that day forth, Utterson desired the society of his surviving friend with the same eagerness. He thought of him kindly; but his thoughts were disquieted and fearful. He went to call indeed; but he was perhaps relieved to be denied admittance; perhaps, in his heart, he preferred to speak with Poole upon the doorstep and surrounded by the air and sounds of the open city, rather than to be admitted into that house of voluntary bondage, and to sit and speak with its inscrutable recluse. Poole had, indeed, no very pleasant news to communicate. The doctor, it appeared, now more than ever confined himself to the cabinet over the laboratory, where he would sometimes even sleep; he was out of spirits, he had grown very silent, he did not read; it seemed as if he had something on his mind. Utterson became so used to the unvarying character of these reports, that he fell off little by little in the frequency of his visits.

1

Incident at the Window

It chanced on Sunday, when Mr. Utterson was on his usual walk with Mr. Enfield, that their way lay once again through the by-street; and that when they came in front of the door, both stopped to gaze on it.

"Well," said Enfield, "that story's at an end at least. We shall never see more of Mr. Hyde."

"I hope not," said Utterson. "Did I ever tell you that I once saw him, and shared your feeling of repulsion?"

"It was impossible to do the one without the other," returned Enfield. "And by the way, what an ass you must have thought me, not to know that this was a back way to Dr. Jekyll's! It was partly your own fault that I found it out, even when I did."

"So you found it out, did you?" said Utterson. "But if that be so, we may step into the court and take a look at the windows. To tell you the truth, I am uneasy about poor Jekyll; and even outside, I feel as if the presence of a friend might do him good."

The court was very cool and a little damp, and full of premature twilight, although the sky, high up overhead, was still bright with sunset. The middle one of the three windows was half-way open; and sitting close beside it, taking the air with an infinite sadness of mien, like some disconsolate prisoner, Utterson saw Dr. Jekyll.

"What! Jekyll!" he cried. "I trust you are better."

"I am very low, Utterson," replied the doctor drearily, "very low. It will not last long, thank God."

"You stay too much indoors," said the lawyer. "You should be out, whipping up the circulation like Mr. Enfield and me. (This is my cousin — Mr. Enfield — Dr. Jekyll.) Come now; get your hat and take a quick turn with us."

"You are very good," sighed the other. "I should like to very much; but no, no, no, it is quite impossible; I dare not. But indeed, Utterson, I am very glad to see you; this is really a great pleasure; I would ask you and Mr. Enfield up, but the place is really not fit."

"Why, then," said the lawyer, good-naturedly, "the best thing we can do is to stay down here and speak with you from where we are."

"That is just what I was about to venture to propose," returned the doctor with a smile. But the words were hardly uttered, before the smile was struck out of his face and succeeded by an expression of such abject terror and despair, as froze the very blood of the two gentlemen below. They saw it but for a glimpse for the window was instantly thrust down; but that glimpse had been sufficient, and they turned and left the court without a word. In silence, too, they traversed the by-street; and it was not until they had come into a neighbouring thoroughfare, where even upon a Sunday there were still some stirrings of life, that Mr. Utterson at last turned and looked at his companion. They were both pale; and there was an answering horror in their eyes.

"God forgive us, God forgive us," said Mr. Utterson.

But Mr. Enfield only nodded his head very seriously, and walked on once more in silence.

8

The Last Night

Mr. Utterson was sitting by his fireside one evening after dinner, when he was surprised to receive a visit from Poole.

"Bless me, Poole, what brings you here?" he cried; and then taking a second look at him, "What ails you?" he added; "is the doctor ill?"

"Mr. Utterson," said the man, "there is something wrong."

"Take a seat, and here is a glass of wine for you," said the lawyer. "Now, take your time, and tell me plainly what you want."

"You know the doctor's ways, sir," replied Poole, "and how he shuts himself up. Well, he's shut up again in the cabinet; and I don't like it, sir — I wish I may die if I like it. Mr. Utterson, sir, I'm afraid."

"Now, my good man," said the lawyer, "be explicit. What are you afraid of?"

"I've been afraid for about a week," returned Poole, doggedly disregarding the question, "and I can bear it no more."

The man's appearance amply bore out his words; his manner was altered for the worse; and except for the moment when he had first announced his terror, he had not once looked the lawyer in the face. Even now, he sat with the glass of wine untasted on his knee, and his eyes directed to a corner of the floor. "I can bear it no more," he repeated.

"Come," said the lawyer, "I see you have some good reason, Poole; I see there is something seriously amiss. Try to tell me what it is."

"I think there's been foul play," said Poole, hoarsely.

"Foul play!" cried the lawyer, a good deal frightened and rather inclined to be irritated in consequence. "What foul play! What does the man mean?"

"I daren't say, sir," was the answer; "but will you come along with me and see for yourself?"

Mr. Utterson's only answer was to rise and get his hat and greatcoat; but he observed with wonder the greatness of the relief that appeared upon the butler's face, and perhaps with no less, that the wine was still untasted when he set it down to follow.

It was a wild, cold, seasonable night of March, with a pale moon, lying on her back as though the wind had tilted her, and flying wrack of the most diaphanous and lawny texture. The wind made talking difficult, and flecked the blood into the face. It seemed to have swept the streets unusually bare of passengers, besides; for Mr. Utterson thought he had never seen that part of London so deserted. He could have wished it otherwise; never in his life had he been conscious of so sharp a wish to see and touch his fellow-creatures; for struggle as he might, there was borne in upon his mind a crushing anticipation of calamity. The square, when they got there, was full of wind and dust, and the thin trees in the garden were lashing themselves along the railing. Poole, who had kept all the way a pace or two ahead, now pulled up in the middle of the pavement, and in spite of the biting weather, took off his hat and mopped his brow with a red pocket-handkerchief. But for all the hurry of his coming, these were not the dews of exertion that he wiped away, but the moisture of some strangling anguish; for his face was white and his voice, when he spoke, harsh and broken.

"Well, sir," he said, "here we are, and God grant there be nothing wrong."

"Amen, Poole," said the lawyer.

Thereupon the servant knocked in a very guarded manner; the door was opened on the chain; and a voice asked from within, "Is that you, Poole?"

"It's all right," said Poole. "Open the door."

The hall, when they entered it, was brightly lighted up; the fire was built high; and about the hearth the whole of the servants, men and women, stood huddled together like a flock of sheep. At the sight of Mr. Utterson, the housemaid broke into hysterical whimpering; and the cook, crying out "Bless God! it's Mr. Utterson," ran forward as if to take him in her arms.

"What, what? Are you all here?" said the lawyer peevishly. "Very irregular, very unseemly; your master would be far from pleased."

"They're all afraid," said Poole.

Blank silence followed, no one protesting; only the maid lifted her voice and now wept loudly.

"Hold your tongue!" Poole said to her, with a ferocity of accent that testified to his own jangled nerves; and indeed, when the girl had so suddenly raised the note of her lamentation, they had all started and turned towards the inner door with faces of dreadful expectation. "And now," continued the butler, addressing the knife-boy, "reach me a candle, and we'll get this through hands at once." And then he begged Mr. Utterson to follow him, and led the way to the back garden.

"Now, sir," said he, "you come as gently as you can. I want you to hear, and I don't want you to be heard. And see here, sir, if by any chance he was to ask you in, don't go."

Mr. Utterson's nerves, at this unlooked-for termination, gave a jerk that nearly threw him from his balance; but he recollected his courage and followed the butler into the laboratory building and through the surgical theatre, with its lumber of crates and bottles, to the foot of the stair. Here Poole motioned him to stand on one side and listen; while he himself, setting down the candle and making a great and obvious call on his resolution, mounted the steps and knocked with a somewhat uncertain hand on the red baize of the cabinet door.

"Mr. Utterson, sir, asking to see you," he called; and even as he did so, once more violently signed to the lawyer to give ear.

A voice answered from within: "Tell him I cannot see anyone," it said complainingly.

"Thank you, sir," said Poole, with a note of something like triumph in his voice; and taking up his candle, he led Mr. Utterson back across the yard and into the great kitchen, where the fire was out and the beetles were leaping on the floor.

"Sir," he said, looking Mr. Utterson in the eyes, "was that my master's voice?"

"It seems much changed," replied the lawyer, very pale, but giving look for look.

"Changed? Well, yes, I think so," said the butler. "Have I been twenty years in this man's house, to be deceived about his voice? No, sir; master's made away with; he was made away with eight days ago, when we heard him cry out upon the name of God; and *who's* in there instead of him, and *why* it stays there, is a thing that cries to Heaven, Mr. Utterson!"

"This is a very strange tale, Poole; this is rather a wild tale, my man," said Mr. Utterson, biting his finger. "Suppose it were as you suppose, supposing Dr. Jekyll to have been — well, murdered, what could induce the murderer to stay? That won't hold water; it doesn't commend itself to reason."

"Well, Mr. Utterson, you are a hard man to satisfy, but I'll do it yet," said Poole. "All this last week (you must know) him, or it, or whatever it is that lives in that cabinet, has been crying night and day for some sort of medicine and cannot get it to his mind. It was sometimes his way — the master's, that is — to write his orders on a sheet of paper and throw it on the stair. We've had nothing else this week back; nothing but papers, and a closed door, and the very meals left there to be smuggled in when nobody was looking. Well, sir, every day, ay, and twice and thrice in the same day, there have been orders and complaints, and I have been sent flying to all the wholesale chemists in town. Every time I brought the stuff back, there would be another paper telling me to return it, because it was not pure, and another order to a different firm. This drug is wanted bitter bad, sir, whatever for."

"Have you any of these papers?" asked Mr. Utterson.

Poole felt in his pocket and handed out a crumpled note, which the lawyer, bending nearer to the candle, carefully examined. Its contents ran thus: "Dr. Jekyll presents his compliments to Messrs. Maw. He assures them that their last sample is impure and quite useless for his present purpose. In the year 18 —, Dr. J. purchased a somewhat large quantity from Messrs. M. He now begs them to search with most sedulous care, and should any of the same quality be left, forward it to him at once. Expense is no consideration. The importance of this to Dr. J. can hardly be exaggerated." So far the letter had run composedly enough, but here with a sudden splutter of the pen, the writer's emotion had broken loose. "For God's sake," he added, "find me some of the old."

"This is a strange note," said Mr. Utterson; and then sharply, "How do you come to have it open?"

"The man at Maw's was main angry, sir, and he threw it back to me like so much dirt," returned Poole.

"This is unquestionably the doctor's hand, do you know?" resumed the lawyer.

"I thought it looked like it," said the servant rather sulkily; and then, with another voice, "But what matters hand of write?" he said. "I've seen him!"

"Seen him?" repeated Mr. Utterson. "Well?"

"That's it!" said Poole. "It was this way. I came suddenly into the theatre from the garden. It seems he had slipped out to look for this drug or whatever it is; for the cabinet door was open, and there he was at the far end of the room digging among the crates. He looked up when I came in, gave a kind of cry, and whipped upstairs into the cabinet. It was but for one minute that I saw him, but the hair stood upon my head like quills. Sir, if that was my master, why had he a mask upon his face? If it was my master, why did he cry out like a rat, and run from me? I have served him long enough. And then . . ." The man paused and passed his hand over his face.

"These are all very strange circumstances," said Mr. Utterson, "but I think I begin to see daylight. Your master, Poole, is plainly seized with one of those maladies that both torture and deform the sufferer; hence, for aught I know, the alteration of his voice; hence the mask and the avoidance of his friends; hence his eagerness to find this drug, by means of which the poor soul retains some hope of ultimate recovery — God grant that he be not deceived! There is my explanation; it is sad enough, Poole, ay, and appalling to consider; but it is plain and natural, hangs well together, and delivers us from all exorbitant alarms."

"Sir," said the butler, turning to a sort of mottled pallor, "that thing was not my master, and there's the truth. My master"— here he looked round him and began to whisper —"is a tall, fine build of a man, and this was more of a dwarf." Utterson attempted to protest. "O, sir," cried Poole, "do you think I do not know my master after twenty years? Do you think I do not know where his head comes to in the cabinet door, where I saw him every morning of my life? No, sir, that thing in the mask was never Dr. Jekyll — God knows what it was, but it was never Dr. Jekyll; and it is the belief of my heart that there was murder done."

"Poole," replied the lawyer, "if you say that, it will become my duty to make certain. Much as I desire to spare your master's feelings, much as I am puzzled by this note which seems to prove him to be still alive, I shall consider it my duty to break in that door."

"Ah, Mr. Utterson, that's talking!" cried the butler.

"And now comes the second question," resumed Utterson: "Who is going to do it?"

"Why, you and me, sir," was the undaunted reply.

"That's very well said," returned the lawyer; "and whatever comes of it, I shall make it my business to see you are no loser."

"There is an axe in the theatre," continued Poole; "and you might take the kitchen poker for yourself."

The lawyer took that rude but weighty instrument into his hand, and balanced it. "Do you know, Poole," he said, looking up, "that you and I are about to place ourselves in a position of some peril?"

"You may say so, sir, indeed," returned the butler.

"It is well, then, that we should be frank," said the other. "We both think more than we have said; let us make a clean breast. This masked figure that you saw, did you recognise it?"

"Well, sir, it went so quick, and the creature was so doubled up, that I could hardly swear to that," was the answer. "But if you mean, was it Mr. Hyde?—why, yes, I think it was! You see, it was much of the same bigness; and it had the same quick, light way with it; and then who else could have got in by the laboratory door? You have not forgot, sir, that at the time of the murder he had still the key with him? But that's not all. I don't know, Mr. Utterson, if you ever met this Mr. Hyde?"

"Yes," said the lawyer, "I once spoke with him."

"Then you must know as well as the rest of us that there was something queer about that gentleman — something that gave a man a turn — I don't know rightly how to say it, sir, beyond this: that you felt in your marrow kind of cold and thin."

"I own I felt something of what you describe," said Mr. Utterson.

"Quite so, sir," returned Poole. "Well, when that masked thing like a monkey jumped from among the chemicals and whipped into the cabinet, it went down my spine like ice. O, I know it's not evidence, Mr. Utterson; I'm book-learned enough for that; but a man has his feelings, and I give you my bible-word it was Mr. Hyde!"

"Ay, ay," said the lawyer. "My fears incline to the same point. Evil, I fear, founded — evil was sure to come — of that connection. Ay, truly, I believe you; I believe poor Harry is killed; and I believe his murderer (for what purpose, God alone can tell) is still lurking in his victim's room. Well, let our name be vengeance. Call Bradshaw."

The footman came at the summons, very white and nervous.

"Put yourself together, Bradshaw," said the lawyer. "This suspense, I know, is telling upon all of you; but it is now our intention to make an end of it. Poole, here, and I are going to force our way into the cabinet. If all is well, my shoulders are broad enough to bear the blame. Meanwhile, lest anything should really be amiss, or any malefactor seek to escape by the back, you and the boy must go round the corner with a pair of good sticks and take your post at the laboratory door. We give you ten minutes, to get to your stations."

As Bradshaw left, the lawyer looked at his watch. "And now, Poole, let us get to ours," he said; and taking the poker under his arm, led the way into the yard. The scud had banked over the moon, and it was now quite dark. The wind, which only broke in puffs and draughts into that deep well of building, tossed the light of the candle to and fro about their steps, until they came into the shelter of the theatre, where they sat down silently to wait. London hummed solemnly all around; but nearer at hand, the stillness was only broken by the sounds of a footfall moving to and fro along the cabinet floor.

"So it will walk all day, sir," whispered Poole; "ay, and the better part of the night. Only when a new sample comes from the chemist, there's a bit of a break. Ah, it's an ill conscience that's such an enemy to rest! Ah, sir, there's blood foully shed in every step of it! But hark again, a little closer — put your heart in your ears, Mr. Utterson, and tell me, is that the doctor's foot?"

The steps fell lightly and oddly, with a certain swing, for all they went so slowly; it was different indeed from the heavy creaking tread of Henry Jekyll. Utterson sighed. "Is there never anything else?" he asked.

Poole nodded. "Once," he said. "Once I heard it weeping!"

"Weeping? how that?" said the lawyer, conscious of a sudden chill of horror.

"Weeping like a woman or a lost soul," said the butler. "I came away with that upon my heart, that I could have wept too."

But now the ten minutes drew to an end. Poole disinterred the axe from under a stack of packing straw; the candle was set upon the nearest table to light them to the attack; and they drew near with bated breath to where that patient foot was still going up and down, up and down, in the quiet of the night. "Jekyll," cried Utterson, with a loud voice, "I demand to see you." He paused a moment, but there came no reply. "I give you fair warning, our suspicions are aroused, and I must and shall see you," he resumed; "if not by fair means, then by foul — if not of your consent, then by brute force!"

"Utterson," said the voice, "for God's sake, have mercy!"

"Ah, that's not Jekyll's voice — it's Hyde's!" cried Utterson. "Down with the door, Poole!"

Poole swung the axe over his shoulder; the blow shook the building, and the red baize door leapt against the lock and hinges. A dismal screech, as of mere animal terror, rang from the cabinet. Up went the axe again, and again the panels crashed and the frame bounded; four times the blow fell; but the wood was tough and the fittings were of excellent workmanship; and it was not until the fifth, that the lock burst and the wreck of the door fell inwards on the carpet.

The besiegers, appalled by their own riot and the stillness that had succeeded, stood back a little and peered in. There lay the cabinet before their eyes in the quiet lamplight, a good fire glowing and chattering on the hearth, the kettle singing its thin strain, a drawer or two open, papers neatly set forth on the business table, and nearer the fire, the things laid out for tea; the quietest room, you would have said, and, but for the glazed presses full of chemicals, the most commonplace that night in London.

Right in the middle there lay the body of a man sorely contorted and still twitching. They drew near on tiptoe, turned it on its back and beheld the face of Edward Hyde. He was dressed in clothes far too large for him, clothes of the doctor's bigness; the cords of his face still moved with a semblance of life, but life was quite gone: and by the crushed phial in the hand and the strong smell of kernels that hung upon the air, Utterson knew that he was looking on the body of a self-destroyer.

"We have come too late," he said sternly, "whether to save or punish. Hyde is gone to his account; and it only remains for us to find the body of your master."

The far greater proportion of the building was occupied by the theatre, which filled almost the whole ground storey and was lighted from above, and by the cabinet, which formed an upper storey at one end and looked upon the court. A corridor joined the theatre to the door on the by-street; and with this the cabinet communicated separately by a second flight of stairs. There were besides a few dark closets and a spacious cellar. All these they now thoroughly examined. Each closet needed but a glance, for all were empty, and all, by the dust that fell from their doors, had stood long unopened. The cellar, indeed, was filled with crazy lumber, mostly dating from the times of the surgeon who was Jekyll's predecessor; but even as they opened the door they were advertised of the uselessness of further search, by the fall of a perfect mat of cobweb which had for years sealed up the entrance. Nowhere was there any trace of Henry Jekyll, dead or alive.

Poole stamped on the flags of the corridor. "He must be buried here," he said, hearkening to the sound.

"Or he may have fled," said Utterson, and he turned to examine the door in the by-street. It was locked; and lying near by on the flags, they found the key, already stained with rust.

"This does not look like use," observed the lawyer.

"Use!" echoed Poole. "Do you not see, sir, it is broken? much as if a man had stamped on it."

"Ay," continued Utterson, "and the fractures, too, are rusty." The two men looked at each other with a scare. "This is beyond me, Poole," said the lawyer. "Let us go back to the cabinet."

They mounted the stair in silence, and still with an occasional awestruck glance at the dead body, proceeded more thoroughly to examine the contents of the cabinet. At one table, there were traces of chemical work, various measured heaps of some white salt being laid on glass saucers, as though for an experiment in which the unhappy man had been prevented.

"That is the same drug that I was always bringing him," said Poole; and even as he spoke, the kettle with a startling noise boiled over.

This brought them to the fireside, where the easy-chair was drawn cosily up, and the tea things stood ready to the sitter's elbow, the very sugar in the cup. There were several books on a shelf; one lay beside the tea things open, and Utterson was amazed to find it a copy of a pious work, for which Jekyll had several times expressed a great esteem, annotated, in his own hand with startling blasphemies.

Next, in the course of their review of the chamber, the search-ers came to the cheval-glass, into whose depths they looked with an involuntary horror. But it was so turned as to show them noth-ing but the rosy glow playing on the roof, the fire sparkling in a hundred repetitions along the glazed front of the presses, and their own pale and fearful countenances stooping to look in.

"This glass has seen some strange things, sir," whispered Poole.

"And surely none stranger than itself," echoed the lawyer in the same tones. "For what did Jekyll"— he caught himself up at the word with a start, and then conquering the weakness — "what could Jekyll want with it?" he said.

"You may say that!" said Poole.

Next they turned to the business table. On the desk, among the neat array of papers, a large envelope was uppermost, and bore, in the doctor's hand, the name of Mr. Utterson. The law-yer unsealed it, and several enclosures fell to the floor. The first was a will, drawn in the same eccentric terms as the one which he had returned six months before, to serve as a testament in case of death and as a deed of gift in case of disappearance; but in place of the name of Edward Hyde, the lawyer, with indescribable amaze-ment, read the name of Gabriel John Utterson. He looked at Poole, and then back at the paper, and last of all at the dead male-factor stretched upon the carpet.

"My head goes round," he said. "He has been all these days in possession; he had no cause to like me; he must have raged to see himself displaced; and he has not destroyed this document."

He caught up the next paper; it was a brief note in the doctor's hand and dated at the top. "O Poole!" the lawyer cried, "he was alive and here this day. He cannot have been disposed of in so short a space; he must be still alive, he must have fled! And then, why fled? and how? and in that case, can we venture to declare this suicide? O, we must be careful. I foresee that we may yet involve your master in some dire catastrophe."

"Why don't you read it, sir?" asked Poole.

"Because I fear," replied the lawyer solemnly. "God grant I have no cause for it!" And with that he brought the paper to his eyes and read as follows:

> "My dear Utterson,—When this shall fall into your hands, I shall have disappeared, under what circumstances I have not the penetration to foresee, but my instinct and all the circumstances of my nameless situation tell me that the end is sure and must be early. Go then, and first read the narrative which Lanyon warned me he was to place in your hands; and if you care to hear more, turn to the confession of
> > "Your unworthy and unhappy friend,
> > "HENRY JEKYLL."

"There was a third enclosure?" asked Utterson.

"Here, sir," said Poole, and gave into his hands a considerable packet sealed in several places.

The lawyer put it in his pocket. "I would say nothing of this paper. If your master has fled or is dead, we may at least save his credit. It is now ten; I must go home and read these documents in quiet; but I shall be back before midnight, when we shall send for the police."

They went out, locking the door of the theatre behind them; and Utterson, once more leaving the servants gathered about the fire in the hall, trudged back to his office to read the two narratives in which this mystery was now to be explained.

9

Dr. Lanyon's Narrative

On the ninth of January, now four days ago, I received by the evening delivery a registered envelope, addressed in the hand of my
colleague and old school companion, Henry Jekyll. I was a good
deal surprised by this; for we were by no means in the habit of
correspondence; I had seen the man, dined with him, indeed, the
night before; and I could imagine nothing in our intercourse that
should justify formality of registration. The contents increased
my wonder; for this is how the letter ran:

"10th December, 18 —.

"Dear Lanyon, — You are one of my oldest friends;
and although we may have differed at times on scientific questions, I cannot remember, at least on my side,
any break in our affection. There was never a day when,
if you had said to me, 'Jekyll, my life, my honour, my reason, depend upon you,' I would not have sacrificed my left
hand to help you. Lanyon, my life, my honour, my reason,
are all at your mercy; if you fail me to-night, I am lost.
You might suppose, after this preface, that I am going to
ask you for something dishonourable to grant. Judge for
yourself.

"I want you to postpone all other engagements for

to-night — ay, even if you were summoned to the bedside of an emperor; to take a cab, unless your carriage should be actually at the door; and with this letter in your hand for consultation, to drive straight to my house. Poole, my butler, has his orders; you will find him waiting your arrival with a locksmith. The door of my cabinet is then to be forced: and you are to go in alone; to open the glazed press (letter E) on the left hand, breaking the lock if it be shut; and to draw out, *with all its contents as they stand*, the fourth drawer from the top or (which is the same thing) the third from the bottom. In my extreme distress of mind, I have a morbid fear of misdirecting you; but even if I am in error, you may know the right drawer by its contents: some powders, a phial and a paper book. This drawer I beg of you to carry back with you to Cavendish Square exactly as it stands.

"That is the first part of the service: now for the second. You should be back, if you set out at once on the receipt of this, long before midnight; but I will leave you that amount of margin, not only in the fear of one of those obstacles that can neither be prevented nor foreseen, but because an hour when your servants are in bed is to be preferred for what will then remain to do. At midnight, then, I have to ask you to be alone in your consulting room, to admit with your own hand into the house a man who will present himself in my name, and to place in his hands the drawer that you will have brought with you from my cabinet. Then you will have played your part and earned my gratitude completely. Five minutes afterwards, if you insist upon an explanation, you will have understood that these arrangements are of capital importance; and that by the neglect of one of them, fantastic as they must appear, you might have charged your conscience with my death or the shipwreck of my reason.

"Confident as I am that you will not trifle with this appeal, my heart sinks and my hand trembles at the bare thought of such a possibility. Think of me at this hour, in a strange place, labouring under a blackness of distress that no fancy can exaggerate, and yet well aware that, if you will but punctually serve me, my troubles will roll away like a story that is told. Serve me, my dear Lanyon, and save

"Your friend, H.J.

"P.S.—I had already sealed this up when a fresh terror struck upon my soul. It is possible that the post-office may fail me, and this letter not come into your hands until to-morrow morning. In that case, dear Lanyon, do my errand when it shall be most convenient for you in the course of the day; and once more expect my messenger at midnight. It may then already be too late; and if that night passes without event, you will know that you have seen the last of Henry Jekyll."

Upon the reading of this letter, I made sure my colleague was insane; but till that was proved beyond the possibility of doubt, I felt bound to do as he requested. The less I understood of this farrago, the less I was in a position to judge of its importance; and an appeal so worded could not be set aside without a grave responsibility. I rose accordingly from table, got into a hansom, and drove straight to Jekyll's house. The butler was awaiting my arrival; he had received by the same post as mine a registered letter of instruction, and had sent at once for a locksmith and a carpenter. The tradesmen came while we were yet speaking; and we moved in a body to old Dr. Denman's surgical theatre, from which (as you are doubtless aware) Jekyll's private cabinet is most conveniently entered. The door was very strong, the lock excellent; the carpenter avowed he would have great trouble and have to do much damage, if force were to be used; and the locksmith was near despair. But this last was a handy fellow, and after two hours' work, the door stood open. The press marked E was unlocked; and I took out the drawer, had it filled up with straw and tied in a sheet, and returned with it to Cavendish Square.

Here I proceeded to examine its contents. The powders were neatly enough made up, but not with the nicety of the dispensing chemist; so that it was plain they were of Jekyll's private manufacture: and when I opened one of the wrappers I found what seemed to me a simple crystalline salt of a white colour. The phial, to which I next turned my attention, might have been about half full of a blood-red liquor, which was highly pungent to the sense of smell and seemed to me to contain phosphorus and some volatile ether. At the other ingredients I could make no guess. The book was an ordinary version book and contained little but a series of dates. These covered a period of many years, but I observed that the entries ceased nearly a year ago and quite abruptly. Here and there a brief remark was appended to a date, usually no more than a single word: "double" occurring perhaps six times in a total of several hundred entries; and once very early in the list and followed by several marks of exclamation, "total failure!!!" All this, though it whetted my curiosity, told me little that was definite. Here were a phial of some salt, and the record of a series of experiments that had led (like too many of Jekyll's investigations) to no end of practical usefulness. How could the presence of these articles in my house affect either the honour, the sanity, or the life of my flighty colleague? If his messenger could go to one place, why could he not go to another? And even granting some impediment, why was this gentleman to be received by me in secret? The more I reflected the more convinced I grew that I was dealing with a case of cerebral disease; and though I dismissed my servants to bed, I loaded an old revolver, that I might be found in some posture of self-defence.

Twelve o'clock had scarce rung out over London, ere the knocker sounded very gently on the door. I went myself at the summons, and found a small man crouching against the pillars of the portico.

"Are you come from Dr. Jekyll?" I asked.

He told me "yes" by a constrained gesture; and when I had bidden him enter, he did not obey me without a searching backward glance into the darkness of the square. There was a policeman not far off, advancing with his bull's eye open; and at the sight, I thought my visitor started and made greater haste.

These particulars struck me, I confess, disagreeably; and as I followed him into the bright light of the consulting room, I kept my hand ready on my weapon. Here, at last, I had a chance of clearly seeing him. I had never set eyes on him before, so much was certain. He was small, as I have said; I was struck besides with the shocking expression of his face, with his remarkable combination of great muscular activity and great apparent debility of constitution, and — last but not least — with the odd, subjective disturbance caused by his neighbourhood. This bore some resemblance to incipient rigour, and was accompanied by a marked sinking of the pulse. At the time, I set it down to some idiosyncratic, personal distaste, and merely wondered at the acuteness of the symptoms; but I have since had reason to believe the cause to lie much deeper in the nature of man, and to turn on some nobler hinge than the principle of hatred.

This person (who had thus, from the first moment of his entrance, struck in me what I can only describe as a disgustful curiosity) was dressed in a fashion that would have made an ordinary person laughable; his clothes, that is to say, although they were of rich and sober fabric, were enormously too large for him in every measurement — the trousers hanging on his legs and rolled up to keep them from the ground, the waist of the coat below his haunches, and the collar sprawling wide upon his shoulders. Strange to relate, this ludicrous accoutrement was far from moving me to laughter. Rather, as there was something abnormal and misbegotten in the very essence of the creature that now faced me — something seizing, surprising and revolting — this fresh disparity seemed but to fit in with and to reinforce it; so that to my interest in the man's nature and character, there was added a curiosity as to his origin, his life, his fortune and status in the world.

These observations, though they have taken so great a space to be set down in, were yet the work of a few seconds. My visitor was, indeed, on fire with sombre excitement.

"Have you got it?" he cried. "Have you got it?" And so lively was his impatience that he even laid his hand upon my arm and sought to shake me.

I put him back, conscious at his touch of a certain icy pang along my blood. "Come, sir," said I. "You forget that I have not yet the pleasure of your acquaintance. Be seated, if you please." And I showed him an example, and sat down myself in my customary seat and with as fair an imitation of my ordinary manner to a patient, as the lateness of the hour, the nature of my preoccupations, and the horror I had of my visitor, would suffer me to muster.

"I beg your pardon, Dr. Lanyon," he replied civilly enough. "What you say is very well founded; and my impatience has shown its heels to my politeness. I come here at the instance of your colleague, Dr. Henry Jekyll, on a piece of business of some moment; and I understood . . ." He paused and put his hand to his throat, and I could see, in spite of his collected manner, that he was wrestling against the approaches of the hysteria —"I understood, a drawer . . ."

But here I took pity on my visitor's suspense, and some perhaps on my own growing curiosity.

"There it is, sir," said I, pointing to the drawer, where it lay on the floor behind a table and still covered with the sheet.

He sprang to it, and then paused, and laid his hand upon his heart: I could hear his teeth grate with the convulsive action of his jaws; and his face was so ghastly to see that I grew alarmed both for his life and reason.

"Compose yourself," said I.

He turned a dreadful smile to me, and as if with the decision of despair, plucked away the sheet. At sight of the contents, he uttered one loud sob of such immense relief that I sat petrified. And the next moment, in a voice that was already fairly well under control, "Have you a graduated glass?" he asked.

I rose from my place with something of an effort and gave him what he asked.

He thanked me with a smiling nod, measured out a few minims of the red tincture and added one of the powders. The mixture, which was at first of a reddish hue, began, in proportion as the crystals melted, to brighten in colour, to effervesce audibly, and to throw off small fumes of vapour. Suddenly and at the same moment, the ebullition ceased and the compound changed to a dark purple, which faded again more slowly to a watery green. My visitor, who had watched these metamorphoses with a keen eye, smiled, set down the glass upon the table, and then turned and looked upon me with an air of scrutiny.

"And now," said he, "to settle what remains. Will you be wise? will you be guided? will you suffer me to take this glass in my hand and to go forth from your house without further parley? or has the greed of curiosity too much command of you? Think before you answer, for it shall be done as you decide. As you decide, you shall be left as you were before, and neither richer nor wiser, unless the sense of service rendered to a man in mortal distress may be counted as a kind of riches of the soul. Or, if you shall so prefer to choose, a new province of knowledge and new avenues to fame and power shall be laid open to you, here, in this room, upon the instant; and your sight shall be blasted by a prodigy to stagger the unbelief of Satan."

"Sir," said I, affecting a coolness that I was far from truly possessing, "you speak enigmas, and you will perhaps not wonder that I hear you with no very strong impression of belief. But I have gone too far in the way of inexplicable services to pause before I see the end."

"It is well," replied my visitor. "Lanyon, you remember your vows: what follows is under the seal of our profession. And now, you who have so long been bound to the most narrow and material views, you who have denied the virtue of transcendental medicine, you who have derided your superiors — behold!"

He put the glass to his lips and drank at one gulp. A cry followed; he reeled, staggered, clutched at the table and held on, staring with injected eyes, gasping with open mouth; and as I looked there came, I thought, a change — he seemed to swell — his face became suddenly black and the features seemed to melt and alter — and the next moment, I had sprung to my feet and leapt back against the wall, my arms raised to shield me from that prodigy, my mind submerged in terror.

"O God!" I screamed, and "O God!" again and again; for there before my eyes — pale and shaken, and half fainting, and groping before him with his hands, like a man restored from death — there stood Henry Jekyll!

What he told me in the next hour, I cannot bring my mind to set on paper. I saw what I saw, I heard what I heard, and my soul sickened at it; and yet now when that sight has faded from my eyes, I ask myself if I believe it, and I cannot answer. My life is shaken to its roots; sleep has left me; the deadliest terror sits by me at all hours of the day and night; and I feel that my days are numbered, and that I must die; and yet I shall die incredulous. As for the moral turpitude that man unveiled to me, even with tears of penitence, I cannot, even in memory, dwell on it without a start of horror. I will say but one thing, Utterson, and that (if you can bring your mind to credit it) will be more than enough. The creature who crept into my house that night was, on Jekyll's own confession, known by the name of Hyde and hunted for in every corner of the land as the murderer of Carew.

HASTIE LANYON

10

Henry Jekyll's Full Statement of the Case

I was born in the year 18 — to a large fortune, endowed besides with excellent parts, inclined by nature to industry, fond of the respect of the wise and good among my fellowmen, and thus, as might have been supposed, with every guarantee of an honourable and distinguished future. And indeed the worst of my faults was a certain impatient gaiety of disposition, such as has made the happiness of many, but such as I found it hard to reconcile with my imperious desire to carry my head high, and wear a more than commonly grave countenance before the public. Hence it came about that I concealed my pleasures; and that when I reached years of reflection, and began to look round me and take stock of my progress and position in the world, I stood already committed to a profound duplicity of life. Many a man would have even blazoned such irregularities as I was guilty of; but from the high views that I had set before me, I regarded and hid them with an almost morbid sense of shame. It was thus rather the exacting nature of my aspirations than any particular degradation in my faults, that made me what I was, and, with even a deeper trench than in the majority of men, severed in me those provinces of good and ill which divide and compound man's dual nature. In this case, I was driven to reflect deeply and inveterately on that hard law of life, which lies at the root of religion and is one of

the most plentiful springs of distress. Though so profound a dou-
ble-dealer, I was in no sense a hypocrite; both sides of me were
in dead earnest; I was no more myself when I laid aside restraint
and plunged in shame, than when I laboured, in the eye of day, at
the furtherance of knowledge or the relief of sorrow and suffering.
And it chanced that the direction of my scientific studies, which
led wholly towards the mystic and the transcendental, reacted
and shed a strong light on this consciousness of the perennial war
among my members. With every day, and from both sides of my
intelligence, the moral and the intellectual, I thus drew steadily
nearer to that truth, by whose partial discovery I have been
doomed to such a dreadful shipwreck: that man is not truly one,
but truly two. I say two, because the state of my own knowledge
does not pass beyond that point. Others will follow, others will
outstrip me on the same lines; and I hazard the guess that man
will be ultimately known for a mere polity of multifarious, incongruous and independent denizens. I, for my part, from the nature
of my life, advanced infallibly in one direction and in one direction only. It was on the moral side, and in my own person, that I
learned to recognise the thorough and primitive duality of man;
I saw that, of the two natures that contended in the field of my
consciousness, even if I could rightly be said to be either, it was
only because I was radically both; and from an early date, even
before the course of my scientific discoveries had begun to suggest the most naked possibility of such a miracle, I had learned
to dwell with pleasure, as a beloved daydream, on the thought of
the separation of these elements. If each, I told myself, could be
housed in separate identities, life would be relieved of all that was
unbearable; the unjust might go his way, delivered from the aspirations and remorse of his more upright twin; and the just could
walk steadfastly and securely on his upward path, doing the good
things in which he found his pleasure, and no longer exposed to
disgrace and penitence by the hands of this extraneous evil. It was
the curse of mankind that these incongruous faggots were thus

bound together — that in the agonised womb of consciousness, these polar twins should be continuously struggling. How, then, were they dissociated?

I was so far in my reflections when, as I have said, a side light began to shine upon the subject from the laboratory table. I began to perceive more deeply than it has ever yet been stated, the trembling immateriality, the mistlike transience, of this seemingly so solid body in which we walk attired. Certain agents I found to have the power to shake and pluck back that fleshly vestment, even as a wind might toss the curtains of a pavilion. For two good reasons, I will not enter deeply into this scientific branch of my confession. First, because I have been made to learn that the doom and burthen of our life is bound forever on man's shoulders, and when the attempt is made to cast it off, it but returns upon us with more unfamiliar and more awful pressure. Second, because, as my narrative will make, alas! too evident, my discoveries were incomplete. Enough then, that I not only recognised my natural body from the mere aura and effulgence of certain of the powers that made up my spirit, but managed to compound a drug by which these powers should be dethroned from their supremacy, and a second form and countenance substituted, none the less natural to me because they were the expression, and bore the stamp of lower elements in my soul.

I hesitated long before I put this theory to the test of practise. I knew well that I risked death; for any drug that so potently controlled and shook the very fortress of identity, might, by the least scruple of an overdose or at the least inopportunity in the moment of exhibition, utterly blot out that immaterial tabernacle which I looked to it to change. But the temptation of a discovery so singular and profound at last overcame the suggestions of alarm. I had long since prepared my tincture; I purchased at once, from a firm of wholesale chemists, a large quantity of a particular salt which I knew, from my experiments, to be the last ingredi-ent required; and late one accursed night, I compounded the el-ements, watched them boil and smoke together in the glass, and when the ebullition had subsided, with a strong glow of courage, drank off the potion.

The most racking pangs succeeded: a grinding in the bones, deadly nausea, and a horror of the spirit that cannot be exceeded at the hour of birth or death. Then these agonies began swiftly to subside, and I came to myself as if out of a great sickness. There was something strange in my sensations, something indescribably new and, from its very novelty, incredibly sweet. I felt younger, lighter, happier in body; within I was conscious of a heady reck-lessness, a current of disordered sensual images running like a millrace in my fancy, a solution of the bonds of obligation, an un-known but not an innocent freedom of the soul. I knew myself, at the first breath of this new life, to be more wicked, tenfold more wicked, sold a slave to my original evil; and the thought, in that moment, braced and delighted me like wine. I stretched out my hands, exulting in the freshness of these sensations; and in the act, I was suddenly aware that I had lost in stature.

There was no mirror, at that date, in my room; that which stands beside me as I write, was brought there later on and for the very purpose of these transformations. The night, however, was far gone into the morning — the morning, black as it was, was nearly ripe for the conception of the day — the inmates of my house were locked in the most rigourous hours of slumber; and I determined, flushed as I was with hope and triumph, to ven-ture in my new shape as far as to my bedroom. I crossed the yard, wherein the constellations looked down upon me, I could have thought, with wonder, the first creature of that sort that their un-sleeping vigilance had yet disclosed to them; I stole through the corridors, a stranger in my own house; and coming to my room, I saw for the first time the appearance of Edward Hyde.

I must here speak by theory alone, saying not that which I know, but that which I suppose to be most probable. The evil side of my nature, to which I had now transferred the stamping efficacy, was less robust and less developed than the good which I had just deposed. Again, in the course of my life, which had been, after all, nine tenths a life of effort, virtue and control, it had been much less exercised and much less exhausted. And hence, as I think, it came about that Edward Hyde was so much smaller, slighter and younger than Henry Jekyll. Even as good shone upon the countenance of the one, evil was written broadly and plainly on the face of the other. Evil besides (which I must still believe to be the lethal side of man) had left on that body an imprint of deformity and decay. And yet when I looked upon that ugly idol in the glass, I was conscious of no repugnance, rather of a leap of welcome. This, too, was myself. It seemed natural and human. In my eyes it bore a livelier image of the spirit, it seemed more express and single, than the imperfect and divided countenance I had been hitherto accustomed to call mine. And in so far I was doubtless right. I have observed that when I wore the semblance of Edward Hyde, none could come near to me at first without a visible misgiving of the flesh. This, as I take it, was because all human beings, as we meet them, are commingled out of good and evil: and Edward Hyde, alone in the ranks of mankind, was pure evil.

I lingered but a moment at the mirror: the second and conclusive experiment had yet to be attempted; it yet remained to be seen if I had lost my identity beyond redemption and must flee before daylight from a house that was no longer mine; and hurrying back to my cabinet, I once more prepared and drank the cup, once more suffered the pangs of dissolution, and came to myself once more with the character, the stature and the face of Henry Jekyll.

That night I had come to the fatal cross-roads. Had I approached my discovery in a more noble spirit, had I risked the experiment while under the empire of generous or pious aspirations, all must have been otherwise, and from these agonies of death and birth, I had come forth an angel instead of a fiend. The drug had no discriminating action; it was neither diabolical nor divine; it but shook the doors of the prisonhouse of my disposition; and like the captives of Philippi, that which stood within ran forth. At that time my virtue slumbered; my evil, kept awake by ambition, was alert and swift to seize the occasion; and the thing that was projected was Edward Hyde. Hence, although I had now two characters as well as two appearances, one was wholly evil, and the other was still the old Henry Jekyll, that incongruous compound of whose reformation and improvement I had already learned to despair. The movement was thus wholly toward the worse.

Even at that time, I had not conquered my aversions to the dryness of a life of study. I would still be merrily disposed at times; and as my pleasures were (to say the least) undignified, and I was not only well known and highly considered, but growing towards the elderly man, this incoherency of my life was daily growing more unwelcome. It was on this side that my new power tempted me until I fell in slavery. I had but to drink the cup, to doff at once the body of the noted professor, and to assume, like a thick cloak, that of Edward Hyde. I smiled at the notion; it seemed to me at the time to be humourous; and I made my preparations with the most studious care. I took and furnished that house in Soho, to which Hyde was tracked by the police; and engaged as a housekeeper a creature whom I knew well to be silent and unscrupulous. On the other side, I announced to my servants that a Mr. Hyde (whom I described) was to have full liberty and power about my house in the square; and to parry mishaps, I even called and made myself a familiar object, in my second character. I next drew up that will to which you so much objected; so that if anything befell me in the person of Dr. Jekyll, I could enter on that of Edward Hyde without pecuniary loss. And thus fortified, as I supposed, on every side, I began to profit by the strange immunities of my position.

Men have before hired bravos to transact their crimes, while their own person and reputation sat under shelter. I was the first that ever did so for his pleasures. I was the first that could plod in the public eye with a load of genial respectability, and in a moment, like a schoolboy, strip off these lendings and spring headlong into the sea of liberty. But for me, in my impenetrable mantle, the safely was complete. Think of it — I did not even exist! Let me but escape into my laboratory door, give me but a second or two to mix and swallow the draught that I had always standing ready; and whatever he had done, Edward Hyde would pass away like the stain of breath upon a mirror; and there in his stead, quietly at home, trimming the midnight lamp in his study, a man who could afford to laugh at suspicion, would be Henry Jekyll.

The pleasures which I made haste to seek in my disguise were, as I have said, undignified; I would scarce use a harder term. But in the hands of Edward Hyde, they soon began to turn toward the monstrous. When I would come back from these excursions, I was often plunged into a kind of wonder at my vicarious depravity. This familiar that I called out of my own soul, and sent forth alone to do his good pleasure, was a being inherently malign and villainous; his every act and thought centred on self; drinking pleasure with bestial avidity from any degree of torture to another; relentless like a man of stone. Henry Jekyll stood at times aghast before the acts of Edward Hyde; but the situation was apart from ordinary laws, and insidiously relaxed the grasp of conscience. It was Hyde, after all, and Hyde alone, that was guilty. Jekyll was no worse; he woke again to his good qualities seemingly unimpaired; he would even make haste, where it was possible, to undo the evil done by Hyde. And thus his conscience slumbered.

Into the details of the infamy at which I thus connived (for even now I can scarce grant that I committed it) I have no design of entering; I mean but to point out the warnings and the successive steps with which my chastisement approached. I met with one accident which, as it brought on no consequence, I shall no more than mention. An act of cruelty to a child aroused against me the anger of a passer-by, whom I recognised the other day in the person of your kinsman; the doctor and the child's family joined him; there were moments when I feared for my life; and at last, in order to pacify their too just resentment, Edward Hyde had to bring them to the door, and pay them in a cheque drawn in the name of Henry Jekyll. But this danger was easily eliminated from the future, by opening an account at another bank in the name of Edward Hyde himself; and when, by sloping my own hand backward, I had supplied my double with a signature, I thought I sat beyond the reach of fate.

Some two months before the murder of Sir Danvers, I had been out for one of my adventures, had returned at a late hour, and woke the next day in bed with somewhat odd sensations. It was in vain I looked about me; in vain I saw the decent furniture and tall proportions of my room in the square; in vain that I recognised the pattern of the bed curtains and the design of the mahogany frame; something still kept insisting that I was not where I was, that I had not wakened where I seemed to be, but in the little room in Soho where I was accustomed to sleep in the body of Edward Hyde. I smiled to myself, and in my psychological way, began lazily to inquire into the elements of this illusion, occasionally, even as I did so, dropping back into a comfortable morning doze. I was still so engaged when, in one of my more wakeful moments, my eyes fell upon my hand. Now the hand of Henry Jekyll (as you have often remarked) was professional in shape and size: it was large, firm, white and comely. But the hand which I now saw, clearly enough, in the yellow light of a mid-London morning, lying half shut on the bedclothes, was lean, corded, knuckly, of a dusky pallor and thickly shaded with a swart growth of hair. It was the hand of Edward Hyde.

I must have stared upon it for near half a minute, sunk as I was in the mere stupidity of wonder, before terror woke up in my breast as sudden and startling as the crash of cymbals; and bounding from my bed I rushed to the mirror. At the sight that met my eyes, my blood was changed into something exquisitely thin and icy. Yes, I had gone to bed Henry Jekyll, I had awakened Edward Hyde. How was this to be explained? I asked myself; and then, with another bound of terror — how was it to be remedied? It was well on in the morning; the servants were up; all my drugs were in the cabinet — a long journey down two pairs of stairs, through the back passage, across the open court and through the anatomical theatre, from where I was then standing horror-struck. It might indeed be possible to cover my face; but of what use was that, when I was unable to conceal the alteration in my stature? And then with an overpowering sweetness of relief, it came back upon my mind that the servants were already used to the coming and going of my second self. I had soon dressed, as well as I was able, in clothes of my own size: had soon passed through the house, where Bradshaw stared and drew back at seeing Mr. Hyde at such an hour and in such a strange array; and ten minutes later, Dr. Jekyll had returned to his own shape and was sitting down, with a darkened brow, to make a feint of breakfasting.

Small indeed was my appetite. This inexplicable incident, this reversal of my previous experience, seemed, like the Babylonian finger on the wall, to be spelling out the letters of my judgement; and I began to reflect more seriously than ever before on the issues and possibilities of my double existence. That part of me which I had the power of projecting, had lately been much exercised and nourished; it had seemed to me of late as though the body of Edward Hyde had grown in stature, as though (when I wore that form) I were conscious of a more generous tide of blood; and I began to spy a danger that, if this were much prolonged, the balance of my nature might be permanently overthrown, the power of voluntary change be forfeited, and the character of Edward Hyde become irrevocably mine. The power of the drug had not been always equally displayed. Once, very early in my career, it had totally failed me; since then I had been obliged on more than one occasion to double, and once, with infinite risk of death, to treble the amount; and these rare uncertainties had cast hitherto the sole shadow on my contentment. Now, however, and in the light of that morning's accident, I was led to remark that whereas, in the beginning, the difficulty had been to throw off the body of Jekyll, it had of late gradually but decidedly transferred itself to the other side. All things therefore seemed to point to this; that I was slowly losing hold of my original and better self, and becoming slowly incorporated with my second and worse.

Between these two, I now felt I had to choose. My two natures had memory in common, but all other faculties were most unequally shared between them. Jekyll (who was composite) now with the most sensitive apprehensions, now with a greedy gusto, projected and shared in the pleasures and adventures of Hyde; but Hyde was indifferent to Jekyll, or but remembered him as the mountain bandit remembers the cavern in which he conceals himself from pursuit. Jekyll had more than a father's interest; Hyde had more than a son's indifference. To cast in my lot with

Jekyll, was to die to those appetites which I had long secretly indulged and had of late begun to pamper. To cast it in with Hyde,
was to die to a thousand interests and aspirations, and to become,
at a blow and forever, despised and friendless. The bargain might
appear unequal; but there was still another consideration in the
scales; for while Jekyll would suffer smartingly in the fires of ab-
stinence, Hyde would be not even conscious of all that he had
lost. Strange as my circumstances were, the terms of this debate
are as old and commonplace as man; much the same inducements
and alarms cast the die for any tempted and trembling sinner; and
it fell out with me, as it falls with so vast a majority of my fellows, that I chose the better part and was found wanting in the
strength to keep to it.

Yes, I preferred the elderly and discontented doctor, surrounded by friends and cherishing honest hopes; and bade a reso-
lute farewell to the liberty, the comparative youth, the light step,
leaping impulses and secret pleasures, that I had enjoyed in the
disguise of Hyde. I made this choice perhaps with some uncon-
scious reservation, for I neither gave up the house in Soho, nor
destroyed the clothes of Edward Hyde, which still lay ready in my
cabinet. For two months, however, I was true to my determination; for two months, I led a life of such severity as I had never
before attained to, and enjoyed the compensations of an approv-
ing conscience. But time began at last to obliterate the freshness
of my alarm; the praises of conscience began to grow into a thing
of course; I began to be tortured with throes and longings, as of
Hyde struggling after freedom; and at last, in an hour of moral
weakness, I once again compounded and swallowed the transforming draught.

I do not suppose that, when a drunkard reasons with himself
upon his vice, he is once out of five hundred times affected by the
dangers that he runs through his brutish, physical insensibility;

386 ROBERT LOUIS STEVENSON

neither had I, long as I had considered my position, made enough allowance for the complete moral insensibility and insensate readiness to evil, which were the leading characters of Edward Hyde. Yet it was by these that I was punished. My devil had been long caged, he came out roaring. I was conscious, even when I took the draught, of a more unbridled, a more furious propensity to ill. It must have been this, I suppose, that stirred in my soul that tempest of impatience with which I listened to the civilities of my unhappy victim; I declare, at least, before God, no man morally sane could have been guilty of that crime upon so pitiful a provocation; and that I struck in no more reasonable spirit than that in which a sick child may break a plaything. But I had voluntarily stripped myself of all those balancing instincts by which even the worst of us continues to walk with some degree of steadiness among temptations; and in my case, to be tempted, however slightly, was to fall.

Instantly the spirit of hell awoke in me and raged. With a transport of glee, I mauled the unresisting body, tasting delight from every blow; and it was not till weariness had begun to succeed, that I was suddenly, in the top fit of my delirium, struck through the heart by a cold thrill of terror. A mist dispersed; I saw my life to be forfeit; and fled from the scene of these excesses, at once glorying and trembling, my lust of evil gratified and stimulated, my love of life screwed to the topmost peg. I ran to the house in Soho, and (to make assurance doubly sure) destroyed my papers; thence I set out through the lamplit streets, in the same divided ecstasy of mind, gloating on my crime, light-headedly devising others in the future, and yet still hastening and still hearkening in my wake for the steps of the avenger. Hyde had a song upon his lips as he compounded the draught, and as he drank it, pledged the dead man. The pangs of transformation had not done tearing him, before Henry Jekyll, with streaming tears of gratitude and remorse, had fallen upon his knees and lifted his clasped hands to God. The veil of self-indulgence was rent from head to foot. I saw my life as a whole: I followed it up from the days of childhood, when I had walked with my father's hand, and through the self-denying toils of my professional life, to arrive again and again, with the same sense of unreality, at the damned horrors of the evening. I could have screamed aloud; I sought with tears and prayers to smother down the crowd of hideous images and sounds with which my memory swarmed against me; and still, between the petitions, the ugly face of my iniquity stared into my soul. As the acuteness of this remorse began to die away, it was succeeded by a sense of joy. The problem of my conduct was solved. Hyde was thenceforth impossible; whether I would or not, I was now confined to the better part of my existence; and O, how I rejoiced to think of it! with what willing humility I embraced anew the restrictions of natural life! with what sincere renunciation I locked the door by which I had so often gone and come, and ground the key under my heel!

The next day, came the news that the murder had been overlooked, that the guilt of Hyde was patent to the world, and that the victim was a man high in public estimation. It was not only a crime, it had been a tragic folly. I think I was glad to know it; I think I was glad to have my better impulses thus buttressed and guarded by the terrors of the scaffold. Jekyll was now my city of refuge; let but Hyde peep out an instant, and the hands of all men would be raised to take and slay him.

I resolved in my future conduct to redeem the past; and I can say with honesty that my resolve was fruitful of some good. You know yourself how earnestly, in the last months of the last year, I laboured to relieve suffering; you know that much was done for others, and that the days passed quietly, almost happily for myself. Nor can I truly say that I wearied of this beneficent and innocent life; I think instead that I daily enjoyed it more completely;

but I was still cursed with my duality of purpose; and as the first edge of my penitence wore off, the lower side of me, so long indulged, so recently chained down, began to growl for licence. Not that I dreamt of resuscitating Hyde; the bare idea of that would startle me to frenzy: no, it was in my own person that I was once more tempted to trifle with my conscience; and it was as an ordinary secret sinner that I at last fell before the assaults of temptation.

There comes an end to all things; the most capacious measure is filled at last; and this brief condescension to my evil finally destroyed the balance of my soul. And yet I was not alarmed; the fall seemed natural, like a return to the old days before I had made my discovery. It was a fine, clear, January day, wet under foot where the frost had melted, but cloudless overhead; and the Regent's Park was full of winter chirrupings and sweet with spring odours. I sat in the sun on a bench; the animal within me licking the chops of memory; the spiritual side a little drowsed, promising subsequent penitence, but not yet moved to begin. After all, I reflected, I was like my neighbours; and then I smiled, comparing myself with other men, comparing my active goodwill with the lazy cruelty of their neglect. And at the very moment of that vainglorious thought, a qualm came over me, a horrid nausea and the most deadly shuddering. These passed away, and left me faint; and then as in its turn faintness subsided, I began to be aware of a change in the temper of my thoughts, a greater boldness, a contempt of danger, a solution of the bonds of obligation. I looked down; my clothes hung formlessly on my shrunken limbs; the hand that lay on my knee was corded and hairy. I was once more Edward Hyde. A moment before I had been safe of all men's respect, wealthy, beloved — the cloth laying for me in the dining-room at home; and now I was the common quarry of mankind, hunted, houseless, a known murderer, thrall to the gallows.

My reason wavered, but it did not fail me utterly. I have more than once observed that in my second character, my faculties seemed sharpened to a point and my spirits more tensely elastic; thus it came about that, where Jekyll perhaps might have succumbed, Hyde rose to the importance of the moment. My drugs were in one of the presses of my cabinet; how was I to reach them? That was the problem that (crushing my temples in my hands) I set myself to solve. The laboratory door I had closed. If I sought to enter by the house, my own servants would consign me to the gallows. I saw I must employ another hand, and thought of Lanyon. How was he to be reached? how persuaded? Supposing that I escaped capture in the streets, how was I to make my way into his presence? and how should I, an unknown and displeasing visitor, prevail on the famous physician to rifle the study of his colleague, Dr. Jekyll? Then I remembered that of my original character, one part remained to me: I could write my own hand; and once I had conceived that kindling spark, the way that I must follow became lighted up from end to end.

Thereupon, I arranged my clothes as best I could, and summoning a passing hansom, drove to an hotel in Portland Street, the name of which I chanced to remember. At my appearance (which was indeed comical enough, however tragic a fate these garments covered) the driver could not conceal his mirth. I gnashed my teeth upon him with a gust of devilish fury; and the smile withered from his face — happily for him — yet more happily for myself, for in another instant I had certainly dragged him from his perch. At the inn, as I entered, I looked about me with so black a countenance as made the attendants tremble; not a look did they exchange in my presence; but obsequiously took my orders, led me to a private room, and brought me wherewithal to write. Hyde in danger of his life was a creature new to me; shaken with inordinate anger, strung to the pitch of murder, lusting to inflict pain. Yet the creature was astute; mastered his fury with a great effort of the will; composed his two important letters, one to Lanyon and one to Poole; and that he might receive actual evidence of their being posted, sent them out with directions that they should be registered. Thenceforward, he sat all day over the fire in the private room, gnawing his nails; there he dined, sitting alone with his fears, the waiter visibly quailing before his eye; and thence, when the night was fully come, he set forth in the corner of a closed cab, and was driven to and fro about the streets of the city. He, I say — I cannot say, I. That child of Hell had nothing human; nothing lived in him but fear and hatred. And when at last, thinking the driver had begun to grow suspicious, he discharged the cab and ventured on foot, attired in his misfitting clothes, an object marked out for observation, into the midst of the nocturnal passengers, these two base passions raged within him like a tempest. He walked fast, hunted by his fears, chattering to himself, skulking through the less frequented thoroughfares, counting the minutes that still divided him from midnight. Once a woman spoke to him, offering, I think, a box of lights. He smote her in the face, and she fled.

When I came to myself at Lanyon's, the horror of my old friend perhaps affected me somewhat: I do not know; it was at least but a drop in the sea to the abhorrence with which I looked back upon these hours. A change had come over me. It was no longer the fear of the gallows, it was the horror of being Hyde that racked me. I received Lanyon's condemnation partly in a dream; it was partly in a dream that I came home to my own house and got into bed. I slept after the prostration of the day, with a stringent and profound slumber which not even the nightmares that wrung me could avail to break. I awoke in the morning shaken, weakened, but refreshed. I still hated and feared the thought of the brute that slept within me, and I had not of course forgotten the appalling dangers of the day before; but I was once more at home, in my own house and close to my drugs; and gratitude for my escape shone so strong in my soul that it almost rivalled the brightness of hope.

I was stepping leisurely across the court after breakfast, drinking the chill of the air with pleasure, when I was seized again with those indescribable sensations that heralded the change; and I had but the time to gain the shelter of my cabinet, before I was once again raging and freezing with the passions of Hyde. It took on this occasion a double dose to recall me to myself; and alas! six hours after, as I sat looking sadly in the fire, the pangs returned, and the drug had to be re-administered. In short, from that day forth it seemed only by a great effort as of gymnastics, and only under the immediate stimulation of the drug, that I was able to wear the countenance of Jekyll. At all hours of the day and night, I would be taken with the premonitory shudder; above all, if I slept, or even dozed for a moment in my chair, it was always as Hyde that I awakened. Under the strain of this continually impending doom and by the sleeplessness to which I now condemned myself, ay, even beyond what I had thought possible to man, I became, in my own person, a creature eaten up and emptied by fever, languidly weak both in body and mind, and solely occupied by one thought: the horror of my other self. But when I slept, or when the virtue of the medicine wore off, I would leap almost without transition (for the pangs of transformation grew daily less marked) into the possession of a fancy brimming with images of terror, a soul boiling with causeless hatreds, and a body that seemed not strong enough to contain the raging energies of life. The powers of Hyde seemed to have grown with the sickliness of Jekyll. And certainly the hate that now divided them was equal on each side. With Jekyll, it was a thing of vital instinct. He had now seen the full deformity of that creature that shared with him some of the phenomena of consciousness, and was co-heir with him to death: and beyond these links of community, which in themselves made the most poignant part of his distress, he thought of Hyde, for all his energy of life, as of something not only hellish but inorganic. This was the shocking thing; that the slime of the pit seemed to utter cries and voices; that the amorphous dust gesticulated and sinned; that what was dead, and had no shape, should usurp the offices of life. And this again, that that insurgent horror was knit to him closer than a wife, closer than an eye; lay caged in his flesh, where he heard it mutter and felt it struggle to be born; and at every hour of weakness, and in the confidence of slumber, prevailed against him, and deposed him out of life. The hatred of Hyde for Jekyll was of a different order. His terror of the gallows drove him continually to commit temporary suicide, and return to his subordinate station of a part instead of a person; but he loathed the necessity, he loathed the despondency into which Jekyll was now fallen, and he resented the dislike with which he was himself regarded. Hence the ape-like tricks that he would play me, scrawling in my own hand blasphemies on the pages of my books, burning the letters and destroying the portrait of my father; and indeed, had it not been for his fear of death, he would long ago have ruined himself in order to involve me in the ruin. But his love of me is wonderful; I go further: I, who sicken and freeze at the mere thought of him, when I recall the abjection and passion of this attachment, and when I know how he fears my power to cut him off by suicide, I find it in my heart to pity him.

It is useless, and the time awfully fails me, to prolong this description; no one has ever suffered such torments, let that suffice; and yet even to these, habit brought — no, not alleviation — but a certain callousness of soul, a certain acquiescence of despair; and my punishment might have gone on for years, but for the last calamity which has now fallen, and which has finally severed me from my own face and nature. My provision of the salt, which had never been renewed since the date of the first experiment, began to run low. I sent out for a fresh supply and mixed the draught; the ebullition followed, and the first change of colour, not the second; I drank it and it was without efficiency. You will learn from Poole how I have had London ransacked; it was in vain; and I am now persuaded that my first supply was impure, and that it was that unknown impurity which lent efficacy to the draught.

About a week has passed, and I am now finishing this statement under the influence of the last of the old powders. This, then, is the last time, short of a miracle, that Henry Jekyll can think his own thoughts or see his own face (now how sadly altered!) in the glass. Nor must I delay too long to bring my writing to an end; for if my narrative has hitherto escaped destruction, it has been by a combination of great prudence and great good luck. Should the throes of change take me in the act of writing it, Hyde will tear it in pieces; but if some time shall have elapsed after I have laid it by, his wonderful selfishness and circumscription to the moment will probably save it once again from the action of his ape-like spite. And indeed the doom that is closing on us both has already changed and crushed him. Half an hour from now, when I shall again and forever reindue that hated personality, I know how I shall sit shuddering and weeping in my chair, or continue, with the most strained and fearstruck ecstasy of listening, to pace up and down this room (my last earthly refuge) and give ear to every sound of menace. Will Hyde die upon the scaffold? or will he find courage to release himself at the last moment? God knows; I am careless; this is my true hour of death, and what is to follow concerns another than myself. Here then, as I lay down the pen and proceed to seal up my confession, I bring the life of that unhappy Henry Jekyll to an end.

ACKNOWLEDGMENTS

This book has been many years in the making, and numerous fantastic people have made it possible by their interest and blessings. I wish space permitted me to thank every one individually, but a few names will have to suffice:

Erin Harris, super-agent extraordinaire, first-rate reader, and friend: you recognized my budding abilities and stuck with me through many projects, endlessly loyal and equally hungry as me. This book exists because of you.

An indebted thank-you to Jenna Johnson for taking a chance on this book, for your scrupulous reads and insightful suggestions; it is a far sharper, more muscular novel thanks to you. Nina Barnett for your savvy assistance in every particular, your availability and dedication. Tracy Roe for your zealous copyediting, for the clarifying final polish you applied. Thank you to the whole talented HMH team for turning this ethereal thing into a reality.

David Leavitt, Padgett Powell, Jill Ciment, Mary Robison, Martin Roper, and Mary Gaitskill, thank you for your skillful instruction over the years. Lee Behlman, for your Victorian expertise and inspiring classes. Adam Vines, Allen Jih, Matthew Ladd, Eric Maxson, Jessica Murray, Elizabeth Kaiser, Stephen Priest,

Dave Reidy, Troy Teegarden, Tanya Underwood, Annie McFadyen, and all my other wonderful Florida friends.

Amant Dewan, Matthew Santiago, James Bucher, Michael Weisberg. Thank you Benjamin Percy, for your writerly advice and support. Angus and Keri Shee, Joe Tuazon, Lauren Tabak, Noah Lichtman, Adam Saltzman. David Walton, Nicky Britt, Lindsay Shoemaker, Jason Kraft, Gala Orba, Stephanie Dykema. Nick Costa. Mikey Troxell — thank you for, oh, everything.

Much gratitude to all my students over the years at Montclair State University, Metro State College of Denver, and Red Rocks Community College for your engagement and vitality, for what you've taught me in return, and for keeping me connected to the world.

To all the family friends I'm lucky to have — Alice Freed, the Marsons, the Citrins, the Jaffes, the Rosens, the Wolfs, Gloria Waldman, Sherry Satterfield — my love and deep appreciation. Thank you to my aunt and uncle Susan and Stan Brim and to my grandparents Edna and Ben Gould.

Mamacita, Linda Gould Levine, I am so fortunate to have you as a reader, your incredibly detailed, academic, ardent (and almost always apt, though I'm loath to initially admit it) responses to everything I write. You have believed in me at every stage of my life and given me the confidence and encouragement to follow the hard, uncertain path of my passion. As have you, old man, Barry Levine; you read everything I write almost instantaneously and with gusto, with your characteristic optimism, sweet consistency, and ever-supportive approval. And my little man, Andrew Levine, thank you for your merciless honesty, your perverse comic relief, your tender heart; for being my lifelong best friend.

Last and most of all, Hilary Hodge, personita favorita. From the start of this project you somehow saw straight into its twisted heart and guided me to it, bearing stoically the ugly brunt of my brooding responses to anything less than absolute applause, reminding me that every writer has suffered through the same process, and never once losing faith that I'd find my way to the triumphant end. You are the soul of this book, and it is for you.

DANIEL LEVINE studied English literature and creative writing at Brown University and received his M.F.A. in fiction writing from the University of Florida. Raised in New Jersey, he now lives in Colorado. This is his first novel. www.danielglevine.com